A HISTORY OF CHRISTIAN THEOLOGY

A HISTORY
OF
CHRISTIAN THEOLOGY

An Introduction

By
WILLIAM C. PLACHER

WESTMINSTER
JOHN KNOX PRESS
LOUISVILLE · KENTUCKY

Copyright © 1983 William C. Placher

Scripture quotations from *The New English Bible* are copyright © The Delegates of the Oxford University Press and the Syndics of the Cambridge University Press 1961, 1970, and are used by permission.

BOOK TEXT DESIGN BY DOROTHY ALDEN SMITH

Published by The Westminster Press ®
PHILADELPHIA, PENNSYLVANIA

20 21 22 23

Library of Congress Cataloging in Publication Data

Placher, William C. (William Carl), 1948–
A history of Christian theology.

Bibliography: p.
Includes index.
1. Theology, Doctrinal—History. I. Title.
BT21.2.P57   1983   230'.09   83–16778
ISBN 0–664–24496–3 (pbk.)

To Eric Dean, David Greene,
Hall Peebles, and Raymond Williams

Teachers, Colleagues, and Friends

CONTENTS

Preface   *9*

1. Introduction   11

2. The Hope of Israel
   Old Testament Background   18

3. The Mission to the Gentiles
   Theology in the New Testament   32

4. The Beginnings of Orthodoxy
   Gnosticism and Its Opponents   44

5. An Alliance with Philosophy
   Apologists, the School of Alexandria,
   and Tertullian   55

6. Truly Human, Truly Divine
   The Trinitarian and Christological
   Controversies   68

7. Light in the East
   Eastern Theology After Chalcedon   88

8. Augustine   108

9. The Path to Salvation
   The Early Middle Ages   122

10. The Fragile Synthesis
    The High Middle Ages   140

11. The Absolute Power of God
    The Late Middle Ages   162

12. Faith Alone, Scripture Alone
    Luther and the Radical Reformers   181

13. The Catholic Reformation
    From Trent to Jansenism and Quietism   200

14. God's Governance
    Calvin and the English Reformation   219

15. Reason and Enthusiasm
    Theology in the Enlightenment   237

16. The City on a Hill
    Theology in the United States,
    1630–1865   255

17. The Claims of History
    The Nineteenth Century   272

18. The End of Western Christendom
    The Twentieth Century   291

Index   *317*

PREFACE

This volume rests upon the work of scholars and translators who have made a host of details of the history of theology available to the nonspecialist. The notes cannot indicate the extent of my indebtedness, which other scholars will easily recognize. For the convenience of readers, I have tried to track down English translations of quotations cited whenever possible.

Many of my teachers—John Charles at Wabash, James McEwen at Aberdeen, Hans Frei, William Christian, Jaroslav Pelikan, Steven Ozment, George Lindbeck, and David Kelsey at Yale—have taught me things which have found their way into these pages. Much of the book was written during a year as a visiting scholar at Stanford, and Van Harvey and the Religious Studies department as well as Robert Hamerton-Kelly, Donald Caughey, and the staff of Stanford Memorial Church made the year pleasant as well as productive. Adult Sunday school classes at First Christian Church and Wabash Avenue Presbyterian Church in Crawfordsville read portions of the manuscript with the eyes of intelligent laypeople. The staff of the Wabash College Computer Center initiated an unpromising student into the mysteries of word-processing. James Heaney was the kind of editor who believed in the book more than I sometimes did myself. I am grateful.

I owe even more to David Blix for his continuing friendship, to my mother for her love and understanding, and to a great many Wabash students for their enthusiasm and patience, which over the years have meant more than they can know. I have returned to my old college as a faculty member, so that those who first taught me theology have become my colleagues and friends, and it is to them that this book is dedicated.

W. C. P.

1

INTRODUCTION

However dogs may bark at me, and pigs grunt, I shall always imitate the writings of the ancients: these shall be my
study, nor, while my strength lasts, shall the sun find me
idle. We are like dwarfs on the shoulders of giants, by
whose grace we see farther than they. Our study of the
works of the ancients enables us to give fresh life to their
finer ideas, and rescue them from time's oblivion and man's
neglect.

—Peter of Blois, writing in the late
twelfth century[1]

Most of us know something, anyway, about the history of Christian
theology. Those who grew up going to church or Sunday school remember at least fragments of Christian history. Even non-Christians
who have grown up in Western culture have encountered the history
of Christian theology as part of the background of political history or
art or literature or whatever. Paul, Augustine, the Trinity, predestination, and the Reformation do not seem totally unfamiliar.

The contexts in which we have learned about this history, however, shape our understanding of it. Churches and Sunday schools
seek primarily to set out the historical foundations of their own
denominations. They therefore tend to present this history as running
in a fairly straight line from the beginnings of Christianity to their
own position (with errors and heresies occasionally falling off to the
sides). To the "secular" historian, on the other hand, theologians
often appear primarily as the villains of the story, standing in the way
of tolerance and intellectual progress.

This book will present the history of Christian theology as an
aspect of intellectual history, a story of people and their ideas. That
leads to a different perspective. For one thing, the story turns out to
be more complicated, more pluralistic than historians only in search

11

of their own roots often admit. Christians have always disagreed about what they ought to believe, and both sides in those disagreements have often made a persuasive case. The study of the history of theology teaches that diversity within Christianity is nothing new. Studying the history of theology on its own terms, rather than only when theology touches on some other branch of history, also teaches greater respect for the intellectual coherence of the theological tradition. This is not simply a story of ignorant bigots fighting against intellectual progress, but of great minds using all their intellectual resources to understand their faith, and shaping much of our culture in the process.

SOME LIMITATIONS AND WARNINGS

Any book has its limitations, and it seems only fair to set out at the start some of the choices that have gone into the making of this book.

1. This is a history of Christian theology, not a general history of Christianity or a general intellectual history of the West. It will say little about church politics, missionary expansion, liturgy, or a host of other topics except as they impinge fairly directly on the history of theology. It will also not wander too far into the history of philosophy, political theory, or art, though these fields and many more can often not be cleanly separated from theology.

2. Theology means the systematic reflection on one's faith. Whenever Christians think about what they believe, they are, in a way, doing theology. Inevitably, though, the historian looks primarily at those who wrote their reflections down and influenced the life and thought of other Christians. According to a common distinction, the history of *theology*, as opposed to the history of *doctrine*, focuses more on the ideas of individual theologians and less on the statements of the institutional church. In attending to the music of Christian history, the history of doctrine pays more attention to the chorus, the history of theology to the soloists. The history of theology therefore inevitably concerns itself with an elite, those who could read and write and had some leisure for reflection, most of them male and the children of reasonable wealth (though some chose to live in extreme poverty). Any intellectual history is in this sense elitist, but the history of theology does always retain a connection with the church—its institutions, its creeds, its liturgies, and its people—so that the history of theology can at least never be the history of *isolated* individuals. The prayers and hopes and doubts of "ordinary" people will generally remain in the background in the following pages, but

they have always shaped the context in which theologians work.

3. Even after defining a topic like the history of theology, a historian still faces a vast quantity of material, and must select some things and ignore others. Any such selection risks many kinds of distortion. Some issues traditionally important in the history of Christian theology do not matter much to most people today, while many people today find concerns scarcely mentioned in traditional histories of theology—Christian attitudes to women, or the relation of Christianity to science, for instance—matters of burning importance. Similarly, a book written in the United States can reasonably give special attention to that country's theology and its roots, but too much such special treatment tends to distort the shape of the story. One can only seek a series of awkward compromises which try to respect the past's own integrity and yet to provide contemporary readers with the things they want to know.

4. The process of selection also risks giving too favorable a portrait of the subject. One tries to present all sides, but the more interesting ideas, the more attractive personalities, the fruitful beginnings as opposed to the dead ends, inevitably exercise a greater fascination, and they will get more than their share of attention in the pages that follow. It is therefore important to remember that Christian theologians have sometimes defended ideas most of us would find repugnant or exceedingly odd. Christian ideals inspired many of the efforts to end slavery, but slave owners quoted the Bible too. Both sides of every war fought by Christians have invoked religious principles. A Christian-inspired conviction that the world had a rational order often inspired scientific advance, but defenders of outdated scientific theories have also appealed to theological premises. In late antiquity, when many philosophers treated anything physical as evil, Christians affirmed the goodness of the physical world as a part of God's creation, but Christianity has led some to deny the value of this world. The very first Christians gave women positions of authority and influence unusual in their society, but in other times Christianity has been cited as a justification for assigning women a subordinate place. Christian theology tolerated and too often encouraged a long history of anti-Semitism, and no responsible history of Christian theology written in the twentieth century can ignore the haunting shadow of the Holocaust.

A history of Christian theology which tries to clarify its logic and its integrity as a tradition inevitably accentuates the positive. There is also a negative side. To be sure, sometimes the old gibe is true: Christianity has not been tried and found wanting; it has been found difficult and not tried. Still, sometimes Christianity itself may have generated its share of the world's evil. At any rate, this warning at the start may allay the suspicions of some that they have started to read a whitewash and remind the unsuspecting that history poses the whole tradition of Christian theology some very hard moral questions.

SOME BASIC THEMES

Like most history worth telling, the history of Christian theology keeps changing directions. Theologians not only come up with new answers, they often ask new questions. The conversion of the Emperor Constantine in the early 300s, for instance, forced Christians to think about the responsibilities of a Christian ruler. Questions about infant baptism, which had been taken for granted for centuries, arose in the sixteenth century. In our own time the role of women in the church has generated a whole set of increasingly debated issues. And so on. Still, some basic issues keep appearing, if in ever-new forms. In particular the affirmation of two important elements of Christian faith often generates a tension which can never be fully resolved. Five such tensions have had particular importance.

1. *The Humanity and Divinity of Christ.* The very first Christians talked about Jesus' birth and his death and his hometown. But they also prayed to him and hoped for salvation through him. They treated him, in short, as both human and divine. Yet Christians always felt that human beings are very different from God. So how could Jesus Christ be both at the same time? From the discussion of the Trinity in the third and fourth centuries, to current debates about the "historical Jesus" and his importance for faith, Christian theologians have wrestled with this problem.

2. *Reason and Revelation.* Christianity began within Judaism, where people believed that God, through the Law and the prophets, had revealed truth about himself and his will to Israel. Christians came to believe that God had revealed himself in Jesus Christ. They soon moved, however, into a Greek culture where philosophers had applied human reason to understanding the structure of the universe, human nature and destiny, and the divine. How should they relate revelation to the conclusions of reason? What could be known by reason, and what had to be accepted by faith? Such questions have survived from Christianity's first contacts with Greek philosophy in the second century, through a long series of medieval debates, through the "rational" religion of the eighteenth century, to the most

recent arguments about the relation of science and the Bible.

3. *Works and Grace.* Christians, according to most theologians, should not be proud of the fact that they have been "saved," they should be grateful to God. They have not earned salvation, for all people are sinners. Rather, they owe salvation to God's grace—God's unmerited love, poured out on the undeserving. If one can be saved only by unmerited grace, if no one can earn salvation, it might seem to follow that our moral efforts do not really matter—even that, as some of Paul's opponents already suggested in the New Testament period, we should "persist in sin, so that there may be all the more grace" (Rom. 6:1). Not so, most theologians have insisted. Our efforts do matter, the moral quality of our lives is important. So we can earn God's grace after all? No, that would lead to pride once more. So this dialectic has continued, from Paul to Augustine through the Middle Ages to the very center of the Reformation debates and still today.

4. *Spirit and Structure.* God's grace works unpredictably. One of the twelve apostles can prove a traitor while Paul, persecutor of the church, turns into one of its greatest missionaries. Yet few Christians have simply stood around waiting for unexpected grace. They have organized churches, with hierarchies and rules. They have designed liturgies and defined sacraments as the vehicles of God's grace. Other Christians have then protested that institutionalization was pretending to limit God's freedom, or that theories of the sacraments were trying to explain an inexplicable mystery. These debates have raged from the time of the Montanists in the second century, to medieval arguments about the papacy and the sacraments, through the Reformation to the present. Christianity cannot exist in history without taking a particular form, but some Christians always resist identifying that form with the action of God.

5. *Church and State.* Christianity began as an illegal sect and in its first centuries suffered intermittent persecution, but throughout most of its history most Christians have lived in countries where they constituted a majority and held political power. The fact that they were Christians, it seemed, ought to shape the way they governed. At the same time, large-scale theocracy—the direct rule of territory by church leaders—has been quite rare in Christian history. The church has influenced the state but has rarely taken it over. That has inevitably generated yet another set of conflicts, from the time of Constantine down to current American debates on prayer in the schools or abortion.

It is not for a historian to judge who is right in these debates, but a historian can note that the tensions have generally been creative.

Those who vote unambiguously for one side or the other—who deny Christ's humanity or divinity, or try to base their beliefs purely on reason or purely on revelation, or whatever—may have the truth, but those who have tried to affirm both sides have usually produced the most interesting theology. If these questions could be settled, then their history would come to an end, and this could be a much shorter book. Many Christian theologians, however, have seen valid insights on both sides of these issues, and their attempts to find a way to preserve all the truth they saw have generated a long and fascinating story.

FOR FURTHER READING

INTRODUCTIONS. The following are good introductory histories of Christianity: Roland H. Bainton, *Christendom*, 2 vols. (Harper & Row, Harper Torchbooks, 1966); Martin Marty, *A Short History of Christianity* (Meridian Books, 1959); Paul Johnson, *A History of Christianity* (Atheneum Publishers, 1979). Johnson's book is the most critical and controversial. For more detail, but still in clear and readable form, one could then turn to the six volumes of The Pelican History of the Church, published by Penguin Books: Henry Chadwick, *The Early Church* (1967); R. W. Southern, *Western Society and the Church in the Middle Ages* (1970); Owen Chadwick, *The Reformation* (1964); Gerald R. Cragg, *The Church and the Age of Reason* (rev. ed., 1970); Alec R. Vidler, *The Church in an Age of Revolution* (1961); Stephen Neill, *Christian Missions* (1964). On Protestantism, see John Dillenberger and Claude Welch, *Protestant Christianity Interpreted Through Its Development* (Charles Scribner's Sons, 1954). Some reference books are: John A. Bollier, *The Literature of Theology* (Westminster Press, 1979); Van A. Harvey, *A Handbook of Theological Terms* (Macmillan Co., 1964); and Alan Richardson (ed.), *A Dictionary of Christian Theology* (Westminster Press, 1969; rev. ed., *The Westminster Dictionary of Christian Theology*, 1983).

COLLECTIONS OF ORIGINAL SOURCES. Hugh T. Kerr, *Readings in Christian Theology* (Abingdon Press, 1966), gathers excerpts from throughout the history of theology. The many volumes of The Library of Christian Classics, published by The Westminster Press, really do include most of the classics of the history of Christian theology through the Reformation. Most of those volumes, along with other sources, will be cited at the end of appropriate chapters.

IMPORTANT BUT MORE DIFFICULT. More specifically on the history of doctrine, the best one-volume work is Hubert Cunliffe-Jones and Benjamin Drewery (eds.), *A History of Christian Doctrine* (Fortress Press, 1980). Jaroslav Pelikan's still-unfinished five-volume *The Christian Tradition,* published by The University of Chicago Press, is more difficult but will be the definitive work of this generation. The three volumes so far completed are: *The Emergence of the Catholic Tradition (100–600)* (1971); *The Spirit of Eastern Christendom (600–1700)* (1974); and *The Growth of Medieval Theology (600–1300)* (1978).

NOTES

1.   Peter of Blois, Letter 92 (to Reginald, Bishop of Bath), in *Patrologia Latina,* ed. by J.-P. Migne, Vol. 207 (Paris: Garnier Fratres, 1904), col. 290. The image of standing on the shoulders of giants is not original with Peter of Blois.

2

THE HOPE OF ISRAEL

My father was a homeless Aramaean who went down to
Egypt with a small company and lived there until they
became a great, powerful, and numerous nation. But the
Egyptians ill-treated us, humiliated us and imposed cruel
slavery upon us. Then we cried to the LORD the God of our
fathers for help, and he listened to us and saw our humilia-
tion, our hardship and distress; and so the LORD brought us
out of Egypt with a strong hand and outstretched arm, with
terrifying deeds, and with signs and portents. He brought
us to this place and gave us this land, a land flowing with
milk and honey.

—Deuteronomy 26:5–9

It may seem odd to begin a history of Christian theology with the
politics and customs of some small tribes living just east of the Mediterranean about 1200 B.C. What does this have to do with Christianity? What does it have to do with theology?

Well, the story of Christianity begins with Jesus, and Jesus was a
Jew: born in a Jewish family, circumcised according to Jewish law,
raised and educated in a Jewish culture. He worshiped at the Temple
and in the synagogues; he chose all his disciples from among his
fellow Jews. Jesus and his first followers set the shape for Christian
theology down the centuries, and they had grown up within Judaism.
They took many of its ideas about God, human beings, nature, and
history for granted. One cannot understand them or what they said
without knowing something about Judaism and the traditions of Israel that lay behind it. (For reasons to be explained below, most
scholars refer to "Judaism" only beginning with Ezra, about 400 B.C.
Before that, it seems safest to talk about "the religion of Israel.")

Yet the records of ancient Israel include almost no "systematic
theology." Mostly, they tell stories, stories about Israel's history. The

theology emerges through those stories and cannot be separated from them. Therefore, while one chapter certainly cannot recount even a summary of the history of Israel, a history of Christian theology has to begin with at least some notes on the beginnings of that history, and the ways in which it made Israel different from its neighbors. Some of the special characteristics of Israel appeared from the outset, but others emerged only gradually, above all through the work of the prophets. So their story will have to come next. That sets the stage for the development of a complex religious tradition called "Judaism" a few centuries before the time of Jesus—and understanding that tradition makes it possible to understand Jesus himself in his historical context.

THE TRIBES OF YAHWEH

Somewhere between 1300 B.C. and 1050 B.C. a group of tribes living between the Jordan River and the Mediterranean Sea began to think of themselves as a single nation—Israel—and to worship a single God they called Yahweh. "Yahweh" is the best modern rendering of the name of God sometimes given as "Jehovah" and translated as "the LORD" in most English Bibles. Pious Jews never pronounced the name aloud. They were surrounded by unfriendly neighbors, and they needed to stick together if they were going to survive. Like many groups before and since, they found that telling a common history gave them a sense of unity. Even today, after all, immigrants seeking new citizenship or college students joining a fraternity or sorority have to learn something about the history of their new community. In reciting that history, they come to be a part of it, and that gives them a sense of belonging. So these tribes began to bind themselves together by telling a common story.

The accuracy of such stories as to detail often scarcely matters. Think of the history most Americans carry around in their heads, for instance: Columbus and Plymouth Rock and Paul Revere's ride and the Declaration of Independence and the Wild West. Skipping over centuries, we forget the hatred the English Protestants at Plymouth would probably have felt for the descendants of Columbus. We treat all these events as a single story of our shared history, which helps define us as a nation. Those left out of that story, as women and minority groups often were, feel themselves alienated from society, and a new generation of historians retells the history more inclusively. So it was with Israel. Each tribe had its legends, its own famous ancestors. Gradually the traditions came to be incorporated in a single story. Abraham, Isaac, Jacob, and Joseph, likely originally the heroes of different tribes, came to be fathers and sons. Apparently the worship of Yahweh had begun among a group fleeing slavery in Egypt, so the story of how Yahweh had led them to their freedom took a central place in the national history.

At first glance, Israel seems in all this very like many other peoples in the ancient Near East. The Hittites and the Edomites and many others also achieved some sort of national unity, also worshiped their own particular deities, and also shaped national histories. But Israel was different, and the difference centered on its religion. First of all, at least in principle, the Israelites worshiped only one God. To be sure, many neighboring nations also recognized one supreme "high God," and the early Israelites did not necessarily deny the existence of other deities; they only said that Israel should worship none but Yahweh. The difference remains dramatic. A fairly typical Babylonian text describing a military campaign refers within a few lines to a host of deities: "Bel . . . Eturkalamma . . . the gods of the city Marad, Ilbaba and the gods of Kish, Ninlil . . . the gods from Borsippa, Kutha . . . and Sippar."[1] The stories of Israel just keep talking about Yahweh. Moreover, even in earliest times, Israel produced almost no statues or physical descriptions of Yahweh. Though the Israelites did refer to Yahweh as "he" rather than "she," unlike many other cultures they did not dwell on their God's virility or other "masculine" characteristics; Yahweh's gender appeared almost exclusively in pronouns. Israel's neighbors found all this bewildering. What did Yahweh look like? Where were his images?

The Israelites also thought of God's *activity* in an unusual way. Other nations of course described their goddesses or gods as acting in history; Marduk, for instance, helped the Babylonians secure prosperity and defeat their enemies. And Israel saw Yahweh at work in the world of nature and the cycle of the seasons. But Yahweh acted *primarily* in the great events of the nation's history, while the deities of neighboring nations generally had *more* to do with safeguarding the repeated annual cycle of vegetation. That meant that, in contrast to divinities whose function was to guarantee that the same thing would keep happening—the yearly flood of the Nile, the appearance of spring—Yahweh made *new* things happen. His people escaped Egypt, they settled a new land, and so on.

Israel's religion thus took particular interest in historical changes in this world. By contrast, it showed startlingly little concern for what happens after death. Egypt provides an obvious contrast, with so much of its religion, and sometimes a significant portion of its national economy, devoted to an obsessive quest for immortality. Apparently the early Israelites lived contentedly with the thought that death is final, survival—if any—being in the shadowy and lifeless realm of Sheol. They rejoiced in Yahweh's benefits in this life and hoped their children and grandchildren would survive and prosper—and that was enough for them.

Israel's God also stood in an unusual relationship with its government. The tribes functioned together for some time without a king—that in itself was unusual in that time and place—and Israel's histories reflect considerable misgivings about the idea of monarchy from the very start. The book of Judges describes the first Israelite to try to become king, Abimelech, as a thoroughly unsavory character who "butchered his seventy brothers, the sons of Jerubbaal, on a single stone block, all but Jotham the youngest, who survived because he had hidden himself" (Judg. 9:5). It was not an auspicious beginning for monarchy, and the story goes on to present a fable in which the olive tree, the fig tree, and the vine all refuse to become king of the plants, while only the thorn bush accepts the job. The historians later tell how, shortly before 1000 B.C., Samuel, the great spokesman of Yahweh, agreed to anoint Saul as Israel's first king only after angry resistance:

> This is the word of the LORD the God of Israel: I brought Israel up from Egypt; I delivered you from the Egyptians and from all the kingdoms that oppressed you; but today you have rejected your God who saved you from all your misery and distress; you have said, "No, set up a king over us." (I Sam. 10:18–19)

To some, the monarchy seemed a betrayal of Yahweh and Israel's liberation. What a contrast with Egypt or a dozen other kingdoms where the ruler was virtually divine. Egyptian Pharaohs did not make mistakes. Saul, on the other hand, appears to us as a bitter if heroic figure, rejected by Yahweh, driven to madness, and sent off to defeat and death. Israel always looked to Saul's successor David as its greatest king, but its story of him frankly portrays a man who disgraced himself over another man's wife and lost control of his own children.

Israel was thus unique, with its belief in one God, who made new things happen, who was the Lord of this world and this life, and who could criticize a king as easily as support him. Yet that uniqueness always faced all sorts of threats. The religions of their neighbors tempted the Israelites away from Yahweh, and under David's successors the government grew more centralized and the court ritual more elaborate, and the worship of Yahweh itself might easily have developed into just another royal cult.

THE FAITH OF THE PROPHETS

More than anyone else, the prophets prevented that. It could be argued that a history of Israel's religion should scarcely mention the prophets, since nearly all of them kept insisting that no one ever listened to them. Yet, however small their influence at the time, the prophets introduced the ideas that would shape the future.

"Prophecy" did not necessarily have anything to do with foretelling the future. The prophets were those who spoke on behalf of Yahweh —to warn, to promise, to advise, to threaten. The first references to prophets have to do with two different sorts of people. Wandering bands of ecstatic prophets went into trances or seizures as if some divine force had seized them. The young Saul, traveling around the countryside, met "a company of prophets coming down from the hill-shrine, led by lute, harp, fife, and drum, and filled with prophetic rapture" (I Sam. 10:5). Many cultures think of such uncontrolled behavior as being connected to the divine in a special way—the madman or the epileptic must be in receipt of special messages from God. On the other hand, there were the official prophets of the royal court and the religious shrines who advised the king. "The king of Israel and Jehoshaphat king of Judah," one account begins, "were seated on their thrones, in shining armour, at the entrance to the gate of Samaria, and all the prophets were prophesying before them" (I Kings 22:10). Such prophets were clearly part of the hired help.

Other nations had ecstatic prophets (who rarely addressed social issues) and court prophets (who often told their employers only what they wanted to hear), but to a unique degree Israel developed something different—prophets who gave advice and warnings, not because someone had hired them, but because they felt a special call from Yahweh himself. Often they criticized the king or the religious ceremonies, and their criticisms began to change Israel's religion.

We tend to take a connection between religion and ethics for granted; one's faith ought to help shape one's moral values. For much of human history, however, worship meant making the proper sacrifices and following the proper ritual; it might have very little to do with morality. In Homer's *Iliad*, for instance, various gods and goddesses punish heroes for failing to offer the proper sacrifices, but they rarely call them to account for moral failings. The prophet Amos, writing about 750 B.C., thus proposed a new idea of proper worship when he declared on behalf of Yahweh,

> I hate, I spurn your pilgrim-feasts;
>   I will not delight in your sacred ceremonies.
> When you present your sacrifices and offerings
>   I will not accept them,
> nor look on the buffaloes of your shared offerings.
> Spare me the sound of your songs;
> I cannot endure the music of your lutes.
> Let justice roll on like a river
> and righteousness like an ever-flowing stream.
>   (Amos 5:21–24)

Yahweh, the prophets increasingly taught, cared about righteousness, not ritual. He had no respect for those who "sell the innocent for silver and the destitute for a pair of shoes . . . grind the heads of the poor into the earth and thrust the humble out of their way" (Amos 2:6), regardless of the sacrifices they performed.

The prophets also made Yahweh less a tribal or national God. Israel had long recognized that it should worship only Yahweh, but at first it assumed that other nations would worship their own deities. Yahweh was Israel's God, but Marduk might be the god of the Babylonians and look after their affairs. Amos, however, declared that Yahweh had brought "Israel up from Egypt, the Philistines from Caphtor, the Aramaeans from Kir" (Amos 9:7). Indeed, he "made the Pleiades and Orion . . . , turned darkness into morning and darkened day into night" (Amos 5:8). Yahweh did not just watch over this particular nation; he ruled all nations, indeed, all the universe.

Later prophets also emphasized Yahweh's relations with individuals. Tribal gods sometimes punished a whole people for one person's sins, or chastened later generations for the evil actions of their ancestors. When the early prophet Elisha denounced King Ahab (about 860 B.C.), for instance, he declared in the name of Yahweh, "All the house of Ahab shall perish and I will destroy every mother's son of his house in Israel" (II Kings 9:8). The Israelites had a traditional saying that when the fathers eat sour grapes, their children taste the sourness, and it sets their teeth on edge. Jeremiah, however (writing about 600 B.C.), looked toward a day when "it shall no longer be said, 'The fathers have eaten sour grapes and the children's teeth are set on edge'; for a man shall die for his own wrongdoing; the man who eats sour grapes shall have his own teeth set on edge" (Jer. 31:29–30). That emphasized personal responsibility and individual relationship with God. Yahweh was becoming at once the God of the whole universe and the God of individuals.

Yahweh had always been a God who acted in history, guiding, rewarding, or punishing his people, but the prophets began to change Israel's understanding of *how* he acted. Earlier stories pictured Yahweh dramatically interfering in the course of events—parting the waters of the sea, or making the sun stand still so that Joshua could win a battle. Many of the prophets now spoke of more "ordinary" events. The Assyrian army won a battle; the Persians conquered the Babylonians. All of that could be explained in terms of politics and military power. Yet the prophet said that Yahweh was at work here too—not interrupting the normal flow of events but guiding all the events of history.

Even with this broader sense of divine action, however, it grew harder to see Yahweh at work in history. Earlier prophets addressed the immediate context: Israel needed to repent right now, or Yahweh would punish the nation. Later prophets grew less confident of Yahweh's imminent intervention. In 721 B.C. an Assyrian army conquered the northern half of the people of Israel. A hundred years later King Josiah, ruling the surviving Kingdom of Judah, instituted major reforms, seeking to return to the proper worship of Yahweh, but then was killed in a disastrous military defeat.

"How long, O LORD, have I cried to thee, unanswered?" asked the prophet Habakkuk.

> I cry, "Violence!", but thou dost not save.
> Why dost thou let me see such misery,
>   why countenance wrongdoing?
>   (Hab. 1:2–3)

Then in 586 Babylonian forces defeated Judah too and led many of its leaders into exile. A faith based on Yahweh's relation with his people found itself with no land, no king, and no Temple.

> By the rivers of Babylon we sat down and wept
>   when we remembered Zion.
> There on the willow trees
>   we hung up our harps,
> for those who carried us off
>   demanded music and singing,
> and our captors called on us to be merry:
>   "Sing us one of the songs of Zion."

How could we sing the LORD's song
in a foreign land?

(Ps. 137:1–4)

About fifty years later a remnant returned to Jerusalem, but something had changed irreversibly. The few prophets after the return from exile spoke mostly about their own inadequacy, and then the tradition of prophecy came to an end.

We cannot see what lies before us,
we have no prophet now;
we have no one who knows
how long this is to last.

(Ps. 74:9)

Somehow, after centuries of tragedy, the sense that Yahweh advised his people and intervened at each stage of their history had lost its plausibility. The relation between God and people would have to be redefined if it was to survive.

ALTERNATIVES WITHIN JUDAISM

When the present looks bleak, people tend to look to the past or to the future. Some Israelites exiled in Babylon argued that Yahweh did not need to keep sending new messages through his prophets, since the Law he had given Moses communicated once and for all everything he wanted or needed to say. Around 400 B.C. a priest named Ezra returned from Babylonia to Jerusalem determined to enforce a rigorous code of law. He particularly emphasized rules that set Israel apart from its neighbors—laws against intermarriage with non-Jews and special customs like circumcision or dietary laws. Reduced in size, without political independence, Israel risked simply disappearing into the morass of the ancient Near East. Ezra and the scholars of the Law who followed him argued that, to survive and preserve their faith in Yahweh, the people would have to emphasize what set them apart. That conscious decision to set themselves apart virtually created a new religion, so that historians begin to talk about "Judaism" rather than "the religion of Israel" when they reach the time of Ezra.

Others in those years after the exile looked to the future. A movement called apocalypticism declared that Yahweh has stopped acting in history so that the evils of the present age can run their course to disaster; only then will he intervene to establish his reign of peace and justice in a new age. The book of Jubilees states this clearly: "For calamity follows on calamity, and wound on wound, and tribulation on tribulation. . . . For all have done evil, and every mouth speaks iniquity. . . . Behold the earth shall be destroyed on account of all their works" (Jubilees 23:13, 17–18).[2] The apocalypticists often claimed that a secret text of great antiquity revealed to them the pattern of all history and the details of the destruction and renewal that lay ahead. Such apocalyptic hopes made it possible to believe in Yahweh's ultimate Lordship over history at a time when he seemed to have abandoned his people. Yahweh was merely waiting for the right moment.

Apocalypticism raised some problems for Israel's religious tradition. Israel's religion had concerned this life, not hope for existence after death. If we dismiss the present age as an evil time, however, and place all our hopes in a future age, then those who live and die, often tragically, before that future arrives seem abandoned by God. Hence the complaint of many:

> "As we die, so die the righteous,
> And what benefit do they reap for their deeds?
> Behold, even as we, so do they die in grief and
>   darkness. . . .
> And henceforth for ever shall they see no light."

"Nevertheless they perished and became as though they had not been, and their spirits descended into Sheol in tribulation." (I Enoch 102:6–8, 11)[3]

At first tentatively, therefore, apocalypticists began to talk about the resurrection of the dead—everyone, even those who had died in the meantime, would receive a reward or punishment when the new age begins. But that remained a matter of debate among Jews. The book of Acts (describing, of course, a much later time) tells how Paul was once brought before a Jewish council. To extricate himself from a tight spot, he declared that he was really on trial because he believed in the resurrection of the dead—and at once his Jewish accusers "fell out among themselves" and "a great uproar broke out" (Acts 23:7–9). The hope of resurrection remained controversial.

Some Jews in the postexilic period did not want to wait for the fulfillment of such hopes and sought to improve their lot here and now by military rebellion. After Alexander the Great conquered the Persian Empire around 330 B.C., his generals divided up the territory, and dynasties based in Egypt (the Ptolemies) and Syria (the Seleucids) fought over the traditional land of Israel. In 168 B.C. a Seleucid king named Antiochus Epiphanes decided to end toleration of the Jewish religion and erected a statue of Zeus in the Temple of Yahweh in Jerusalem. Out in one village an old priest named Mattathias watched in horror as a fellow Jew offered the first sacrifice at a pagan shrine "and in a fury of righteous anger rushed forward and slaughtered the traitor on the very altar" (I Macc. 2:24). Mattathias and his sons, one of them named Judas Maccabeus, fled to the hills and began a guerrilla war that eventually established an independent Jewish state. Political independence at long last was not the fulfillment of Israel's hopes, however, for some of the Maccabean rulers proved quarrelsome and corrupt. When the Roman general Pompey turned up in 69 B.C., one faction even solicited his support, and the Romans conquered the Maccabean kingdom without much resistance.

By the time of Jesus, Judaism had thus become quite diverse. Jews had spread throughout the Roman Empire and even beyond its borders, and many of them modified their faith to fit in with the culture around them. At Elephantine in southern Egypt, for instance, a colony of Jews survived for centuries, worshiping the mother-goddess as well as Yahweh at their own temple. Also in Egypt, in the great city of Alexandria, the Jewish philosopher Philo made important connections between Judaism and Greek philosophy, connections that influenced some early Christian theology, as we shall see in the next chapter. Even within the traditional land of Israel, there were conflicting parties. The Sadducees watched over the rituals of the Temple at Jerusalem. The Pharisees piously pursued a scrupulous obedience to the Law. The Zealots urged military revolt against the Romans. Many groups dreamed of a coming apocalypse; in recent years the discovery of the Dead Sea Scrolls has disclosed a good deal about one such community, at Qumran, which retreated from society to a desert monastery to practice ritual purity and await the coming great conflict in which the armies of Yahweh would defeat his enemies. They baptized new members and honored a great leader, the "Teacher of Righteousness"—both points suggesting interesting parallels with Christianity, parallels whose exact significance scholars continue to debate. Most ordinary people probably "belonged" to none of these groups in a formal way but felt the influence of all of them in varying degrees.

A generation after Jesus' death the disastrous revolt of A.D. 66 to 71 discredited Zealot military ambitions and apocalyptic dreams. Jerusalem lay in ruins, and all the hopes for a kingdom of Yahweh seemed destroyed as well. As in the time of Ezra, the scholars of the

Law saved Judaism, and the Pharisaic rabbis (teachers) became the intellectual leaders of Judaism for many centuries to come. The Pharisees' comments on the Law began the traditions of Judaism as we know it today.

JESUS IN CONTEXT

Jewish apocalypticism survived mainly among Christians. Basic Christian terms like "Messiah" and "Son of Man" developed in the context of Jewish apocalyptic, though Christians often exaggerate the importance of such ideas in Judaism. Hearing the Old Testament passages that seem to look forward to the coming of the Messiah so often every Christmas season, one tends to forget what a small portion of Israel's Scriptures those selections represent. Still, Messianic expectations certainly do run a long way back in Israel's history. The word "Messiah" in Hebrew (*Christos* in Greek) means "the anointed one." Originally it could apply to any king ceremonially sanctioned by Yahweh. Samuel poured oil on the heads of Saul and David in a ritual of anointing and giving Yahweh's blessing. As kings became weak and corrupt and then the monarchy came to an end, however, the focus shifted from the present ruler to a great future king who would restore prosperity, justice, and peace to Israel—a Messiah, a great political and military champion of Yahweh and leader of the people.

Others had different hopes. The book of Daniel told of a vision of cosmic wonders and conflicts, and of their culmination:

> I was still watching in visions of the night and I saw one like a son of man coming with the clouds of heaven; he approached the Ancient in Years and was presented to him. Sovereignty and glory and kingly power were given to him, so that all people and nations of every language should serve him; his sovereignty was to be an everlasting sovereignty which should not pass away, and his kingly power such as should never be impaired. (Dan. 7:13–14)[4]

This "Son of Man" is a heavenly figure, descending at the head of armies of angels, quite unlike the human, political Messiah.

Historians cannot determine the interrelations among these hopes or their relative importance by the time of Jesus. The Qumran community apparently hoped for several different Messianic figures. Jesus certainly entered a society full of expectations and looking for a person to give shape to its dreams. His message responded to that apocalyptic context. The first words Mark quotes from Jesus are, "The time has come; the kingdom of God is upon you; repent, and believe the Gospel" (Mark 1:15), and the Gospels keep returning to the image of the coming kingdom of God. But how will the kingdom come? Sometimes the New Testament has Jesus describe a grand cataclysm that will give birth to the new age, with the imagery of Daniel's vision.

> But in those days, after that distress, the sun will be darkened, the moon will not give her light; the stars will come falling from the sky, the celestial powers will be shaken. Then they will see the Son of Man coming in the clouds with great power and glory, and he will send out the angels and gather his chosen from the four winds, from the farthest bounds of earth to the farthest bounds of heaven. (Mark 13:24–27)

In other passages the kingdom of God is within us, a change in human lives already begun under the impact of Jesus' preaching. To some extent these pictures seem inconsistent. Is the kingdom a private experience already happening or a spectacular public event that still lies in the future? Perhaps one of the Gospels' most common images of the kingdom preserves something of both ideas. The kingdom, we read again and again, is like a seed, already planted and now germinating in secret, but still waiting to emerge and burst forth in flower in the future. Christians ever since, at any rate, have sought to preserve both ways of talking about the kingdom: a transformation already experienced in their hearts, and a transformation of the world yet to come.

The more we learn of the Judaism of Jesus' time, through new discoveries like the Dead Sea Scrolls or more careful study of documents long available, the more difficult it becomes to make radical distinctions between most of his teaching and that of his Jewish contemporaries. Too many Christian historians, for instance, have contrasted Jesus' message of love with "narrow Jewish legalism." Some Pharisees may have become so obsessed with fulfilling the details of the law that they forgot about caring for their neighbors— it is a problem not unknown among Christians—but the greatest of the early Pharisaic rabbis, Hillel, Jesus' contemporary, proclaimed: "What is hateful to yourself do not do to your neighbor. That is the entire Torah. All the rest is commentary."[5] That seems identical with Jesus' commandment to love.

The most distinctive feature of Jesus' teaching, indeed, seems to have been the role of Jesus himself, yet on just this point the Gospels offer puzzling indications. Particularly in Mark, for instance, whenever people recognize Jesus as the Messiah, Jesus tells them to keep this a secret. Jesus often speaks of the "Son of Man" (Daniel's apocalyptic hero), but nearly always in the third person and the future tense. Did he think of himself as the Son of Man?

Even a rather skeptical historian, however, will probably admit some features of Jesus' teaching about himself. He claimed a special authority, it seems, and a special relationship with God. Bystanders in the Gospels remark that he speaks with authority, and, in a culture where most took the Law as God's definitive word, Jesus did not just interpret the Law. He sometimes modified it: "You have heard that it was said . . . But I say to you . . ." To a first-century Jew, that represented a very strong claim to speak on God's behalf. Further, Jesus apparently thought that people's response to him personally would determine their relation to the coming kingdom of God. Following Jesus led into the kingdom.

The themes of Jesus' teaching are important, but of course he was more than a teacher. All the Gospels put the end of his life at the dramatic center of his story. Here all the hopes of Israel come together—he is the king of the Jews, the greatest of the suffering prophets. Yet Jesus transformed those expectations. He did not lead Israel to victory over Rome. Indeed, one of the remarkable features of the narratives of his last days is that his increasing isolation makes it impossible to identify him with any one "side" or cause. The Roman governor sentenced him as a Jewish rebel, but the leaders of Judaism also turned against him. He attacked the powerful on behalf of the poor, but in the end the mob too called for his blood. His own disciples ran away; Peter denied him. He did not go to his death agony as a representative of Jews, or of the poor, or of Christians, but alone, and thus, according to Christian faith, as a representative of all.

FOR FURTHER READING

INTRODUCTIONS. B. Davie Napier, *Song of the Vineyard*, rev. ed. (Fortress Press, 1981), provides a well-written and thoughtful survey of Old Testament literature. Bernhard W. Anderson, *Understanding the Old Testament* (Prentice-Hall, 1975), is a widely used and reliable textbook. O. Jessie Lace (ed.), *Understanding the Old Testament*

(Cambridge: Cambridge University Press, 1972), offers several useful introductory essays.

IMPORTANT BUT MORE DIFFICULT. Two excellent recent histories of ancient Israel: John Bright, *A History of Israel,* 3d ed. (Westminster Press, 1981), and Siegfried Herrmann, *A History of Israel in Old Testament Times,* tr. by John Bowden (Fortress Press, 1981). William F. Albright, *The Biblical Period from Abraham to Ezra* (Harper & Row, Harper Torchbooks, 1963), provides a quick summary of that history. Albright's *From the Stone Age to Christianity* (Doubleday & Co., Anchor Books, 1957), sets ancient Israel in a larger historical context, with particular emphasis on archaeological evidence. Gerhard von Rad, *Old Testament Theology,* 2 vols., tr. by D. M. G. Stalker (Edinburgh: Oliver & Boyd, 1962, 1965), seems to me the most impressive scholarly summary of that field at the moment. On Jesus, a standard work is Günther Bornkamm, *Jesus of Nazareth,* tr. by Irene and Fraser McLuskey (Harper & Row, 1975). The views set forth in the present volume, in this and much else, have been most deeply influenced by Hans W. Frei, *The Identity of Jesus Christ* (Fortress Press, 1975), and Wolfhart Pannenberg, *Jesus—God and Man,* tr. by Lewis L. Wilkins and Duane A. Priebe, 2d ed. (Westminster Press, 1977).

NOTES

1. "The Babylonian Chronicle," in D. Winton Thomas (ed.), *Documents from Old Testament Times* (London: Thomas Nelson & Sons, 1958), p. 82.

2. R. H. Charles (ed.), *The Apocrypha and Pseudepigrapha of the Old Testament,* Vol. 2 (Oxford: Clarendon Press, 1913), p. 48.

3. Ibid., p. 274.

4. I have substituted the literal Hebrew "son of man" where the *New English Bible* has "man."

5. Quoted in Jacob Neusner, *From Politics to Piety* (KTAV Publishing House, 1979), p. 13.

3

THE MISSION TO THE GENTILES

Christian theology is a series of footnotes to St. Paul.
                                        —Sydney Ahlstrom[1]

A short time after Jesus' death about A.D. 30, a handful of his followers began to proclaim him as their resurrected Lord. Within a hundred years, thousands of people from Rome to Mesopotamia shared that faith. But their first century was a time of conflict and change as well as growth for Christians. At first they eagerly awaited Jesus' return in glory at almost any moment, but two generations later that expectation had, for many, receded into the background. All of the very first Christians were Jews, but well before 130 a clear majority came from a Gentile background. Throughout this period, Christians were struggling to find ways to explain who Jesus was and why he was so important. Those issues will be the major themes of this chapter.

The books of the New Testament come out of that first century after Jesus' death. While Christians today often read them for religious inspiration or moral guidance, and while scholarship studies the text and ideas of each book, this chapter will instead approach the New Testament with the eye of a historian of theology. These books are virtually the only records we have of Christianity's beginnings. What do they tell us about the general trends in earliest Christian theology?

One figure—Paul—dominates the story they give us. Over half of the New Testament was written by him or his followers. He cannot have been an easy man to live with. Arrogant, argumentative, and— if we can believe tradition—short, bald, and ugly, he had more enemies than friends even among fellow Christians. He didn't much care.

Five times the Jews have given me the thirty-nine strokes; three times I have been beaten with rods; once I was stoned; three times I have been shipwrecked, and for twenty-four hours I was

adrift on the open sea. I have been constantly on the road; I have
met dangers from rivers, dangers from robbers, dangers from my
fellow-countrymen, dangers from foreigners. . . . If boasting there
must be, I will boast of the things that show up my weakness.
. . . I am well content, for Christ's sake, with weakness, contempt,
persecution, hardship, and frustration; for when I am weak, then
I am strong. (II Cor. 11:24–26, 30; 12:10)

As a devout Jew, Paul had at first even joined in the persecution of
Christians. Then he had an experience so overpowering that it made
him a Christian and changed his life forever. The book of Acts tells
how he saw a blinding light and heard the voice of Christ from
heaven, but Paul himself never described the experience at all. Whatever happened, it led him to proclaim that Christ can change our lives
in so fundamental a way that nothing else matters. "There is no such
thing as Jew and Greek, slave and freeman, male and female; for you
are all one person in Christ Jesus" (Gal. 3:28). That conviction made
Paul the enemy of anyone who wanted to set apart those who kept
Jewish law, or those who spoke in tongues, or those who counted
themselves a spiritual elite, or anybody else, as better than their
fellow Christians. In defending his faith in the unity of all Christians
in Christ, he developed much of the foundation of Christian theology.

Yet the New Testament is not just Paul's story. Bishop Stephen
Neill has entitled his introduction to the New Testament *Jesus
Through Many Eyes,* and that makes well an important point. The
first Christians were diverse; they understood their faith in diverse
ways, and the New Testament preserves a record of that diversity.
Reading it as a historian of theology, one comes to recognize the
different expectations concerning Christ's return, the different ideas
about the relations between Christianity and Judaism, and the different pictures of Jesus it reflects. Christians who are nervous about
diversity of belief should probably not read the New Testament carefully—or, then again, perhaps they should.

THE SECOND COMING

Consider the question of Christ's return. Some Jewish apocalyptic
writers had expected that a Messianic figure would come, end the
present age, establish the kingdom of God, and raise the dead to
receive their rewards and punishments. Jesus' followers believed that
he had been raised from the dead, but the present age seemed to be
continuing, and certainly no general resurrection had occurred. No
one had expected an isolated resurrection in the midst of history, and

no one knew quite what to make of it. At first many Christians expected Jesus to return at any moment. They were surprised and disturbed when some Christians died and Jesus had still not yet come again. In First Thessalonians (possibly the earliest writing in the New Testament) Paul reassured them, explaining, "We believe that Jesus died and rose again; and so it will be for those who died as Christians; God will bring them to life with Jesus. . . . We who are left alive until the Lord comes . . . shall join them" (I Thess. 4:14–15, 17). He seems to assume that Jesus will return before the deaths of many of his readers ("we who are left alive until the Lord comes"). That expectation moved into the background in Paul's later writings, but he never explicitly abandoned it. His notorious advice that it is best not to marry, for instance, rested in part on the conviction that the tribulations of the end of this age are at hand, and this is no time to have to worry about a family (see II Cor. 7).

The odd thing is that Paul, and many other early Christians, began with a conviction that Jesus was about to return, and then gradually realized that they had been wrong, without that realization ever shaking their faith. Some historians have found this so improbable that they have declared the "crisis of the delay of the Second Coming" the central issue in early Christian theology,[2] but there is no evidence that any such crisis occurred. The expectation that he would soon return had at first been part of faith in Christ, but it turned out not to be essential to that faith.

In some New Testament books a different point of view is already taken for granted. The author of Luke and Acts,[3] for example, consciously presented the history of early Christianity as a story of the expansion and progress of the faith, with the expectation that that expansion would continue for a long time, with Christ returning only at its culmination far in the future. He has rejected the expectations of an imminent Second Coming and indeed the whole apocalyptic view of the present age as an evil time getting steadily worse. The author of the Gospel of John, on the other hand, thought that Christ had *already* come in glory. His life had been a triumph, and the new age has already begun in Jesus' preaching and the faith it has generated. That hardly leaves a place for a *second* coming.

But apocalyptic hopes did not die away either. Apocalyptic imagery and visions of Christ's return fill the book of Revelation. Scholars continue to debate when that book was written, but most agree that II Peter is one of the latest books of the New Testament—yet it too conveys a powerful hope that Christ will soon return. One simply cannot trace a single trend on this issue. Some Christians in the New

Testament period thought that Christ was about to return; others did not. Christians ever since have held both views—and all can find New Testament support for their positions.

JEWS AND GREEKS

The "delay" of Christ's return, then, did not provoke a crisis; the question of Christianity's relationship to Judaism did. The very first Christians in Jerusalem had grown up Jews, and both they and their Jewish neighbors at first assumed that, even if they believed Jesus to be the Messiah, they remained Jews. True, from the very start they baptized new members and repeated Jesus' words at the Last Supper as they shared bread and wine—the ritual that would become the Eucharist or Communion or the Lord's Supper, though in the earliest church it usually took place within the context of a common meal rather than as a separate rite. But one could find baptisms and ritual meals among Jewish groups like the Qumran community. None of that needed to place them outside Judaism.

But Judaism itself, as the last chapter suggested, was a complicated thing. Even at the start, when all Christians were Jews, they were different kinds of Jews, and those differences created problems. Acts 6 reports the first real conflict in the Christian community. A group of twelve served as the leaders of the Christians in Jerusalem. Peter acted as chairman at first, though later Jesus' brother James seems to have taken over this role. "The Twelve" all spoke Aramaic, a language closely related to Hebrew, but some Christians came from among the Greek-speaking Jews. The Christian community distributed free food among its widows, and the Greek-speaking Jewish Christians complained that, since the Twelve took charge of this, they did not get their fair share. The community therefore elected seven deacons, all with Greek names, to supervise charity.

But was this really just an argument over free food? Jews who spoke Greek were more open to outside influences and less committed to Jewish traditions. It seems probable that, when they became Christians, they would be more likely to move away from Jewish customs altogether. At any rate, the Jews had apparently tolerated the first Christians, but now Jewish leaders turned against these Greek-speaking Jewish Christians and executed their leader Stephen, one of the seven deacons. Apparently this group represented a more fundamental challenge to Judaism.

That execution raised the level of conflict between Jews and Christians, conflict made worse by their legal situation. In order to control politically subversive or morally dubious cults, the Roman Empire required that religions receive government authorization. Judaism was a *religio licita,* an authorized religion, and the first Christians claimed to be Jews. Indeed, they insisted that since Jesus had been the Messiah, only those who accepted him were truly faithful to Judaism. Understandably, Jews rejected this interpretation and denied that Christians were still part of Judaism. This had the effect of making Christians subject to persecution as members of an illegal religion. Some Christians responded with attacks on the blindness of the Jews. When Christianity was an oppressed minority fighting for its life, such attacks were understandable, but their inclusion in the New Testament preserved them for later centuries when Christians dominated and Jews were the minority facing persecution. The same words in a different context had a tragically different meaning.

The initial persecution had driven the Greek-speaking Jewish Christians from Jerusalem, and only the Christians more faithful to Jewish tradition remained there. Then, between 66 and 71, the Jews rebelled against Roman domination, and the Romans defeated them and destroyed the city of Jerusalem. Traditional Jewish-Christian communities, however, survived in Palestine and Syria. The Gospel of Matthew and the letter of James, although written in Greek, probably indicate some characteristic concerns of these communities. Matthew mentions at nearly every turn how Jesus fulfilled some prophecy in the Jewish Scriptures and emphasizes how Jesus had come to fulfill the Law rather than to destroy it, and James insists that a Christian must lead a morally righteous life (that is, follow the Law) as well as having faith. The authors of both seem to be writing out of a Jewish tradition and addressing a Jewish-Christian audience.

In later centuries we catch glimpses of Palestinian or Syrian Jewish Christianity, but by then it seems far outside the Christian mainstream. Christianity began its rapid expansion when it preached to Gentiles as well as Jews, and when it made it clear that you did not have to become a Jew in order to become a Christian. That shift began with the Greek-speaking Jewish Christians who fled Jerusalem, and Paul became its greatest leader. He had been brought up a pious Jew, "circumcised on my eighth day, Israelite by race, of the tribe of Benjamin, a Hebrew born and bred; in my attitude to the law, a Pharisee" (Phil. 3:5). But his conversion to Christianity left him convinced that differences between Jews and Gentiles did not matter in the unity of Christ. He assured Gentile converts that they need not be circumcized or follow Jewish dietary regulations and other laws. Many Jewish Christians, however, continued to observe their ancestral customs, and that meant that Jewish and Gentile Christians could not even eat a meal together, for the Gentile would destroy the Jew's ritual purity. Christ ought to have set us free from all that, Paul insisted. No set of rules, no list of good deeds, can make a human being truly worthy in the sight of God, but Christ's liberating good news is that God loves us anyway, in spite of our unworthiness. "Christ died for us while we were yet sinners, and that is God's own proof of his love towards us" (Rom. 5:8). The unity of those who have faith in Christ is therefore far more important than adherence to any law. To some Jewish Christians, such indifference to the Law seemed a betrayal of their heritage, and Paul had to go to Jerusalem to negotiate an agreement with James and the Jerusalem leaders. Luke's account of the result differs from Paul's own (compare Acts 15 and Galatians 2), but it is at least clear that everyone acknowledged Paul's right to preach to Gentiles and invite them to become Christians without accepting all of Jewish law.

Paul then began to face an opposite problem among Gentile converts, who were eager to believe that Christianity freed them from any moral or religious responsibilities at all. To the flotsam and jetsam of a tough Greek port like Corinth, that sounded like a great idea. If God's grace, his unmerited love for us, comes to us even when we are sinners, they asked, "Shall we [not] persist in sin, so that there may be all the more grace?" (Rom. 6:1). Of course not, Paul replied. We cannot earn God's love, but, having received it anyway, we strive in gratitude to become "dead to sin and alive to God, in union with Christ Jesus" (Rom. 6:11). No one with faith in Christ will want to continue sinning.

Sin, in other words, could injure Christ's community as easily as excessive regard for the Law could. Even special spiritual gifts, if misused, could prove disruptive. Many early Christians saw visions or spoke prophecies or spoke in tongues (crying out words of unknown languages under the inspiration of the Spirit). Paul acknowledged the genuineness of all these gifts, and indeed declared he was "more gifted in ecstatic utterance than any of you" (I Cor. 14:18), but he insisted on their secondary importance. These gifts could divide the community or distract people from Christ if not subjected to some control. "If your ecstatic utterance yields no precise meaning, how can anyone tell what you are saying? You will be talking into the air. . . . You are, I know, eager for gifts of the Spirit; then aspire above all to those which build up the church" (I Cor. 14:9, 12). Paul had found a great liberation in a sense of unity in Christ, and therefore he would limit freedom which threatened that unity—whether by separating

Jews from Gentiles, disrupting the community through sin, or creating an elite with special spiritual gifts.

Some of Paul's critics today, however, charge that his acceptance of many of the values and attitudes of his time and culture really destroyed his vision of freedom. For instance, he refused to grant women equality in the church or in society. He condemned homosexual activity. He urged that Christians treat their slaves well, but did not demand that they free them. He called for obedience to all governmental authority, since "there is no authority but by act of God, and the existing authorities are instituted by him; consequently anyone who rebels against authority is resisting a divine institution" (Rom. 13:1–2).

For an understanding of Paul's views on these and other matters we ought to judge what he says in the context of his own time. In a society where some religious groups did not even admit women as members, for instance, it is striking how often Paul's letters singled out women as among the leaders and special friends to whom he extended greetings. Most of his contemporaries thought that in marriage a man simply owned his wife; Paul's comments on marriage nearly always emphasized the equality of the relationship: "The husband must give the wife what is due to her, and the wife equally must give the husband his due. The wife cannot claim her body as her own; it is her husband's. Equally, the husband cannot claim his body as his own; it is his wife's (I Cor. 7:3–4). In Paul's time, that was a radical idea.

Similarly, in our society, when Christians often have vast political influence, Paul's emphasis on simply obeying the government may seem regrettably indifferent to the need to work for social change. When one remembers that Paul wrote as a member of a tiny sect with no political power at all, living under a dictatorship that suspected Christians of insurrectionist tendencies, however, it gets a bit unreasonable to expect him to have led a political reform campaign. One would likewise have to know much more than a hasty reading reveals about the economic and social realities of ancient slavery (a slavery, by the way, that had nothing to do with race) before judging how useful it would have been to urge its abolition. The issue of homosexual practices is unclear in a different way, for Paul merely mentioned in passing, as part of a list of the evils of his time, that among sinful pagans males are filled with lust and behave indecently with other males (Rom. 1:27), without explaining just what he meant or why he opposed such behavior. At any rate, an understanding of Paul's thinking ought to begin with his central themes of freedom and unity in

Christ, and to think about limits he seems to impose on such freedom and unity (whether one wants to follow him or criticize him at such points), remembering the cultural context in which he wrote.

THE BEGINNINGS OF CHRISTOLOGY

Paul had found in Jesus Christ the basis for his new understanding of his life and the world. Who was Jesus that he should make such a difference? That was an important and difficult question not just for Paul but for all the earliest Christians. For one thing, they shaped their first answers in terms of Jewish culture and history. But when they proclaimed to Greeks or other non-Jews that Jesus was the long-awaited Messiah or the Son of Man promised by Daniel, their new audience found this totally unfamiliar. "Christ," the Greek translation of "Messiah," which for Greek-speaking Jews conveyed a sense of centuries of expectation, among Gentiles soon came to serve as little more than part of Jesus' name. Christians had to find new ways of identifying Jesus.

Even Judaism, to be sure, included many different hopes, and no one can be sure just how they were connected by the time of Jesus. Christians combined and modified them in a variety of ways. Jesus was, they said, the Messiah, descended from David—but not the sort of political or military leader many Jews had expected. Jesus was the apocalyptic Son of Man, now raised from the dead and soon to return in glory to inaugurate the new age of God's kingdom. That pointed to two stages of Christ's existence: his earthly life and his triumphant return. The first Christians probably left it at that, but soon some began to ask about the time before Jesus' birth and the time between his resurrection and his second coming. Paul had already offered a four-stage account. Jesus Christ (1) was with God before birth, then (2) lived a life on earth, and now (3) dwells with God in heaven awaiting (4) his second coming.

> For the divine nature was his from the first; yet he did not think to snatch at equality with God, but made himself nothing, assuming the nature of a slave. Bearing the human likeness, revealed in human shape, he humbled himself, and in obedience accepted even death—death on a cross. Therefore God raised him to the heights and bestowed on him the name above all names, that at the name of Jesus every knee should bow. (Phil. 2:6–10)

Talking about Christ's existence before birth thus not only filled out the story; it also identified Christ more clearly with God and opened up a new dimension of Christ's obedience and sacrifice for us. Not only did he go to the cross; he had voluntarily submitted to becoming a human being. Matthew and Luke talked about Christ's becoming human in a different way, in the story of the virgin birth, which neither Paul nor Mark's Gospel mentioned. This provided a new way of expressing Jesus' special relationship with God. In traditional Judaism, calling someone the "Son of God" might mean only that he served God's will with particular faithfulness. Christians now claimed more. Jesus was the Son of God in the sense that he had no human father.

Still, this did not yet address the full problem of explaining Jesus' importance to people who knew nothing of Jewish traditions. To do that, Christians had to borrow from other cultures. The "mystery cults" provided one helpful context. To understand their significance one needs to know a bit about the history of Greek religion. Much of traditional Greek religion had centered on the goddesses and gods of the city-states. Each small, independent city-state offered public sacrifices to its deities in hopes of securing peace and prosperity. These cults did not offer the individual much sense of personal relationship with the deities, and, like the religion of early Israel, they concerned this life and had little to say about what happens after death. In the fifth and fourth centuries B.C., many Greeks began to find these civic cults inadequate, and after Alexander the Great effectively ended the independence of the Greek city-states in the late fourth century B.C., ceremonies tied up with political activities that no longer existed seemed to lose their point.

The mystery cults—some imported, some homegrown in Greece—offered something many Greeks found spiritually more satisfying. Those who joined a mystery cult underwent a secret initiation. There they learned the story of a deity who had died but then risen to new life; and they became somehow united with that deity, so that they too would rise to new life after death. The mysteries offered a personal connection with a deity and a hope beyond death, and the emphasis on membership gave people a sense of belonging in a society where many traditional institutions had collapsed. All this provided Christians with an obvious analogy. Join our fellowship, they could say, and become one with Christ, participating in ceremonies of baptism and the sharing of bread and wine, and you, like Christ, will be raised from the dead.

If the mystery cults provided a ready analogy to explain Christianity, however, they could easily do more harm than good if a Christian failed to recognize the ways in which Christianity differed. Many of those differences went back to Christianity's Jewish roots. One could, for instance, join a number of different mystery cults, almost as easily as joining any private club today, and continue to worship the deities of one's city besides. Christians, like Jews before them, demanded that new followers turn away from all other cults and worship only one God. Like prophets such as Amos, Christians also expected that their faith would make an ethical difference. The mystery cults might encourage the development of some virtues, but they cared principally about participation in the rituals. Christianity called for love and sharing and a transformation of one's life. In addition, the mystery cults' stories of dying and rising gods took place—if one could locate them at all in time and space—in a vague, far-distant past; they really served to symbolize eternal truths about the ever-repeated cycles of birth and death. Christians, on the other hand, talked about a specific death and resurrection in quite recent times, a once-for-all event that had altered the course of history forever.

Another analogy from the world beyond Judaism that Christians could use, with caution, involved the savior cults of great rulers. When a great king defeated an enemy or conquered new territory and established order, peace, and justice, people often proclaimed him their "savior" and instituted ceremonies of worship. Christians talked of Christ as their savior and explained how he had transformed their lives and their world more fundamentally than any great ruler could do. Of course they also had to emphasize the difference between wealthy and powerful rulers and this humble carpenter's son who died on a cross.

Some Jews had already made connections with Greek thought, and Christians could draw on those resources too. The last chapter briefly mentioned Philo, a contemporary of Jesus who lived in Alexandria in Egypt. Earlier Jewish writers had talked about the Wisdom of God or the Word of God as if these were, not separate deities, of course, but divine powers with a kind of activity of their own. Philo took up these ideas, especially the Word of God (in Greek, the *Logos*). After all, think how important God's Word is in the Hebrew Scriptures. In Genesis, God creates by speaking—through a Word. Yahweh's Word comes to the prophets. Greek philosophers also talked about the Word, the Logos. It is hard to generalize about the roles this concept played in quite different systems, but the Logos usually meant a rational principle that orders the universe and, when we think properly, guides our understanding. That rational Logos described by the philosophers, Philo said, is the creating and prophetic Word of Yahweh, not a second God, but a special kind of manifestation of God.

The author of John's Gospel had probably not read Philo, but he drew on the same ideas to explain who Jesus was:

> When all things began, the Word already was. The Word dwelt with God, and what God was, the Word was. The Word, then, was with God at the beginning, and through him all things came to be; no single thing was created without him. . . . So the Word became flesh; he came to dwell among us, and we saw his glory, such glory as befits the Father's only Son, full of grace and truth. (John 1:1–3, 14)

In Jesus, God's creative and prophetic Word—related to God as a son is to a father—became a human being. For a long time the use of such language led scholars to think John was written in a Greek context and probably as late as the second century. As the extent to which such ideas already existed within Judaism becomes clearer, however, the Gospel of John keeps looking earlier and more Jewish, though its account of Jesus Christ as the Logos came to be terribly important in later interactions between Christianity and Greek philosophy.

These brief comments certainly do not exhaust the riches of New Testament accounts of Jesus. The letter to the Hebrews, for instance, developed an elaborate account of Christ as the new high priest who is also the perfect sacrifice. Paul talked about Christ as the second Adam, who restored humanity just as the first Adam corrupted it. Perhaps, however, this is enough to make the point. The first Christians all shared a sense that Christ had transformed their lives and indeed the whole world. They were confident that God had been working in Christ. Just as they developed varied theories about Christ's return and the relation of Christianity and Judaism, so they were willing to use the widest range of images and concepts to convey what Christ is and does, drawing on all the resources of the cultures around them. It did not occur to them to say that Christians could talk about Jesus in only one way. In the succeeding generations, however, those who followed them would find it necessary to put some limits on that freedom in interpreting their faith.

FOR FURTHER READING

INTRODUCTIONS. For a general introduction to the New Testament, Norman Perrin and Dennis C. Duling, *The New Testament: An Introduction,* 2d ed. (Harcourt Brace Jovanovich, 1982), provides a great scholar's synthesis of recent scholarship, revised by one of his students. James L. Price, *Interpreting the New Testament* (Holt, Rinehart & Winston, 1961), is a widely used college text. Robert M. Grant, *A Historical Introduction to the New Testament* (Harper & Row, 1963), offers the emphasis suggested by its title.

IMPORTANT BUT MORE DIFFICULT. Rudolf Bultmann, *Primitive Christianity in Its Contemporary Setting,* tr. by Reginald H. Fuller (Meridian Books, Living Age Books, 1956), provides a straightforward discussion of the historical context by the greatest New Testament scholar of this century. F. F. Bruce, *Paul: Apostle of the Heart Set Free* (Wm. B. Eerdmans Publishing Co., 1978), is a recent, thorough biography of Paul from a theologically conservative standpoint. Günther Bornkamm's *Paul,* tr. by D. M. G. Stalker (Harper & Row, 1971), gathers the conclusions of recent German scholarship. For a most thoughtful and balanced account of Paul, see Krister Stendahl, *Paul Among Jews and Gentiles* (Fortress Press, 1976).

NOTES

1. Sydney E. Ahlstrom, *Theology in America* (Bobbs-Merrill Co., 1967), p. 23.
2. See, for instance, Martin Werner, *The Formation of Christian Dogma,* tr. by S. G. F. Brandon (Harper & Brothers, 1957).
3. Scholars debate the authorship of the Gospels endlessly. For convenience I will sometimes refer to "Luke" or "John" without implying that these were the names of the people who wrote those books.

4

THE BEGINNINGS OF ORTHODOXY

Our birth is but a sleep and a forgetting:
The soul that rises with us, our life's star,
Hath had elsewhere its setting,
And cometh from afar.
            —William Wordsworth[1]

"Orthodoxy" is not a popular word. To many it carries with it images of book-burning and the tortures of the Inquisition. Since many theologians of the first several centuries of Christianity worked to define orthodoxy (the word literally means "straight opinion," in contrast to heresy, a "choice" that diverges from straight opinion) it would be easy to write them off as narrow-minded bigots. Still, consider this analogy: Manufacturers carefully preserve their legal rights to the names of their products, and with good reason. While Christian faith is a good bit more important than commercial products, early Christians faced similar concerns. They thought they had good news that could transform one's life and change the world. When they encountered someone proclaiming a different message in the name of Jesus Christ, they wanted to rush in and say, "No, that really is not Christianity"—or, more formally, "Our message is orthodox; that is heresy." At first it was not clear who had the right to say that, or how to settle a dispute between competing claims to orthodoxy. By the end of the second century, however, most Christians had agreed that some interpretations of Christianity, especially those known under the labels of Gnosticism, Montanism, and Marcionism, were heresies. In reaching those decisions they defined their faith more carefully, established a hierarchical organization, and began to define some writings as "Scripture." In trying to stay the same, Christianity had changed.

GNOSTIC DREAMS

In moments of frustration, children often fantasize that they have been separated from their real parents. Sent to their room for punishment or denied some toy, they imagine they belong to an ideal family somewhere else, and that they are living among strangers because of a dreadful mistake. At the beginning of the Christian era, many people felt that sort of alienation from the world around them. Economic decline and social chaos made it harder for them to achieve success or security. The ordinary citizen had no impact on a vast and autocratic empire, and the old order of the cults and cultures of city-states and small kingdoms had vanished. People felt that they did not belong where they were, and from the first to the fourth centuries, all around the eastern half of the Mediterranean, many turned to Gnosticism. "Gnosis" means "knowledge" or "wisdom," and the Gnostics claimed to have a secret wisdom concerning the true nature and destiny of the spiritual elect: "who we were, and what we have become, where we were or where we were placed; whither we hasten, from what we are redeemed, what birth is and what rebirth."[2] Each Gnostic group had its own theory, but nearly all contrasted the soul, which is the true self and which endures through many lifetimes, with the body, in which the soul has somehow become entrapped. Each Gnostic system told a different story about how the soul had fallen into the body and how it could be freed.

The "Hymn of the Pearl," probably written in Egypt in the second century, provides a good example. The hero, son of a great king in the East, is sent by his father to Egypt on a dangerous quest for the One Pearl.

> If thou go down to Egypt
> And bring the one pearl
> Which is in the midst of the sea,
> In the abode of the loud-breathing serpent,
> Thou shalt put on (again) thy splendid robe ...
> And with thy brother, our next in rank,
> Thou <shalt be heir> in our kingdom.

So the lad goes off to Egypt in disguise, but the Egyptians recognize him as a foreigner.

> But from some cause or other
> They perceived that I was not their countryman,
> And they dealt with me treacherously

> And gave me to eat of their food.
> And I forgot that I was a king's son
> And I served their king.
> And I forgot the pearl
> For which my parents had sent me.
> And because of the heaviness of their <food>
> I fell into a deep sleep.

Back home, his parents hear the bad news and send a magic letter that wakes the boy from his sleep.

> I remembered that I was a son of kings
> And my noble birth asserted itself. . . .
> And I snatched away the pearl
> And turned about, to go to my father's house.
> And their dirty and unclean garment
> I took off and left in their land,
> And directed my way <that I might come>
> To the light of our homeland, the East.[3]

That story conveys the central Gnostic theme. If some people, the members of an elite of true spiritual origin, feel out of place in this world, it is because they are; they have forgotten their true selves and become enmeshed in bodies.[4] Yet if they are among those whose true home lies elsewhere, they need only hear the truth about themselves in order to recover their identities. "Therefore if one has knowledge, he is from above. If he is called, he hears, he answers, and he turns to him who is calling him, and ascends to him."[5]

Until quite recently, scholars knew about the Gnostics only through a few fragments and the reports of their opponents. Little of their own work seemed to have survived. Then in 1945, near a village called Nag Hammadi, an Egyptian peasant found an old jar full of papyrus books. In recent years, following adventures full of blood feuds, smuggling, conspiracies, and last-minute rescues, these Gnostic texts have finally been published, and, far more than before, we can hear the Gnostics speak for themselves. This new information makes it harder than ever to generalize about Gnosticism. Its various forms apparently owed intellectual debts to Greek thought, Jewish apocalypticism, and religious traditions from throughout the Near East. While Gnostics generally agreed that good souls had become entrapped in a cycle of rebirths in evil bodies, they found it harder to explain how evil had arisen in the first place. Some pictured the universe as a battleground between good and evil, adopting a view labeled "dualism." The world contains such a mix of good and evil that it could not all have been created by a good God. Evil forces must be at work as well, and each of us must fight within ourselves a battle in the cosmic war between good and evil. Other Gnostics thought that everything had begun as good, and evil had emerged only gradually through processes of decay and forgetting. Gnostic theologies often listed a vast number of different ranks of deities, and in part this seems an effort to bridge the gap between primordial good and present evil by sheer quantity of intervening stages.

Gnostics also disagreed among themselves about ethics. They agreed that our bodies are not part of our true selves, but some therefore rigorously denied the body and all its desires in order to purify the soul. Others, at least if we can believe their opponents, held that since the body is not part of the essential self, bodily pleasures do not really touch us, and we may as well indulge ourselves to the full.

Gnosticism stood in a complex relationship to Christianity, neither quite inside nor quite separate. Gnostic themes antedated Christianity, but many Gnostics were, or at least claimed to be, Christians. They proclaimed Jesus as the savior who brings the secret wisdom that teaches us how to escape this evil world. Other Christians argued that Gnosticism distorted the Christian message. Gnosticism, they said, offered hope only to members of a spiritual elite. Further, Christians ought to believe that this world is the good creation of a good God. Gnostics taught that our bodies and all the material world are evil or illusory. "Do not think the resurrection is an illusion," one of the Nag Hammadi texts warns, "Indeed, it is more fitting to say that the world is an illusion."[6] For the Gnostics, this world was a place to be escaped or ignored; other Christians thought we should enjoy the world as it is and work to make it better. Most Gnostics, convinced of the evil of the world of matter, denied that Christ could have had a physical body. Some denied that he had been born of a woman (or said that at most he had "passed through Mary as water passes through a pipe"[7]), and few admitted that he had suffered or died. Perhaps his soul had escaped his body at the last minute. Some Gnostics interpreted Mark 15:34 as the body's cry, "My spirit, my spirit, why have you abandoned me?" Perhaps someone else (Simon of Cyrene, mentioned in the Gospels as carrying Jesus' cross, was a popular candidate) had been crucified in Jesus' place.

> It was another, Simon, who bore the cross on his shoulder. It was another on whom they placed the crown of thorns. But I was rejoicing in the height over all the wealth ... of their error, of their empty glory. And I was laughing at their ignorance.[8]

Since the Gnostics rejected the world of matter themselves, they could not believe that God had fully entered into it.

The New Testament already contains warnings against Gnosticism. Writing to the Colossians, Paul referred to a Gnostic group that worshiped "invisible orders of thrones, sovereignties, authorities, and powers" and advised, "Do not let your minds be captured by hollow and delusive speculations, based on traditions of man-made teaching and centered on the elemental spirits of the universe and not on Christ" (Col. 1:16; 2:8). As a way of refuting Gnosticism, John's Gospel emphasized that the Word became flesh, though much Johannine imagery, especially its contrasts between light and darkness, brings Gnosticism to mind. Soon, however, warnings proved inadequate. Even when a majority of Christians rejected Gnosticism, the Gnostics replied that they alone knew the secret wisdom passed down to the inner circle of believers. To refute such claims, their opponents had to identify the innermost circle, the most authoritative Christians, and show that they were not Gnostics. That forced Christians to define more precisely who spoke with authority. In the earliest days in Jerusalem authority had rested in "the Twelve," but that body was unique to Jerusalem. The pastoral letters in the New Testament (I and II Timothy and Titus) apparently describe the situation in the second half of the first century in communities founded by Paul. They refer to officials called bishops (literally "overseers") and presbyters (literally "elders"). Rather confusingly, however, I Timothy 3 seems to distinguish a single bishop from a subordinate group of elders, while Titus 1 apparently equates the two terms. Perhaps the situation varied from community to community, with one person in charge in some places and a sort of committee in others.

A generation or two later, about 110, Ignatius, the bishop of Antioch in Syria, described a situation in which each Christian community had a bishop, and the bishop was in charge. In a series of letters Ignatius wrote as he traveled under arrest to Rome to face martyrdom, he declared:

> I am already battling with beasts on my journey from Syria to Rome. . . . I am in chains with ten leopards around me—or at least with a band of guards who grow more brutal the better they are treated. . . . May I find joy in the beasts that have been made ready for me. . . . Fire and cross and battling with wild beasts, the breaking of bones and the mangling of members, the grinding of my whole body, the wicked torments of the devil—let them all assail me, so long as I get to Christ Jesus.[9]

Facing suffering himself, he found strength in the thought that he was following Christ's example, and therefore he had special reason to oppose Gnostic theories that Christ had not suffered or died.

> And so be deaf when anyone speaks to you apart from Jesus Christ, who was of the race of David, the son of Mary, who was truly born and ate and drank, who was truly persecuted under Pontius Pilate and was really crucified and died.[10]

Ignatius also drew strength from the Eucharist, which he declared to be the "medicine of immortality and the antidote against death."[11] Of course the church hierarchy administered the Eucharist, and Ignatius emphasized the importance of that hierarchy. If the Gnostics appealed to secret tradition, Ignatius countered with the authority of the bishops. "We ought to regard the bishop as we would the Lord Himself."[12] "All who belong to God and Jesus Christ are with the bishop."[13] Why listen to the bishops? Because they inherit the authority Christ gave to the apostles. About 170 another bishop, Irenaeus (of Lyons in southern France), explicitly stated the doctrine of "apostolic succession": Christ chose the apostles, who chose a first generation of bishops, who chose their successors, and so on. If Christ had had any secret wisdom to teach, these people would know it—and they were not Gnostics.

FROM CHARISMA TO HIERARCHY

Ignatius and Irenaeus had defined authority in a new way. In the earliest stages of Christianity, the Holy Spirit might speak through anyone. Paul, for instance, emphasized that he owed his authority to no one but Christ. Anyone could speak in tongues or see a vision, and other Christians would listen with respect. Leadership was "charismatic," depending on the gifts given by the Spirit. In the second century, on the other hand, those who had seen a vision or expressed an "inspired" new idea might be silenced if what they said contradicted the authority of the bishop. This shift produced inevitable conflicts. *The Teaching of the Twelve Apostles,* a manuscript discovered in 1883 which seems to describe the situation among early Christians in Syria, pictures a sort of plague of wandering charismatic prophets. The author advises:

> Let every apostle who comes to you be received as the Lord. But he shall not remain more than one day. But, if necessary, let him remain a second day. But, if he stays for three, he is a false prophet. . . . Not everyone who speaks in the spirit is a prophet,

but only if he follows the conduct of the Lord. . . . And, whoever
says in spirit: "Give me money," or anything like it, do not listen
to him. But, if he asks that it be given to others in need, let no
one judge him.[14]

This writer could not deny the authority of inspired prophets, but he
wanted to get them out of the way as quickly as possible, so that the
existing leadership could restore normalcy.

Still, charismatic leadership had its defenders, and that defense
took clearest shape in Montanism. Montanus lived in Asia Minor in
the middle of the second century. He claimed that when he fell into
a trance, the Holy Spirit spoke directly through him. The church
historian Eusebius quoted a thoroughly nasty account by an anonymous critic of Montanism:

A recent convert named Montanus . . . was filled with spiritual
excitement and suddenly fell into a kind of trance and unnatural
ecstasy. He raved, and began to chatter and talk nonsense.
. . . Then he secretly stirred up and inflamed minds closed to the
true Faith, raising up in this way two others—women whom he
filled with the sham spirit, so that they chattered crazily, inop-
portunely, and wildly, like Montanus himself.[15]

The Montanists could have replied with some justice that the very
first Christians had sometimes behaved in the same "crazy" and
"inopportune" fashion. Indeed, in a number of ways the Montanists
sought to return to earliest Christianity, with more spontaneous
styles of worship, more rigorous ethical demands, and a more vivid
expectation of the imminent end of the world. Incidentally, as the
quotation from Eusebius indicates, they thought the Spirit could
speak through women as well as men. The very first Christians, the
Montanists, and some Gnostics all gave significant authority to
women, in part simply because the Spirit might speak through anyone. As Christians turned to a hierarchical leadership, they accepted
the general pattern of the society around them, in which leaders were
male and religions with women priests were often associated with
the excesses and emotionalism of cults of sexual deities.

In many ways, then, the Montanists sought a return to primitive
Christianity, but on the central issue their opponents rightly accused
them of innovation. The Montanists claimed that their revelations
direct from the Holy Spirit could supersede the authority of Jesus or
Paul or anyone else. If Montanism had triumphed, Christianity would
have lain at the mercy of the prophets of each new generation. Rejecting that possibility and turning back to Christ and the first apostles

for authority, however, implied that the Holy Spirit had once spoken in a way that it no longer did. That idea in turn led very gradually to the formation of a "canon" of Scripture.

To the very first Christians, "Scripture" meant the Jewish Scriptures, which they considered God's Word and which they read during their worship. They began, at first rather casually, to add Christian texts. A letter from Paul or a story about Jesus carried great authority, but the nature of that authority and exactly which writings possessed it remained undefined.

Part of the impetus to clarify this point came from a young Christian named Marcion who moved from Asia Minor to Rome in 144. He had a good bit of money and made a generous gift to the Roman Christian community. As one might expect, at first he received an enthusiastic welcome. Soon, however, the Roman Christians began to find his ideas disturbing. If God is good, Marcion asked, would he really have created a world as full of evil and suffering as this one? When we read about the angry, harsh, bloodthirsty God of the Jewish Scriptures, does that sound like Jesus' loving Father? Marcion offered a simple solution to such puzzles: There are two Gods, one either evil or merely without mercy and a bit incompetent (surviving sources leave Marcion's view on this unclear), who created the world and is the God described in the Old Testament; the other a good God and the Father of Christ ("the one a judge, fierce and warlike, the other mild and peaceable, solely kind and supremely good"[16]).

Historians often classify Marcion with the Gnostics, but he differed in important ways. Gnostic salvation calls us back to our true home, while Marcion thought that this evil world *is* our true home. Marcion held that the good God had had no relationship at all with us or anything else in the world until he sent Christ his Son. (If he were really so good and so powerful, Marcion's opponent Tertullian sarcastically observed, "Marcion's God ought to have created at least a solitary vegetable" in all that time before the coming of Christ.[17]) For Marcion, God's prior noninvolvement meant that in Christ God is not restoring us to our rightful place but offering undeserved salvation out of pure love, and we should not try to learn some secret wisdom but accept that love in gratitude and simple faith. The great church historian Adolf von Harnack once remarked that Marcion was the only person in the early church who understood Paul, and he misunderstood him. It is true that many Christians in the second century sought to win salvation through careful obedience to law or the penetration of some secret wisdom. Marcion's call for faith in God's unmerited love does come as a refreshing breath of Pauline Christianity. Nevertheless, he also treated this world as a purely evil place, not the creation of the good God, and denied Christ's human birth. In the year 29, he said, Christ suddenly appeared, full grown; however, rather oddly, Marcion did accept Christ's crucifixion and death.

Above all, Marcion broke Christianity's connection with Judaism. The history of Israel and the Jewish Scriptures had no significance for him, since they concerned a different God. He also rejected Christian writings that affirmed continuity with Judaism. He took edited versions of Paul's letters, Luke, and Acts and declared them the only authoritative Scriptures. His opponents insisted that that was far too limited. Christians had already been developing an informal sense of Scripture, but Marcion's radical proposal forced them to clarify their thinking.

Yet the process took a long time. A fragment written in Rome about 190 lists roughly our New Testament, but it omits Hebrews and possibly (the text is unclear) one of Peter's letters and one of John's, and it adds the Wisdom of Solomon and the Apocalypse of John. The book of Revelation also remained long in dispute. The first surviving catalog that exactly corresponds to today's New Testament dates as late as 367. In the end the criterion of selection appealed to the principle used against the Montanists: the Holy Spirit had spoken to the first generation of Christians in a special way. Therefore the New Testament included only books thought to have been written by an apostle or the student of an apostle. For centuries, though, Christians got on without a precise canon (a list of books that are counted as Scripture). From the start they recognized that some writings communicated God's Word with special authority, but they approached the matter with a freedom that long made it unnecessary to agree on a specific list.

In this respect and others one could present the second century as a tragic story of Christianity's loss of freedom. Christians created a more structured leadership and began to define Scripture more carefully. They distrusted claims of the immediate working of the Holy Spirit, and they accused some of their fellow Christians of heresy. Given the biases of their society, the move to more hierarchical leadership increased male dominance. Yet it is easier to regret these tendencies than to see how they could have been avoided. The goodness and importance of this world and continuity with Judaism are important themes in Christian thought. Much of subsequent popular Christianity has taught that our bodies are evil and urged us to turn away from the earth and place all our hopes in heaven—ideas that come more out of Gnosticism than from the New Testament. In that context, one might wish that the second century had attacked Gnosticism even more forcefully. Affirming what is right seems often to entail denouncing what is wrong and running the risk of becoming more rigid. In spite of its struggles to define orthodoxy, early Christianity remained remarkably flexible. Confronted with Greek philosophy, for instance, Christians proved eager and adaptable about appropriating its insights.

FOR FURTHER READING

INTRODUCTIONS. Elaine Pagels, *The Gnostic Gospels* (Random House, Vintage Books, 1981), looks at Gnosticism with particular attention to political and feminist implications in the light of the Nag Hammadi discoveries.

COLLECTIONS OF ORIGINAL SOURCES. The Nag Hammadi texts are now available in translation in James M. Robinson (ed.), *The Nag Hammadi Library* (Harper & Row, 1977). James Stevenson (ed.), *A New Eusebius: Documents Illustrative of the History of the Church to A.D. 337* (London: S.P.C.K., 1957), provides a good collection of excerpts from early Christian writers, as does Henry Bettenson, (ed.), *Early Christian Fathers* (Oxford University Press, 1969). Cyril C. Richardson (ed.), *Early Christian Fathers* (Westminster Press, 1953), offers longer, and therefore usually more helpful, selections.

IMPORTANT BUT MORE DIFFICULT. Hans Jonas, *The Gnostic Religion* (Beacon Press, 1958), remains possibly the most philosophically profound book on Gnosticism. Recent discoveries have confirmed the Jewish connections of Gnosticism identified in Robert M. Grant, *Gnosticism and Early Christianity* (Columbia University Press, 1959).

NOTES

1. William Wordsworth, "Ode: Intimations of Immortality from Recollections of Early Childhood," in Thomas Hutchinson (ed.), *The Poetical Works of Wordsworth* (London: Oxford University Press, 1936), p. 460.
2. Clement of Alexandria, *Extracts from the Works of Theodotus* 78.2, tr. by Robert Pierce Casey (London: Christophers, 1934), p. 89.

3. The Acts of Thomas, tr. by R. McL. Wilson, in *New Testament Apocrypha*, ed. by Edgar Hennecke and Wilhelm Schneemelcher (Westminster Press, 1963, 1965), Vol. 2, pp. 499–501.

4. Arnobius of Sicca, *The Case Against the Pagans* 2.16, tr. by George E. McCracken (Newman Press, 1949), Vol. 1, p. 129.

5. The Gospel of Truth 1.22, tr. by George W. MacRae, in James M. Robinson (ed.), *The Nag Hammadi Library* (Harper & Row, 1977), p. 40.

6. The Treatise on Resurrection 48.10–16, tr. by Malcolm L. Peel, in Robinson, *The Nag Hammadi Library*, pp. 52–53.

7. Irenaeus, *Against Heresies* 1.7.2; quoted in Jaroslav Pelikan, *The Emergence of the Catholic Tradition (100–600)* (University of Chicago Press, 1971), p. 90.

8. The Second Treatise of the Great Seth 56.9–20, tr. by Joseph A. Gibbons, Roger A. Bullard, and Frederik Wisse, in Robinson, *The Nag Hammadi Library*, p. 332.

9. Ignatius, To the Romans 5, in *The Apostolic Fathers*, tr. by Francis X. Glimm, Joseph M.-F. Marique, and Gerald G. Walsh (Christian Heritage, 1947), p. 110.

10. Ignatius, To the Trallians 9, ibid., p. 104.

11. Ignatius, To the Ephesians 20, ibid., p. 95.

12. Ibid., 6, p. 89.

13. Ignatius, To the Philadelphians 3, ibid., p. 114.

14. *The Teaching of the Twelve Apostles* 11, ibid., pp. 180–181.

15. Eusebius, *The History of the Church* 5.16, tr. by G. A. Williamson (New York University Press, 1966), pp. 218–219.

16. Tertullian, *Against Marcion* 1.6.1, tr. by Ernest Evans (Oxford: Clarendon Press, 1972), p. 15.

17. Ibid., 1.11.5, p. 28. Translation revised.

5

AN ALLIANCE WITH PHILOSOPHY

Philosophy was given to the Greeks . . . [as] a
schoolmaster to bring the Hellenic mind . . . to Christ.

—Clement of Alexandria[1]

What indeed has Athens to do with Jerusalem? . . . Away
with all attempts to produce a mottled Christianity of Stoic,
Platonic, and dialectic composition.

—Tertullian[2]

Israel worshiped a God who could grow angry, who changed his
mind, a God involved in history, who cared so much about one group
of people that their apostasies drove him to fits of impatience. The
greatest philosophers of Greece spoke of an unchanging divine principle, far removed from our world, without emotion, unaffected by
anything beyond itself. Improbably enough, Christian theology came
to identify these two as the same God; this may be the single most
remarkable thing to have happened in Western intellectual history.
Some have dismissed it all as a terrible mistake, but the intellectual
fertility that resulted makes that hard to do. At any rate, a number
of theologians of the second and third centuries, confronted with
Greek culture, undeniably tried to reinterpret Christian faith in terms
of the most important ideas of that era. Whether facing the discoveries of modern science or the traditions of non-European societies,
Christians in subsequent centuries have rarely been as daring.

THE GOD OF THE PHILOSOPHERS

Even before the time of Christ, intellectuals throughout the Roman
Empire had faced a discrepancy between their most profound
thoughts about the divine and their religious traditions. Philosophers

of Greece and Rome had spoken of a single divine principle, beyond description, beyond partisanship. Though mythology might lead to important insights about human beings and their world, as it has even for modern psychology, the petty jealousies and sexual peccadilloes of its deities seemed increasingly embarrassing, and the cult of sacrificing to this or that god or goddess had come to seem more like bribery than worship. For many, philosophical thought had made mythological religion appear morally and intellectually unacceptable. In this situation, Christians in effect said, "We have a religion, but its understanding of God is more like philosophy than mythology." They sought an alliance with classical philosophy against popular religion.

Philosophy (the word means "love of wisdom" and also included what we would call natural science and political theory) had been a Greek invention, an attempt to understand the nature of reality, the ideal government, or the way to lead a good life, not by accepting traditions or myths from the past, but by the application of human reason. Two schools of Greek philosophy, Platonism and Stoicism, deeply influenced early Christian thought.

Four hundred years before the time of Jesus, Plato's teacher Socrates had faced a moral crisis in Greek culture. Traditionally, the Greeks had believed that their laws and morality were the creation of the gods, built into the natural order of things. Just as stones naturally fall, so killing or incest is naturally wrong. However, as they encountered other cultures with different moral values, and as their political upheavals led to changes in their laws, many Greeks came to feel that each society invents its own standards of right and wrong. As a character in one of Plato's dialogues puts it, justice is the right of the stronger—whoever has enough power or influence can make up the rules and enforce a certain definition of justice or any other virtue. Socrates rejected that variety of cynical relativism. No matter how large or powerful a majority may be, when it proclaims that brutal killing is right, or that the ugly is beautiful, or that two plus two equals five, such statements remain false. Absolute standards of good and truth exist regardless of anyone's opinions, and we must try to be true to them. Socrates preferred to suffer execution rather than abandon his quest for truth.

As with Jesus later, Socrates wrote nothing. We know about his philosophy principally through the dialogues written by his student Plato, in which Socrates usually appears as the main character, though Plato probably originated many of the ideas he expresses. Beginning with Socrates' belief in absolute values like justice and beauty, Plato developed his theory of "forms." He contrasted the world of changing particular things that we observe through our senses with a world of eternal, unchanging forms, and he said that particular things are what they are by "participation" in these forms. A government may replace just laws with unjust ones, but the "form" of justice remains unchanged, and a particular law is just to the degree that it matches up to that form. Similarly, the brown table at which I am now writing may be painted green or chopped into kindling, but the forms of "brown" and "table" remain unaltered.

Obviously, we don't learn about the forms through our senses, for the senses observe only changing particular objects, and Plato rather distrusted the senses as a path to truth anyway. How then can we know what "justice" really means if we have never experienced perfect justice? Drawing in part on the mystery religions, Plato answered such questions with his theory of recollection. Our souls have passed through a long cycle of rebirths, he explained, and in knowing the forms we only recollect what we knew in a previous existence where, untrammeled by the body and its limitations, our souls knew the forms directly. Therefore, in searching for knowledge, we ought to turn away from the senses and try to recover the truth that lies within our souls; in turning away from the passions and distractions of our bodies and the physical world, we will also purify our true selves.

Such a philosophy has obvious religious implications, and Plato vigorously attacked traditional mythology for its corrupting stories of quarrelsome deities. In subsequent generations, his followers further emphasized the religious side of his thought, partly because they had given up Plato's own hope for political reform and sought instead escape from the concerns of this world. They dedicated themselves to purifying their souls, so that they might know the forms directly. Some even sought a unity deeper than the forms, an indescribable first principle beyond all comprehensibility or differentiation, at the base of all things. The greatest of the neo-Platonists, Plotinus, who lived around A.D. 200, achieved mystical experiences in which the soul seemed to lose its identity by merging into the One.

The soul looks upon the wellspring of Life, wellspring also of Intellect, beginning of Being, fount of Good, root of Soul. . . . There, indeed, it was scarcely vision, unless of a mode unknown; it was a going forth from self, a simplifying, a renunciation. . . . This is the life of gods and of the godlike and blessed among

men, liberation from the alien that besets us here, a life taking
no pleasure in the things of earth, the passing of solitary to
solitary.[3]

That dream has haunted mystics ever since, though one feels all the
despair of late antiquity in that search for a "life taking no pleasure
in the things of earth." Plotinus' One influences the world by provid-
ing an unattainable ideal; the One never acts, let alone in particular
historical events, and does not care about our affairs or anything else.
One of Plotinus' students remarked that his teacher "seemed
ashamed of being in the body";[4] the concerns of this world were not
for him. He died saying, "I am striving to give back the Divine in me
to the Divine in the All."[5]

Many philosophers of another tradition, Stoicism, shared that
ideal. Stoicism began, several centuries before Christ, with ethical
concerns. In a chaotic world of vast empires, it seemed impossible to
change external things for the better. All one can control, the Stoics
said, are the attitudes with which one faces the inevitable. A tyrant
may kill us, but we can face death bravely. We may have a frustrating
life, but we still can do our duty. We cannot control whether we will
have a pleasurable life, but we can control whether we will lead a
virtuous life, and we must seek virtue by learning to accept our
destiny. Indeed, many Stoics said, if we really understood the inter-
relatedness of things, we would realize that even our pains and troubles serve a higher good. As the Stoic emperor Marcus Aurelius put
it: "Nothing is injurious to the part, if it is for the advantage of the
whole. . . . Everything harmonizes with me which is harmonious to
thee, O Universe. Nothing for me is too early nor too late, which is
in due time for thee."[6] The Stoics thought that a rational principle
guides the whole universe, and that each of us contains, within our
reason, a spark or seed of that cosmic rationality which they often
called the Logos, the "Word" (a term we have already met in Philo
and the Gospel of John). Thus they valued the "natural," which is in
tune with the Logos; and they emphasized, in a world where many
still dismissed foreigners as less than fully human, the relatedness of
all human beings, for we all share in the same universal Logos.

Stoics and Platonists differed on important issues. The Platonists,
for instance, sharply contrasted the realm of souls and forms with the
material world, while the Stoics said that souls too were material,
albeit an odd and hard-to-observe sort of matter. Still, at the popular
level both philosophies pointed in many of the same directions—
denial of or indifference to bodily pleasures, discovery of the truth by

looking inward to the soul rather than outward through the senses, and the search for ultimate unity. Obviously such themes, and the eloquence and sophistication with which they were presented, attracted many Christians. Equally obviously, they introduced ideas about God, human beings, and the world that could lead to some changes in what Christians believed.

THE APOLOGISTS

The apologists (the word means "defenders") were among the first to explore the connections between Christianity and philosophy. Beginning in the second century, a number of Christians addressed defenses of Christianity to the emperor or to the educated public generally, arguing that Christians should not be persecuted, and refuting charges made against them. Some charges grew out of popular rumors. The apologists had to explain, for instance, that Christian references to eating flesh and blood did not mean they practiced cannibalism, and their talk of love did not mean they had wild orgies. Christians were not disloyal citizens just because they refused to worship the emperor, and their prayers for the end of the world did not mean they hated all their neighbors. In a world where most people worshiped all sorts of deities, the Christian refusal to do so led to the charge that they were atheists, and the apologists had to explain how this was not so. More fundamentally, most educated Greeks and Romans thought of Christianity as a lower-class superstition from an obscure frontier province. The apologists had to make it seem intellectually respectable, and that usually meant relating it to philosophy.

One early apologist, Justin Martyr, who came from Palestine, settled in Rome, and was killed under persecution about 165, presented Christianity as the best of philosophies. He told how he had studied with many different philosophers without finding satisfaction, until one day a mysterious old man taught him about Christian faith. "My spirit was immediately set on fire, and an affection for the prophets, and for those who are friends of Christ, took hold of me; while pondering on his words, I discovered that his was the only sure and useful philosophy. Thus it is that I am now a philosopher."[7] Justin emphasized philosophy's continuity with Christianity and its Jewish roots. He thought the philosophers had gotten most of their best ideas by reading the Jewish Scriptures. "Everything the philosophers and poets said in speaking about the immortality of the soul, or retribution after death, or speculation on celestial matters, or other similar doctrines, they took from the Prophets."[8] Moreover, he said, the philosophers teach us that the reason in every human being participates in the universal Logos, and we learn from the Gospel of John that in Jesus Christ the Logos became flesh. Therefore, whenever people use their reason, Christ, the Logos, is already at work: "We have been taught that Christ was the First-begotten of God, and we have indicated above that he is the Word of whom all mankind partakes. Those who lived by reason are Christians, even though they have been considered atheists."[9] Thus Justin counted Socrates a Christian. On the other hand, he launched vitriolic attacks against Greek and Roman myths, which he described as the work of demons who had stirred people up to kill both Socrates and Christ. Previously the word "daemon" had simply meant a spirit, whether good or bad; Justin helped give it the bad connotation it has for us. Philosophy and Christianity, both products of the Logos, must band together to fight the evils of demonic religion.

While praising philosophy, Justin claimed that Christianity is better than Platonism or Stoicism, for Christ revealed directly and clearly, in a way ordinary people could understand, what philosophers had only glimpsed and expressed in convoluted ways. This knowledge now had a new power to change lives. "There was no one who believed in Socrates so much as to die for his teaching, but not only philosophers and scholars believed in Christ . . . but also workmen and men wholly uneducated, who scorned all glory, and fear, and death."[10] At the same time he admitted that a philosophically sophisticated Christianity could not take some parts of the Bible literally.

> For, the Ineffable Father and Lord of all neither comes to any place, nor walks, nor sleeps, nor arises, but always remains in His own place, wherever it may be. . . . He surveys all things, knows all things, and none of us can escape his notice. Nor is he moved who cannot be contained in any place, not even in the whole universe.[11]

Like most people who try to find a compromise, Justin has faced attacks from both sides. Philosophers say he oversimplified Platonism; Christians have accused him of modifying faith to suit philosophy. Both charges contain an element of truth, but Justin did try to think about Christianity in terms of the best ideas of his time.

That task continued in Alexandria in Egypt, one of the richest and most cosmopolitan cities of the empire. Already around the time of

Jesus, Philo and others had made it a center of dialogue between Judaism and Greek thought. We do not know who brought Christianity to the city, but it arrived early and soon spread to all social classes. That produced a problem in teaching the faith to new converts, for inevitably the well educated would have different questions and respond best to a different approach than the illiterate. Around 160 a man named Pantaenus apparently set up a special school for intellectually sophisticated converts, though the nature of this school remains a matter of scholarly debate. We know almost nothing about Pantaenus except for the intriguing report that he had visited India, but a number of the works of his student and successor Clement, who died about 214, survive.

Clement of Alexandria was a civilized, cultivated man who wrote about table manners and how much makeup one should use, as well as about theology. Like Justin, he attacked Greek mythology, but with a kind of cheerful humor. "It is," he joked, "a majestic Zeus that you portray, Homer. . . . Yet, my good man, if you but let him catch a glimpse of a woman's girdle, even Zeus is exposed and . . . put to shame."[12] Clement was not, he said, like so many Christians "who are frightened at the Hellenic philosophy, as children are at masks."[13] He called for tolerance. After all, "The way of truth is . . . one. But into it, as into a perennial river, streams flow from all sides."[14] Many of his students came from wealthy families; Clement reassured them that, as long as they did not value it too highly, they need not give away their money. "Can you also rise superior to your riches? Say so, and Christ does not draw you away from the possession of them; the Lord does not grudge."[15] Unlike most of his contemporaries, Clement went out of his way to emphasize the equality of men and women in their relationship with God, and he even used feminine imagery of God: "We, believing in God, flee to the Word, 'the care-soothing breast' of the Father. And he alone, as is befitting, supplies children with the milk of love, and those only are truly blessed who suck this breast."[16]

While Clement knew a good bit of philosophy, the next great writer from the school of Alexandria, Origen, was his clear intellectual superior—indeed, one of the greatest minds in the history of Christianity. Origen, who lived from about 185 to about 254, was not the sort of man about whom people feel neutral. He feuded with many of his contemporaries and was denounced as a heretic after his death, but no one has ever exerted more influence on Greek-speaking Christianity. As a teenager, Origen had seen his father dragged off to martyrdom and had to be restrained from following. As a young man, according to one story, he found that he provoked scandal by giving private lessons on the Bible to women. Concerned that nothing should interfere with his work, he read in Matthew's Gospel how some have made themselves eunuchs for the kingdom of heaven, and decided to end all cause for scandal by castrating himself.

From earliest childhood, Origen devoted himself to the study of the Bible. Even as a boy, his student and biographer reported, "he was not satisfied with reading the sacred words in a simple and literal manner, but sought something further, and busied himself, even at that age, with deeper speculations, troubling his father with questions as to what could be the inner meaning of the inspired Scripture."[17] He continued to cause trouble by pursuing the inner meanings of Scripture all his life. Partly (perhaps Gnostic influence was at work here) he suspected that the deepest truth always remains hidden at first and reveals itself only to long reflection. Often, though, Origen looked for a hidden meaning simply because it seemed that the obvious meaning could not be true:

> What man of intelligence will believe that the first and the second and the third day, and the evening and the morning, existed without the sun and moon and stars? . . . And who is so silly as to believe that God, after the manner of a farmer, "planted a paradise eastward in Eden." . . . And when God is said to "walk in the paradise in the cool of the day" . . . I do not think anyone will doubt that these are figurative expressions which indicate certain mysteries through a semblance of history and not through actual events.[18]

Clearly, he said, we must look for a figurative meaning when the Bible says things about God which, taken literally, "would not be believed of the most savage and unjust of men."[19] Moreover, sometimes it takes a knowledge of languages to disclose the real meaning of the Bible. "The story of Adam and his sin," for instance, "will be interpreted philosophically by those who know that 'Adam' means 'human being' in the Hebrew language, and that in what appears to be concerned with Adam, Moses is speaking of the nature of man."[20]

Origen's interpretations sometimes point up the influence Platonism had on him. He often dismissed the material world as unimportant in order to concentrate on the affairs of disembodied souls. Still, unlike most of the Platonists, he did not turn away from history to concern himself only with eternal truths. He believed that history is important, that in history souls fall into sin and are redeemed. Our present lives and indeed all human affairs, however, are only a small part of a vast cosmic saga. One reason for so expanding the scope of history concerned the problem of evil. Some good people suffer; some evil people seem lucky all their lives. Can that be fair? Origen's belief in the existence of all sorts of angels and demons provided another dimension to this question: Why do some souls get to be archangels while others find themselves human beings or even demons? According to Origen, all souls must have started out equal—otherwise God would be unfair. God gave these souls freedom, however, and that meant they could misuse God's gifts. In varying degrees they did so, and they suffer the consequences of their actions, being born and reborn in various bodies, living various existences, as they get the sort of life they earned the last time around. In all of this, however, God is at work. Without depriving any of us of freedom, he guides history so that everything finally turns out for the best.

> God . . . in providing for the salvation of his entire creation . . . has so ordered everything that each spirit or soul . . . should not be compelled by force against its free choice to any action except that to which the motions of its own mind lead it . . . and at the same time that the motions of their wills should work suitably and usefully together to produce the harmony of a single world.[21]

God is, as it were, a musician so gifted that he can weave all our spontaneous melodies into one harmony.

Origen's belief that all souls achieve salvation in the end led to attacks against him—in his own time and ever since—from those who insist that the Bible teaches that some stay in hell forever. Although probably no one in history has written more biblical commentaries, he is often accused of turning too much away from the Bible to Greek thought. Still, he did not just make connections between Christianity and Platonism; he really forged a new philosophy. Accepting Plato's view that our souls are our real selves and that we are born in new bodies again and again, he made history important in a way that Plato had not, as a process in which God gives freedom to parts of his creation and then guides them all to salvation without destroying that freedom. Further, Origen rejected the God of the philosophers, indifferent to the world of change and untouched by emotion. "The Father himself and God of all is long-suffering, merciful and pitiful," he wrote. "Has he not then in a sense passions? The Father himself is not impassible. He has the passion of love."[22]

A PROTEST

The last chapter indicated how the increasingly hierarchical leadership of Christianity produced a protest by the Montanists. Not surprisingly, efforts to relate Christian faith to Greek philosophy, and to Greek and Roman culture generally, brought forth protest too, and this found its most eloquent spokesman in Tertullian, a North African Christian writing about 200. Tertullian thought that Christians should have little to do with the society around them. In one treatise he imagined the "pallium"—the cloak which was sometimes a distinctive garb of Christians—as proclaiming to the world, "I owe no duty to the forum, the election-ground, or the senate house: I am no judge, no soldier, no king: I have withdrawn from the populace. My only business is with myself."[23] Like other apologists, Tertullian insisted that Christians would be peaceful citizens, but he saw them as observers, not participants in society. Government service required an oath to the divine emperor. How could Christians call the emperor God? How could a Christian, dedicated to peace and love, join the army or serve on a jury and vote to send someone to prison or death? Christ "shrank back from becoming a king. . . . Let even this fact help to remind you that all the powers of the world are not only alien to, but enemies of, God. . . . One soul cannot be due to two masters— God and Caesar. . . . The image of Caesar . . . is on the coin . . . and the image of God . . . is on man . . . , so . . . render to Caesar indeed money, to God yourself. Otherwise, what will be God's if all things are Caesar's?"[24]

He took much the same attitude to possible relations between Christianity and philosophy. It may be significant that Tertullian was the first important Christian author to write in Latin. As the old joke says, the Greeks built metaphysical systems, and the Romans built roads. Tertullian did sometimes reflect a practical Roman's impatience with Greek subtleties, but more than that he distrusted any compromises of the faith. "What indeed has Athens to do with Jerusalem?" he demanded. "What concord is there between the Academy and the Church? . . . Away with all attempts to produce a mottled Christianity of Stoic, Platonic, and dialectic composition. . . . With our faith, we desire no further belief."[25] Faith needs no help from philosophy. Why should a Christian try to be "reasonable"? "The Son of God was crucified; I am not ashamed because men must be ashamed of it. And the Son of God died; it is by all means to be believed because it is absurd. And He was buried, and rose again; the fact is certain, because it is impossible."[26] To be sure, Tertullian could praise Plato's doctrine of immortality and admire the Stoic Seneca, and he wrote his attacks on culture in a wonderfully polished style. For all that, he delivered a powerful warning against all those who want to modify Christian faith because it fails to fit somebody's theory of what a reasonable or up-to-date religion ought to be.

Tertullian also became involved in a debate about how rigorously Christian communities could impose ethical standards on their members. Apparently in the early second century most Christians had believed that baptism effected freedom from prior sins, but that a Christian must not commit a major sin *after* baptism. A Roman Christian named Hermas, writing somewhere before 150, reported that a vision had revealed to him that after baptism we were entitled to one falling away—but only one. Then Callistus, who became bishop of Rome in 217, argued that the church should be like Noah's ark, which took in all the animals. He thought the community should help its members become better, not exclude those who fell short of the highest standards. Thus we should forgive Christians who sin as long as they sincerely repent. The horrified Roman theologian Hippolytus considered this a betrayal of Christian ideals, and he broke away and founded a separate group. The issue was complicated by a debate about the Trinity, and by a dubious episode in Callistus' past, in which he had been accused of embezzlement. Tertullian, not surprisingly, shared Hippolytus' horror at compromises of Christian purity. He argued for rigorous standards for church membership and even expressed considerable support for the Montanists—historians continue to debate whether he actually joined them—as preservers of proper Christian standards. Here too he fought for a faith that did not bend to the winds of the society around it.

The issues raised by Tertullian and Origen remain alive today. Some Christians attack the intellectual life, and much of the world around them, in the name of Christ, as if one had to stop thinking in order to be a good Christian. Others seem eager to modify their faith to suit the current cultural fashion. Tertullian warns of the dangers of compromising faith to make it socially acceptable. The school of Alexandria shows how Christians can use all the intellectual resources of the world around them to proclaim their faith. In the generations immediately after Origen and Tertullian, Christians demonstrated that they had learned both lessons. In struggling to define what they believed about Christ, they fought off compromise and also created a theory of great intellectual sophistication.

FOR FURTHER READING

INTRODUCTIONS. Much has been written on Greek philosophy. The relevant sections of Bertrand Russell, *A History of Western Philosophy* (Simon & Schuster, 1945), while sometimes eccentric, are always entertaining. Henry Chadwick, *Early Christian Thought and the Classical Tradition* (Oxford University Press, 1966), contains introductory essays on Justin, Clement, and Origen.

COLLECTIONS OF ORIGINAL SOURCES. Plato's dialogues are available in a host of translations. Jason L. Saunders, *Greek and Roman Philosophy After Aristotle* (Free Press, 1966), gathers some important Stoic and neo-Platonic texts. Stevenson's *A New Eusebius* and Bettenson's *Early Christian Fathers,* mentioned in the last chapter, have good excerpts from the writers discussed here. J. E. L. Oulton and Henry Chadwick (eds.), *Alexandrian Christianity* (Westminster Press, 1954), and S. L. Greenslade (ed.), *Early Latin Theology* (Westminster Press, 1956), both in The Library of Christian Classics, have longer selections.

IMPORTANT BUT MORE DIFFICULT. Frederick Copleston, *A History of Philosophy,* Vol. 1, Parts 1 and 2 (Doubleday & Co., Image Books, 1962), is the standard introductory history. A. H. Armstrong (ed.), *The Cambridge History of Later Greek and Early Medieval Philosophy* (London: Cambridge University Press, 1967), provides careful studies of neo-Platonists, Stoics, and others. L. W. Barnard, *Justin Martyr* (London: Cambridge University Press, 1967), is a balanced account. Charles Bigg, *The Christian Platonists of Alexandria* (Oxford: Clarendon Press, 1913), and Charles N. Cochrane, *Christianity and Classical Culture* (London: Oxford University Press, 1944), remain classics.

NOTES

1. Clement of Alexandria, *The Miscellanies* 1.5, in *The Ante-Nicene Fathers,* ed. by Alexander Roberts and James Donaldson, Vol. 2 (Wm. B. Eerdmans Publishing Co., 1962), p. 305.

2. Tertullian, *The Prescription Against Heretics* 7, tr. by Peter Holmes, in *The Ante-Nicene Fathers,* Vol. 3 (Wm. B. Eerdmans Publishing Co., 1963), p. 246.

3. Plotinus, *The Enneads* 6.9.9 and 11, tr. by Stephen MacKenna, 3d ed. (London: Faber & Faber, 1962), pp. 622, 624–625.

4. Porphyry, *On the Life of Plotinus* 1, ibid., p. 1.

5. Ibid., 2, p. 2.

6. Marcus Aurelius, *Meditations* 10.6 and 4.23, tr. by G. Long, in Whitney J. Oates (ed.), *The Stoic and Epicurean Philosophers* (Modern Library, 1940), pp. 563, 511.

7. Justin Martyr, *Dialogue with Trypho* 8, in *Saint Justin Martyr,* tr. by Thomas B. Falls (Christian Heritage, 1948), p. 160.

8. Justin Martyr, *First Apology* 44, ibid., p. 81.

9. Ibid., 46, p. 83.

10. Justin Martyr, *Second Apology* 10, ibid., p. 130.

11. Justin Martyr, *Dialogue with Trypho* 127, ibid., pp. 345–346.

12. Clement of Alexandria, *Exhortation to the Greeks* 2, in *Clement of Alexandria,* tr. by G. W. Butterworth (G. P. Putnam's Sons, 1919), p. 67.

13. Clement of Alexandria, *The Miscellanies* 6.10, ibid., p. 498.

14. Ibid., 1.5, p. 305.

15. Clement of Alexandria, *The Rich Man's Salvation,* ibid., pp. 317, 319.

16. Clement of Alexandria, *The Instructor* 1.6, in *The Ante-Nicene Fathers,* Vol. 2, p. 220.

17. Quoted in Eusebius, *The Ecclesiastical History* 6.2, tr. by J. E. L. Oulton (G. P. Putnam's Sons, 1932), Vol. 2, p. 13.

18. Origen, *On First Principles* 4.3.1 (Greek text), tr. by G. W. Butterworth (Harper & Row, Harper Torchbooks, 1966), p. 288.

19. Ibid., 4.2.1, p. 271.

20. Origen, *Contra Celsum* 4.40, tr. by Henry Chadwick (Cambridge: Cambridge University Press, 1965), p. 216. I have altered the translation rather freely, since Chadwick's literal version makes it sound at first as if "Adam" is a Greek word.

21. Origen, *On First Principles* 2.1.2 (Latin text), ibid., p. 77.

22. Origen, *Homilies on Ezekiel* 6.6; quoted in Charles Bigg, *The Christian Platonists of Alexandria* (Oxford: Clarendon Press, 1913), p. 197.

23. Tertullian, *On the Pallium* 5, tr. by S. Thelwell, in *The Ante-Nicene Fathers,* Vol. 4 (Wm. B. Eerdmans Publishing Co., 1956), p. 11.

24. Tertullian, *On Idolatry* 18, 19, and 15, tr. by S. Thelwell, in *The Ante-Nicene Fathers,* Vol. 3, pp. 72, 73, 70.

25. Tertullian, *The Prescription Against Heretics* 7, ibid., p. 246.

26. Tertullian, *On the Flesh of Christ* 5, tr. by Peter Holmes, ibid., p. 525.

6

TRULY HUMAN, TRULY DIVINE

> Every place in the city is full of them: the alleys, the cross-roads, the forums, the squares. Garment sellers, money changers, food vendors—they are all at it. If you ask for change, they philosophize for you about generate and ingenerate natures. If you inquire about the price of bread, the answer is that the Father is greater and the Son inferior. If you speak about whether the bath is ready, they express the opinion that the Son was made out of nothing.
>
> —Gregory of Nyssa's despairing comment on the pervasiveness of theological debate in the city of Constantinople[1]

By the early third century, most Christians had come to believe that Christ was both human and divine. That conviction had not come easily. Then as now, many people, when confronted with a poor carpenter's son suffering on a cross, thought that God could not possibly be like that. Important factors in Christianity's background reinforced that instinct. The monotheism they inherited from Judaism made Christians nervous about saying that Christ was divine yet not identical with God the Father. That sounded like belief in two Gods. The Greek philosophical tradition with which Christianity had struck an alliance taught that the divine cannot change or suffer—so how could a crucified human being be divine?

In the second century, many Gnostics and others had concluded that Christ had not really been a human being—he only seemed to be. Historians call this view Docetism (from a Greek word meaning "to seem"). Most Christians, however, eventually came to feel that Docetism would turn Jesus' life into a sort of trick, an illusion. Moreover, Christians who believed that Christ's suffering and death on the cross saved them from their sins feared that if Christ had only *seemed* to suffer and die, then they could only *seem* to be saved.

68

What about the other alternative? Perhaps Jesus was not divine. Some early Jewish Christians apparently thought of him as no more than a great man, a prophet and teacher, or perhaps one of Yahweh's angels. But in most of the books in the New Testament Christ's divinity was already implied, whether by the story of the virgin birth in Matthew and Luke, or by John's references to the divine Logos, or by Paul's account of Christ's preexistence in equality with God. The earliest surviving Christian sermon outside the New Testament firmly proclaimed: "Brethren, we must think of Jesus Christ as we do of God . . . and we must not think lightly of our salvation. For when we think little of him, we also hope to receive little."[2] That was the point, really. Christians prayed to Christ, they worshiped him, and they trusted in him for salvation. If Christ was only a man, or even an angel, that trust seemed misplaced. Only God never changes; only God is all-powerful. For believers to be ultimately secure, trust in Christ needed to be trust in God.

Such reflections produced general agreement among Christians by the late second century that Christ was both human and divine, but that agreement only laid the foundation for centuries of debate, above all concerning two questions: If Christ was divine, what was his relation to God the Father? If Christ was both human and divine, how were humanity and divinity related within him? The Council of Nicea in 325 and the doctrine of the Trinity which developed in its wake tried to answer the first question; the Council of Chalcedon in 451 addressed the second. Before tracing the history of these debates, it may be helpful to set out the rules of the game. How did Christians decide what to believe? How did you win an argument if you were a third- or fourth-century theologian? Three principles guided the debate.

1. *Do not contradict the Bible.* Christians continued to debate just which books belonged in the New Testament, but they recognized the general authority of Scripture and tended to reject theories that seemed to contradict it.

2. *Do not interfere with the liturgy.* Christians will generally leave theologians alone, considering them harmless enough, but theologians who tell them to stop praying as their parents taught them risk instant unpopularity.

3. *Do not threaten the means of salvation.* As already noted, early Christians affirmed Christ's divinity and humanity in part because saying that Christ had only seemed to be human, or had not been truly divine, had threatened their confidence in their

salvation. That concern continued to shape subsequent debates. To understand its impact requires a digression on how Christians thought Christ had saved them.

THE MEANS OF SALVATION

Many Gnostics, as well as apologists like Justin Martyr, spoke of Christ primarily as a teacher, one who saved us by telling us things we had forgotten or never known. Jesus taught us how to live, or explained our true nature. To many Christians, however, that picture of Christ as teacher seemed incomplete. If it was just a matter of imparting information, why couldn't God simply have sent an angel or a prophet? Even more, why would a teacher need to suffer and die on a cross? Irenaeus, the bishop of Lyons in southern France in the late second century who developed the theory of apostolic succession, sought the basis for a fuller account of Christ's saving work in Paul's references to Christ as the second Adam. When Adam, out of pride and disobedience, sinned, something went wrong with humanity. Christ put things right. He undid what Adam had done by living a human life of humility and obedience, even to death. Historians call this the theory of recapitulation (Christ repeated Adam, only in reverse), and it has undergirded most accounts of the work of Christ ever since. Accepting recapitulation, however, left a need to define what Adam had done wrong and how Christ put it right.

According to one view, Adam had yielded to Satan's trickery and obeyed him rather than God, thereby putting humanity under Satan's lordship. Christ then freed us by defeating Satan. According to some accounts he even used trickery to defeat trickery. Since Adam had voluntarily submitted to Satan, so the argument went, Satan had legitimate rights over all Adam's descendants. Since God is completely just, he could not simply ignore those rights. But God had never submitted to Satan, so Satan had no rights over God. Now Christ looked like a mere human being, and therefore Satan, deceived, tried to seize him. Since Christ was also divine, Satan thereby overreached his rights. Now all deals were off, and God could legitimately punish Satan by freeing humanity from his power. In the vivid words of the fourth-century theologian Gregory of Nyssa, "The Deity was under the veil of our nature, so that, as with ravenous fish, the hook of the Deity might be gulped down along with the bait of flesh."[3] Augustine later said the same thing: "The cross of the Lord became a trap for the Devil; the death of the Lord was the food by which he was ensnared."[4] Such imagery captured the drama and conflicts of salvation and portrayed a God acting in love to save humanity while remaining perfectly just, even to respecting the rights of Satan, but it raised some awkward questions. Did Satan really have a legitimate power over humanity, a power God had to respect until Satan went too far? Did Christ accomplish our salvation through trickery?

Another version of recapitulation used the language of sacrifice and the law courts. Adam had disobeyed God and thereby damaged humanity's relationship with God. When one betrays a friend, something must be done to mend that friendship. Similarly, in the Old Testament, people who had sinned offered a sacrifice to signify their repentence and restore their fellowship with God. In law, one might have to pay a penalty to an injured party to redress the injury done —and one did people an injury if one failed to give them their due honor or respect. Our disobedience has distorted our relationship with God and left us owing God a penalty for the injury we have done his honor. Christ's suffering and death represent a sacrifice on our behalf, a payment for our sin.

This theory too posed some problems. We expect Satan to be nasty, so it comes as no surprise when Christ has to suffer to overcome his power, but we might think God would be willing to forgive us without demanding the price of such suffering. Moreover, the idea that "Christ" pays a penalty to "God" risks implying a separation between them that either denies Christ's divinity or else posits the existence of two Gods. Yet, like the imagery of victory over Satan, this language explained Christ's work in a way that reconciled divine love and divine justice.

Behind these and other versions of the theory of recapitulation lay an assumption about the unity of "humanity" that owed much to Platonic philosophy. Most of us today take a kind of individualism for granted, and we find it hard to understand why something Adam did should affect all human beings. Plato, however, had taught that only universal terms like "justice" and "humanity" have an independent reality. Particular laws or human beings are just or human only to the degree that they participate in those universal forms. Adam's sin, therefore, did not just corrupt Adam; it corrupted all humanity, and therefore humanity needs to be transformed. When Christ became human, he united humanity with divinity, and thus all of us, as participants in humanity, began to share in divinity. As Origen put it, "With Jesus human and divine nature began to be woven together, so that by fellowship with divinity human nature might become divine."[5] Today we retain only slight touches of this way of thinking—as when, for instance, a fellow countryman does something unusually heroic or shameful and we feel proud or guilty, as if this act had altered what it is to be a citizen.

Different accounts of recapitulation thus offered different theories of what Christ did for us: he freed us from Satan, he healed our relationship with God by making a sacrifice or payment, or he transformed our humanity by uniting it with divinity. A particular theologian might appeal to two or all three, though the language of sacrifice was more popular among Latin-speaking Christians, and that of union with divinity more common in the Greek world. All these accounts of what Christ does repeatedly played an important role in defining who Christ is. That leads us back to the main theme of this chapter, the question of what it meant to call Christ both human and divine.

THE ROAD TO NICAEA

Most Christians had come to believe that Christ was divine as well as human, and they had always believed that there is only one God, but did this mean that Christ was simply identical with that one God? Not exactly. Three theologians living in Rome about 200—Noetus, Praxeas, and Sabellius—encountered problems when they proposed such a simple identification. "Do you see," Noetus asked, "how the Scriptures proclaim one God? And as this is clearly exhibited . . . I am under necessity . . . to make this One the subject of suffering. For Christ was God."[6] "What evil, then, am I doing in glorifying Christ?" he wanted to know. "We know in truth one God; we know Christ."[7] What evil was he doing? A number of his contemporaries did not hesitate to tell him. Above all, they said, "Sabellians" like Noetus contradicted the Bible. Hilary of Poitiers set out the specifics 150 years later:

> If he dares, let Sabellius proclaim the Father and the Son as one and the same. . . . He will at once hear from the Gospels, not once or twice, but frequently: "This is my beloved Son in whom I am well pleased." He will hear: "The Father is greater than I." He will hear: "I go to the Father." He will hear: "Father, I give thee thanks" and "Father, glorify me."[8]

In other words, the New Testament repeatedly distinguished between the Father and the Son. Christ prayed to his Father. Therefore, Christ cannot be identical with the Father.

That leads back to the old question: If Christ is divine but is not the Father, are there not two Gods? Tertullian looked for a way out of this problem with a series of metaphors. "God sent forth the Word," he explained, ". . . just as the root puts forth the tree, and the fountain the river, and the sun the ray." Therefore we can distinguish between Father and Son, just as we can distinguish between sun and the ray of light flowing from it, but they are not two separate things.

> For the root and the tree are distinctly two things, but correlatively joined; the fountain and the river are also two forms, but indivisible; so likewise the sun and the ray are two forms, but coherent ones. Everything which proceeds from something else must needs be second to that from which it proceeds, without being on that account separated.[9]

This recognized the New Testament distinction between Father and Son without leading to belief in two Gods.

Unfortunately, these metaphors, used by Origen and many other writers as well, contained a hidden problem. If the Father was the sun and Christ merely one ray coming out of the sun, then Christ was clearly subordinate to the Father. Tertullian admitted as much: "For the Father is the entire substance, but the Son is a derivation and portion of the whole as He Himself acknowledges: 'My Father is greater than I.' "[10] The difficulties of this view became clear only in the theories of Arius, a priest living in Alexandria around 300, whom tradition has cast as the villain of this story. Arius wanted to make it absolutely clear that the Son is not identical with the Father. Only the Father, he said, is eternal; the Son is subordinate to the Father and was created at some point in time.

> The Word of God was not from eternity, but was made out of nothing. . . . Wherefore there was a time when he did not exist, inasmuch as the Son is a creature and a work. . . . He is neither like the Father as it regards his essence, nor is by nature either the Father's true Word, or true Wisdom, but indeed one of his works and creatures.[11]

Having a genius for propaganda, Arius set his favorite slogan to a popular tune, and soon half of Alexandria was singing, "There was a time when the Son was not."

Arius encountered a remarkable opponent. If there is not already a patron saint of stubbornness, Athanasius would be the logical candidate. At the beginning of the Arian dispute, he was in his early twenties, secretary to the bishop of Alexandria. He had, according to tradition, unusually dark skin, a hooked nose, and a red beard, and he was so small that his opponents called him a dwarf. He never,

ever, gave in on anything. He once grabbed the bridle of the Emperor Constantine's horse and refused to let go until Constantine had conceded a theological point. Before he died at about eighty, he had become bishop of Alexandria, had been exiled five times to every corner of the empire, had hidden for years in the deserts of Egypt, had received popular ovations greater than those given any military hero, and had taken on every opponent from the emperor on down.

Arius taught that the Son had been created in time. Athanasius insisted that the Son was begotten eternally. The conflicts between *creating* and *begetting,* and between *in time* and *eternally* shaped their debate.

Judaism had drawn a sharp line between God and God's creation. Therefore, Athanasius argued, if the Son was created, the Son was on the wrong side of that line and could not be divine. The Arians protested that they did believe in the Son's divinity. Even if they could do so consistently, Athanasius replied, they would then believe in two divine beings, one uncreated and the other created. That would mean they believed in two Gods. "Either they must own that He is not true God, because He Himself is one of the creatures, or if, from regard for the Scriptures, they will go on to call Him a God, it is impossible for them to deny that there are two Gods."[12]

According to Athanasius, the Son was not created but "begotten." Anything created is made out of a separate material; a pot, for instance, has nothing substantial in common with the potter who made it. "Begotten," or "born from," on the other hand, implies that the Son comes out of the Father as a child comes out of its parents' substance. But calling Christ begotten makes him divine and not a creature. Thus calling the Son begotten implied that (and this became the crucial term for Athanasius) the Son was "of the same substance" (in Greek, *homoousios*) with the Father.

At the same time, Athanasius warned, the begetting of the Son is not like the begetting of a human child. "The generation of the Son is not like that of a man, which requires an existence after that of the Father.... But the nature of the Son of God being infinite and eternal, His generation must, of necessity, be infinite and eternal too."[13] The Son was not begotten in time; his relation with the Father is eternal. Therefore Athanasius could not accept Arius' slogan that "There was a time when the Son was not." A Christ who had come into existence, he insisted, had already undergone change and might change again. If Arius was right, he said, "there is the same nature in the Son as there is in us. He is liable to change and variation; He may turn into evil ways if He is so inclined; His nature, like ours, is mutable."[14] If our confidence in our salvation rests in a Christ who may change, then it cannot be secure, and for Athanasius a Christ who had come into existence was necessarily a Christ who might change again.

Both Arius and Athanasius won considerable support, and that aroused the concern of the Emperor Constantine. A short time before, Constantine had become a Christian. Whatever his motives—a notorious historical puzzle—he clearly had hoped for Christian support in holding his fragile empire together. While Christians probably constituted only 10 to 20 percent of the empire's population, they had an enthusiasm and organization very appealing to an emperor who needed all the help he could get. Imagine, then, his dismay when he found that his new allies were torn by a dispute he could never quite understand. "Having made a careful inquiry into the origin and foundation of these differences," he wrote to the leaders of both sides, "I find the cause to be of a truly insignificant character, and quite unworthy of such fierce contention."[15] Constantine therefore called over three hundred bishops together in a council at Nicaea. This first official council of the whole church condemned the Arians and wrote a statement of faith, the Nicene Creed, which declared that Christ was "begotten, not created," and "of the same substance as the Father."[16] Athanasius had won.

THE TRINITY

Or so it seemed. At first glance, Nicaea appeared to have settled the question, but further arguments broke out almost at once. For one thing, though the Arians had lost a battle, they continued to fight the war. Later in Constantine's reign and even more under his son Constantius they secured considerable imperial support. Even worse, it soon emerged that those who had signed the Nicene Creed could not agree on what it meant. The crucial debate centered on the statement that the Son was "of the same substance" *(homoousios)* with the Father. Perhaps an analogy can clarify the issue. Suppose I told you that the paperweight on my desk is made from the marble from which the Parthenon is constructed—the same substance. You might think I meant "the same substance" in the sense of "the same type of marble," or you might think I had crept up to the Parthenon late one night and chipped off a piece of *that very substance.* Most of the bishops at Nicaea interpreted *homoousios* in the first sense. In effect, they thought that human beings, trees, and rocks are made of changing, destructible stuff, while the Father is made of eternal, unchanging stuff, and the Son is made of the same sort of stuff as the Father.

Athanasius, on the other hand, insisted that the Son was of the *very same substance* as the Father. He charged his opponents with abandoning the Nicene Creed by replacing "of the same substance" with "of similar substance" (in Greek, the change is from *homoousios* to *homoiousios*—an iota's worth of difference). That led away from monotheism, since it implied the existence of two separate beings, both made of divine substance.

The difficulty for Athanasius concerned all those New Testament passages which made a distinction between the Father and the Son, which had earlier been the crucial problem for the Sabellians. How could the Son pray to the Father, or the Father be greater than the Son, if they were *homoousios?* If Athanasius' position were to triumph, as it eventually did, someone would have to explain how the Father and the Son could be "of the same substance" yet not identical. To add further complications, a similar debate had developed concerning the Holy Spirit. The traditional formula of baptism "in the name of the Father and of the Son and of the Holy Spirit," which carried the authority of both Scripture and liturgy, seemed to imply that whatever was said about the Father and Son ought to be said about the Holy Spirit too. The works of the Spirit played an extremely important role in the early church; however, for a long time theologians had devoted little attention to it. As early as 200 Tertullian called the Spirit "God,"[17] but no Christian writing in Greek did so until the late fourth century. The Nicene Creed tersely declared, "We believe . . . in the Holy Spirit," without any further comment. Still, the ideal solution concerning the relation of Father and Son clearly ought to accommodate the Holy Spirit as well.

The task of developing that solution fell to three theologians from Cappadocia, in what is now northern Turkey—Basil, his brother Gregory of Nyssa, and their friend Gregory of Nazianzus. Together, these three Cappadocians had all the resources needed in intellectual controversy. Basil and Gregory came from a remarkable family. Their sister Macrina may have been its most powerful personality. She devoted herself to an ascetic life, shamed Basil out of his youthful pride in his oratorical abilities, and comforted Gregory on Basil's death. Gregory's account of her own deathbed conversation portrays a woman of deep piety and formidable theological learning. Basil was the organizer in the family, with all the gifts of a great military commander. He founded a famous monastery, and the rules he set down for his monks still regulate life in most Greek monasteries. One senses Basil's spirit in a letter he wrote describing the site of his monastery; he reserved his greatest enthusiasm for its military advantages: "There is one entrance to it, of which we are the master."[18] His brother Gregory of Nyssa, on the other hand, was a poet and a dreamer. For a long time he drifted through life without either a career or much religion, but he eventually found a deep faith. If faith came to Basil as a call to battle, however, Gregory heard it as an invitation to love whispered to the soul.

> When she has torn herself from her attachment to sin, and by that mystic kiss she yearns to bring her mouth close to the fountain of light, then does she become beautiful, radiant with the light of truth. . . . Like a steed she races through all she perceives by sense or by reason; and she soars like a dove until she comes to rest with longing under the shade of the apple tree. . . . Then she is encompassed by a divine night during which the spouse approaches but does not reveal Himself.[19]

Such visions of speeding beyond sense and reason drew on the neo-Platonic tradition, but Gregory brought to them an emotion uniquely his own. With love, everything ought to be simple. When Basil feuded with a friend and they refused to speak to each other, Gregory forged a letter of apology from the friend to Basil. Basil was furious when he found out, but the quarrel had been mended, and Gregory never thought he had done anything wrong.

If Gregory of Nyssa added the insight of a poet to his brother's determination, their friend Gregory of Nazianzus brought the skills of a great orator. In his youth he went off to study at the pagan university at Athens, full of ambition for a career in public speaking. He met Basil, and it changed his life. "I sought there eloquence," he wrote many years later, "and found happiness, for I found Basil. I was like Saul, who in searching for asses found a kingdom."[20] Basil tested their friendship severely. Needing bishops he could trust to vote on his side, he arranged Gregory's appointment to a tiny village in the middle of nowhere. Completely unsuited for pastoral work, Gregory soon retired in discouragement. Doubts about his own faith evidently always haunted him, but when the issue hung in the balance, he yielded again to Basil and went to Constantinople, the imperial capital, and delivered a brilliant series of orations that secured the triumph of the Nicene Creed.

The Cappadocians saved *homoousios* theology by making a terminological distinction. The problem was how to define the difference among Father, Son, and Spirit if they were "of the same substance." Using terminology that went back to Origen, the Cappadocians said that God was one *ousia* but three *hypostaseis* (hypostases). Now an ordinary dictionary might well define both *ousia* and *hypostasis* as "substance." Indeed, both the Nicene Creed and some of Athanasius' works treated them as synonyms, but the Cappadocians distinguished between them. Consider three people: Peter, Mary, and John. Each of them is a particular individual (a *hypostasis*), but the three are all human beings; they share a common essence or substance *(ousia)* of humanity. If you point to Peter and ask, "What is that?" there are two appropriate answers: "That is Peter" (a particular individual or *hypostasis*) or "That is a human being" (a substance or *ousia*). Similarly, Christ is "the Son" *(hypostasis)* and "God" *(ousia)*—a different *hypostasis* than the Father, but "of the same substance" *(homoousios)*, just as the Nicene Creed had said.

This interpretation created an obvious difficulty. We would count Peter, Mary, and John as three human beings. Analogically, should we count the Father, Son, and Spirit as three Gods? Of course not, the Cappadocians replied. God is a special case, in at least two ways. First, we think of three people as separate in part because they might disagree, act on different motives, or pursue different goals. The three divine *hypostaseis,* however, always act in perfect concord. Second, in other cases we can distinguish the separate individuals from the stuff of which they are made because they are subject to change. Basil used the example of three copper coins, which can be melted down into a single lump of copper, and then, perhaps, recast as four coins. Thus we distinguish the particular number of coins from the copper out of which they were made. The three divine *hypostaseis,* on the other hand, are the only form the divine *ousia* has ever taken or could ever take. It therefore makes no sense to think about the substance of divinity apart from the three particular forms it takes. Divinity just *is* these three *hypostaseis,* and so in this case in an important way we cannot think of the "oneness" as something different from the "threeness." Therefore, there are not three separate Gods.

The Cappadocians explained how God is a special case, but it is also important to remember that they were deeply influenced by Platonic philosophy, with its insistence that the universal form is more real than the particular individual. Even with three human beings or three copper coins, they probably saw more underlying unity than we do. Modern theologians often have a tough time restating their theory of the Trinity in plausible form apart from those Platonic assumptions. Another problem with Cappadocian Trinitarianism was that it depended so much on particular words that one could hardly express it in any language but Greek. Since the time of

Tertullian, Latin-speaking Christians had made a parallel distinction between three *personae* (Father, Son, and Holy Spirit) and one *substantia*. Unfortunately, *substantia* is the literal Latin translation of *hypostasis* (both words mean "that which stands under"), so horrified Latin-speaking Christians read Greek references to "three *hypostaseis*" as meaning "three *substantiae*." Eventually, the two linguistic halves of Christianity decided that they were just using different words to say the same thing. As Augustine put it, "For the sake, then, of speaking of things that cannot be uttered, that we may be able in some way to utter what we are able in no way to utter fully, our Greek friends have spoken of one essence, three substances; but the Latins of one essence or substance, three persons."[21]

In fact, this agreement between Greeks and Latins on terminology may have covered up a fundamental difference. Greek theology always began with the Father, Son, and Holy Spirit. Greek-speaking Christians, for instance, generally addressed prayers to one particular *hypostasis*, not just to God. For them, the problem was how to unite the three *hypostaseis* in one *ousia*. Latin-speaking Christians, on the other hand, began with the unity of one God. Their problem lay in explaining how that *substantia* could involve three *personae*. Their choice of terms is revealing. The word *persona* can, like *hypostasis*, mean "particular individual," but it can also refer to a character in a play or even the mask an actor wore to play a particular part. In short, Greeks emphasized the threeness, Latins the oneness. If Greek Trinitarianism risked so emphasizing the distinctions that it ended up with three Gods, Latin Trinitarianism risked treating the *personae* as merely masks or roles and denying any real distinction at all.

As Augustine remarked, all these theories sought to speak of things that cannot be uttered, and the Trinity is a favorite target of critics out to show the logical incoherence of Christianity. It should at least be acknowledged that fourth-century theologians knew that one does not equal three. They were trying to avoid conclusions they thought dangerously wrong. Sabellianism apparently contradicted Scripture, for the New Testament distinguished between the Father and the Son. Arianism seemed to lead to belief in two divinities and the horrifying possibility that Christ might change in unpredictable ways. Anyone who tries to distinguish between Father and Son and avoid Sabellianism, however, while preserving an identity of substance between them and avoiding Arianism, will inevitably move toward something like the doctrine of the Trinity.

THE ROAD TO CHALCEDON

If the doctrine of the Trinity clarified, at least up to a point, the relations among Father, Son, and Spirit, it said nothing about another issue—the relation between the human and the divine in Christ. Christ was divine, but he was also a human being. Given how different humanity is from divinity, how could he be both at the same time? Gregory of Nyssa admitted that he did not know. "We are not capable," he wrote, "of detecting how the Divine and the human elements are mixed up together. The miracles recorded permit us not to entertain a doubt that God was born in the nature of man. But how—this, as being a subject unapproachable by the processes of reasoning, we decline to investigate."[22] As with other issues, however, some theologians developed ideas that forced their fellow Christians to define their faith more precisely in order to show why these ideas were wrong. In this case, the debate became intertwined with the jealousy between Alexandria in Egypt and Antioch in Syria, two of the greatest cities of eastern Christianity. To set out all the terms at the start: The "Logos-flesh Christology" of Alexandria, pushed to an extreme, turned into Apollinarianism. The "two-natures Christology" of Antioch, pushed to an extreme, became Nestorianism. An Alexandrian attack on Nestorianism pushed in its turn to an extreme developed into Monophysitism. The Council of Chalcedon in 451 found a compromise that most Christians accepted, but the Nestorians and the Monophysites continued to hold the allegiance of many.

Alexandria: Logos-Flesh Christology and Apollinarianism. Ever since the days of Philo, the divine Word, the Logos, had been one of the dominant ideas in Alexandrian thought. In trying to understand the relation of human and divine in Christ, therefore, Alexandrians started with the Gospel of John's assertion that the Word became flesh. As Athanasius put it, "The Word of God . . . took a human body to save and help men, so that having shared our human birth, He might make men partakers of the divine and spiritual nature."[23] In the late 300s another Alexandrian, named Apollinaris, tried to clarify what that meant. That had proved a dangerous thing to attempt in the past, and so it proved again. Ordinary human beings, Apollinaris explained, have a body and a mind. Christ had a human body, but in him the divine Logos took the place of a human mind. "The Word became flesh without assuming a human mind; a human mind is subject to change and is the captive of filthy imaginations; but He was a divine mind, changeless and heavenly."[24]

Theodore of Mopsuestia, the great leader of the theologians of Antioch, accused Apollinaris of contradicting Scripture. The New Testament described Christ as "afraid" and "growing in wisdom." Now these statements apply to Christ's mind: "It is obvious that the body did not grow in wisdom." Therefore, unless the Apollinarians claimed that during Jesus' boyhood the divine Logos grew in wisdom —a view which "not even these men are so impudent as to maintain in their wickedness"[25]—they must acknowledge that Christ had a human mind, not just a human body.

Apollinaris offered a compromise. The human mind, he explained, is composed of parts. Its lower elements feel fears and emotions, while reason dwells in its highest part. Christ had not only a human body but also the lower parts of a human mind; the Logos replaced only the human reason. Theodore responded that the real problem concerned salvation, and there this compromise did not help. Since Christ saved humanity by uniting it with divinity, only those parts of us which have been united with divinity in Christ will be saved. Therefore, if Christ lacked a human reason, then human reason has not been united with divinity and was not saved. In the words of Gregory of Nazianzus, "If anyone has put his trust in Him as a Man without a human mind, he is really bereft of mind, and quite unworthy of salvation. For that which He has not assumed He has not healed; but that which is united to His Godhead is also saved."[26]

Antioch: Two-Natures Christology and Nestorianism. Theodore's arguments carried the day, and the Council of Constantinople in 381 condemned Apollinaris, but a condemnation alone did not solve the problem. Theodore had to offer an alternative theory of the relation of human and divine in Christ. Like the Cappadocians, he introduced a distinction in terminology. Christ, he said, had two natures *(physeis)* in one person *(prosōpon)*. At first, it was not clear just what these terms meant, but Theodore tried to explain. He believed that Christ was fully human. He did not just have a human body; he felt emotions and pains as we do. On the other hand, everyone acknowledged that divinity could not suffer or change. Theodore explained this by treating each "nature" as a subject to which one could assign different predicates. When Christ wept or feared, that was the human nature; when he performed miracles or forgave sins, that was the divine nature.

Nestorius, who became patriarch of Constantinople in 428, encountered problems because he followed out all the implications of this two-natures Christology, especially on the issue of Mary, the mother or bearer of God. For at least a hundred years, Christians had been praying to Mary, "the bearer of God." Irenaeus and other theologians had described Mary as the second Eve who undid the sin of the first Eve just as Christ, the second Adam, undid the sin of the first Adam. Popular piety revered Mary. Nestorius gladly honored her, but he insisted that no one should call her the "bearer of God," for being born was something that had happened to Christ's human nature. Calling Mary "the mother of God" would be like saying that God is two years old, two years after Jesus' birth; it applied a predicate of the human nature to the divine nature. One could, Nestorius offered, call Mary "the bearer of Christ."

When theologians interfere with popular piety, they rouse opposition, and Nestorius soon found himself under bitter attack as a defamer of the Virgin Mary. To add to his troubles, his chief opponent was Cyril of Alexandria, one of the nastiest controversialists in the history of theology. Cyril had succeeded his uncle as patriarch of Alexandria and stopped at nothing in defense of Alexandria and of himself. When he died, one of Cyril's contemporaries wrote to a friend:

> At last with a final struggle the villain has passed away. . . .
> Observing that his malice increased daily and injured the body
> of the Church, the Governor of our souls has lopped him off like
> a canker. . . . His departure delights the survivors, but possibly
> disheartens the dead; there is some fear that under the provoca-
> tion of his company they may send him back again to us. . . . Care
> must therefore be taken to order the guild of undertakers to place
> a very big and heavy stone on his grave to stop him coming back
> here.[27]

Even if it is difficult to like him, however, one must admit that Cyril put some legitimate questions to Nestorius. Nestorius argued that Christ must be fully human so that all of humanity could be joined with divinity and saved, yet he so emphasized the distinction between the two natures that it was hard to see how humanity and divinity really came together at all. Further, Nestorius agreed that Christ's suffering on the cross contributed to our salvation, but, according to this sharp distinction between the two natures, only the humanity, not the divinity, suffered. He therefore seemed to imply that we owe our salvation to a human being, not to God. A council of bishops was called to meet at Ephesus in 431, with Cyril in charge, to discuss these matters. Bad weather delayed the arrival of Syrian bishops sympathetic to Nestorius, but Cyril refused to wait for them. With the help of a troop of Egyptian monks who threatened recalcitrant bishops, he secured the condemnation of Nestorius.

Alexandria Again: Monophysitism. Victory accomplished, Cyril began to have second thoughts. Both Theodore of Mopsuestia and Nestorius had taught that Christ has two natures in one person. Cyril, characteristically unwilling to compromise, at first insisted on Christ's oneness in every respect: one person *(prosōpon)*, one nature *(physis)*, one particular individual *(hypostasis)*. Gradually, however, he came to admit that after all, Christ had been both human and divine, and one needed some word to talk about that duality. He conceded that it was possible to speak of "two natures" as long as acknowledgment was made of only one person and one *hypostasis*. What really mattered to Cyril was that, because of the union of the two natures in one *hypostasis*, predicates belonging to one nature could be applied to the other. (The technical Latin term for this is *communicatio idiomatum,* the interchange of attributes.) Thus, for example, although Christ suffered as a human being and worked miracles as God, and although Mary had borne a human being, one could say (contrary to Nestorius) that the divinity had suffered and the humanity had worked miracles, and that Mary had borne the divinity. Humanity and divinity so came together in Christ as to justify such an exchange of predicates.

Cyril's insistence on the *communicatio idiomatum* still gave grounds for the condemnation of Nestorius, for one could apply the human predicate of "being born" to the divine nature and thereby say that Mary gave birth to God; but Cyril's switch from one to two natures left some of his own supporters stranded. Shortly after Cyril's death in 444, an elderly monk named Eutyches blundered onto the scene. He seems to have been fuzzy on a great many theological points, but he was absolutely sure that Christ had only one nature. Cyril's successor at Alexandria, Dioscurus, who had all of Cyril's faults and none of his virtues, regretted that Cyril had conceded anything at all to his opponents and seized on Eutyches as the symbolic hero of the cause of "one nature" *(mono- + physis).* Dioscurus presided over a council at Ephesus in 449 that vindicated Eutyches and condemned any reference to "two natures" after Jesus' birth, but the carryings on at this "Robber Council" created a major scandal. Dioscurus refused to let his opponents speak at all and used an army of monks to handle anyone who threatened to cause trouble. The pope's representative barely escaped back to Rome with his life.

Many "Monophysite" Christians, loyal to the traditions of Alexandria and Cyril's earlier views, accepted the conclusions of the Robber Council, but other Christians found both the condemnation of two natures and the way it had been accomplished disturbing. They arranged another council, at Chalcedon in 451, to straighten things out. The bishops at Chalcedon based their conclusions in part on a letter Pope Leo I had written from Rome to the Robber Council. Dioscurus, needless to say, had not allowed anyone there to read it. In the Definition of Chalcedon the bishops rejected Monophysitism and, basically, returned to Cyril's later position. Two natures, human and divine, coexist in one person, and the oneness of the person makes it appropriate to apply the predicates of either nature to the other (the *communicatio idiomatum*). By this time, every phrase had its importance.

Following the Holy Fathers we all with one voice confess our Lord Jesus Christ one and the same son . . . , truly God and truly man, the same consisting of a reasonable soul and a body, of one substance with the Father as touching the Godhead, of one substance with us as touching the manhood . . . , born of the Virgin Mary, the Mother of God . . . , to be acknowledged in two natures, without confusion, without change, without division, without separation.[28]

"Reasonable soul" rejects the Apollinarian view that Christ lacked a human soul. "Of one substance" opposes the Arians.

"The Mother of God" is against Nestorius. "In two natures" rejects Eutyches and the Monophysites.

Other debates followed, but Chalcedon provides a good point to stop and review. No doubt the intricate precision of the Chalcedonian definition signals an impressive accomplishment, but what does it— or the debate that went before it—matter?

There are two sorts of answers to that question, political and theological. Politically, in all the conflicts between Alexandria and Antioch, Rome always came out on the winning side, and the use of Pope Leo's letter as the basis for the settlement at Chalcedon added to the prestige of the bishop of Rome as the arbiter of orthodoxy. The papal authority that has endured until today grew in part out of these debates. Second, after the Nestorians were condemned at Ephesus in 431, they did not just disappear. A strong Nestorian church spread from Syria to China and survived for centuries. Small communities of Nestorians indeed still exist today. Similarly, after the condemnation of "one nature" at Chalcedon in 451, Monophysite Christians remained numerous in Egypt and adjoining territories. The "orthodox" Christians who accepted Chalcedon persecuted both Nestorians and Monophysites. When Islam began to spread from Arabia in the 600s and 700s, many Nestorians and Monophysites found the Muslims more tolerant than their Christian opponents, and the inheritors of Chalcedon often showed little interest in coming to the aid of "heretics." Perhaps nothing could have stopped the Muslim expansion, but it is intriguing to speculate on whether a theologically united Christianity might have produced a stronger defense and even kept much of the Middle East Christian. If so, then the results of the theological controversies of the fourth and fifth centuries have had an impact that continues down to today's headlines.

Theologically, it is admittedly sometimes tempting to dismiss all these debates as a quibbling over details. But by and large Christians avoided definitions until they felt their salvation stood under threat. For Ignatius of Antioch, going off to face suffering and death in the confidence that Christ had taken that road before him, it was not quibbling to reject the Docetist view that Christ had only seemed to suffer and die. Athanasius thought that Arianism implied that Christ might change and turn evil; he did not consider that point trivial. Apollinaris' view that Christ had not had a human mind posed a real threat to people who hoped for the transformation of their humanity because it had been united with divinity, and who did not want to leave their minds behind. Pious believers praying to Mary, the bearer of God, found Nestorianism deeply disturbing. And so on. To be sure, some aspects of the Trinity and the union of humanity and divinity in Christ remain always a mystery. But that is no excuse for not trying to understand what one can understand, particularly when challenges to faith raise hard questions and demand clarification. In such a context, the Christological discussions represent a great accomplishment. It was in a way the last great accomplishment of an intellectually united Christianity. Nicaea and Chalcedon drew on the work of theologians from all parts of the Christian world; subsequent theological debates tended to take place in either the East or the West.

FOR FURTHER READING

INTRODUCTIONS. For a rare combination of entertaining biographies and serious theological discussion, see Robert Payne, *The Holy Fire* (Harper & Row, 1957). Biographical comments in this chapter have closely followed Payne.

COLLECTIONS OF ORIGINAL SOURCES. Many of the crucial primary texts are collected in three books: William G. Rusch (ed.), *The Trinitarian Controversy* (Fortress Press, 1980); Edward Rochie Hardy (ed.), *Christology of the Later Fathers,* in The Library of Christian Classics (Westminster Press, 1954); Richard A. Norris, Jr., and William G. Rusch (eds.), *The Christological Controversy* (Fortress Press, 1980). J. Stevenson (ed.), *Creeds, Councils, and Controversies* (London: S.P.C.K., 1972), continues the collection of primary sources begun in the same author's *A New Eusebius,* mentioned above in Ch. 4.

IMPORTANT BUT MORE DIFFICULT. Possibly the best detailed account of Christology and other theological developments in the early church is J. N. D. Kelly, *Early Christian Doctrine* (London: Adam & Charles Black, 1958). Edmund J. Fortman, *The Triune God* (Westminster Press, 1972), provides a running summary of positions throughout the development of the doctrine of the Trinity. R. A. Norris, *Manhood and Christ* (Oxford: Clarendon Press, 1963), is a now-classic rehabilitation of the orthodoxy of Theodore of Mopsuestia.

NOTES

1.   Gregory of Nyssa, *Oration on the Deity of the Son and the Holy Spirit,* in *Patrologia Graeca,* ed. by J.-P. Migne, Vol. 46, (Paris: Garnier Fratres, 1863), col. 558.

2.   *The So-called Second Letter of Clement* 1, in *The Apostolic Fathers,* tr. by Edgar J. Goodspeed (Harper & Brothers, 1950), p. 85.

3.   Gregory of Nyssa, *The Great Catechism* 24, tr. by William Moore and Henry A. Wilson, in *A Select Library of the Nicene and Post-Nicene Fathers,* 2d Ser., ed. by Philip Schaff and Henry Wace, Vol. 5 (Christian Literature Co., 1893), p. 494.

4.   Augustine, Sermon 263.1, in *Sermons on the Liturgical Seasons,* tr. by Mary Sarah Muldowney (Fathers of the Church, 1959), p. 392.

5.   Origen, *Contra Celsum* 3.28, tr. by Henry Chadwick (Cambridge: Cambridge University Press, 1965), p. 146.

6.   Hippolytus, *Against the Heresy of One Noetus* 2, tr. by J. H. Macmahon, in *The Ante-Nicene Fathers,* ed. by Alexander Roberts and James Donaldson, Vol. 5 (Wm. B. Eerdmans Publishing Co., 1957), p. 224.

7.   Noetus, quoted in ibid., 2, p. 223.

8.   Hilary of Poitiers, *On the Trinity* 2.23, tr. by Stephen McKenna (Fathers of the Church, 1954), p. 53.

9.   Tertullian, *Against Praxeas* 8, tr. by Peter Holmes, in *The Ante-Nicene Fathers,* Vol. 3 (Wm. B. Eerdmans Publishing Co., 1963), p. 603.

10.   Ibid., 9, pp. 603–604.

11.   Letter of Alexander, bishop of Alexandria, summarizing the Arian position; quoted in Socrates, *Ecclesiastical History* 1.6, tr. by A. C. Zenos,

in *A Select Library of the Nicene and Post-Nicene Fathers*, 2d Ser., Vol. 2 (Christian Literature Company, 1890), p. 4.

12. Athanasius, *Orations Against the Arians* 3.16, in *The Orations of S. Athanasius* (London: Griffith Farran; no date or translator given), p. 198.

13. Ibid., 1.14, p. 25.

14. Ibid., 1.5, p. 15.

15. Constantine, *Letter to Alexander the Bishop and Arius the Presbyter;* quoted in Eusebius, *Life of Constantine* 2.68, tr. by Ernest Cushing Richardson, in *A Select Library of the Nicene and Post-Nicene Fathers*, 2d Ser., Vol. 1 (Christian Literature Co., 1890), p. 516.

16. The Nicene Creed, in *Creeds of the Churches*, ed. by John H. Leith (Aldine Publishing Co., 1963), pp. 30–31.

17. Tertullian, *Against Praxeas* 13, in *The Ante-Nicene Fathers*, Vol. 3, p. 608.

18. Basil, Letter 14, to Gregory his companion, in *Saint Basil: Letters*, tr. by Agnes Clare Way (Catholic University of America Press, 1951), p. 47.

19. Gregory of Nyssa, *Commentary on the Canticle* 1001, in *From Glory to Glory: Texts from Gregory of Nyssa's Mystical Writings*, tr. by Herbert Musurillo (Charles Scribner's Sons, 1961), pp. 247–248.

20. Quoted in Robert Payne, *The Holy Fire* (Harper & Row, 1957), p. 139.

21. Augustine, *On the Trinity* 7.4.7, tr. by W. G. T. Shedd, in *A Select Library of the Nicene and Post-Nicene Fathers*, 1st Ser., ed. by Philip Schaff (Charles Scribner's Sons, 1900), p. 109.

22. Gregory of Nyssa, *The Great Catechism* 11, in *From Glory to Glory*, p. 486.

23. Anthony, quoted in Athanasius, *Life of Anthony* 74, tr. by Mary Emily Keenan, in *Early Christian Biographies*, ed. by Roy J. Deferrari (Catholic University of America Press, 1952), p. 199.

24. Apollinaris, *Letter to the Bishops Exiled at Diocaesarea* 2; quoted in G. L. Prestige, *Fathers and Heretics* (London: S.P.C.K., 1948), p. 111.

25. Quoted in R. A. Norris, *Manhood and Christ* (Oxford: Clarendon Press, 1963), p. 204.

26. Gregory of Nazianzus, Letter 101, to Cledonius the priest, against Apollinaris, tr. by Charles Gordon Browne and James Edward Swallow, in *A Select Library of the Nicene and Post-Nicene Fathers*, 2d Ser., Vol. 7 (Christian Literature Co., 1894), p. 440.

27. Theodoret of Cyr, Letter 180; quoted in Prestige, *Fathers and Heretics*, p. 150. The authenticity of this letter is disputed, but I find it irresistible.

28. The Definition of Chalcedon. See Leith, *Creeds of the Churches*, pp. 35–36, for another translation.

7

LIGHT IN THE EAST

When we arrive at perfection . . . God no longer comes to us, as before, without image or appearance . . . , but He makes Himself seen in His simplicity formed in light without form, incomprehensible, ineffable. I can say no more. . . . He who is God by nature holds converse with those He has made gods by grace, as a man talks with his friends, face to face.

—Symeon the New Theologian[1]

On a map of the countries around the Mediterranean, draw a line between Italy and Yugoslavia, down the Adriatic, and through western Libya. In the Roman Empire west of that line, the language of government and intellectual life was Latin; to the east it was Greek. For several hundred years after the time of Christ, that distinction did not matter much to Christians. The empire was united, and even in the West Christianity attracted its first converts from among those who spoke Greek. Beginning around 300, however, the empire began to divide into two halves politically. By 400 some theologians in the West, Augustine for one, could scarcely read Greek, and Christians in the East paid little attention to Latin theology. Within a hundred years after Chalcedon (451), differences in the languages people spoke, the theologians they read, and the issues they cared about had divided Christianity. Technically, the church split only when the Pope and Patriarch of Constantinople excommunicated each other in 1054, but that act only made official a division that had existed for centuries.

This chapter will concern the theology of Eastern Christianity. For most Protestants and Roman Catholics, this is unfamiliar territory, and part of the task will be simply to introduce issues and a cast of characters as important in their own tradition as "justification by faith" or Thomas Aquinas are in the West. It will be, above all, a story of emperors and mystics. When Constantine converted to Christianity early in the fourth century, he moved his capital east from Rome to Byzantium, which he renamed Constantinople, so it was in the East that Christians struggled for the first time to determine the relations proper between the church and a Christian ruler. In the West the prestige of the emperor dwindled rapidly, and the last Roman emperor gave up his throne in 476. Byzantine emperors ruled in the East until 1453, and they continued to play an important role in the life of the church. Opposition to them came primarily from the monasteries, where a great mystical tradition helped nurture the courage to challenge even an emperor. Emperors and monastic theologians came into conflict first on Christological issues and then on the role of icons, but questions about the relation of the church to a Christian ruler played an important role all along. This chapter will first look at those conflicts, then turn to the foundations of Eastern theology, and finally summarize some of the theological differences between East and West.

EMPERORS AND ICONS

The first Christians were a small minority, mostly of the lower class, living under an autocratic government that viewed them with suspicion. Nothing could have been less relevant to their situation than thinking about the ethical questions that face those who have political power. Their worry was survival. The New Testament reflects a variety of attitudes to Roman authority. In Romans 13, Paul urged obedience to the authorities, and Luke went out of his way to show Roman officials as friendly to Christians. The book of Revelation's allegorical references to Rome as "Babylon," on the other hand, scarcely disguise its hopes for the destruction of a corrupt empire. Roman policy encouraged such ambivalence. Christianity was technically an illegal religion, but with brief exceptions persecution was a local phenomenon of short duration rather than a consistent imperial policy. Christians could hope that they would be left in peace as a reward for good behavior. The Apologists offered repeated assurances that Christians would be loyal citizens, but for most Christians that loyalty did not imply active participation in government, much less military service. By the late second century, and possibly earlier, a few were fighting in the army, but Tertullian disapproved,[2] and Origen argued that Christians could serve the empire better with their prayers than with swords.[3] Some Christians thought that the gospel called them to pacifism on principle, but for others the reason was that they felt like outsiders, onlookers.

Then in the early 300s the Emperor Constantine converted to Christianity. In one generation, Christians went from suffering persecution to sharing in the centers of power. Not surprisingly, some Christians thought that with Constantine's conversion the kingdom of God had arrived on earth and put no limits on their praise of the new Christian emperor. The church historian Eusebius, for instance, declared that this rather tough old soldier was the viceroy of God, continually inspired by God, the interpreter of the Word, who, "emulous of his Divine example, having purged his earthly dominion from every stain of impious error, invites each holy and pious worshiper within his imperial mansions, earnestly desiring to save with all its crew that mighty vessel of which he is the appointed pilot."[4] Constantine did not hesitate to accept whatever praise and authority came his way. He called together the Council of Nicaea on his own authority, and he expected that bishops would report theological disputes to him, since it was to him that God "has entrusted the direction of all human affairs."[5] Eusebius reported how,

> on the occasion of his entertaining a company of bishops, he let fall the expression, "that he himself too was a bishop," addressing them in my hearing in the following words: "You are bishops whose jurisdiction is within the church: I also am a bishop, ordained by God to overlook those outside the church."[6]

Characteristically, Eusebius recounted this startling claim to church authority in a tone of unqualified admiration.

In the tendency to identify the leadership of the emperor with the rule of God, the doctrine of *oikonomia* stood open to particular abuse. *Oikonomia,* corresponding to our "economy" more in sound than in meaning, originally referred to God's plan for salvation, but it gradually became more specific. If application of some church law would interfere with God's plan for salvation, one could appeal to the principle of *oikonomia* and break the law for the sake of the larger good. Basil, for instance, said that baptism by heretics is in general invalid, but in a particular case, if rebaptism would be disruptive and impractical, one could accept the heretical baptism for the good of God's overall purposes.[7] When applied to actions of the emperor, the principle of *oikonomia* could function like appeals to "national security" in our own time. Someone would say that God was working through the emperor, and any criticism of the imperial order might interfere with God's plans. *Oikonomia* could justify either the church's silence or its support of the most dreadful imperial behavior. Not all Christians agreed that the actions of a Christian emperor must stand unquestioned. Many especially objected to imperial interference in church affairs. Even under Constantine's son Constantius, his adviser Bishop Hosius had warned him: "Do not meddle in church affairs nor give orders on them. Rather take instruction from us. . . . As we are not permitted to govern the world" so the emperor is not permitted to perform the functions of a priest.[8]

In the course of a series of theological debates, first on Christology and then on iconoclasm, Byzantine theologians fought to set limits on imperial power over the church. Christological debates came first. The Council of Chalcedon in 451 had left Christians divided between those who accepted the council's assertion that Christ has two natures and the Monophysites, who did not. In the 540s Emperor Justinian sought some kind of compromise between the two positions. Justinian was one of the greatest of the Byzantine emperors: he reconquered much of Italy, and his collection of Roman law, the Justinian code, remains one of the great legacies of Roman culture. When he turned to theology, he persuaded the Second Council of Constantinople, which met in 553, to try to win over the Monophysites by condemning Theodore of Mopsuestia, the greatest theologian of the school of Antioch and the champion of the "two natures" language which had been ratified at Chalcedon. Justinian also disliked Origen, whom he suspected of selling Christian theology out to Greek philosophy, and the council apparently (the records are unclear) condemned Origen as well.

Clearly the emperor took the lead in these actions, but Justinian recognized some limits on his authority. His law code declared:

> There are two greatest gifts which God, in his love for man, has granted from on high: the priesthood and the imperial dignity. The first serves divine things, the second directs and administers human affairs; both, however, proceed from the same origin and adorn the life of mankind. . . . If the priesthood is in every way free from blame and possesses access to God, and if the emperors administer equitably and judiciously the state entrusted to their care, general harmony will result, and whatever is beneficial will be bestowed upon the human race.[9]

That did recognize that the priesthood and the emperor had separate missions, but it left the emperor with vast powers, and Justinian reserved the right to approve church officials and rule on theological issues.

He did not succeed, however, in reuniting the Monophysites to the Chalcedonian Christians. Such a union was achieved briefly in Egypt in 633, but the task of agreeing on how many natures Christ has proved finally insurmountable. Some suggested asking instead how many wills Christ has. Perhaps the natural inclination is to say that he had one will; anything else smacks of schizophrenia. One theologian of the period, Macarius of Antioch, firmly declared, "I will never say two natural wills . . . , even if I were to be torn limb from limb and cast into the sea."[10] Monothelitism (the belief that Christ has only one will, from mono-+ thelēma, "one will"), however, soon ran up against two now-familiar problems. First, it seemed to contradict Scripture. When Christ prayed, "Not my will but thine be done," he distinguished between two wills, and positing two divine wills would destroy the unity of the Trinity. Thus Christ must have had a human as well as a divine will. Second, there was the problem of salvation. The great theologian John of Damascus quoted yet again the famous passage from Gregory of Nazianzus, "That which has not been assumed cannot be healed."[11] If Christ did not have a human will, then the human will, which is the starting point of our sin, has not been joined with divinity and therefore has not been saved. "If he did not assume a human will, that in us which suffered first has not been healed."[12] In 681, therefore, the Third Council of Constantinople declared that Christ has two wills.

This rather obscure debate continues to play a significant role in the history of theology principally because of the role of Pope Honorius I. The popes in Rome had preserved an unblemished record of always coming out on the winning side of theological controversies, but this time Pope Honorius apparently came down firmly in favor of "one will," though most Christians since, including the Roman Catholic Church, have judged this heretical. The evidence contains some ambiguities, but Catholic historians trying to defend the doctrine of papal infallibility find Honorius one of their most awkward cases.

Emperors had gotten somewhat involved in these Christological disputes, but it was imperial initiatives that began the iconoclastic debates, and emperors and empresses were at the center of a quarrel that nearly tore Byzantine Christianity apart. The issues can only be understood against the background of early Christian attitudes to images. While recent archaeology has discovered a few exceptions, in general Jews took the commandment against making graven images to mean that they should not make any pictures or statues of their God. In a time when most art was religious, they therefore tended not to make any pictures or statues at all. The first Christians followed that example. In part it was probably because they were too poor to decorate churches elaborately, but religious motives also played a role. Eusebius rebuked Constantine's sister when she asked him for a picture of Christ.[13] Since Christ was divine, such an image would violate the Ten Commandments. Many Christian artists substituted the image of a lamb to avoid picturing Christ.

Gradually customs changed. Church decorations grew more elaborate, and pictures offered a good way of teaching illiterate believers about the faith. Images of Christ, Mary, and the saints became common in churches, and praying before them came to be an important part of the devotional life of many Christians. Some, however, still felt disturbed about such images, and the Emperor Leo the Isaurian, who ruled from 717 to 741, insisted that they were blasphemous and set out to destroy them. His son Constantine V stepped up the attack. Some historians have attributed their iconoclasm (image-breaking) to Muslim influence, but the evidence seems shaky. They were military leaders with a loyal army from the provinces, and such figures— Oliver Cromwell comes to mind—often have a Puritan streak suspicious of the elaborate art of the cities. Moreover, the iconoclasts had a legitimate concern: Many people, especially those with little education, probably did worship the icons rather than using the icons as a way of worshiping God.

The iconoclastic controversy dominated Byzantine theology from the early 700s until the mid 800s. The various victories and defeats, which usually depended on shifts in imperial power, grew far too complicated to trace here. The debates occasioned important works from two of the greatest of Eastern theologians, John of Damascus (643 to about 750) and Theodore of Studios (759–826), who attacked iconoclasm and argued for limits on imperial power in theology.

At a time when imperial authority had imposed iconoclasm on the empire, John of Damascus lived beyond the emperor's threats, under Muslim rule. Although a Christian, he had at an early age succeeded his father as one of the principal officials of the Muslim court in Syria. Then he met a Christian slave named Cosmas who wanted to live as a monk, and John gave up all his wealth and power to follow Cosmas into the monastic life. He later wrote a moving story of friendship called *Barlaam and Joasaph,* which conveys his affection for Cosmas. For John, the incarnation represented the crucial argument against iconoclasm. "In former times, God, without body or form, could in no way be represented. But today, since God has appeared in the flesh and lived among men, I can represent what is visible in

God."[14] Nearly a century later, Theodore of Studios made the same point. Like John, he had given up much wealth for the monastic life, but, far from retreating to the desert, he had moved to a monastery in the heart of Constantinople. There he led a steady barrage of criticism of the imperial court. Banished for denouncing an emperor's marriage as contrary to church law, he returned only to be banished twice more for his attacks on iconoclasm. To deny that one can paint a picture of Christ is, Theodore insisted, to deny Christ's humanity. "Man has no characteristic more fundamental than this, that he can be represented in an image; that which cannot be represented in this way is not a human being."[15] Defenders of icons like John and Theodore admitted the possibility of their misuse. Worship or adoration *(latreia),* they said, should be offered only to the three hypostases of the Trinity; an icon, like an emperor or any person one respected, deserved only honor or veneration *(timē).* But the possibility of abuse is no excuse for forbidding images altogether. If Christ was a human being, then it is possible to paint a picture of him.

Both John and Theodore argued that the emperors had no business interfering in theological debates anyway. "Political prosperity," John wrote, "is the business of the Emperor; the ecclesiastical organization belongs to the pastors and teachers, and to take it out of their hands is to commit an act of robbery."[16] Theodore emphasized that even the emperor must be subject to the law. "Either the emperor is God, for divinity alone is not subject to the law, or there is anarchy and revolution. For how can there be peace if there is no law valid for all?"[17] One could not drag in the principle of *oikonomia* to bend the law to suit the emperor's convenience. The defeat of iconoclasm, therefore, did more than establish the veneration of icons—which, as those familiar with the Orthodox churches will know, has been an important part of Eastern Christianity ever since. It set limits on the ruler's power to interfere in the affairs of the church and established the rights of theologians, like the prophets of ancient Israel, to protest the ruler's actions in the name of their faith.

DEIFIED HUMANITY
AND THE UNKNOWABLE GOD

It was their spiritual life that gave monks like John and Theodore the courage to stand up to emperors, and their mystic experience also played a crucial role in shaping their theologies. In the West, the lists of great mystics and great theologians overlap, but in the East they are virtually identical. Tradition dominated much of Byzantine theology, but while Eastern writers may sometimes seem trapped in repeating traditional formulas, those formulas expressed what they had come to know intimately in their own spiritual lives.

Many Eastern theologians believed that theology could never venture far from personal experience because no words can adequately talk about God. The true knowledge of God, Gregory of Nyssa once wrote, "is the seeing that consists in not seeing, because that which is sought transcends all knowledge, being separated on all sides by incomprehensibility."[18] Such a vision of the incomprehensible cannot really be communicated to another; you have to experience it for yourself. One major source of this theology of divine incomprehensibility was the work of "Dionysius the Areopagite," known to modern scholarship as Pseudo-Dionysius. The author of these great mystical texts remains unknown, though most scholars today guess that they were written in Syria, perhaps as late as the sixth century, but throughout most of Christian history they were considered the work of a first-century convert of Paul himself, with all the authority that that conveyed. Dionysius proclaimed the superiority of "negative theology." We can describe only what God is not, not what God is. What God is can be known only when "we worship with reverent silence the unutterable Truths and . . . approach that Mystery of Godhead which exceeds all Mind and Being."[19]

One of the most influential Byzantine theologians, Maximus the Confessor (580–662), wrote a famous commentary on Dionysius. Maximus insisted that we cannot say anything about God, not even that God exists. "The two names of Being and Non-Being ought both to be applied to God, although neither of them really suits Him. . . . He possesses an existence that is completely inaccessible and beyond all affirmation and negation."[20] Therefore, the best speech about God is silence, and the profoundest knowledge of God lies in humble ignorance. "For the ignorance about God on the part of those who are wise in divine things is not a lack of learning, but a knowledge that knows by silence that God is unknown."[21]

After reading the insistent declarations of Dionysius and Maximus that we cannot describe or understand God, it comes as a shock to hear Eastern theologians saying that we can *become* God, but they returned to this theme again and again. The idea that Christ saves us by joining humanity with divinity had always been especially important among Greek-speaking Christians. With Athanasius, they believed that "he became man that we might become divine."[22] To use a very weak analogy, when someone not of royal blood becomes a king, perhaps a bit of that royal prestige might rub off on his relatives.

But such analogies cannot really capture for our individualistic age the power this imagery had in a time steeped in Platonic thought, when the universal "humanity" seemed more "real" than particular human individuals. By being both human and divine, Christ had changed forever what it means to be human.

For Eastern theologians, deification was not, however, just something Christ had done once for all of humanity, but a process that could shape the life of each person. God is love, and in becoming more loving we come to be more like God, so that we come to realize within ourselves the deification of humanity that Christ first made actual. "Love, the divine gift," Maximus the Confessor wrote, "perfects human nature until it makes it appear in unity and identity with the divine nature."[23]

In that process of deification through love we play an active role. In the words of John of Damascus:

> God gave us the power to do what is good; but he also made us free, in order that the good might come both from him and from us; for whoever chooses the good receives God's collaboration to do the good, so that having preserved what is natural to us, we might receive what is supernatural—incorruptibility and deification.[24]

Such an emphasis on human efforts does not mean that we can win salvation apart from God's grace. As Maximus put it: "No creature is capable of deification by its own nature, since it is not capable of grasping God. This can happen only by the grace of God."[25] Nevertheless, in comparison with Latin theology, the East put more emphasis on the human contribution. The next chapter will describe Augustine's claim that we are saved by the grace of God alone, without regard to our works. That would have seemed too extreme to most Eastern theologians. It is not that the two halves of Christianity disagreed on specific issues so much as that they thought about these matters in different ways. Western theologians thought in terms of states. With Adam's initial sin, humanity had fallen into a state of sin. Christ redeems us, bringing us into a state of grace. The emphasis falls on the moment of conversion, in which one moves from one state to the other. Eastern theology, on the other hand, tended to think in terms of processes. We move gradually toward deification. Since most Western theologians thought of salvation as occurring at the moment of conversion, they could say that human works had no part in it and still leave an important place for human efforts after conversion in response to God's grace. Eastern theologians, on the other hand, thought of deification as a process that continues throughout one's life. Therefore they had to build human works into that process or there would be no place for our moral efforts at all.

These two central themes of Eastern theology—the incomprehensibility of God and salvation through deification—seem incompatible. One of the reasons God cannot be understood is that God is utterly simple and cannot be analyzed into component parts. Yet in deification we become parts of God. More generally, talk of divine incomprehensibility pushes God ever farther away from us, while the hope of deification brings God ever closer. Maximus the Confessor sought to resolve these puzzles with a compromise: "All that God is except for an identity in *ousia* ["substance" or "essence," the key word in Trinitarian debates] one becomes when one is deified by grace."[26] That left room for deification while preserving God's *ousia* as unapproachable. But, particularly if God is utterly simple, what could there be in God other than *ousia?*

Late Byzantine theology sought to respond to this and other problems with the doctrine of the divine *energeiai* ("actions" or "operations"), fully developed by the greatest theologian of the period, Gregory Palamas, who died in 1359. In the now-familiar pattern, Gregory grew up in the emperor's court, even becoming the ward of the emperor, and then gave all that up for the austere life of a monk. He did not, however, manage to retire from the conflicts and problems of the world. How could we know, much less become, God, Gregory wondered, if God's essence is utterly incomprehensible? Earlier theologians had contrasted God's essence, Father, Son, and Holy Spirit, one and utterly unknowable, with God's creatures, made in time and separate from God. Gregory proposed an intermediate classification, the *energeiai* of God. Scripture talks about God's Love, God's Knowledge, the Divine Light. These are distinct from the essence of God. We can talk about them separately and experience them—God's love, for instance—even though God's essence remains unapproachable, but they are not creatures, for they are eternal and come from God rather than being made of some separate substance. "From his *energeiai*," Basil the Cappadocian had written nearly a thousand years before, "we know our God; we do not undertake to approach his substance itself. His *energeiai* come down to us, but his substance remains inaccessible."[27] Now Gregory Palamas developed that theme. "The divine and uncreated grace and *energeiai* of God is, being indivisibly divided, like the sun's ray, which warms and lightens and vivifies and increases its own splendor in what it enlightens, and shines forth in the eyes of its beholders."[28] Through the divine *energeiai* we can come to know God, although God's essence remains unknowable, and we can move forward toward deification by participating in those *energeiai*.

These *energeiai* were not just a topic for abstract discussion; for centuries the monks on Mt. Athos, where Gregory lived for a time, had claimed to experience the Uncreated Light, one of the divine *energeiai*. These Hesychast monks (*hēsychia* means "inward quiet," "stillness") evolved some special techniques of prayer, including continuous repetition of the "Jesus prayer" ("Jesus Christ, Son of God, Savior, have mercy upon me") and controlled breathing of a sort we would associate with yoga. Around the year 1000 one Hesychast, Symeon the New Theologian, had an astounding experience while saying the Jesus prayer. According to his own later report,

> one day he was saying the prayer . . . when suddenly a divine light shone on him from above, filling the place entirely. The young man lost all awareness, he forgot that he was in a house or under a roof, for he saw, all around him, nothing but light . . . and he himself, so it seemed to him, had become light.[29]

This was, he grew convinced, the light that Peter, John, and James had seen surrounding Jesus at the transfiguration—not sunlight, or the product of any created thing at all, but the divine, uncreated light that streams forth as one of God's *energeiai*. When the Hesychast monks, many of whom had similar experiences, spoke of such matters, Symeon insisted: "We do not speak of things of which we are ignorant, but we bear witness to that which we know. For the light already shines in the darkness, in the night and in day, in our hearts and minds."[30]

Like others in Christian history who believe they are given special gifts (some of those who "speak in tongues," for instance), some Hesychasts started to believe that whoever had not shared their special experience was not among the saved. "Those who have not seen this Light, have not seen God: for God is Light," Symeon wrote. "Those who have not received this light, have not yet received grace, for in receiving grace, one receives this divine light, and God himself."[31] Those who had received the light—some went on to claim— did not need the usual sacraments and ministry of the church.

Gregory Palamas' contemporary Barlaam launched a violent attack on the Hesychasts. Barlaam had been educated in logic and philosophy in Italy, and he had little patience with theology based primarily on tradition and mystical experience. He said that theology ought to apply the tools of philosophical analysis, not just repeat what had been handed down from the past; and he ridiculed the Hesychasts as people who hoped to find God by staring at their navels. Barlaam had charm and intellectual brilliance, and he had performed several successful diplomatic missions. Powerful forces at the imperial court supported his attempt to put an end to Hesychast practices. Finally, Gregory Palamas arrived from his monastery to face Barlaam in debate, and by most accounts he demolished him. In contrast to Barlaam's appeals to logical analysis, Gregory defended theological reliance on tradition. Mere logic, he said, could not penetrate the nature of God. We must trust in what has been handed down through the community of faith. He also defended the use of physical disciplines in prayer. "When God is said to have made man according to His image," he explained, "the word *man* means neither the soul by itself nor the body by itself, but the two together."[32] Therefore our efforts toward salvation appropriately involve the body as well as the soul.

> It is not out of place to teach, especially with beginners, people to look at themselves, and by means of breathing to send the mind back inside themselves. . . . People who undertake this struggle continually find their mind flying off as soon as it has been collected. . . . That is why some have recommended control of inhalation and exhalation and holding the breath a little, so as to hold the mind too.[33]

As his cautious language here suggests, Gregory trimmed the excessive claims of the Hesychasts. Their prayers represented one path to salvation, he said, but not the only one, and they should not be pursued to the exclusion of sacraments and other Christian activities. Even at that, Gregory found stiff resistance from Barlaam's supporters, and the issues became intertwined with a bitter fight over the succession to the imperial throne. The Eastern Orthodox Church finally accepted Gregory's views and considers him one of its greatest saints. He represented a kind of culmination of that long tradition of monastic theologians who challenged theological error and imperial power from the confidence that grew out of their mystical experience. Still, although his theology grew out of mystical insights, Gregory himself always insisted that none of his words could adequately capture what the mystic encounters. "Theology is as far from the vision of God in light," he wrote, "and as distinct from intimate conversation with God, as knowledge is different from possession; to say something about God is not equivalent to meeting with God."[34]

THE FIRST ROME, THE SECOND ROME,
AND THE THIRD ROME

A history of Christian institutions might devote much attention to the official breaks between the Eastern and Western churches—the Eastern Orthodox and the Roman Catholic, to use the usual modern names. When the two groups actually separated, however, they had long had little to say to each other. It is more important, therefore, to the history of theology to describe the different ways of thinking that had long existed in the two halves of Christianity. Hesychasm and iconoclasm, for instance, never emerged as important issues in the West, while the East never really debated predestination.

In the late 800s, Photius, the patriarch of Constantinople, denounced Western theories of the procession of the Holy Spirit, a point to be explained below, and the pope excommunicated him, but the breach was soon healed. The pope and the patriarch of Constantinople excommunicated each other in 1054, and that split endured. In 1438–39, however, representatives from both sides met in the Council of Florence and for a moment seemed to have achieved an agreement. Both groups had reasons to want unity. A Turkish army virtually surrounded Constantinople, and the emperor hoped for help from the West, far more likely if Christians loyal to the pope did not consider Constantinople a city of excommunicated heretics. The pope, on the other hand, faced a challenge to his authority from a rebellious council, and thought he could establish his own position more securely by pulling off the coup of uniting Christian East and West. An outline of the debates at the Council of Florence provides a good summary of the issues that had come to divide Roman and Byzantine theology.

Several issues proved fairly easy to settle. Eastern Christians used leavened bread in the Eucharist; Westerners used unleavened. The East allowed married men to become priests. The two sides disagreed on the moment in the liturgy in which the bread and wine became Christ's body and blood. Rome taught that on death the condemned go to hell and the saints go to heaven, but people who have been saved but have not yet done full penance for their sins go for a time to purgatory. Many Eastern Christians believed in purgatory, but they did not find it clearly mentioned in the Scriptures and were unwilling to require that all Christians should believe in it. On these problems East and West could agree to disagree.

The real theological debate concerned the "procession of the Holy Spirit." As the last chapter explained, the Nicene Creed had rejected

Arianism by saying, among other things, that Christ was "begotten, not created." That relation of "begetting" established that the Son was not a creature, essentially unrelated to the Father, but of the same substance with the Father. The doctrine of the Trinity declared that the Holy Spirit was also of the same substance with the Father, but Scripture clearly spoke of Christ as the "only begotten Son" of the Father. The Father, therefore, could not beget the Holy Spirit as well. Gregory of Nazianzus had proposed another word: "procession." "The Holy Spirit is truly Spirit, coming forth from the Father indeed, but not after the manner of the Son, for it is not by Begetting but by Procession (since I must coin a word for the sake of clearness)."[35] As Gregory's parenthesis suggests, no one knew quite what "procession" meant, but the Council of Constantinople in 381 adopted a creed that is in essence the form of the Nicene Creed most churches use today and that declared that the Son was begotten of the Father while the Holy Spirit proceeded from the Father.

East and West soon began to think about these intra-Trinitarian relations differently. Eastern theologians thought of the Father as the principle of unity, with the Son and the Spirit coming forth from the Father in their different ways. In the West, Augustine's influence led people to think of the Spirit as the primary basis of Trinitarian unity. To Augustine, the Spirit represented love, and just as love binds the church together on earth, so the Spirit is the love which binds together Father and Son. "The Holy Spirit . . . is neither of the Father alone, nor of the Son alone, but of both; and so intimates to us a mutual love, wherewith the Father and the Son reciprocally love one another."[36] Therefore, Augustine said, the Spirit proceeds not just from the Father, but "from the Father and the Son," and after about 800, Western Christians generally recited the creed adopted at Constantinople with the addition of the word *filioque* ("and the Son"). Greek Christians objected to this on two counts. First, they opposed any tampering with the creed, particularly one about which they had never been consulted. Second, the "double procession" of the Holy Spirit seemed to them to deny the single basis of unity for the Trinity in the Father and to subordinate the Spirit to the Son. Some even unkindly suggested that it would make the Spirit the Father's Grandson. The two points of view were really operating with different metaphors, each communicating an insight; unfortunately the implications of their metaphors seemed to contradict each other.

Most of the debate at Florence concerned the *filioque*, and eventually the council reached a compromise. Some important Eastern theologians had said that the Spirit proceeds "through the Son";

many distinguished theologians in the West had said "from the Son."
Well, the council concluded, these inspired minds could not have
disagreed, and therefore the two phrases must mean the same thing.
True, the West had added something to the creed, but after all the
Council of Constantinople itself had modified the Nicene Creed. Each
half of Christianity could continue to say the creed in its own way.

Only one of the Greek delegates rejected this compromise, but,
when they returned home, the rest were greeted as traitors. Much of
the anger grew out of Greek bitterness against the West. Crusaders
from the West had roamed around Byzantine territory for several
centuries by this time, generally doing more harm than good, and in
1204 a crusading army had viciously sacked Constantinople and imposed a period of Latin rule there. Behind their theological arguments,
Eastern Christians nursed quite justifiable grudges.

A more specific problem concerned the position of the pope. Rome
had been the unchallenged leading church in the West, tracing its
authority back to both Peter and Paul, and Western Christians had
come to think of the pope, the bishop of Rome, as the head of the
whole church, the court of final appeal. Chapter 9 will tell that story
in more detail. Christians in the East, on the other hand, assigned
preeminence to the five patriarchs of Rome, Constantinople, Alexandria, Jerusalem, and Antioch, and insisted on a council of the
church as the ultimate authority. They would acknowledge Rome as
first among equals, and, like Theodore of Studios, many Eastern
theologians praised Rome as "the one and only help in recurrent
crises . . . , the pure and genuine source of orthodoxy . . . , the distinct
calm harbor for the whole church from every heretical storm."[37] But
they would not accept the pope as the sole head of the church. After
all, Peter had been only one of the apostles, and, if it came to that,
Peter had led the church at Jerusalem and Antioch before he ever
went to Rome. The conflict emerged dramatically at the outset of the
Council of Florence, when the patriarch of Constantinople discovered
that the pope expected him to genuflect and kiss the pope's foot.

> From where does the Pope get this right? What council gave it to
> him? . . . If he is the successor of Peter, we are the successors of
> the other Apostles. Did they kiss the feet of Peter? . . . If the Pope
> wants a brotherly embrace, following the ancient custom of the
> church, I will embrace him. If he will not accept that, I will
> abandon everything and go home.[38]

In the end, the pope settled for an embrace, but in private, so that no
one would see this compromise of his dignity.

This basic conflict over authority, compromised at Florence, re-emerged almost at once, and Florence turned out to have offered the last chance for a union of papal Rome and imperial Constantinople. Less than twenty years later, in 1453, the Turks conquered Constantinople, and the Eastern empire ended forever. Eastern Christianity of course survived under sometimes tolerant Muslim rulers, but the simple struggle for survival left little time for original theology. The best educated writers of this period had usually studied in the West and brought Western ideas to their own tradition. After the Reformation, a few even sought to build bridges to Protestantism, the new enemy of their old enemies at Rome. In the seventeenth century, one patriarch of Constantinople, Cyril Lucaris, adopted many of the ideas of John Calvin, but most Eastern Christians quickly repudiated Lucaris.

After the fall of Constantinople, Eastern Christianity grew most of all in Slavic lands. Missionaries had gone there centuries earlier, converting the Bulgars in 864 and the Russians, at least according to legend, in 988. According to the traditional story, Prince Vladimir of Kiev in Russia sent some nobles to the Moslems, the Jews, and the Eastern and Western Christians to choose the best faith, and the emissaries returned in awe at the liturgy they had witnessed in Constantinople.

> We know not whether we were in heaven or on earth. For on earth there is not such splendor or such beauty and we are at a loss to describe it. We only know that God dwells there among men, and their service is fairer than the ceremonies of other nations. For we cannot forget that beauty.[39]

The Russians decided that this was the religion for them. (In fairness, perhaps it should also be noted that they supposedly rejected Islam at once on hearing that the prophet forbids alcohol: "Drinking is the joy of the Russians, we cannot do without it."[40])

Early Slavic Christianity followed Byzantine theology closely, but the missionaries, unlike those of Rome, translated the liturgy into the native languages. The missionary saints Cyril and Methodius virtually created written Slavic language, and the fact that each nation had a Christianity in its own tongue made for a strong identification of faith and nation, particularly when, under the rule of one conqueror or another, there was little other basis for a sense of national identity.

Russian Christianity in particular came to consider itself the inheritor of the tradition of Rome and Constantinople. The theologian Philotheus of Pskov wrote of Czar Basil III early in the sixteenth century, "He is on earth the sole emperor of the Christians, the leader of the Apostolic Church which stands no longer in Rome or in Constantinople, but in the blessed city of Moscow. . . . Two Romes have fallen, but the third stands."[41]

Russia inherited not only the dream of imperial glory but also the ideal of Christian monasticism and self-denial. The Russian tradition, however, was less one of active monastic protest than of the passive acceptance of suffering. The greatest of Russia's saintly heroes were Prince Boris and Prince Gleb, the sons of the Prince Vladimir who converted Russia to Christianity. When their evil brother murdered them to seize the throne, they welcomed their agonizing deaths. "Glory to Thee," Boris cries in the legend, "for Thou hast vouchsafed me to flee the seductions of this deceptive life. . . . They treated me like a lamb for consumption. Thou knowest, my Lord, that I do not resist, do not object." His brother Gleb tells the hired ruffians who come to kill him, "If you wish to satiate yourselves with my blood, I am in your hands and in those of my brother your prince."[42] The retelling of this story generation after generation must have had a profound impact on Russian attitudes. Even centuries later in the novels of Tolstoy and Dostoevsky one encounters that admiration of passive suffering in the face of injustice. Yet even today one also finds Christian protest, rooted in a deep spirituality, against the injustices of those in power. In the writings and example of someone like Alexander Solzhenitsyn, for instance, if Marxist commissars have replaced Christian emperors, the ideal of the mystic who protests against the evil ruler, the tradition of Maximus the Confessor, John of Damascus, and Theodore of Studios, such an important part of the vision of Eastern Christianity, lives on.

FOR FURTHER READING

INTRODUCTIONS. The best historical survey at an introductory level is John Meyendorff, *Byzantine Theology* (Fordham University Press, 1974). Steven Runciman, *The Byzantine Theocracy* (Cambridge: Cambridge University Press, 1977), describes church and state in Byzantium in an enjoyable style.

IMPORTANT BUT MORE DIFFICULT. Since so little material is available in English, attention should be drawn again to two works mentioned at the end of the introduction. Given the author's vast erudition and the limited sources available in Western languages in this area, Jaroslav Pelikan, *The Spirit of Eastern Christendom (600–1700)* (University of Chicago Press, 1974), may well be the most important volume of Pelikan's five-volume history of doctrine. The chapter on Byzantine theology by Kallistos Ware in Hubert Cunliffe-Jones and Benjamin Drewery (eds.), *A History of Christian Doctrine* (Fortress Press, 1980), is an unusually clear introduction. Vladimir Lossky, *The Mystical Theology of the Eastern Church* (London: James Clarke & Co., 1957), offers the profound insights of an important theologian of this tradition. G. P. Fedotov, *The Russian Religious Mind,* 2 vols. (Harper & Row, Harper Torchbooks, 1960), is the classic work on Russian Christianity. John Meyendorff has also written *Christ in Eastern Christian Thought* (Corpus Books, 1969), and *A Study of Gregory Palamas* (London: Faith Press, 1962).

NOTES

1. Symeon the New Theologian, Homily 90; quoted in Vladimir Lossky, *The Mystical Theology of the Eastern Church* (London: James Clarke & Co., 1957), p. 232.

2. Tertullian, *On the Pallium* 5, tr. by S. Thelwell, in *The Ante-Nicene Fathers,* ed. by Alexander Roberts and James Donaldson, Vol. 4 (Wm. B. Eerdmans Publishing Co., 1956), p. 11.

3. Origen, *Contra Celsum* 8.73, tr. by Henry Chadwick (Cambridge: Cambridge University Press, 1965), p. 509.

4. Eusebius, *The Oration in Praise of the Emperor Constantine* 2, tr. by Ernest Cushing Richardson, in *A Select Library of the Nicene and Post-Nicene Fathers,* 2d Ser., ed. by Philip Schaff and Henry Wace, Vol. 1 (Christian Literature Co., 1890), p. 583.

5. Quoted in Steven Runciman, *The Byzantine Theocracy* (Cambridge: Cambridge University Press, 1977), p. 13.

6. Eusebius, *The Life of Constantine* 4.24, tr. by Ernest Cushing Richardson, in *A Select Library of the Nicene and Post-Nicene Fathers,* 2d Ser., Vol. 1, p. 546.

7. Basil, Letter 188, to Amphilochius, in *Letters,* tr. by Agnes Clare Way (Fathers of the Church, 1955), Vol. 2, p. 11.

8. Athanasius, *History of the Arians,* in *Patrologia Graeca,* ed. by J.-P. Migne, Vol. 25 (Paris: Garnier Fratres, 1884), col. 748; quoted in Runciman, *The Byzantine Theocracy,* p. 27.

9. Justinian, *Corpus juris civilis,* Novella 6; quoted in John Meyendorff, *Byzantine Theology* (Fordham University Press, 1974), p. 213.

10. Quoted in Jaroslav Pelikan, *The Spirit of Eastern Christendom* (University of Chicago Press, 1974), p. 70.

11. John of Damascus, *The Orthodox Faith* 3.6, in *Writings,* tr. by Frederic H. Chase, Jr. (Fathers of the Church, 1958), p. 280, quoting Gregory of Nazianzus, Letter 101.

12. John of Damascus, *On the Two Wills in Christ* 28, in *Patrologia Graeca*, Vol. 95 (Paris: Garnier Fratres, 1864), col. 161; quoted in Pelikan, *The Spirit of Eastern Christendom*, p. 75.

13. Eusebius, Letter 2, to Constantia, in *Patrologia Graeca*, Vol. 20 (Paris: Garnier Fratres, 1857), col. 1545; quoted in Runciman, *The Byzantine Theocracy*, p. 65.

14. John of Damascus, *First Oration on Images*, in *Patrologia Graeca*, Vol. 94 (Paris: Garnier Fratres, 1864), col. 1236; quoted in Meyendorff, *Byzantine Theology*, p. 45.

15. Theodore of Studios, *Refutation of the Impious Poems of the Iconoclasts*, in *Patrologia Graeca*, Vol. 99 (Paris: Garnier Fratres, 1903), cols. 444–445; quoted in Pelikan, *The Spirit of Eastern Christendom*, p. 128.

16. John of Damascus, *Second Oration on Images*, in *Patrologia Graeca*, Vol. 94, col. 1296; quoted in Philip Sherrard, *The Greek East and the Latin West* (London: Oxford University Press, 1959), p. 26.

17. Theodore of Studios, *Letters*, Book 1, Letter 36, in *Patrologia Graeca*, Vol. 99, col. 1032; quoted in Meyendorff, *Byzantine Theology*, p. 57.

18. Gregory of Nyssa, *The Life of Moses* 2.163, tr. by Abraham J. Malherbe and Everett Ferguson (Paulist Press, 1978), p. 94.

19. Dionysius the Areopagite, *On the Divine Names* 1.3, tr. by C. E. Rolt (Macmillan Co., 1920), p. 54.

20. Maximus the Confessor, *Mystagogia*, in *Patrologia Graeca*, Vol. 91 (Paris: Garnier Fratres, 1865), col. 664; quoted in Sherrard, *The Greek East and the Latin West*, p. 40.

21. Maximus the Confessor, *Scholia on the "On the Divine Names" of Dionysius the Areopagite* 7.1, in *Patrologia Graeca*, Vol. 4 (Paris: Garnier Fratres, 1889), col. 341; quoted in Pelikan, *The Spirit of Eastern Christendom*, p. 34.

22. Athanasius, *On the Incarnation of the Word* 54, in *Contra Gentes, and De Incarnatione*, tr. by Robert W. Thomson (Oxford: Clarendon Press, 1971), p. 269.

23. Maximus the Confessor, *Book of Ambiguities* 41, in *Patrologia Graeca*, Vol. 91, col. 1308; quoted in Lossky, *The Mystical Theology of the Eastern Church*, p. 214.

24. John of Damascus, *On the Two Wills in Christ*, in *Patrologia Graeca*, Vol. 95, col. 149.

25. Maximus the Confessor, *Questions to Thalassius on the Scripture* 22, in *Patrologia Graeca*, Vol. 90 (Paris: Garnier Fratres, 1865), col. 321; quoted in Pelikan, *The Spirit of Eastern Christendom*, p. 11.

26. Maximus the Confessor, *Book of Ambiguities* 41, in *Patrologia Graeca*, Vol. 91, col. 1308; quoted in ibid., p. 267.

27. Basil, Letter 234, to Amphilochius, in *Letters*, Vol. 2, p. 160.

28. Gregory Palamas, *Physical, Theological, Ethical and Practical Chapters;* quoted in Sherrard, *The Greek East and the Latin West*, pp. 37–38.

29. Symeon the New Theologian, *Catechesis* 22, in *Sources Chrétiennes*, Vol. 104, ed. by Basile Krivochéine (Paris: Les Editions du Cerf, 1964), p. 372.

30. Symeon the New Theologian, Homily 129.2; quoted in Lossky, *The Mystical Theology of the Eastern Church*, p. 218.

31. Ibid.

32. Gregory Palamas, *Prosopopoeiae*, in *Patrologia Graeca*, Vol. 150

(Paris: Garnier Fratres, 1865), col. 1361; quoted in Timothy Ware, *The Orthodox Church* (Harmondsworth, Middlesex: Penguin Books, 1964), p. 225.

33. Gregory Palamas, *Triads* 1.2.7; quoted in John Meyendorff, *A Study in Gregory Palamas* (London: Faith Press, 1962), p. 145.

34. Ibid., 1.3.42, p. 168.

35. Gregory of Nazianzus, *Oration on the Holy Lights* 12, tr. by Charles Gordon Browne and James Edward Swallow, in *A Select Library of the Nicene and Post-Nicene Fathers*, 2d Ser., Vol. 7 (Christian Literature Co., 1894), p. 356. I have modified the translation to fit the terminology I have been using.

36. Augustine, *On the Trinity* 15.17.27, tr. by Arthur West Haddan, in *A Select Library of the Nicene and Post-Nicene Fathers*, 1st Ser., ed. by Philip Schaff, Vol. 3 (Charles Scribner's Sons, 1900), p. 215.

37. Theodore of Studios, Letter 2.12, in *Patrologia Graeca*, Vol. 99, col. 1153; quoted in Pelikan, *The Spirit of Eastern Christendom*, p. 155.

38. Sylvester Syropoulos, *History* 4.33, in *Les "Mémoires" du Sylvestre Syropoulos*, ed. by V. Laurent (Paris: Editions du centre national de la recherche scientifique, 1971), pp. 232–234.

39. Quoted in G. P. Fedotov, *The Russian Religious Mind* (Harper & Row, Harper Torchbooks, 1960), Vol. 1, p. 372.

40. Ibid., p. 353.

41. Quoted in Baron Meyendorff and Norman H. Baynes, "The Byzantine Inheritance in Russia," in *Byzantium*, ed. by Norman H. Baynes and H. St. L. B. Moss (Oxford: Clarendon Press, 1948), p. 385.

42. Quoted in Fedotov, *The Russian Religious Mind*, Vol. 1, pp. 99, 101.

8

AUGUSTINE

AUGUSTINE: I desire to know God and the soul.
REASON: Nothing more?
AUGUSTINE: Absolutely nothing.[1]

More than anyone else, Augustine shaped Western theology and made it different from the traditions of the East. For the Western half of the church throughout the Middle Ages his authority stood second only to that of Scripture. Historians have with some justice described the Reformation as a struggle between two sides of Augustine: Protestantism began with his doctrine of grace, and the Roman Catholic response grew out of his doctrine of the church. Descartes began modern philosophy with a series of arguments paraphrased from Augustine, and much of Freud reads like an extended commentary on Augustine's *Confessions*. For better or worse, today's thinking about God, or human personalities, or history, or sex still owes him a great deal. Above all, while we read many early Christian thinkers merely out of historical interest, Augustine often speaks as our contemporary, a modern somehow out of place. For all these reasons, Augustine deserves a chapter to himself. Few theologians have so consciously related their thought to their lives, and, because of Augustine's influence, the pattern of his life became a model for Christians ever after. A chapter on Augustine, therefore, needs to begin with biography.

MONICA'S SON

He was born in 354 in Tagaste, in the Roman province of North Africa. His mother Monica was a devout Christian; his father Patricius remained a pagan throughout Augustine's childhood. But Augustine later wrote of his mother: "She earnestly endeavored, my

God, that you rather than he should be my father."[2] That remark correctly suggests some strange and powerful psychological tensions at work, and Augustine, looking back over his life in his *Confessions,* reported them with remarkable candor. He mentioned his father's death only in passing, and two years after it happened, but Monica never left his thoughts. At one point he secretly fled aboard ship all the way to Italy to try to escape her.

The tensions in Augustine's society equaled those in his family. He belonged to a Latin-speaking aristocracy spread thin over North Africa; the Berber peasants out in the countryside felt no loyalty to Rome. Augustine never quite fit in anywhere. He never learned the "native" language spoken by most North Africans, yet even at the end of his life the cultured Julian of Eclanum could dismiss him as "that African." In his youth the burden of taxation imposed by the military demands of the empire was already driving much of the middle class into bankruptcy. He died with a barbarian army surrounding his city, and within a few generations North Africa, the breadbasket that had fed the empire, was eroding into desert wasteland.

During Augustine's childhood, however, Roman order must have seemed eternal, and a young man could train himself with the expectation of a successful career. The education of future lawyers and officials concentrated on perfecting an elegant and ornate style of writing and speaking. In retrospect it would seem more than a little false. As boys, Augustine observed,

> what we liked to do was play, and for this we were punished by those who were themselves behaving in just the same way. But the amusements of older people are called "business," and when children indulge in their own amusements, these older people punish them for it. . . . I doubt whether any good judge of things would say that it was a good thing for me, as a boy, to be beaten for playing some ball game simply on the grounds that by playing this game I was impeded in my studies, the point of which was that I should be able to perform, when I grew older, in some game more unbecoming still.[3]

Still, he did well in school, mastering Latin style, though he never learned much Greek and most Greek theology always remained a closed book to him.

When he was sixteen, his father ran short of money, and Augustine had to stay out of school for a year. He fell in with a local teen-aged gang, and one night they stole some pears from a neighbor's tree. Augustine's critics often ridicule the exquisite sensitivity that can agonize for pages over this boyhood prank, but what horrified him was not the magnitude of what he had done—he committed his share of worse sins—but the realization that he had sought evil purely for its own sake. Most philosophers of his day agreed with Plato that everyone seeks the good. We do evil only out of ignorance, when we mistake a lesser good for a greater. In this case, a Platonist would say the good of satisfying hunger seemed greater than the good of respecting property. But he and his friends were not hungry, Augustine protested, and they had pears of their own anyway.

> Our real pleasure was simply in doing something that was not allowed. . . . The evil was foul, and I loved it; I loved destroying myself; I loved my sin—not the thing for which I had committed the sin, but the sin itself.[4]

Any adequate philosophy or theology must face up to the sad fact that sometimes we choose the evil precisely because doing evil attracts us.

When Augustine went back to school in Carthage, he soon found more exciting things to do than stealing pears.

> I came to Carthage, and all around me in my ears were the sizzling and frying of unholy loves. I was not yet in love, but I loved the idea of love, and from a hidden want I hated myself for not wanting more. . . . It was a sweet thing to me both to love and to be loved, and more sweet still when I was able to enjoy the body of my lover.[5]

Since a socially ambitious young man did not want to marry too soon and burden his career with a lower-class wife, Augustine took a mistress, and they soon had an illegitimate son.

Of course his mother had raised him a Christian, though like many of his contemporaries who saved the cleansing power of baptism until the approach of death when it could do the most good, he had not been baptized. Gradually, he abandoned his mother's faith. At seventeen he read Cicero's *Hortensius,* an exhortation to the study of philosophy, and it inspired him with a longing to devote his life to the search for truth, but at first that scarcely led him toward Christianity. Partly because of Tertullian's influence, the North African church emphasized accepting authority rather than using reason in religious matters, and the available translations of the Bible were in an inelegant Latin. Christianity did not seem the religion for a young intellectual.

For a time Manicheanism attracted him. Mani, who lived in Baby-

lon and Persia in the 200s, had founded a religion that spread from
Europe to China and for several centuries rivaled Christianity. It
combined elements from many different traditions: from Christianity
a belief in Christ as savior, from Buddhism an order of ascetic monks,
and above all, from traditional Persian religion a dualism of good and
evil. Like many Gnostics, the Manicheans believed that this world,
with all its evils, could not have been entirely created by a good God.
There must be two deities, an evil one who created the material
world, and a good one who created spirits. Every human being struggles between these forces of darkness and light. Because they believed that the stars determine our destinies, the Manicheans studied
a good bit of astronomy, and Augustine found their scientific interests, and their general appeal to reason, more appealing than his own
Christian background.

> They said we were terrified by superstition, and that faith was
> demanded of us before reason, while they, on the other hand,
> were forcing faith on no one without first hunting for and disen-
> tangling the truth. Who would not be enticed by these promises?
> And would there not be special enticement for a youthful mind
> desirous of truth, and yet haughty and talkative in disputations?[6]

He never joined the inner elite of vegetarian monks, but for nine years
he belonged to the outer circle of "hearers."
    Then the commitment to reason which had led him to the Mani-
cheans began to lead him away. He discovered some contradictions
in their astronomical theories. This puzzled the local Manicheans, but
they assured Augustine that the famous bishop Faustus would answer all his questions. Then Faustus at last came to town and proved
to be a man far less educated than Augustine himself. Augustine
began to face even harder problems. Manichean astrology assumed
that the stars control our actions, but do we really lack free will in
the way that that would imply? If an astrologer's slave did something
wrong and blamed it on the course of the stars, Augustine reflected,
his master would reply, "You idiot, do you think that's good enough
for the boss just because it's good enough for the customers?"[7]
    When they were not blaming the stars, Manicheans blamed their
bodies. Our souls are pure and good, they said; it's just that they are
entrapped in evil bodies. Looking back on this period of his life,
Augustine saw that "it gratified my pride to think that I was blame-
less. . . . I liked to excuse myself and accuse something else—something that was in me, but was not really I. But in fact I was wholly
I."[8] He himself, not his stars or even just his body, had wanted to steal

those pears or make love to his mistress. Manicheanism came to look increasingly like a series of inadequate excuses.

Then Augustine discovered Platonism, and it changed his life. It offered this passionate intellectual a vision of eternal truth and a call to turn away from sensual pleasures and purify his soul. Years later, as a Christian bishop, he remarked that with the change of only a few words the Platonists would all become Christians, and all his life he retained the Platonist conviction that we find the truth by turning away from the senses and the physical world to look inward. Yet he also described the Platonists as being like people who see a great city on the opposite shore but lack any means of crossing the water. At this point in his life, he ruefully admitted, his prayer had been, "Make me chaste and continent—but not yet."[9] Platonism provided the vision of a pure life devoted to truth, but it did not give him the moral strength to live that life.

Increasingly successful in his career as a teacher of rhetoric, he went to Milan, the imperial capital, where he heard the sermons of Ambrose, the local bishop, who preached an intellectually sophisticated Christianity he had never encountered before. His friends told him inspiring stories of Christian monks who had given up everything to go off to the desert in search of God. He knew what he ought to do, what he wanted to do, but he couldn't do it. Then one afternoon near the end of August 386, he was in a garden in Milan, with a Bible lying nearby.

> Suddenly a voice reaches my ears from a nearby house . . . and in a kind of singsong the words are constantly repeated: "Take it and read it. Take it and read it." At once . . . I . . . rose to my feet, being quite certain that I must interpret this as a divine command to me to open the book and read the first passage which I should come upon. . . . I snatched up the book, opened it and read in silence the passage upon which my eyes first fell: not in rioting and drunkenness, not in chambering and wantonness, not in strife and envying, but put on the Lord Jesus Christ, and make not provision for the flesh in concupiscence. I had no wish to read further; there was no need to. For immediately I had reached the end of this sentence it was as though my heart was filled with a light of confidence and all the shadows of my doubt were swept away.[10]

He received baptism and withdrew with his mother, his son, and some friends to a life of prayer and study, but conversion did not bring him peace. For many Christians, such a dramatic conversion would have been the end of the story, except for living happily ever after, but Augustine insisted that doubts and temptations never magically go away. They haunted him all his life. When he returned to Africa, he feared that some town would choose him as its bishop, a post for which he felt totally unworthy. He even refused to enter cities where the bishop had recently died, for fear of being drafted, but eventually the bishop of Hippo enlisted him as his assistant and then successor, and he found himself in the midst of every theological dispute in an unusually disputatious province.

AGAINST THE DONATISTS

Any North African bishop in the late fourth century faced the problem of Donatism. During the last great persecution, the Romans had demanded that Christians hand over copies of the Bible to be destroyed. Some Christians, even some priests and bishops, had done so to save their lives. After the persecution ended, people began to ask whether these "traitors" (*traditores,* "those who handed over") could validly administer the sacraments. That raised two larger issues. First, as indicated at the end of Chapter 5, above, Christians had long debated the place of sinners in the church. Should the Christian community expel them in order to maintain its purity or keep them in order to offer guidance and help? Second, Christians increasingly thought of their priests as a special class, set apart by their power to administer the sacraments. Did that mean that priests should be judged by different standards? Since the days of Tertullian, North African Christians had generally believed in rigorous criteria for church membership. Combined with the growing sense of priests as people set apart, that left many skeptical that a *traditor* could really be a priest. When it turned out that one of the bishops who had ordained the bishop of Carthage in 312 had been a *traditor,* a rigorist party declared the ordination invalid and proclaimed a man named Donatus bishop instead. By Augustine's time, two generations later, most cities in North Africa had two competing bishops, with a majority of the people probably loyal to the "Donatists." Donatism apparently drew most of its support from the Berber peasantry, while its opponents came primarily from the Latin-speaking upper classes. Guerrilla war ensued, and the rhetoric of both sides resembled the propaganda of such conflicts throughout history: the Donatists protested against persecution, and their opponents denounced them as terrorists.

Both sides appealed to the legacy of Cyprian, the famous bishop of Carthage back in the mid-200s. He had borrowed and developed much of Tertullian's thought, toning down its rhetoric, and applied his considerable gifts as an administrator to strengthening the church as an institution. His martyrdom in 258 had sealed his reputation as the great hero of North African Christianity.

On the one hand, Cyprian had warned against the dangers of corrupt priests. "All are, indeed, involved in sin," he had written, "who have been contaminated by the sacrifice of a blasphemous and unjust priest."[11] That seemed to support Donatist rigorism. On the other hand, he had always insisted on the importance of preserving the unity of the church: "Nor can he who forsakes the church of Christ attain the rewards of Christ. He is a stranger; he is profane; he is an enemy. He can no longer have God for his Father who has not the church for his mother."[12] Since North African Christians had come to be divided, Augustine argued, either the Donatists or their opponents must be guilty of forsaking the church. But the true church must be universal, spread throughout the world, while the Donatists existed only in North Africa and were not in communion with Christians elsewhere. Therefore they must be the guilty party, subject to Cyprian's condemnation.

The most effective argument against Donatism, however, involved a more practical concern. If the Donatists were right, and a priest's sin renders the sacraments he performs invalid, then, if a priest (or the bishop who ordained him, or the bishop who had ordained that bishop) was secretly an unrepentant sinner, then those he had ministered to were not really married, did not receive Communion, were not truly baptized, and so on. Most leaders of the church agreed with Augustine that we cannot ask people to have so much depend on the unknowable moral purity of the priesthood. In securing the condemnation of the Donatists, Augustine made it clear that a priest's authority rests on his proper ordination, not his personal virtue. That made Christian authority purely hierarchical, dependent only on one's place in an institutional structure, but it gave people priests whose legitimacy they could trust.

Augustine at first expected to persuade the Donatists by his arguments. When their opposition continued, some of his allies urged that the Roman authorities be asked to force them to conform, but Augustine initially opposed the idea. He thought the use of force in religious matters produces at best hypocritical conformity and at worst more bitter rebellion. Then he changed his mind and urged the emperor to confiscate Donatist property and assess fines until they returned to the fold. Apparently bands of Donatists were roaming the countryside and intimidating their opponents, and Augustine felt justified in calling on the government to maintain public order. Further, a few former Donatists evidently thanked him for having pressured them out of their errors, and he concluded that properly applied sanctions might not be such a bad idea after all.[13] His decision has often been cited as the beginning of a thousand years of all the horrors of the Inquisition, and that goes too far, but calling in the army to enforce a theological decision did set a precedent that would haunt Christendom.

AGAINST THE PELAGIANS

About the time Augustine was winning his victory over the Donatists, a British monk named Pelagius was reading Augustine's *Confessions* with mounting dismay. Like many a provincial just arrived in the big city, Pelagius had been horrified by the low moral standards of Christians in Rome. Even worse, they scarcely seemed to care about their faults. He feared that Augustine justified all this spiritual laziness by telling how he had been unable to reform his life, radically unable to do anything about his sin, until God seized him in the midst of his sins. God holds us responsible for our sins, Pelagius argued, and that would scarcely be fair unless we have the power to stop sinning. Of course we need God's help, but we should get to work at once trying to be better. God helps those who help themselves. Not so, Augustine protested. God helps those who *cannot* help themselves.[14] Perhaps morality came easily to Pelagius, but Augustine had himself experienced being so trapped in sin that one lacks even the will to try to escape. "For after the will itself freely sins, we are thrown into necessity, into which we descend from that starting point."[15] An addict may freely choose to take his drug, but it does not follow that he has the power to stop. All sin is like that, Augustine insisted. It begins in choice and ends in slavery. Besides—if we could save ourselves, why did Christ have to suffer and die for us?

Out of such reflections, Augustine forged his doctrine of predestination. Through grace, God saves some people in spite of their inability to help themselves. Nothing they have done merited that salvation. Yet Scripture insists that God's grace does not extend to all. There are goats as well as sheep; some are consigned to eternal fire. God must therefore simply decide to save some and leave others, no worse in their characters, to the consequences of their sins.

Is that unfair? Augustine argued that everyone sins, everyone deserves punishment. God gives some better than they deserve, but no one gets less. The whole theory may make God seem arbitrary, but at least it keeps people from being proud. No one can claim to have earned salvation; it is an undeserved gift for which one can only be grateful.

The justice of God's predestination depends on the claim that everyone is a sinner deserving punishment. But, whether he turned to Scripture or to simple observation, Augustine thought that point easy to prove. Even in infancy we are selfish, proud, unloving. "I myself," Augustine remarked, "have seen and known a baby who was envious; it could not yet speak, but it turned pale and looked bitterly at another baby sharing its milk."[16] A baby's moral values in an adult would produce a monster. Why do human beings come into the world so corrupt? Augustine explained it as the inheritance of original sin. When Adam pridefully turned away from God, he brought us all into sin. On this point, Augustine could appeal to the general practice of infant baptism for support. Everyone agreed that adult baptism washed away sins. Why baptize infants unless they carry a burden of sin too? Since they have not had time to accumulate sins of their own, they must have inherited them. Picking up an idea from Cyprian, he went on to ask why Christ had been born of a virgin. Somehow the usual sexual means of conception must pass on sin, so that Christ, in order to be free of sin, had to be born in a different way. The first sin created lust, for Adam and Eve at once felt the need to cover their nakedness. The corruption of their souls infected their bodies, and the process of human conception passes that infection down to all their descendants.

For Augustine, then, human sexuality has been steeped in sin ever since Adam. Yet it is worth noting that he insisted that Adam and Eve had once known sex free from sin; sexuality is God's creation and not evil in itself.[17] Moreover, he knew that it is not "as if the only sins you could commit were those in which you use your genitals."[18] In a sinful state, sex is tainted by lust, but hunger is likewise corrupted by gluttony, accomplishment by pride, and relaxation by sloth. The real problem is that our reason ought to control our will, which should in turn regulate our desires, but in sin everything is reversed. Desires direct the will, and a corrupted reason tries to rationalize the results. Admittedly lust was Augustine's favorite example of this sad process, partly because it had been the cause of his own greatest struggles. But beyond that, he considered it the most vivid example of desire's mastery of reason. A persuasive argument can stop even a glutton in the middle of a meal, but a pause for discussion at the height of desire is the stuff of farce.

Near the end of Augustine's life, his views on predestination and original sin faced bitter attack from Julian, the young, elegant bishop of Eclanum, whose parents had been Augustine's friends. Julian minced no words in denouncing a picture of God as holding infants guilty of inherited sin.

"Tiny babies," you say, "are not weighed down by their own sin, but they are burdened with the sin of another." Tell me then, tell me, who is this person who inflicts punishment on innocent creatures? . . . You answer God. God, you say. . . . You have come so far from religious feeling, from civilized thinking, so far, indeed, from mere common sense, in that you think that the Lord God is capable of committing a crime against justice such as is hardly conceivable among barbarians.[19]

Augustine never knew quite how to answer. He had written desperately to the great Bible translator Jerome a long catalog of the sufferings of children, crying out at the end:

God is good, God is just, God is almighty: only a madman doubts this. . . . Doubtless when their elders suffer these afflictions we are wont to say either that their goodness is being tested . . . or that their sins are being punished. . . . But these are older people. Tell me what we are to answer about children.[20]

Jerome didn't know what to respond, and Augustine never found an answer. He stuck to what he did know. The world is not the simple place Julian would like it to be. Even if you do not believe in original sin, infants still suffer the agonies of disease and starvation; the goodness of God is not easily understood. Augustine knew that his own salvation owed nothing to his own efforts. God had rescued him when he had found himself unable to make the right efforts. Not everyone is so lucky. God must predestine some to salvation, regardless of their lack of merit, and they receive his grace. He abandons the others to their sins. More than that we cannot know. The Julians of this world would like to think that of course God will choose the decent folk like us, but we too are sunk in our sins, and God may not see things the way we do.

This choice of God is certainly hidden from us. . . . Even if it should be perceptible to some men, I must admit that, in this matter, I am incapable of knowing. I just cannot find what criterion to apply in deciding which men should be chosen to be saved by grace. If I were to reflect on how to weigh up this choice, I myself would instinctively choose those with better intelligence or less sins, or both; I should add, I suppose, a sound and proper education. . . . And as soon as I decide on that, He will laugh me to scorn.[21]

AGAINST THE PAGANS

In 410 Alaric and his army of Visigoths conquered and pillaged the city of Rome. Refugees fled to North Africa, and many of the non-Christians among them argued that Rome had fallen to defeat because it had abandoned its ancestral deities for Christianity. In a massive book, *The City of God,* Augustine replied with an alternative interpretation of history. Since the beginning of time, he said, humanity has been divided into two cities: the city of man, whose history is traced in the rise and fall of empires, fame, wealth, and human accomplishments, and the city of God, the company of those who love and serve God. It is the character of their love that divides people into these two cities:

> These two loves of which the one is holy, the other impure; the one sociable, the other self-centered; the one concerned for the common good for the sake of the heavenly society, the other subordinating the common good to self-interest for the sake of a proud lust for power . . . have brought about the distinction among mankind of the two cities.[22]

It is not, Augustine emphasized, that it is wrong to love the things of this world. "I do not blame you; I do not criticize you, even if this life is what you love."[23] The point is how to order your loves. "What God has made for you is good; but some goods are great, others small; there are worldly goods, spiritual goods, temporal goods, yet all are good, because the good God made them good. Therefore it is said in Scripture: Order me in love."[24] Those who belong to the city of God love all the things of this world, but they love God first.

It is fascinating, in *The City of God,* to watch Augustine struggle with his ambivalence toward Rome. He admired its history of courage and sacrifice; he acknowledged its great accomplishments; he knew how much he himself owed to its intellectual traditions. Yet he could not forget just how much blood had been shed to achieve that greatness.

> Is it reasonable and wise to glory in the extent and greatness of the empire when you can in no way prove that there is any real happiness in men perpetually living amid the horrors of war, perpetually wading in blood? Does it matter whether it is the

blood of their fellow citizens or the blood of their enemies? It is still human blood, in men perpetually haunted by the bloody spectre of fear and driven by murderous passions. The happiness arising from such conditions is a thing of glass, of mere glittering brittleness. One can never shake off the horrible dread that it may suddenly shiver into fragments.[25]

The Romans in their pride had sought power and wealth and fame. Well, they ruled the world, the wealth of empire poured in, the greatest poets sang their praises. "They have no right to complain of the justice of the true and supreme God. They have received their reward."[26] If they wanted an eternal reward, they should have turned from the things of this world to seek it.

So much for the city of man. Augustine refused to trace the history of the city of God to his own time. It is the secret history of the world, known only to God. God reveals a part of this history in the Bible, but without the divine guidance of Scripture, no human being should try to trace just where God is at work in history. Many of Augustine's contemporaries followed Eusebius in seeing the Christian empire as the work of God's providence. A few tried to identify the signs of Christ's imminent second coming. Both styles of interpretation survive among Christians today: there are those who see Christ at work in the victories of "Christian nations," and those who match up current events with passages in the book of Revelation. Augustine would have none of it. Biblical revelation shows us how God once worked in history—through suffering, and in spite of the failings of the sinful people who serve him—and faith tells us that God continues to work that way in our time, but how and where and through whom is not for us to know.

In this as in much else those who like neat systems will always find Augustine frustrating. Against the Manicheans, he insisted on human freedom in the face of claims that the stars direct our actions. Against the Pelagians, he said that human freedom has been entrapped in sin ever since Adam. Against the Donatists, he defended the institutional church no matter what its moral imperfections as the vehicle of God's grace through the sacraments, but in The City of God he said that no one can know for certain where God is at work in our time, and his doctrine of predestination leaves our destiny totally dependent on God's mysterious will, without regard for human efforts or human institutions. If charged with inconsistency, he would have replied that this is how God had worked in his life. The church and the sacraments helped him, but God converted him when he had turned away from them. He spent his life struggling, but God saved him when all his struggles had failed. "Give me a lover, and he will feel what I say. Give me one that longs, one that hungers, give me one that is on pilgrimage in this wilderness . . . give me such a one, and he will understand what I mean."[27]

FOR FURTHER READING

INTRODUCTIONS. Peter Brown, *Augustine of Hippo* (University of California Press, 1967), is more difficult than most introductory books so far listed, but it is an absolutely superb intellectual biography. On a simpler level, see Warren Thomas Smith, *Augustine* (John Knox Press, 1980).

COLLECTIONS OF ORIGINAL SOURCES. The best place to begin is with Augustine's *Confessions,* tr. by Rex Warner (New American Library, Mentor-Omega Books, 1963). Augustine wrote an amazing number of books; some good collections of more important excerpts are: Whitney J. Oates (ed.), *Basic Writings of Saint Augustine,* 2 vols. (Baker Book House, 1981); John H. S. Burleigh (ed.), *Augustine: Earlier Writings* (Westminster Press, 1953); and John Burnaby (ed.), *Augustine: Later Works* (Westminster Press, 1955). J. Patout Burns (ed.), *Theological Anthropology* (Fortress Press, 1981), provides documents from both sides of the Pelagian controversy and some other texts that set the whole debate in its historical context.

IMPORTANT BUT MORE DIFFICULT. Roy W. Battenhouse (ed.), *A Companion to the Study of St. Augustine* (Oxford University Press, 1955); Gerald Bonner, *St. Augustine of Hippo* (Westminster Press, 1963); John Burnaby, *Amor Dei* (London: Hodder & Stoughton, 1938); Etienne Gilson, *The Christian Philosophy of St. Augustine* (Random House, 1960); R. A. Markus, *Saeculum: History and Society in the Theology of St. Augustine* (Cambridge: Cambridge University Press, 1970).

NOTES

1. Augustine, *Soliloquies* 1.2.7, in *The Soliloquies of Saint Augustine,* tr. by Thomas F. Gilligan (Cosmopolitan Science & Art Service Co., 1944), p. 17.
2. Augustine, *Confessions* 1.11, tr. by Rex Warner (New American Library, Mentor-Omega Books, 1963), p. 29.
3. Ibid., 1.9, p. 27.

4. Ibid., 2.4, p. 45.

5. Ibid., 3.1, p. 52.

6. Augustine, *The Advantage of Believing* 1.2, tr. by Luanne Meagher, in *The Writings of Saint Augustine*, Vol. 2 (CIMA Publishing, 1947), p. 392.

7. Augustine, *Exposition of the Psalms* 140.9, in *Patrologia Latina*, ed. by J.-P. Migne, Vol. 37 (Paris: Garnier Fratres, 1885), col. 1821.

8. Augustine, *Confessions* 5.10, op. cit., p. 104.

9. Ibid., 8.7, p. 174.

10. Ibid., 8.12, pp. 182–183.

11. Cyprian, Letter 67, Cyprian and the bishops at the Council of Carthage to Felix, Aelius, and their people, in *Letters (1–81)*, tr. by Rose Bernard Donna (Catholic University of America Press, 1964), p. 233.

12. Cyprian, *On the Unity of the Church* 6, tr. by Ernest Wallis, in *The Ante-Nicene Fathers*, ed. by Alexander Robertson and James Donaldson, Vol. 5 (Wm. B. Eerdmans Publishing Co., 1957), p. 423.

13. Augustine, *The Retractions* 2.31, tr. by Mary Inez Bogan (Catholic University of America Press, 1968), p. 129.

14. Ibid., 1.12.4 (numbered 1.13.4 in *Patrologia Latina*), pp. 52–53.

15. Augustine, *Against Fortunatus the Manichean* 1.22, in *Patrologia Latina*, Vol. 42 (Paris: Garnier Fratres, 1886), col. 124.

16. Augustine, *Confessions* 1.7, op. cit., p. 24.

17. Augustine, *Against Julian* 4.8.49, tr. by Matthew A. Schumacher (Fathers of the Church, 1957), p. 210.

18. Augustine, *Exposition of Genesis According to the Letter* 10.13.23, in *Patrologia Latina*, Vol. 34 (Paris: Garnier Fratres, 1887), col. 417.

19. Augustine, *Unfinished Work Against Julian;* quoted in Peter Brown, *Augustine of Hippo* (University of California Press, 1967), pp. 391–392.

20. Augustine, Letter 166.16, to Jerome, in *Letters*, Vol. 4, tr. by Wilfred Parsons (Fathers of the Church, 1955), p. 21.

21. Augustine, *On Diverse Questions to Simplicianus* 1.22, in *Patrologia Latina*, Vol. 40 (Paris: Garnier Fratres, 1887), col. 127; quoted in Brown, *Augustine of Hippo*, p. 156.

22. Augustine, *Exposition of Genesis According to the Letter* 11.15.20, in *Patrologia Latina*, Vol. 34, col. 437.

23. Augustine, Sermon 297.4, in *Patrologia Latina*, Vol. 38 (Paris: Garnier Fratres, 1865), col. 1360.

24. Augustine, Sermon 21.3, Ibid., col. 114.

25. Augustine, *The City of God* 4.3, tr. by Gerald G. Walsh et al. (Doubleday & Co., Image Books, 1958), p. 87.

26. Ibid., 5.15, p. 112.

27. Augustine, *Homilies on the Gospel of John* 26.4 (various translators), in *Library of the Fathers* (Oxford: John Henry Parker, 1848), pp. 402–403. Translation altered.

9

THE PATH TO SALVATION

When we compare the present life of man on earth with
that time of which we have no knowledge, it seems to me
like the swift flight of a single sparrow through the banquet-
ing-hall . . . on a winter's day. . . . In the midst there is a
comforting fire to warm the hall; outside the storms of winter rain or snow are raging. This sparrow flies swiftly in
through one door of the hall and out through another.
. . . Even so, man appears on earth for a little while; but of
what went before this life or of what follows, we know
nothing. Therefore, if this new teaching has brought any
more certain knowledge, it seems only right that we should
follow it.

> —Advice given by a counselor of King Edwin of
> Northumbria when the first Christian mission-
> aries visited in the early seventh century[1]

Though *The City of God* pointed beyond Rome to an eternal kingdom,
Augustine had lived and written as a Roman, the product of a culture
that had endured a thousand years. Within a hundred years of his
death, the empire no longer survived in the West, and trade, law, and
every aspect of civilization underwent profound changes. Christianity too had to change. Many of the empire's invaders knew nothing
of Christianity; some had been converted initially by Arians. Teaching them would not be easy, for the literacy rate declined rapidly, and
economic changes forced people out of the large cities and back to
farms. Rural society could not support elaborate churches or communities of intellectual discussion. Christians needed to refine their
faith into a clear, simple message. In its first centuries Christianity
had had to prove its intellectual respectability to a sophisticated
Roman world; now sophisticated theology had to find new ways to
communicate with less educated people in a society where different

theological issues had become important.

In the absence of large cities or royal courts, monasteries provided the largest and most stable communities, and the leadership of Christianity fell increasingly to monks and nuns. Theologians naturally explored issues related to monasticism, particularly the value of asceticism and celibacy, and the relation between monastic calls to heroic moral efforts and Augustine's denial that human works could contribute to salvation. The sacraments and the cults of Mary and the saints proved the most vivid ways of making faith vivid and comprehensible to ordinary people, and they generated another set of theological questions. In a period of changes in political structures, the church also needed to clarify its authority in relation to that of the state.

Those three general issues—the rise of monasticism, the theology of sacraments and saints, and the relations between church and state —will be the themes of this chapter. The centuries from A.D. 400 to A.D. 1000, which will be surveyed here, can seem a remote time most unlike today, but that judgment to some extent reflects the particular perspective of Europeans and North Americans. Twentieth-century Christianity is growing fastest in Africa and Latin America, and there it struggles to fit Christian faith into a tribal society and to define the relations of church and state in an often brutal context. Those were also the issues that concerned early Medieval Christians.

MONASTICISM

In 271 a wealthy young Egyptian named Antony heard a sermon on the text, "If you would be perfect, go, sell what you possess and give to the poor, and you will have treasure in heaven." He heard and obeyed, living the rest of his life in prayer and fasting in the desert. As a very old man, he came to know Athanasius, the theological defender of the *homoousios* doctrine, who wrote a *Life of Antony* which inspired men and women throughout the Christian world to follow Antony's example. Of course some people had always moved away from human society in hopes of drawing nearer to God. Elijah and John the Baptist had gone to the desert; Jesus himself, the Gospels report, spent forty days in the wilderness. But the third and fourth centuries saw a real burst of flight into the solitary life of self-denial. Why?

For one thing, earlier Christians had faced persecution and ridicule wherever they lived; they remained outsiders even in the midst of society. After Constantine, as Christianity became socially respectable, those who sought a heroic life had to find new ways of testing themselves. In addition, many of the philosophies and popular religions of late antiquity preached the need to turn away from the physical world and subdue the body in order to purify the soul. At the same time, punitive taxation, economic collapse, and social chaos made the escape from ordinary life unusually tempting. One legend of the time tells how

> Abba Olympios of the Cells was tempted to fornication. His thoughts said to him, "Go, and take a wife." He got up, found some mud, made a woman and said to himself, "There is your wife, now you must work hard in order to feed her." So he worked giving himself a great deal of trouble. The next day, making some mud again, he formed it into a girl and said to his thoughts, "Your wife has had a child, you must work harder so as to be able to feed her and clothe your child." So he wore himself out doing this, and said to his thoughts, "I cannot bear this weariness any longer." They answered, "If you cannot bear such weariness, stop wanting a wife." God, seeing his efforts, took away the conflict from him and he was at peace.[2]

The desert could offer escape as well as a place of testing.

From the start the ascetic life attracted both women and men. The monks and nuns practiced all sorts of austerities—going without food or sleep for weeks, living in filth or among insects and vermin, dwelling for decades on the tops of columns—but celibacy usually served as the central symbol of bodily self-denial. It was an ideal that the culture of the time took for granted. Indeed, it came as a surprise when, in the 390s, a Roman Christian named Jovinian wrote a pamphlet arguing that unmarried Christians are not superior to those who marry, nor are those who fast better than those who eat and drink while giving thanks to God, for on the day of judgment all faithful Christians will enjoy an equal degree of blessedness.[3] Jerome, the author of the great Vulgate translation of the Bible into Latin, replied that Adam and Eve had married only after their sin, while Joshua, Elijah, and John the Baptist hadn't married at all. True, Peter had married, but that was before he met Jesus, and anyway Jesus loved John, who had not married, more than Peter. Even the pagans admired chastity. Besides, marriage is disagreeable, and wives plague and deceive their husbands.[4] Jerome made an even more forceful case in support of female chastity. Reading all this today, it is tempting to write it off as the expression of Jerome's own pathology, but he expressed values and beliefs widespread at the time. Already in 306 the Council of Elvira had declared that bishops, priests, and deacons must remain unmarried. Christian theologians did not have to go around urging people to deny the desires of their bodies. If anything, they spent more time trying to modify the excesses of asceticism and reminding people that Christianity did affirm the goodness of the physical world as a part of God's creation.

Soon the wilderness in Egypt and Syria bloomed with a very odd crop of vegetation. Some early monks and nuns lived alone, but they gradually formed communities that needed rules. In the early 300s Pachomius organized a male community in Egypt, while his sister Mary presided over a group of women, and they set out a pattern of discipline and daily life followed by many other communities. Basil's rule for his monastery in Asia Minor also had considerable influence. Monasticism spread throughout the East and also to Gaul and thence to Ireland, where for several centuries the Irish monks preserved the highest intellectual standards in Western Europe. Simply because monks provided stable communities in a chaotic world and were willing to go anywhere, they soon took over much of the intellectual and missionary leadership of the church.

The most important figure in monasticism in the West was Benedict of Nursia, who was born about 470. He fled his wealthy Italian family to live a solitary life in the wilderness, but other monks soon gathered around him, and he wrote a rule for their common life. Benedict provides a good example of the unpredictability of historical influence. His rule borrowed heavily from earlier sources and rarely achieved eloquence. Benedict himself probably never supervised more than a few dozen monks and had little impact on his contemporaries. Yet by the time of Charlemagne around 800 nearly all the monasteries in the West followed Benedict's rule, and it has probably guided the details of more human lives than any other document. Its greatest virtue is its common sense. In setting out a daily round of prayer, work, and study, Benedict always sought moderation. He explained at the outset:

> We are about to open a school for God's service, in which we hope nothing harsh or oppressive will be directed. For preserving charity or correcting faults, it may be necessary at times, by reason of justice, to be slightly more severe. Do not fear this and retreat, for the path to salvation is long and the entrance is narrow.[5]

He could be severe, as in forbidding private property: "No one, without the abbot's permission, shall dare give, receive or keep *anything* —not book, tablet, or pen—nothing at all. Monks have neither free will nor free body, but must receive all they need from the abbot."[6] Yet he could also gently advise, "When they arise for the Divine Office, they ought to encourage each other, for the sleepy make many excuses,"[7] and he carefully limited the excesses of asceticism. There is symbolism in the fact that Benedict's monastery was founded in 529, the year in which the emperor Justinian closed the last philosophical school in Athens and was in the midst of his great codification of Roman law. Monasteries would be the schools of Europe, setting out the laws of salvation, for centuries to come.

The monastic ideal urged people to strive heroically for salvation. That raised some awkward questions about Augustine's insistence that human efforts cannot contribute to our salvation, which comes only through God's predestined grace. John Cassian, who did much to bring monasticism to the West in the early 400s, argued that both God's grace *and* human efforts play an important role in salvation. He and other critics of Augustine focused on two points. First, Augustine said that no one can do good apart from grace, but non-Christians obviously do perform good deeds. Second, the theory of predestination seemed to imply that Christ died only for those predestined to salvation, but in fact Christ died for all. "How can we imagine without grievous blasphemy," John Cassian demanded, "that He does not generally will *all* men, but only *some* instead of *all* to be saved?"[8] Of course grace is necessary for salvation, Augustine's critics acknowledged, but people can begin to move toward salvation without it, and God offers it to everyone, though some turn it down.

Augustine's defenders, like Caesarius, the bishop of Arles in southern France, replied that this makes God look ineffectual. Does John Cassian mean that God wants to save everybody, but can't quite manage it? No one can resist grace if it is offered, Caesarius insisted; God therefore must not offer it to everyone. And without grace, human beings cannot truly do good. As the Synod of Orange, with Caesarius presiding, declared in 529, "The grace of God is not granted in response to prayer, but itself causes prayer to be offered for it"; and, "Undeserved grace precedes meritorious works."[9] That looked like a victory for the Augustinian theory that grace must come first, but the bishops gathered at Orange never mentioned predestination. They proclaimed Augustine as their hero, but practical people out to raise the moral tone of a half-Christian continent could scarcely bring themselves to dismiss the value of human efforts toward salvation altogether.

That meant trouble for anyone who tried to defend Augustine on every point, as a Saxon monk living in France named Gottschalk found out in the early 800s. Gottschalk had been packed off to a monastery as a child, and he hated it. He wrote profoundly moving lyric poetry on religious themes, but nonetheless sought continually for permission to abandon the life of a monk. Then he read Augustine and began to push the theory of predestination to its limits. He agreed with Caesarius that human beings can do no good apart from grace. "None of us," he said, "is able to use free will to do good, but only to do evil."[10] We do good only when God takes control of our wills. God has predestined some to salvation, others to damnation. Christ died only for some, and there is nothing the others can do about it.

Gottschalk's opponents, led by Hincmar of Reims, managed to have him condemned at the Council of Quiercy in 853. The council declared that Christ died for all, and, while God has predestined punishment for those who reject grace, he has not predestined those who will receive that punishment. They sent Gottschalk off to prison. From time to time, someone would bring him out to see if he had changed his mind. He always asked for some Augustine to read and then produced a statement of faith as uncompromising as ever—and back to prison he went. "And so," Hincmar grimly observed, "he concluded an unworthy life with a death that was worthy of it, and he departed into his own place."[11]

Gottschalk's opponents at one point turned to John Scotus Eriugena, an Irish monk who had achieved a better knowledge of Greek than anyone had acquired in the West for several centuries. Working in virtual isolation, he had developed a complex and original theology based in part on Platonic philosophy. They wanted Scotus Eriugena to write a decisive refutation of Gottschalk, but they received a cure that struck them as worse than the disease. God suffuses all the world, Eriugena said; "all things are in him, since he himself is all things."[12] Like Augustine, he identified evil with nonexistence. Everything that God creates is good, and therefore evil must be, not an existing thing, but a negation or limitation of something that does exist.

Gottschalk had said that God predestines some people to damnation. Hincmar protested that God would never do that. He said that God predestines the elect to salvation, but does not predestine the condemned. Gottschalk thought this was simply silly: predestining one group inevitably implied the predestining of the other. Scotus Eriugena agreed with Hincmar, but for a reason distinctly his own: since sin and evil do not "exist," they cannot be predestined by God. On another issue, Gottschalk argued that people could do good only with grace. Hincmar replied that non-Christians obviously do good deeds. Scotus Eriugena agreed with both, for *everyone*, including non-Christians, receives some grace. "There is truly no rational nature that is utterly lacking in any gift of grace."[13]

The underlying issue concerned what "grace" means. Gottschalk thought of grace as God's original and utterly mysterious predestinating choice. Scotus Eriugena thought of grace as the overflowing power of God's love, which suffuses all that exists. Most people, like Hincmar, wanted something more tangible. Neither Eriugena's metaphysical subtleties nor Gottschalk's uncompromising doctrine of predestination presented grace in a way that seemed to touch their lives on a practical level. Increasingly, they thought of grace most often as something to be obtained through the sacraments.

SACRAMENTS AND SAINTS

In the early Middle Ages the definition of "sacrament" remained vague. Christians believed that some actions symbolize and convey God's grace in a special way, but they might use the word "sacrament" of anything from baptism to saying the Lord's prayer to Israel's crossing of the Jordan River. The current Roman Catholic doctrine that there are seven sacraments did not become official until the Council of Florence in 1438.

Long before that, everyone agreed that the Eucharist was a sacrament, but even here they could not agree on how to describe what happened in it. A council of the Eastern church at Nicaea in 787 affirmed the real presence of Christ's body and blood in the bread and wine, but, although Western bishops had been present, this view was not at first clearly accepted in the West.[14] In 831, however, a French theologian named Paschasius Radbertus firmly declared that in the Eucharist the bread and wine cease to be bread and wine and become the body and blood of Christ, the same body that was born of Mary and died on the cross.

Western hesitation to agree with Radbertus owed something to the fact that Augustine had warned against taking Jesus' words at the Last Supper too literally. Christ spoke of spiritual things, he had explained, and the bread and wine certainly convey his grace to our spirits, but that need not imply anything about what happens on the material level. Radbertus' contemporary Ratramnus appealed to Augustine's authority when he said that the body of Christ is a heavenly, divine thing which cannot be present in visible form on the altar.[15] Two hundred years later, Berengar of Tours (died 1088) made the same point. The bread and wine, he said, become Christ's body and blood "not materially but spiritually."[16] After all, what we eat looks like bread and tastes like bread, so it must *be* bread. The body of Christ is not something that can be divided up into little pieces. Besides, think how much bread has been consumed by now in the course of Christian worship. Even if Christ's body had been as big as a tower or mountain, it would have been used up long ago.[17]

In the end, however, Radbertus' more literal approach carried the day. In making the grace of God vivid to ordinary people, theories of spiritual presence fell far short of the assertion that "this is no longer bread and wine, but Christ's body and blood." Widespread popular reports of seeing a small human body miraculously appear on the altar contributed to the most literal interpretation possible. Berengar's eleventh-century opponents, Lanfranc and Guitmond of Aversa, made the essential point: in their inner or essential nature the bread and wine stop being what they were before and become the body and blood of Christ. Later Aristotelian terminology called this process "transubstantiation." Aristotle had taught that in the ordinary course of things substances remain the same while their properties change. Thus, for instance, water can freeze into ice, changing its property from liquid to solid while it remains the same substance. In the Eucharist, according to the theory of transubstantiation, the reverse miraculously occurs: the properties remain the same, but the substance changes. What we eat still looks and tastes like bread, but it has become the body of Christ. The Fourth Lateran Council declared this a doctrine of the church in 1215.

The same search for vivid symbols of the working of grace helped shape the cult of the saints. Although the Eucharist provided the most direct sort of contact with Christ, he seemed increasingly remote to many early Medieval folk. They wanted to pray to someone a bit more approachable, and they increasingly turned to Mary and the saints.

At least as early as the second century, Christians had paid special honor to martyrs as heroes of the faith. Interest in their relics grew naturally enough. Even modern secular people can stare in awe at the memorabilia of great patriots, which seem to have a special sort of power. How much more that could be true in an age when everyone took all sorts of miraculous powers for granted. In 386 Ambrose, the bishop of Milan who had such an influence on Augustine, discovered the bodies of two martyrs beneath the site of his new cathedral and thus began a burst of interest in the relics of martyrs which spread, especially throughout Gaul. In the early 400s, however, a certain Vigilantius denounced the cult of martyrs as superstition. When people die, he said, they remain asleep until the last judgment, and therefore the martyrs are now asleep and cannot hear our prayers; special attention to bits of bone or clothing is sheer superstition. Jerome marshaled a whole series of theological arguments—and insults—against Vigilantius, but in the face of the rapid growth of popular piety, such arguments were scarcely needed.

In part the cult of martyrs served to wean people away from the worship of pagan gods. Pope Gregory I advised a missionary to England in 601:

> The temples of the idols ... should not be destroyed, but ... altars constructed, and relics deposited. ... And, since they are wont to kill many oxen in sacrifice to demons, they should have also some solemnity of this kind in a changed form ... on the anniversaries of the holy martyrs whose relics are deposited there. ... For it is undoubtedly impossible to cut away everything at once from hard hearts, since one who strives to ascend to the highest place must needs rise by steps or paces, and not by leaps.[18]

Vivid stories of their martyrdoms brought the martyrs alive to people. These heroes now lived with Christ; it seemed reasonable for Christians to ask them to intercede on their behalf.

After the end of persecution, some people still seemed to have the same kind of sanctity that the martyrs had had. His biographer wrote of the monk Martin of Tours, who died in 397, "Although the character of our times could not ensure him the honor of martyrdom yet he will not remain destitute of the glory of a martyr, because both by vow and virtues he was alike able and willing to be a martyr."[19] But who decided that people like Martin deserved to be saints just like the martyrs? Even in the days of martyrdom, it had been a problem that heretics could also die for their faith, but now the identity of those on whom Christians could call with the confidence that they are with Christ grew even harder to determine. Still, for centuries saints were proclaimed informally by local bishops or popular acclamation; only in 993 did a candidate named Ulrich of Augsburg go through a formal process of "canonization," in which papal officials studied his life for evidence of piety and verified miracles produced by prayers to him since his death. Then the pope officially proclaimed him a saint, subjecting the cult of the saints to a form of institutional control.

Mary had an even more special place in Christian piety. Even in the early Christological debates, Nestorius roused all sorts of opposition when he urged people to stop calling Mary "the God-bearer." A number of theological developments increased Mary's importance to Christian faith. Augustine's theory that sexual intercourse passes down the taint of original sin made the virgin birth crucial to Christ's freedom from sin, and Mary's role thus became necessary to the accomplishment of our salvation. Further, Christ seemed increasingly the remote judge rather than the forgiving savior. In the 700s one theologian urged praying to Mary "because we cannot find anyone more powerful . . . for placating the wrath of the judge."[20] An English Franciscan writing about 1320 only expressed an idea that had become common long before:

> We ought to imitate the man who has incurred the king's anger. What does he do? He goes secretly to the queen and promises a present. So when we have offended Christ, we should first go to the Queen of heaven and offer her, instead of a present, prayers, fasting, vigils, and alms; then she, like a mother, will come between us and Christ, the father who wished to beat us, and she will throw the cloak of mercy between the rod of punishment and us, and soften the king's anger against us.[21]

Specific theological claims about Mary gradually followed. The New Testament declared that Mary was a virgin, and Ambrose and Augustine had both believed that she remained a virgin all her life, even after Jesus' birth. A Lateran council at Rome proclaimed this as doctrine in 649, but just what it meant remained open to debate, often in rather startling gynecological detail. Paschasius Radbertus, the champion of the real presence of Christ's body and blood in the Eucharist, argued that Mary could not have remained a virgin if Christ had been born in the normal way. Therefore, just as the risen Christ passed through closed doors, so the infant Christ passed miraculously through the closed womb of the Virgin.[22] Ratramnus, who also accused Radbertus of vulgar literalism on the Eucharist, dismissed such a birth as a "monstrosity" that risked denying Christ's real humanity.

Other debates concerned whether Mary had ever sinned and whether her body had been raised to heaven at her death, either after her death or without her actually dying. Only in the nineteenth and twentieth centuries has the Roman Catholic church officially promulgated the doctrine of the immaculate conception (Mary's birth miraculously free from the taint of original sin) and that of the assumption (the lifting of Mary's body to heaven at her death). Some theologians eager to honor Mary opposed these specific doctrines as innovations, but they were already popular ideas in the Middle Ages.

In a number of ways, then, the early medieval church sought to make the path to salvation clearer to its people. It qualified the extremes of Augustine's theory of predestination to leave a place for human efforts. It made Christ's presence more real in the Eucharist, and it offered more accessible approaches to grace through prayer to Mary and the saints. But it was the system of penance that most helped to guide people's lives. The first Christians had assumed that Christians should not, and usually would not, commit sins after baptism. Many began to postpone baptism to cover as many sins as possible. As Augustine and others realized, however, as long as we "remain in this life . . . if we say that we have no sin, we deceive ourselves, and the truth is not in us."[23] But what were Christians to do when they sinned?

Gradually a system of penance emerged. For quite minor sins, an individual could pray and repent in private. But by the third century those who had committed more substantial sins were supposed to request admission to the order of penitents, who wore special clothing and sat in a special section of the church, usually excluded from Communion and devoting themselves to prayers, almsgiving, and strict continence for the period of their penance, which might last anywhere from the forty days of Lent to several years. As Boniface, a great eighth-century missionary to Germany, put it, penance was a "second form of cleansing after the sacrament of baptism, so that the evils we do after the washing of baptism may be healed by the medicines of penance."[24] Usually one could undergo penance only once, and therefore people who had been through the process had to lead careful lives thereafter, usually remaining celibate and avoiding occupations that might lead to sin—such as being a soldier, a charioteer, an actor, or a magistrate. Before long, penance suffered the same fate baptism had earlier. As Caesarius of Arles complained in the sixth century, "People say, 'When I am grown old I will undertake penance. When I am grown old or am desperately ill, then I will ask for penance.' "[25]

Beginning in the 500s, Irish monks developed an alternative. In part they drew on the pagan customs of their land, where confessors or spiritual advisers and payments to an injured party had long played an important part in the legal system. In part they appealed to monastic tradition, in which monks had always confessed their faults to the abbot on a regular basis. They created a private and repeatable penance. The sinner went contritely to a priest, confessed sin, carried out an assigned penance—and could return for the same process after further sins. A series of "penitentials," or penitential manuals, listed appropriate penalties for various sins. These could be quite specific, and reading them provides a useful corrective for anyone who thinks that human sexual activity has grown more imaginative over the centuries. The penalties demanded seem extraordinarily severe today, but the first protests against the penitentials grew out of the fear that assigning a specific penalty made sinning altogether too easy. Nevertheless, repeatable penance provided a remarkably effective tool for ethical discipline, and the use of such manuals spread throughout Europe. Together with baptism and regular Communion, penance provided a sacramental system that guided people's lives.

POPES AND EMPERORS

Such guidance of every aspect of people's lives naturally augmented the church's power, and increasingly the nature of that power needed clarification, particularly the pope's relation to other church leaders and the relation between church and state. These matters took a very different shape in the West than in the East. After 476 no emperor remained in the West, and the emperor in Constantinople, while retaining some authority in theory, seemed weak and far away. At the same time, the bishop of Rome, the pope, had come to have an authority no churchman in the East could match. Rome as a city had much on its side: the traditional authority of the empire's capital, the heritage of Peter as its first bishop, a record of coming out on the winning side of theological disputes, and the best-kept archives in the world, which enabled it to cite evidence and historical documents that supported its position. In the East, Alexandria, Antioch, and Constantinople vied for power, but no other city challenged Rome in the West. In 343 the Council of Sardica endorsed the preeminence of the bishop of Rome because he "upheld the memory of St. Peter,"[26] and in 380 Emperor Theodosius declared the faith "which the apostle of God, St. Peter, has delivered to the Romans and which is now professed by the pontiff Damasus [the bishop of Rome at the time] and the bishop of apostolic sanctity Peter of Alexandria" to be the official religion of the Roman Empire.[27] Seventy years later the Council of Chalcedon made Pope Leo's letter the basis of its settlement, proclaiming that "Peter has spoken through the mouth of Leo." The Eastern bishops at Chalcedon, however, also gave great authority to the patriarch of Constantinople and implied that papal rights rested on Rome's political importance and on the decisions of councils. The popes insisted that they inherited their primacy from Peter and it did not depend on any councils or political arrangements. All this set the context for the debates at the Council of Florence that have been described in Chapter 7.

Whatever controversies continued between East and West, however, the popes ruled the church in the West—but how far did the authority of the church extend? In the East, such debates usually concerned whether the church was independent of the emperor, but in the West popes made claims, not just to independence, but to superiority over all other rulers. In the later 400s, for instance, Pope Gelasius wrote to Emperor Anastasius:

> Two there are, august emperor, by which this world is chiefly ruled, the sacred authority of the priesthood and the royal power. Of these the responsibility of the priests is more weighty in so far as they will answer for the kings of men themselves at the divine judgement. . . . Although you take precedence over all mankind in dignity, nevertheless you piously bow the neck to those who have charge of divine affairs and seek from them the means of your salvation.[28]

In practice, the popes of this period simply lacked the power to assert any such authority. They depended for protection on rulers who would not look kindly on claims of papal superiority. Still, in the background their claims survived. In 800 Pope Leo III crowned Charlemagne emperor of the West. Apparently Charlemagne had not known about the ceremony in advance and felt angry when the pope unexpectedly placed a crown on his head, for he feared an implicit papal claim to choose or approve emperors.

For the time being, though, nothing came of it. The 800s and 900s saw one of the most corrupt periods in papal history, and most popes found themselves too involved in local Roman politics and the mere struggle for survival to pursue any wider claims. In addition, the rise of the feudal system increasingly complicated the question of church authority. Feudalism filled the vacuum left by the collapse of strong central government. How could an ordinary person feel safe? Generally, you found some powerful lord in your neighborhood and promised him loyalty, as well as a portion of your crops or the offer to fight in his army, in return for a promise of protection. The resulting interlocking system of obligations held early medieval Europe together. The church needed protection too, for its people, its buildings, and its land, and so local church leaders commonly promised loyalty to neighboring kings or nobles. They in turn needed the help of church officials, who were often virtually the only people who could read and write, in carrying out their business. All this could serve mutual convenience, but it could also lead to abuses. A priest or bishop might owe more loyalty to the local noble than to the church, and the noble might claim the right to appoint or approve the appointment of church officials. Many attacked the legitimacy of "lay investiture," in which a layman gave a bishop the staff which symbolized his office; it seemed to turn bishops into government functionaries. Even worse, it could lead to "simony," the buying of church offices, when a lord offered to sell a bishopric to the highest bidder. (The name comes from Simon Magus who, in the book of Acts, offered to buy the power to work miracles from the apostles.)

Strong papal leadership might break this pattern of abuse, but the popes themselves were weak and corrupt. In 1046, when Emperor Henry III went from Germany to Rome to be crowned, he found three "popes" claiming the office, none of them particularly worthy of it. Henry threw out all three, appointed his own candidate, and encouraged papal reform. From the imperial point of view, he succeeded all too well, for the reformed papacy began to ask what right an emperor had to appoint a pope anyway and to rediscover the old claims that a pope really ought to be superior to any king or emperor. When Hildebrand, the leader of the reformers, became Pope Gregory VII in 1059, he went to work on two fronts.

First he sought to clear out clerical abuses. He urged people not to attend Eucharists conducted by a priest who was living with a mistress. His supporter Cardinal Humbert even maintained that priests who had bought their offices and were thus guilty of simony could not validly administer the sacraments. Ordination conveys grace, and grace must be given freely, he argued. Those who had purchased ordination had not received it freely, he said. "Therefore they do not receive grace . . . but if they do not receive it they do not have it; if they do not have it they cannot give it."[29] That struck even most of the reformers as going too far. It raised the same problem Augustine had diagnosed in Donatism. If the validity of a sacrament could be destroyed by some fault of the priest, how could people ever be sure they were really receiving the sacraments? The reform movement had to strike a delicate balance. It had to denounce corrupt priests forcefully enough to produce reform without attacking them so strongly that it destroyed people's confidence in the system of church and sacraments, which was often available to them only through the work of a corrupt priest.

It was easier to assert the superiority of the church to other powers. Again, Cardinal Humbert put the point in the most unqualified terms:

The priesthood is analogous to the soul and the kingship to the body, for they cleave to one another and need one another and each in turn demands services and renders them to another. It follows from this that, just as the soul excels the body and commands it, so too the priestly dignity exceeds the royal.[30]

Pope Gregory VII claimed the right to intervene anywhere, to depose, transfer, or replace bishops, call synods and general councils, depose emperors, and release people from allegiance to their rulers. Faced with a corrupt church, tied in so many ways to governmental structures, he believed that only such powers could get the job of reform done. To Emperor Henry IV, however, this seemed an attempt to make the pope the absolute monarch of Europe. Henry rejected Gregory's claims, and Gregory excommunicated him, declaring further that good Christians ought to support the German nobles who were rebelling against their emperor. At first Gregory seemed to be winning, but then Henry traveled to Italy and knelt in the snow outside the pope's castle for three days, begging forgiveness. As a priest, Gregory could not ignore a repentant sinner, so he lifted the excommunication. Henry rushed back to Germany and defeated his enemies. The issue remained unsettled. In theory, everyone agreed that the church and empire or kingdoms had separate tasks, both given by God. But in practice, when the church owned vast stretches of land and provided many governmental officials, it was hard to know where to draw the line between the two. Gregory saw lay investiture as illegitimate interference in the church, but to Henry it seemed necessary to have some right to choose his own leading landowners and officials.

In the early 1100s Pope Paschal II proposed a dramatic solution. Let the church give up all its property; let priests and bishops return to being simple pastors of souls, living on free gifts from the faithful. Not surprisingly, the bishops reacted in horror, and perhaps justifiably so. Paschal offered an idealistic way of freeing the church from the bonds of power, but in the tough world of feudalism a bishop without property might be even more vulnerable to outside control. In any event, the Concordat of Worms in 1122 ended the lay investiture controversy on a different basis. Emperors renounced the right to present bishops with the ring and staff that symbolized their office. Bishops would be elected without imperial interference, but the ruler would be present at the election and would recognize the chosen candidate.

Conflicts between church and state soon emerged, however, in new and more sophisticated forms. On a variety of issues, indeed, from church authority to sacramental theology, Christians were discovering that they needed tools to define more precisely what they believed. Beginning around 1000, "scholasticism," the theology developed in new schools and universities, began to develop those intellectual tools. At the same time, the struggle to reconcile the church's need for power with the Christian ideal of poverty and self-sacrifice became even more dramatic. Those intellectual and political issues will be the theme of the next chapter.

FOR FURTHER READING

INTRODUCTIONS. Surveys by great scholars in the field include: David Knowles, *Christian Monasticism* (McGraw-Hill Book Co., World University Library, 1969); Walter Ullmann, *A Short History of the Papacy in the Middle Ages* (London: Methuen & Co., 1972); Peter Brown, *The Cult of the Saints* (University of Chicago Press, 1981).

COLLECTIONS OF ORIGINAL SOURCES. George E. McCracken (ed.), *Early Medieval Theology*, in The Library of Christian Classics (Westminster Press, 1957), collects many texts from the period. Helen Waddell, *The Desert Fathers* (London: Constable & Co., 1936), offers a collection of fascinating texts by and about the early monks, with a beautiful brief introduction. Edward Peters, *Monks, Bishops and Pagans* (University of Pennsylvania Press, 1975), includes documents that give the flavor of the transition from the ancient to the medieval world. John T. McNeill and Helena M. Gamer have brought the texts from early penitentials together in *Medieval Handbooks of Penance* (Octagon Books, 1965). Brian Tierney, *The Crisis of Church and State 1050–1300* (Prentice-Hall, 1964), includes excerpts from the central documents on its topic, with fine introductions.

IMPORTANT BUT MORE DIFFICULT. Jaroslav Pelikan, *The Growth of Medieval Theology (600–1300)* (University of Chicago Press, 1978), focuses on doctrinal developments to the exclusion of philosophical and political issues, but within those limits is indispensable. See also Eric Waldram Kemp, *Canonization and Authority in the Western Church* (London: Oxford University Press, 1948), and A. J. Macdonald, *Berengar and the Reform of Sacramental Doctrine* (Richwood Publishing Co., 1977).

NOTES

1. Bede, *A History of the English Church and People* 2.13, tr. by Leo Sherley-Price (Harmondsworth, Middlesex: Penguin Books, 1968), p. 127.
2. *The Sayings of the Desert Fathers*, tr. by Benedicta Ward (London: A. R. Mowbray & Co., 1975), p. 135.
3. Jerome, *Against Jovinianus* 1.3, tr. by W. H. Fremantle, *A Select Library of the Nicene and Post-Nicene Fathers*, 2d Ser., ed. by Philip Schaff and Henry Wace, Vol. 6 (Christian Literature Co., 1893), p. 348.
4. Ibid., 1.41–46, pp. 379–382.
5. Benedict of Nursia, *The Rule of St. Benedict*, prologue, tr. by Anthony C. Meisel and M. L. del Mastro (Doubleday & Co., Image Books, 1975), p. 45.
6. Ibid., ch. 33, p. 76.
7. Ibid., ch. 22, p. 70.
8. John Cassian, *The Conferences* 13.7, tr. by Edgar C. S. Gibson, *A Select Library of the Nicene and Post-Nicene Fathers*, 2d Ser., Vol. 11 (Christian Literature Co., 1894), p. 425.
9. Canons of the Synod of Orange (529), canons 3 and 18; quoted in Adolf von Harnack, *History of Dogma*, tr. by Neil Buchanan, Vol. 5 (Little, Brown & Co., 1899), pp. 258–259.
10. Quoted in Florus of Lyons, *On the Three Epistles* 21, in *Patrologia Latina*, ed. by J.-P. Migne, Vol. 121 (Paris: Garnier Fratres, 1880), cols. 1022–1023; quoted in Jaroslav Pelikan, *The Growth of Medieval Theology (600–1300)* (University of Chicago Press, 1978), p. 83.
11. Hincmar of Reims, *On the Deity as One and Not Three* 19, in *Patrologia Latina*, Vol. 125 (Paris: Garnier Fratres, 1879), col. 618; quoted in Pelikan, op. cit., p. 7.
12. John Scotus Eriugena, *Homily on the Prologue of the Gospel of John* 11; quoted in Pelikan, op. cit., p. 102.
13. John Scotus Eriugena, *Commentary on the Gospel of John* 3.9; quoted in Pelikan, op. cit., p. 104.
14. See G. G. Coulton, *Five Centuries of Religion*, Vol. 1 (Cambridge: Cambridge University Press, 1923), pp. 103–104.
15. Ratramnus, *De corpore et sanguine Domini* 9.19.72; quoted in A. J. Macdonald, *Berengar and the Reform of Sacramental Doctrine* (Richwood Publishing Co., 1977), p. 240.
16. Berengar, *Epistle to Adelman;* quoted in Macdonald, op. cit., p. 248.
17. Berengar, *De sacra coena* (Hildesheim: Georg Olms Verlag, 1975), pp. 171, 45; Peter the Venerable quoted the remark about Christ needing to have been as big as a tower or mountain in *Treatise Against Peter of Bruis*, in *Patrologia Latina*, Vol. 189 (Paris: Garnier Fratres, 1890), col. 799. See Macdonald, *Berengar and the Reform of Sacramental Doctrine*, pp. 304–310.
18. Pope Gregory I, Letter 76, to Mellitus, Abbot, tr. by James Barmby, in *A Select Library of the Nicene and Post-Nicene Fathers*, 2d Ser., Vol. 13 (Christian Literature Co., 1898), p. 85.
19. Sulpicius Severus, Letter 2; quoted in Eric Waldram Kemp, *Canoniza-*

tion and Authority in the Western Church (London: Oxford University Press, 1948), p. 21.

20. Ambrose Autpert, Sermon 208.11, in *Patrologia Latina*, Vol. 101 (Paris: Garnier Fratres, 1865), col. 2134; quoted in Pelikan, *The Growth of Medieval Theology*, p. 69.

21. *Fasciculus morum;* quoted in Coulton, *Five Centuries of Religion*, Vol. 1, p. 140.

22. Paschasius Radbertus, *On the Parturition of Saint Mary* 1.51; quoted in Pelikan, *The Growth of Medieval Theology*, pp. 73–74.

23. Augustine, *Faith, Hope, and Charity* 17.64, tr. by Louis A. Arand (Newman Press, 1947), pp. 65–66.

24. Boniface, Sermon 8.1, in *Patrologia Latina*, Vol. 89 (Paris: Garnier Fratres, 1863), col. 858; quoted in Pelikan, *The Growth of Medieval Theology*, p. 32.

25. Caesarius of Arles, Sermon 257, in *Patrologia Latina*, Vol. 39 (Paris: Garnier Fratres, 1865), col. 2219; quoted in R. C. Mortimer, *The Origins of Private Penance in the Western Church* (Oxford: Clarendon Press, 1939), p. 126.

26. Quoted in Walter Ullmann, *A Short History of the Papacy in the Middle Ages* (London: Methuen & Co., 1972), p. 8.

27. Ibid., p. 9.

28. Quoted in Brian Tierney, *The Crisis of Church and State 1050–1300* (Prentice-Hall, 1964), pp. 13–14.

29. Ibid., p. 34.

30. Humbert, *Three Books Against the Simoniacs;* quoted in Tierney, op. cit., pp. 41–42.

10

THE FRAGILE SYNTHESIS

Thus the seven liberal arts like servant wenches came prying into the sacred and state banquet chamber of their mistress [theology] and, as if checked in their wanton ways and disciplined under the annoyed and strict surveillance of the word of God, were ordered to sit down; previously they had wandered all about like obscene, chattering, verbose girls, doing nothing except acting out of indiscreet curiosity.

—Rupert of Deutz, writing in the twelfth century[1]

People who should know better still sometimes dismiss the medieval period in Europe as "the Dark Ages." Admittedly, in the seventh and eighth centuries, and (after temporary advances under Charlemagne) again in the tenth century, the pressures of invasions and economic collapse forced most Western Europeans to concentrate on the immediate task of survival. As we have seen in the preceding chapter, this affected everything, theology included. Christians had to make their message simple and vivid and preserve the basic truths of their faith. After the year 1000, however, medieval Europe produced remarkable accomplishments in fields as diverse as architecture, literature, law, and philosophy. The lights had come back on. Theology faced the new challenges of a time of intellectual sophistication. Precision and completeness now became as important as simplicity and clarity, and theologians constructed edifices as complex as Gothic cathedrals.

Cultural advances brought the church power and wealth as well as intellectual accomplishment. Some Christians wondered if this was really a good thing. Jesus had lived a life of poverty, preaching to simple fisherfolk. How did that fit with the grandeur of the papal court or the vast cathedrals—or the scholars studying philosophy and writing huge theological tomes? The Franciscan poet Jacopone da Todi declared:

> Plato and Socrates may contend
> And all the breath in their bodies spend,
> Arguing without an end—
> What's it all to me?
> Only a pure and simple mind
> Straight to heaven its way doth find;
> Greets the King—while far behind
> Lags the world's philosophy.[2]

Others, however, pointed out that God had created human reason, and presumably he wants us to use and develop it as fully as we can. They ridiculed those who, "wanting to have company in their ignorance . . . want us to believe like peasants and not to ask the reason behind things."[3] True faith, they said, will only grow stronger the more thoughtfully we examine it.

Theology in the eleventh, twelfth, and thirteenth centuries thus developed amid tensions, tensions shaped in part by the different institutional contexts in which theologians worked. A theologian writing in a monastery sought above all to meditate on the meaning of the faith. Someone writing in a university aimed at defending his views in intellectual debate. Different styles of theology would result. Two new groups founded at the beginning of the thirteenth century, the Dominicans and the Franciscans, sought to combine the best of both these worlds. They would commit themselves to a special spiritual discipline, but they would be active in the world rather than withdrawing to contemplation. Their approaches differed. The Dominicans began as preachers and teachers and put more emphasis on intellectual analysis, while the Franciscans always retained more of their founder's love of contemplation. Still, both Dominicans and Franciscans, like earlier monks and university teachers, found that their particular tasks and concerns shaped the character of their theologies.

In their different ways, they were all trying to fit together faith and reason, the church and the world, the gospel of Christ and the complicated society in which they lived. It was not an easy task, and during this period the world came to seem less a seamless whole. A genius might find a way of balancing all these tensions, but they did not go away.

SCHOLARS AND LOVERS

The most original thinker of the eleventh century, Anselm, a monk who was born in Italy and educated in France and who ended his life as Archbishop of Canterbury, illustrates monastic theology at its best. He stood firmly in the Augustinian tradition, believing that faith must precede understanding. "Unless you believe," he insisted, "you will not understand."[4] "For I do not seek to understand in order to believe, but I believe in order to understand. For I believe even this: that I shall not understand unless I believe."[5] Only faith in Christ provides the perspective from which one can see the world aright.

At the same time, Anselm saw few limits to what reason could achieve when guided by faith. His "ontological argument" for the existence of God, for instance, has fascinated philosophers ever since.

"Ontology" refers to the study of being, and the ontological argument rests on an analysis of God's being. Aquinas and Kant attacked this argument; Descartes and Leibniz defended it, and the debate continues. (Given Bertrand Russell's fame as an atheist, I cannot resist quoting him: "One day in 1894, as I was walking along Trinity Lane . . . I saw in a flash (or thought I saw) that the ontological argument is valid. I had gone out to buy a tin of tobacco; on my way back, I suddenly threw it up in the air, and exclaimed as I caught it: 'Great Scott, the ontological argument is sound.' "[6] He later recovered.)

Several recent commentators have argued that Anselm actually presented two different arguments, but their case becomes fairly technical and does not concern the relation of faith and reason, which is under discussion here. Anselm began with the assumption that even those who deny God's existence must have some idea of what the word "God" means. Otherwise, how could they know what they are denying? If atheists and skeptics know what "God" means, then God exists in their understandings. Among other things, everyone understands God to be "something than which nothing greater can be thought." We cannot conceive of anything greater than God. Anselm further assumed that it is greater to exist in reality than merely to exist in the understanding. For instance (this is not his example), tornadoes represent a greater danger to my house than dragons do —not because dragons would lack destructive force, but because dragons exist only in human imaginations, while tornadoes, alas, exist in reality as well. From these assumptions, the argument follows:

1. "Something than which nothing greater can be thought" exists in the understanding. [Even the atheist knows what "God" means.]

2. It is greater to exist in reality than merely to exist in the understanding.

3. Suppose that "something than which nothing greater can be thought" existed only in the understanding. Then it would be possible to think of something even greater, namely, an entity otherwise identical which also existed in reality.

4. But this is impossible, since by definition it is impossible to think of something greater than "something than which nothing greater can be thought."

5. Therefore "something than which nothing greater can be thought" must exist in reality as well as in the understanding.

6. Since God is "something than which nothing greater can be thought," God exists in reality.[7]

The argument leaves many readers uncomfortable. One has a sense of being tricked, but even trained logicians cannot agree on where or whether it goes wrong. For nearly a thousand years now, Anselm's interpreters have debated not only about whether he succeeded but also about what he sought to accomplish. He seems to be offering an argument that should persuade even the atheist, yet the argument comes in the context of a prayer, and Anselm always retained his Augustinian conviction that faith must precede understanding.

A similar puzzle arises in connection with Anselm's discussion of the work of Christ. Chapter 6 discussed the theory that Christ saved humanity by tricking the devil and freeing us from the devil's power. That had come to be the most common image of Christ's work in the early Middle Ages, but not for Anselm. "Was it in order to deceive the Devil" that Christ became human? he asked. "Surely, Truth deceives no one," and Christ represents truth.[8] Anselm explained in a different way (to quote the title of his book) *Why God Became Man*. The devil dropped out of the picture; the problem concerned humanity and God. In sinning, we have broken our obligations to God and dishonored him. We owe God a debt, and, though God in his mercy would like to forgive us, as the foundation of perfect justice he cannot simply overlook sin. "Without satisfaction (i.e., without voluntary payment of the debt) God cannot forgive unpunished sin and the sinner cannot arrive at happiness."[9] Perhaps we could do extra work to make up for our sins? But we owe God everything; we ought to be perfect, and we cannot be better than perfect or give God more than everything. "If even had I not sinned I would . . . owe to God myself and whatever I can do, I have nothing with which to make payment for my sin."[10] Only God could do something above and beyond what God requires. Only God's voluntary submission to suffering could pay our debts, yet human beings have run up this debt, so justice would be satisfied only if a human being paid it. Therefore, if both justice and mercy are to be served, God must become a human being, so that "one and the same [individual] . . . would pay through his human nature what this nature ought to pay and would be able through his divine nature to do what was required."[11] Only Christ, both human and divine, can save us.

Anselm's critics sometimes find all this too legalistic. They also charge that the picture of Christ suffering to pay the debt required by God the Father risks so contrasting Father and Son as to threaten the unity of the Trinity. Still, Anselm's account made particularly good sense in the context of the system of penance, which had accustomed people to thinking of sin as a debt incurred and requiring compensation. Most fascinating is that at the outset Anselm announced, "This book goes on to prove by rational necessity—Christ being removed from sight, as if there had never been anything known about him— that no man can possibly be saved without him."[12] Like the ontological argument, this makes extraordinary claims for human reason. When later theologians sought to clarify what reason can know apart from faith, they sometimes regarded Anselm as the most daring champion of pure reason, but the scope of reason apart from faith was never his concern. He always started with faith, but he sought to understand his faith, and no one has ever used reason more ambitiously in that task.

A generation or two later Peter Abelard, who died in 1142, found that faith and reason did not always fit so naturally together. Abelard gained his fame, not amid the contemplative life of a monastery, but in the thick of intellectual debates at the University of Paris. The new style of disputation there suited him. As a student, he amazed his friends by giving a brilliant lecture on matters he had scarcely studied and on his first try. "It was not my custom," he explained, "to advance through practice but through talent."[13] He put together a book entitled *Yes and No* which juxtaposed passages from Scripture and from famous theologians supporting both sides of a whole series of theological issues. He insisted that he sought only clarification, not any weakening of respect for authority, but his enemies mistrusted this arrogant young genius who tossed all these contradictions to his admiring students.

Abelard agreed with Anselm that Christ did not save us by tricking the devil, but he also rejected Anselm's theory that Christ's suffering pays off our debt to God. "How cruel and wicked it seems," he wrote, "that anyone should demand the blood of an innocent person as the price for anything . . . , still less that God should consider the death of his Son so agreeable that by it he should be reconciled to the whole world!"[14] What sort of brutal sadist is God, that the death of his Son should be so pleasing to him? Abelard preferred to think of Christ as the expression of God's love, inspiring a love in return from us:

> Through this unique act of grace manifested to us—in that his Son has taken upon himself our nature and persevered therein, in teaching us by word and example even unto death—he has more fully bound us to himself by love; with the result that our hearts should be enkindled by such a gift of divine grace, and true charity should not now shrink from enduring anything for him.[15]

Critics have often said that this reduced Christ to no more than an inspiring example, leaving the real work of earning our salvation to us. Yet Abelard always insisted that we can love God only because he first loved us. God's love in Christ does not merely encourage us; it makes our love possible.

Abelard knew about love. At the height of his career he fell in love with a young girl named Heloise. Her unsuspecting uncle welcomed the great teacher's offer to instruct his niece, and soon, "under the pretext of work we made ourselves entirely free for love. . . . There was more kissing than teaching; my hands found themselves at her breasts more often than on the book."[16] The uncle found out. Heloise fled. Abelard agreed to marry her in secret. Apparently he was not a priest and could legally have married, but celibacy remained so strong an ideal that a public marriage would have destroyed his reputation. Eventually the furious uncle hired some local toughs to castrate Abelard, and Abelard sent Heloise off to a convent before retiring to a monastery himself. As Heloise had predicted, "If we do this, one fate finally awaits us: we shall both be ruined and sorrow will thereby pierce our hearts equal in intensity to the love with which they are now aflame."[17] Abelard urged her to devote her life to God, and she followed all the external rigors of her discipline, but she could not repent. "So sweet to me were those delights of lovers which we enjoyed in common that they cannot either displease me nor hardly pass from my memory. . . . And when I ought to lament for what I have done I sigh rather for what I have had to forego."[18] She lived out the life of a saintly prioress, but she insisted she acted out of love for Abelard, not for God.

Naturally Abelard's critics took full advantage of the scandal, and none more so than Bernard of Clairvaux. Bernard again represents the monastic tradition, and to set him in his proper context, something needs to be said about how monasticism had been developing. From the time of Charlemagne around 800, the Rule of St. Benedict had guided nearly all the monasteries in the West, but monks had often not followed it very well. Many pious persons left money to monasteries, which sometimes became quite rich, and monks, who had sometimes been sent off to this life by their parents, often preferred enjoying monastic wealth to following monastic discipline. The Benedictine tradition left each community completely independent, and that made it very difficult to reform a corrupt monastery. In 910 some monks dedicated to complete obedience to Benedict's rule founded a new community at Cluny and began a new system. Whenever monks went out from Cluny to found a new monastery, it remained under the rule of the abbot of Cluny. This tightly controlled network of Cluniac communities produced a burst of reforming energy that contributed to the fight against corruption under Pope Gregory VII mentioned in the last chapter. Cluny itself soon grew rich, however, and a single abbot found it difficult to supervise many scattered communities. In 1098 still another group of reforming monks set themselves up, this time at a wild spot in a French forest called Citeaux. The Cistercian monasteries which began at Citeaux found an alternative to the absolute independence of the original Benedictines and the centralized authority of Cluny: the abbots of all Cistercian monasteries met regularly to discuss problems and set policy.

The Cistercians accomplished a spiritual revival, in part because they attracted a young man named Bernard. He was full of paradoxes. Devoted to withdrawal from the world, he became, all by himself, a major force in European politics. Indifferent alike to philosophy and beauty—when asked to describe the design of the church where he had worshiped for years, he admitted that he had never noticed—he wrote works of philosophical penetration and stylistic elegance. Dedicated to love and to the Virgin Mary, he attacked his opponents violently and enthusiastically preached crusades. He denounced anyone, from the pope on down, who betrayed or compromised his vision of the Christian ideal. "The walls of the church are aglow," he exclaimed, "but the poor of the church go hungry. The stones of the church are covered with gold, while its children are left naked. The food of the poor is taken to feed the eyes of the rich."[19] He orchestrated a campaign against Abelard, vilifying his character and attacking his theory that, as Bernard saw it, Christ lived and died "for no other purpose than that he might teach us how to live by his words and example."[20]

The conflict between Bernard and Abelard exemplifies the tension between the monastery and the university. Anselm had found the monastery the ideal place to pursue reason's inquiries, but Abelard and others had taken theology into the disputatious, potentially skeptical world of the university. If the future of Christian intellectualism lay in that direction, Bernard wanted no part of it. Still, it was not obvious that such a choice had to be made. At the Abbey of St. Victor in Paris a series of theologians combined the deepest faith and mystical experience with a wide-ranging interest in new philosophical developments. Bernard's contemporary Hugh of St. Victor insisted on the value of every kind of knowledge: "Learn everything; you will see afterwards that nothing is superfluous."[21] But he also asserted that the highest good of life lies in the mystic vision of God, possible only with the help of grace. A generation later, Richard of St. Victor, who died in 1173, applied philosophical analysis even to understanding the Trinity, yet he also wrote moving and influential guides to the mystic life. The "Victorines" retained Anselm's sense of a faith so confident that it could encompass the whole world of knowledge.

Even Bernard did not simply attack new ideas, nor were anger and suspicion his principal motivations. All his impatience with his opponents and his own self-denial—he nearly killed himself with austerities—grew out of a lover's passion. He did not reverence God as a great ruler, he once explained: "Let someone filled with horror or stupor or fear or wonder be content with reverence; where there is love all these are unimportant."[22] He taught a mystic discipline that moved gradually away from love of self toward the disinterested love of God:

> As a drop of water seems to disappear completely in a big quantity of wine, even assuming the wine's taste and color; just as red, molten iron becomes so much like fire it seems to lose its primary state; just as the air on a sunny day seems transformed into sunshine . . . , so it is necessary for the saints that all human feelings melt in a mysterious way and flow into the will of God.[23]

It is ironic that only one of Bernard's contemporaries has left us a record expressing such pure love—and Heloise loved Abelard rather than God.

HERETICS AND FRIARS

Among his many campaigns, Bernard helped organize a crusade against a group called the Cathari (or Albigensians) in southern France. The Cathari rejected both the physical world and the institutional church. Indirectly, they may have had connections with the Manicheans whom Augustine had fought centuries before, and they echoed many of the old Gnostic themes: God created only spirits; an evil being made bodies and other physical objects; Christ only appeared to have a body and did not really suffer. The Cathari rejected all the corruption of this world, and they won popular support by their attacks on the corrupt clergy. As noted in the last chapter, reformers like Pope Gregory VII had to walk a thin line between tolerating corrupt priests and attacking them so violently as to destroy people's confidence in the sacraments and the church. The Cathari had no such inhibitions and insisted that corrupt priests could not convey the grace of God. Their own leaders often led lives of extreme self-denial, sometimes even starving themselves to death in an ultimate rejection of the material world. Ordinary people hoped that a blessing on their deathbed from one of these "perfect ones" would assure their salvation or at least a chance to become perfect themselves in their next life.

Some scholars have traced a profound influence of the Cathari on our culture, noting that the troubadours, who contributed so much to the ideals of knighthood and romantic love, began in Cathari circles. The more immediate influence of the Cathari on the church, however, grew out of the need for new weapons to oppose them. Crusading armies could kill them but, then as now, could not win the people's hearts and minds. The wealth and aristocratic background of many bishops separated them from the populace. Monks withdrew from the world, and too many priests had little education or ability. Around 1200 a Spaniard named Dominic created an order of "friars." Like monks, his friars, the Order of Preachers, or Dominicans, dedicated themselves to a religious life, but instead of withdrawing to contemplation, they secured a good education and then traveled about in the world preaching. Local bishops sometimes distrusted them, and monasteries sensed an implied criticism of their own life, but in the face of opposition the Dominicans served an important function and soon spread throughout Europe.

A contemporary of Dominic named Francis grew up the son of a merchant in the Italian town of Assisi, leading a life of irresponsible youth, preparing to fight a local war, and learning all the latest French love songs. Then he sold some of his father's goods and gave the money to the poor. His angry father accused him of theft. Francis went before the local bishop to renounce all claims to his inheritance, stripping himself naked to give back his father's clothes. Someone gave him a ragged old cloak, and he went off, singing, to dedicate himself like a knight to Lady Poverty. Francis soon attracted followers, and he demanded absolute poverty of them. "If we have possessions," he explained, "we shall need arms to protect them. And from this arise disputes and quarrels, and the love of God and of one's neighbor is much hindered."[24] When Francis asked Pope Innocent III for permission to organize his followers as friars traveling around the countryside begging for their food and preaching faith in Christ, the answer would have been hard to predict. Not long before the church had condemned a man named Peter Waldo for organizing a group of poor lay preachers rather like the Franciscans, and Francis' ideal of absolute poverty implied a criticism of the church's wealth and power. The story goes that Pope Innocent had a dream in which a great church began to collapse, until a little man in a ragged brown cloak held it up and kept it from falling. In any event he authorized the Franciscans, and Francis in turn always remained respectful of papal authority.

That authority eventually challenged his ideal of poverty. Already in Francis' lifetime he largely withdrew from leadership, and at his death his successor, the ambitious Brother Elias, built a huge church to honor him. As the friars grew in number, it became harder for them to support themselves by begging, and in order to be effective preachers they needed education, which meant owning books and pens and paper. Church authorities nervously insisted that a good Christian need not be poor. Some of Francis' followers, however, soon known as "spiritual Franciscans," continued to feel that owning anything betrayed the ideal of Francis and of Christ. Some of them developed an interest in the works of Joachim of Fiore, an Italian monk who had lived in the 1100s. Joachim had sought the hidden meaning of history, writing works full of numerical symbols. He divided history into three great ages: the Age of the Father, ruled by law, in which people were to work and marry and the ideal was the Old Testament patriarch; the Age of the Son, ruled by grace, in which people were to learn and the ideal was the priest who teaches; and the Age of the Spirit, ruled by love, in which people were to praise God and the ideal is the monk filled with the love of God. Some have traced the influence of Joachim's tripartite patterning of history all the way down to the nineteenth-century philosopher Hegel and to Karl Marx. In the thirteenth century the spiritual Franciscans thought that the Age of the Spirit had begun in their time, with Joachim the new John the Baptist and Francis the new Christ. Just as Christ had overthrown the law, so they would now overthrow the institutional church.

Their opponents proved too strong for them. The church denied that Christ and his apostles had lived a life of absolute poverty. A fascinating debate over the meaning of the New Testament had weighed the fact that the apostles had a treasury against the fact that Judas was in charge of it. John of Parma, the Franciscan leader most sympathetic to the spirituals, had to resign and stand trial. Though the Franciscan ideal has continued to exercise its power, most Christians did not feel that their faith required them to pull out of the economic system of their society. After the persecution of Christianity's first centuries and the hard times of the early Middle Ages, Christians in the thirteenth century could be comfortable as never before. In quite different ways, both the enmity of the Cathari toward the physical world and the Franciscan ideal of poverty challenged that comfort. But the church decided to accept the world and the structures of its society. Similarly, Christian theology eventually decided to accept much of the world's philosophy.

ARISTOTLE AND AQUINAS

The introduction of Aristotle into Western Europe in the 1200s complicated the relation between theology and philosophy. In the early 500s a Christian named Boethius had translated several of Aristotle's works, mostly on logic, into Latin, but only in the late 1100s and 1200s did scholars in Sicily and Spain translate his greatest philosophical and scientific texts, some from Greek and some from Arabic versions in which Muslim philosophers had been studying Aristotle for centuries. These translations had an impact reminiscent of those science fiction stories in which the world suddenly encounters a civilization far in advance of its own. Aristotle had systematically answered the widest range of questions on everything from ethics to physics to biology. Students flocked to the universities advertising that they taught Aristotle. For Christian theologians, all this posed at least two problems. First, the whole Augustinian tradition had taught that only faith provided the standpoint from which one could understand the world correctly. Since Aristotle had not been a Christian, how had he managed to understand so much? Second, most theologians had drawn on the idea, going back to Aristotle's teacher Plato, that the road to knowledge involves turning away from the senses and looking inward to the truths known by the soul. Aristotle, on the other hand, taught that all knowledge begins with sense observation.

Some thinkers, like Siger of Brabant, a famous teacher at Paris, wholeheartedly adopted the views of both Aristotle and the famous Arabic commentator on his works, Averroës. These "Latin Averroists" encountered particular difficulties because on several points where Aristotle's meaning was unclear, Averroës had interpreted him in the way least compatible with Christianity. In a notoriously obscure discussion of the soul, for example, Aristotle seemed to say that the "active intellect," the part of our minds which does our thinking and which can survive our deaths, is not separate in each individual, but all human beings share a single active intellect. At least Averroës read it this way. Christianity seemed to teach that souls survive death as individuals to receive rewards and punishments, and that would not be possible if we all share one active intellect. Similarly, Averroës thought of everything as predetermined in a way that seemed to leave no room for human freedom, in which Christianity believed. Averroës himself had treated religion rather condescendingly as a way of looking at the world suitable for people who were not clever enough to understand philosophy. The Latin Averroists rarely went that far, at least in public, but they often protected themselves by claiming to be no more than good historians. They were not asserting the *truth* of anything which contradicted faith, they insisted, but as philosophers their job was to report what Aristotle and Averroës had said, whether it was ultimately true or not. One sometimes suspects their sincerity in this; but if indeed their claim is to be believed, they risked turning the study of philosophy into an antiquarianism teaching only the opinions of Aristotle, not the truth about the world. Yet at first glance the alternative for an Aristotelian would seem to be to abandon faith altogether.

Some church officials therefore forbade the teaching of Aristotle. Some theologians attacked him, claiming that he had not really understood the world so well. The great Franciscan theologian Bonaventure, for instance, argued that, while we can learn from Aristotle on many matters of detail, on a number of basic issues he was simply wrong. For example, Aristotle taught that the world has existed eternally, while Christians believe that God created the world, and that before creation it did not exist. Further, Aristotle denied the separate existence of Platonic forms. For Plato or Augustine, human laws or institutions, to take an example, are "just" to the extent that they resemble or participate in the form of justice, which for Augustine exists in the mind of God. Aristotle thought that justice exists only *in* particular laws and institutions, not somehow separately. To Bonaventure, that meant that God could influence the world only as a first cause who initially created it or as a final goal for which to aim. God could not provide the pattern that shapes creation at every moment. Bonaventure disagreed, developing a vision of all creation as emanating from and then gradually returning to God. The goal of creation "is to be returned, as in an intelligible circle, to its first Principle in whom it will be completed and beatified."[25] Human beings, as spiritual creatures, represent the means through which creation is turning to God. "For since all these creatures were ordained toward the same noble form, the rational soul, once souls have attained their final state of rest, all other things besides must come to completion and repose."[26]

Thomas Aquinas refused either to reject Aristotle or to follow him in everything, and in developing another approach he defined the relation between faith and reason in a new way. In contrast to the cosmic vision of things characteristic of the Franciscan Bonaventure, Aquinas, as a Dominican, depended more on careful argument and analysis. Few authors' works convey so misleading an impression of their lives. His writing flows like a calm stream of argument, carefully considering each objection before formulating his own answer, but the story of his life reads like pure melodrama. When as a boy he decided to become a Dominican, his family kidnapped him and tried to force him to change his mind. He traveled around Europe, always on foot, to participate in theological discussions. In 1256 or 1257, at the age of thirty or so, he became the Dominican professor of theology at the University of Paris at a time when most of the Paris faculty was seeking to drive the Dominicans and Franciscans, whom they disliked and mistrusted, out of the university. Indeed, it took virtually a direct order from the pope to secure his job. He then devoted his career to championing Aristotle at a time when many church officials still considered Aristotle a dangerous anti-Christian influence. Shortly after his death the bishop of Paris condemned a whole series of points he had taught as contrary to the Christian faith. Simply to survive, he learned to keep his thoughts and his emotions to himself. According to later stories at least, his fellow students had thought him rather stupid, for he almost never spoke, and it may be psychologically significant that his handwriting was totally illegible. But once he reached his conclusions, he spoke out fearlessly.

To start with, Aquinas distinguished what we can know by reason from what we can know by revelation. Learning about the habits of fish, for instance, does not require turning to prayer or the Bible. One might better consult the biological works of Aristotle or conduct a scientific experiment. On such matters, human reason provides the answer. On the other hand, if I want to know about the Trinity or the sacraments, neither my reason nor Aristotle's can provide the answer. We know about such things only because God has revealed them. Aquinas thought that some truths are available through both reason and revelation. Philosophers can prove that God exists, for instance, but God has also revealed his existence. There is a good reason for this duplication. The philosophical arguments are complex and require some education and intelligence to understand, but everyone needs to know that God exists in order to be saved. We cannot expect the ploughman in the field to study philosophy for the sake of his salvation. "We also stood in need of being instructed by divine revelation even in religious matters the human reason is able to investigate. For the rational truth about God would have appeared only to few, and even so after a long time and mixed with many mistakes; whereas on knowing this depends our whole welfare, which is in God."[27]

If Thomas distinguished between truths known through reason and those known through revelation, he did not think that reason and revelation can ever contradict each other, since both come from God. As an example, the Latin Averroists noted that reason as represented by Aristotle taught the eternity of the world in contrast to the biblical doctrine of creation, but Aquinas thought he could show on *philosophical* grounds that Aristotle was wrong to be certain of the world's eternity. Reason cannot settle this question one way or the other. Revelation, by telling us that God created the world, does not contradict reason but adds to it.

For Aquinas that is only one case of the relation between nature and grace. "Gifts of grace are added to those of nature in such a way that they do not destroy the latter, but rather perfect them; wherefore also the light of faith . . . does not destroy the natural light of cognition."[28] Augustine had usually contrasted grace with sin; Aquinas gave the state of "nature" new attention. Nature provided a way of understanding human abilities and accomplishments apart from a specifically Christian context. Even apart from grace, the "natural" person could find meaning in existence and try to lead a virtuous life. Aristotle, after all, had described a just government and called people to a life devoted to contemplation, culminating in contemplation of God. Still, in addition to the fact that human natural ends often get corrupted by sin, even in an uncorrupted form they would be incomplete. "Although man has a natural inclination toward his ultimate end, he cannot attain it by natural means but by grace only."[29] Aristotle knew that the highest good of a human being lies in the contemplation of God, but only grace makes that contemplation possible. Yet grace does not destroy nature but perfects it.

As mentioned earlier, Aristotle had posed a further problem for theologians by arguing that knowledge begins with sense observation, not with turning inward away from the senses. Here Aquinas agreed with him. We need to sort out what the senses tell us before we can arrive at knowledge, but the senses do provide the starting point. Aquinas' ways of arguing for the existence of God illustrate this point. As a good Augustinian, Anselm had ignored the senses and focused on the idea of God in our souls as the basis for the ontological argument. Aquinas began with what we observe in the world. To take one of his arguments, we see change in the world around us, but we notice that change in any object is produced by change in some other object. The baseball flies through the air only because the bat swung to hit it.

> Some things in the world are certainly in the process of change. This we plainly see. Now anything in the process of change is being changed by something else. . . . Moreover, this something else, if in process of change, is itself being changed by yet another thing; and this last by another. Now we must stop somewhere, otherwise there will be no first cause of the change, and, as a result, no subsequent causes. . . . If the hand does not move the stick, the stick will not move anything else. Hence one is bound to arrive at some first cause of change not itself being changed by anything, and this is what everybody understands by God.[30]

Aquinas followed a similar pattern through four other arguments, beginning with a series of things we observe and tracing that series to God as its first or highest element.

Of course we cannot observe God through our senses. Therefore, while Aquinas thought that a philosopher can show that God exists, he doubted that reason can tell us much about God's nature. "We cannot know what God is, but only what he is not," he wrote; "we must therefore consider the ways in which God does not exist rather than the ways in which he does."[31] "This is the ultimate in human knowledge of God: to know that we do not know him."[32] Aquinas discussed the nature of God at some length, but his analysis mostly shows what we cannot say about God—we cannot put limits on God, we cannot think of God as divided into parts, and so on. Still, God did create the universe, and God's creatures bear some relation to their creator. Thus Aquinas thought we can use words like "being," "wisdom," and "goodness," whose meaning we learn from observing God's creatures, in an *analogous* sense of God. But he emphasized that it is only an analogy; these words do not mean the same thing when applied to God.

Aquinas' insistence that knowledge begins with the senses was only one side of a new value he gave to human bodies. Platonic philosophy had inspired the greatest Christian theology for over a thousand years, but the Platonic goal of freeing our souls from our bodies had always fit a bit awkwardly with the Christian hope of bodily resurrection. The joyous news of Easter was that our bodies will be raised to eternal life, but a Platonist didn't *want* a body eternally. Here Aristotle fit Christianity better. Aristotle had distinguished between the "matter" and the "form" of a substance. In a bronze statue, the bronze is its matter and the figure it represents is its form. Aristotle, and Aquinas, taught that the soul is the form of the body. We should not think of the soul and body as two separate things, any more than we think of the bronze and its shape as two separate things; rather, the soul is the ordered arrangement that makes these material elements into a human being. In an argument too technical to explain here, both Aristotle and Aquinas concluded that souls (Aristotle said one part of the soul) can exist apart from bodies, but they rejected freeing the soul from the body as the ultimate goal for human beings. Aquinas thought that disembodied souls exist until Christ's second coming and the general resurrection, but he believed that finally we will and should exist as embodied souls.

This new attitude toward the body influenced Aquinas' ethics. In a time that idealized celibacy, he praised the married life too, and not just for "spiritual" reasons. "Married friendship," he wrote, "is useful, delightful, and honorable. It serves to provide for domestic life. It brings the delight of sex and the physical pleasures animals have."[33] He opposed social structures like polygamy which perpetuate inequality between men and women, for "friendship consists in an equality."[34] Aquinas looked favorably at physical desires, including sexual desires, since they are "natural," part of human nature as God created it. Today many people associate that Aristotelian language of "what is natural" with condemnations of birth control or homosexuality as "unnatural." It is at least worth remembering that in Aquinas' thought it functioned primarily to oppose those who praised celibacy as the only truly suitable Christian life. Here too he thought grace added to nature rather than opposing it.

All in all, Thomas Aquinas combined a remarkable set of attitudes. He withdrew into depths of mystic contemplation, but he praised the physical world. He sought to speak with great precision about God, but he emphasized most of all how little we can say about God. He died before the age of fifty; not long before, he had stopped writing altogether, leaving his greatest work incomplete. After a mysterious vision, he told a friend that, in comparison with what he had now seen, all that he had written seemed as worthless as straw.

SOME POLITICAL IMPLICATIONS

Aquinas' political discussions led to some fascinating implications. He can be plausibly cast as either a conservative or a radical. All law, he said, has to begin with God. An eternal law within the mind of God defines what is right and wrong. Our human reason can understand a part of that eternal law, and this participation in the eternal law by human reason is "natural law." Particular human laws should seek to accomplish the purposes of this natural law. On the one hand, this implies that all law comes from God and ought to be obeyed as a religious duty; on the other hand, it means that, if a purported "law" is not consistent with natural law, then it is not really a law at all. Aquinas was emphatic about this. "When the ruler taxes his subjects rather for his own greed or vanity than the common benefit . . . [or] when, although meant for the common good, laws are inequitably dispensed, these are outrages rather than laws."[35] That could easily justify a good many revolutions.

In Aquinas' own time, however, the most influential application of his ideas concerned the relations between church and state. The Concordat of Worms in 1122 had ended lay investiture, establishing a considerably greater independence of the church from outside influences. At about the same time a series of able popes was solidifying papal power. As the preceding chapter noted, popes had long claimed a special kind of authority over all rulers, and at last they seemed in a position to put those claims into practice. Pope Innocent III, elected about 1200, certainly intended to try:

> To me is said in the person of the prophet, "I have set thee over nations and over kingdoms, to root up and to pull down, and to

waste and to destroy, and to rebuild and to plant." . . . You see then who is this servant set over the household, truly the vicar of Jesus Christ, successor of Peter, anointed of the Lord, a God of Pharaoh, set between God and man, lower than God but higher than man, who judges all and is judged by no one.[36]

The pope, he said, had the right to approve or reject any king or emperor. After all, church officials crowned rulers. "If the princes elected as king a sacrilegious man or an excommunicate, a tyrant, a fool, or a heretic . . . ought we to . . . crown such a man? Of course not."[37]

Many of his contemporaries viewed Innocent's claims with alarm. For one thing, medieval people had a strong sense of precedent; the whole feudal system rested on a complex system of traditional rights. Whatever claims might have been made in theory, in practice previous popes had not exercised the rights Innocent now claimed. Further, besides this general claim to authority all over Europe, the pope directly ruled a good bit of central Italy. As a ruler with a territorial interest of his own, he inevitably came into conflict with other rulers, who saw him then as a rival or opponent and therefore could not accept him as an overlord. The tentative emergence of the nation-state and a sense of national identity gradually increased papal problems. In the eleventh century debates on lay investiture or even in the arguments with Innocent III around 1200, one almost never encounters the accusation that the pope is a "foreigner" who should stay out of "our affairs." Around 1300, however, Pope Boniface VIII engaged in a series of disputes with King Philip IV of France, and this time Philip could count on support from people who considered themselves loyal to France and resented the idea of sending money off to Rome or accepting papal interference in French business.

Boniface claimed the same vast authority that Innocent III had asserted a hundred years earlier. Clergy should not pay taxes to the king or otherwise obey royal commands without papal permission. "If the earthly power errs it shall be judged by the spiritual power, if a lesser spiritual power errs it shall be judged by its superior, but if the supreme spiritual power errs it can be judged only by God and not by man."[38] While Innocent had encountered resistance, however, Boniface experienced defeat; at one point some troops from the French king virtually kidnapped him. In part his failures arose from his own personality: he was an old man who suffered from painful gallstones and bursts of temper that alienated even his supporters.

But the new sense of nationalism made papal claims less acceptable to many in any event.

Some of Aquinas' ideas also contributed to changing attitudes toward papal authority. For Augustinians, all knowledge begins with faith. Similarly, all authority could be traced on up to the pope. Aquinas, however, had taught that reason has its own independent tasks and integrity; the biologist need not invoke faith but can look to Aristotle or his own experiments. Applying a parallel, that suggested that the state had its own independent tasks and authority, over which the church should exercise no supervision. To be sure, the church guides us toward eternal salvation, which is a higher goal than the earthly peace and happiness which is the goal of the state, and thus in a sense the church is "higher" than the state, but the state remains independent. As one of Aquinas' students, John of Paris, put it: "There were kings in France before there were Christians. Therefore neither the royal power nor its exercise is from the pope but from God and from the people who elect a king by choosing either a person or a royal house."[39] Monarchy and papacy, like reason and revelation, trace their separate authorities directly to God.

Both Aquinas' defenders and his critics generally see him as the culmination of the Middle Ages, who fit everything together in a grand synthesis in which monastic contemplation and university argumentation came perfectly together. In a sense, however, he achieved that synthesis by tearing things apart. For a thousand years, Christians had thought of their world as a single ordered hierarchy. All knowledge began with faith; all authority depended on the church's blessing. All truth and all authority, Aquinas agreed, come ultimately from God, but in this world he separated the realms of reason and revelation, church and state. Once that separation had been made in principle, it grew steadily wider.

FOR FURTHER READING

INTRODUCTIONS. For a remarkable survey of some central issues in less than a hundred pages by the greatest historian of medieval philosophy, see Etienne Gilson, *Reason and Revelation in the Middle Ages* (Charles Scribner's Sons, 1938). Gilson's *The Spirit of Medieval Philosophy* (Charles Scribner's Sons, 1936) surveys the scene at greater length. G. K. Chesterton, *St. Thomas Aquinas* (Doubleday &

Co., Image Books, 1956), is sometimes dated or eccentric but never dull. For a survey of the whole period, Jeffrey Burton Russell, *A History of Medieval Christianity* (Thomas Y. Crowell Co., 1968).

COLLECTIONS OF ORIGINAL SOURCES. A range of important texts, mostly from the eleventh and twelfth centuries, are collected in Eugene R. Fairweather (ed.), *A Scholastic Miscellany*, in the Library of Christian Classics (Westminster Press, 1956). Brian Tierney, *The Crisis of Church and State 1050–1300* (Prentice-Hall, 1964), offers texts and helpful introductions on church-state relations. Thomas Gilby has gathered together passages from Aquinas organized by topic in *St. Thomas Aquinas: Philosophical Texts* (London: Oxford University Press, 1951), and *St. Thomas Aquinas: Theological Texts* (London: Oxford University Press, 1955). Longer selections are collected in A. M. Fairweather (ed.), *Nature and Grace: Selections from the Summa Theologica* (Westminster Press, 1954), and *Introduction to Saint Thomas Aquinas*, ed. by Anton C. Pegis (Modern Library, 1965). The important texts of Anselm are gathered in *Saint Anselm, Basic Writings*, tr. by S. N. Deane (Open Court Publishing Co., 1966).

IMPORTANT BUT MORE DIFFICULT. On Anselm, see Jasper Hopkins, *A Companion to the Study of St. Anselm* (University of Minnesota Press, 1972), and R. W. Southern, *Saint Anselm and His Biographer* (Cambridge University Press, 1963). On Abelard, see Richard E. Weingart, *The Logic of Divine Love* (Oxford: Clarendon Press, 1970). On Aquinas, there are so many books that one scarcely knows where to start. I have found the most useful to be M.-D. Chenu, *Toward Understanding Saint Thomas*, tr. by A.-M. Landry and D. Hughes (Henry Regnery Co., 1964).

NOTES

1. Rupert of Deutz, *De Trinitate et operibus eius;* quoted in M.-D. Chenu, *Nature, Man, and Society in the Twelfth Century*, tr. by Jerome Taylor and Lester K. Little (University of Chicago Press, 1968), p. 304.
2. Jacopone da Todi, translated in Anne Macdonell, *Sons of Francis* (G. P. Putnam's Sons, 1902), p. 369.
3. William of Conches, *Philosophy of the World* 1.23, in *Patrologia Latina*, ed. by J.-P. Migne, Vol. 172 (Paris: Garnier Fratres, 1894), col. 56; quoted in Chenu, *Nature, Man, and Society in the Twelfth Century*, p. 11.
4. Anselm of Canterbury, *The Incarnation of the Word* 1, in *Anselm of Canterbury*, ed. and tr. by Jasper Hopkins and Herbert Richardson, 3 vols. (Toronto: Edwin Mellen Press, 1976), Vol. 3, pp. 11–12, quoting Isa. 7:9.
5. Anselm of Canterbury, *Proslogion*, ch. 1, in *Anselm of Canterbury*, Vol. 1, p. 93.
6. Bertrand Russell, "My Mental Development," in Paul Arthur Schilpp

(ed.), *The Philosophy of Bertrand Russell* (Tudor Publishing Co., 1944), p. 10.
   7.   Anselm of Canterbury, *Proslogion* 2, in Hopkins and Richardson, *Anselm of Canterbury,* Vol. 1, pp. 93–94.
   8.   Anselm of Canterbury, *A Meditation on Human Redemption,* in ibid., p. 138.
   9.   Anselm of Canterbury, *Why God Became Man* 1.19, in Hopkins and Richardson, *Anselm of Canterbury,* Vol. 3, p. 85.
   10.   Ibid., 1.20, p. 88.
   11.   Ibid., 2.17, p. 127.
   12.   Ibid., preface, p. 43.
   13.   Peter Abelard, *The Story of Abelard's Adversities,* ch. 3, tr. by J. T. Muckle (Toronto: Pontifical Institute of Medieval Studies, 1954), p. 22.
   14.   Peter Abelard, *Exposition of the Epistle to the Romans,* in Eugene R. Fairweather (ed.), *A Scholastic Miscellany* (Westminster Press, 1956), p. 283.
   15.   Ibid.
   16.   Peter Abelard, *The Story of Abelard's Adversities,* ch. 6, ibid., p. 26.
   17.   Ibid., ch. 7, p. 34.
   18.   Heloise, The Fourth Letter, in *The Letters of Abelard and Heloise,* tr. by C. K. Scott Moncrieff (Alfred A. Knopf, 1942), p. 81. Some scholars claim that Heloise's letters were written by Abelard or by some anonymous figure well after the event, but I find their arguments unpersuasive.
   19.   Bernard of Clairvaux, *An Apologia to Abbot William* 12.28, tr. by Michael Casey, in *The Works of Bernard of Clairvaux,* Vol. 1 (Cistercian Publications, 1970), pp. 65–66.
   20.   Bernard of Clairvaux, *Treatise Against Several Erroneous Chapters by Peter Abelard,* in *Patrologia Latina,* Vol. 182 (Paris: Garnier Fratres, 1897), col. 1067; quoted in Richard E. Weingart, *The Logic of Divine Love* (Oxford: Clarendon Press, 1970), p. 202.
   21.   Quoted in Frederick Copleston, *A History of Philosophy,* Vol. 2 (Newman Press, 1952), p. 175.
   22.   Bernard of Clairvaux, *On the Song of Songs,* Sermon 83, tr. by Irene Edmonds, in *The Works of Bernard of Clairvaux,* Vol. 4 (Cistercian Publications, 1980), p. 182.
   23.   Bernard of Clairvaux, *On Loving God* 10.28, tr. by Robert Walton, in *The Works of Bernard of Clairvaux,* Vol. 5 (Cistercian Publications Consortium Press, 1974), p. 120.
   24.   *The Legend of the Three Companions* 35; quoted in John Moorman, *A History of the Franciscan Order* (Oxford: Clarendon Press, 1968), p. 13.
   25.   Bonaventure, *The Breviloquium,* tr. by José de Vinck, *The Works of Bonaventure,* Vol. 2 (St. Anthony Guild Press, 1966), p. 80.
   26.   Ibid., p. 292.
   27.   Thomas Aquinas, *Summa Theologiae* 1a.1.1, tr. by Thomas Gilby, Vol. 1 (Blackfriars, 1964), p. 7.
   28.   Thomas Aquinas, *Commentary on the Trinity* 3.2, in *The Trinity, and The Unicity of the Intellect,* tr. by Rose Emmanuella Brennan (B. Herder Book Co., 1946), p. 59.
   29.   Thomas Aquinas, *Commentary on Boethius' "On the Trinity"* 6.4 ad 18m; quoted in Etienne Gilson, *The Spirit of Thomism* (P. J. Kenedy & Sons, 1964), p. 57.

30. Thomas Aquinas, *Summa Theologiae* 1a.2.3, tr. by Timothy McDermott, Vol. 2 (Blackfriars, 1964), pp. 13, 15.

31. Ibid., 1a.3, prologue, Vol. 2, p. 19.

32. Thomas Aquinas, *Disputed Questions on the Power of God* 7.5. ad 4; quoted in Josef Pieper, *The Silence of St. Thomas* (Pantheon Books, 1957), p. 37.

33. Thomas Aquinas, *Commentary on the Nicomachean Ethics of Aristotle* 8, lecture 12; quoted in Thomas Gilby (ed.), *Thomas Aquinas, Theological Texts* (London: Oxford University Press, 1955), p. 385.

34. Thomas Aquinas, *On the Truth of the Catholic Faith* 3.124, tr. by Vernon J. Bourke (Doubleday & Co., Image Books, 1956), p. 152.

35. Thomas Aquinas, *Summa Theologiae* 1a-2ae.96.4, tr. by Thomas Gilby, Vol. 28 (Blackfriars, 1964), p. 131.

36. Innocent III, *Sermon on the Consecration of a Pope,* in *Patrologia Latina,* Vol. 217 (Paris: Garnier Fratres, 1890), cols. 657–658; quoted in Brian Tierney, *The Crisis of Church and State 1050–1300* (Prentice-Hall, 1964), pp. 131–132.

37. Innocent III, *Venerabilem;* quoted in Tierney, op. cit., pp. 133–134.

38. Boniface VIII, *Unam sanctam;* quoted in Tierney, op. cit., p. 189.

39. John of Paris, *Tractatus de potestate regia et papali;* quoted in Tierney, op. cit., p. 208.

11

THE ABSOLUTE POWER OF GOD

Time of mourning and temptation,
  Age of envy, torment, tears,
Time of languor and damnation,
  Age of last declining years,
Time of falseness, full of horror,
  Age of lying, envy, strife,
Time without true judgment, honor,
  Age of sadness, shortening life.

—Eustache Deschamps, writing
in the fourteenth century[1]

Europe had a difficult time in the fourteenth century. Chronic inflation drove many of the poor into starvation. The Black Death carried off a third of the continent's population. England and France began a hundred years of warfare. For a generation rival popes claimed the allegiance of Christians, each excommunicating those who acknowledged the other, and a popular legend had it that during all this time no one entered heaven. Amid such crises even the world described by Aquinas, in which reason supported revelation, and church and state worked together for the good of humanity, seemed increasingly implausible. "Faith" and "reason" split farther apart. A newly dominant philosophy called "nominalism" raised questions about the order that earlier philosophers had thought to be built into the universe. The nominalists believed that much of the way we order the world rests on our own choice, not on a natural and eternal design. Applied to theology, nominalism could make our salvation seem more arbitrary and more individual; it undercut the old ways of making Christ's work seem an appropriate way of saving all humanity. In the same period disputes among popes and councils weakened confidence in the church as the vehicle of salvation. As the fifteenth century began, some Christians turned away in disgust from the increasingly complicated theological debates and the conflicts of church politics and sought simply to lead decent and pious lives, with more concern for this world and human problems. It may have been a bad time to live through, but the fourteenth and fifteenth centuries are fascinating to study, for all these problems produced creative theological responses.

NOMINALISM

Philosophic developments in the late Middle Ages had an important impact on theology. An explanation of those developments has to begin by defining two basic terms—"realism" and "nominalism." It is easiest to begin with an example: As I look out my window just now, I see three clouds. They are quite different in shape, size, and color, yet I call all three "clouds." How can I give the same name to different things? A *realist,* like Plato or Augustine, would say that there exists some "form" or "universal" of what a cloud is, perhaps in an eternal realm of forms, perhaps in the mind of God, and those three things up in the sky are all clouds because they all resemble that form or universal. It is as if God has drawn up a blueprint for clouds, and anything counts as a cloud if it roughly corresponds to that blueprint. A *nominalist* denies the separate existence of such forms or universals. Only particular individual objects exist; forms or universals are not real entities, they are just names *(nomina).* I apply the same name ("cloud") to those three things because people who speak English have agreed to do so, but there is no single correct way of dividing up the world. We might, for instance, have agreed to use one word for both fog and white clouds and quite another word for the dark clouds of a thunderstorm. An extreme realist might say, "That's wrong, because there's an eternal form of cloud, and our classifications ought to correspond to the eternal order of things," but a nominalist would reply: "There isn't any eternal order of classification. We divide things into categories for our own convenience, and there's no right or wrong to it."

Realism dominated the early Middle Ages, but under Aristotle's influence Aquinas sought a compromise. "Ideas are in God for the purpose of knowing and making," he wrote, "but . . . singulars have acts of existence more truly than universals do, because the latter subsist only in singulars."[2] In other words, there is no "universal idea of cloud" existing independently, but just particular clouds. Nevertheless, God has always thought of clouds as belonging to a single class, so when we apply a single name to all of them, we are following a divine order, not creating one of our own.

Aquinas emphasized the importance of universals in another way too, by insisting that we can have knowledge only of forms or universals. I have *sensations* when I stare at that thing in the sky, according to Aquinas, but I have no *knowledge* until I go beyond that particular object to a form or universal and say, "Oh, that's a cloud." This might seem an odd theory. Surely, someone could protest, "I know my brother Sam, and Sam is a particular individual, not a universal." But what you *know,* Aquinas would reply, is that Sam is bearded, blond, intelligent, and so on, and "beardedness," "blondness," and "intelligence" are all universal terms. In all this, Aquinas meant to establish that we do not invent an order to the universe; there's an objective order out there, and in our knowing we find it.

John Duns Scotus, a Franciscan born in Scotland around 1266, near the end of Aquinas' life, disagreed with Aquinas on a number of points. First, he developed a very technical theory of the role of universals, according to which it is possible to know an individual. I do not just know blondness, beardedness, and intelligence, I know my brother Sam. Second, Aquinas had taught that we can know a number of truths, like the existence and some attributes of God, by either reason or revelation. Scotus had a more rigorous standard of philosophic proof, and he rejected some of Aquinas' arguments on religious matters. He did not deny the conclusions; he simply said that these are things we can know only by faith, not through reason. Third, Aquinas' discussions of God usually began with God's *intellect;* Scotus focused on God's *will.* Aquinas would approach a problem by asking what God would reasonably do. Scotus doubted that we can figure out God's reasoning. We have to look and see what God has willed to do. To the question, "Why does his will will?" Scotus answers, "There is no reason except that will is will."[3] Aquinas had taught that if Adam had not sinned, the incarnation would not have happened—there would have been no reason for God to become a human being. Scotus said that God would have become incarnate in any event, as the only way of perfectly expressing his love of humanity. For Scotus the incarnation became a pure expression of God's loving will, not something God did for a reason.

In all these new ideas, Scotus introduced a greater element of the arbitrary. As universals became less important to theories of knowledge, our ordering of the world seemed more our own invention and less the discovery of God's plan. If reason has a smaller role in theology and God's will comes more to the fore, then theology becomes more a matter of believing what is revealed and less a matter of applying reason to see the logic of things. The universe stops looking so much like a rationally ordered whole. Scotus argued with great precision, but his conclusions ultimately implied a smaller role for reason and argument in theology. In that respect, he has more in common with the earlier Franciscan Bonaventure, and his emphasis on faith and contemplation, than with the greater role given reason by the Dominican Aquinas.

Another Franciscan, William of Ockham, continued that tradition of using reason to show reason's limitations. Historians used to classify Ockham as the greatest of the nominalists. Some recent scholars, noting the differences between Ockham and more extreme forms of nominalism, refuse to call him a nominalist at all. But Ockham certainly did develop several of the themes already mentioned in directions characteristic of nominalism. He was born, near London, sometime in the 1280s, and died in 1347. He joined the Franciscans and studied at Oxford but never taught there. No one knows why, but it seems likely he failed to get a job because he had angered someone in authority. He often did. At any rate, someone at Oxford denounced him to the pope, and Ockham had to go to the papal court at Avignon in France to defend himself.

Unfortunately, he arrived in the midst of a campaign by Pope John XXII against the Franciscans. In the last chapter we saw how in the thirteenth century the spiritual Franciscans lost their struggle to require their members to live in absolute poverty. At that time a compromise had distinguished between "ownership" and "use." The Franciscans preserved their ideal of poverty in theory by "owning" nothing, with the understanding that they *used* things legally owned by friends of the order or by the pope. John XXII resented Franciscan criticisms of the wealth of the church, particularly since they often had the use of the wealth they were criticizing. He denied the distinction between ownership and use and, in effect, ordered the Franciscans not to be poor any more. A number of leading Franciscans, including Ockham, fled to the court of Emperor Louis in Bavaria, who was himself feuding with the pope, and Ockham spent much of his life under papal excommunication writing propaganda for the emperor.

Ockham's theology began with a sense of the absolute power of God. God can do anything that doesn't involve a logical contradiction —an exception Ockham made only because it makes no sense to talk about something that is logically contradictory. God can take Saul, the persecutor of the church, and make him a saint. He can intervene and make anything happen, no matter how contrary to the usual laws of nature. He can declare acts we would normally consider sinful to be virtuous. "An act is called meritorious because it is accepted by God," and God can accept whatever he wants.[4] Theology therefore cannot begin with what God ought to do or reasonably would do; it must stick to the revelation of what God has in fact done.

Ockham is most famous among philosophers for a principle called "Ockham's razor," according to which we should not posit the existence of more entities than we need to explain the data we have—the razor "shaves off" unnecessary entities. Suppose, for instance, that I arrive home to discover the living room in a shambles and my badly trained dog hiding from me under the bed. I would not immediately conclude that a burglar must have broken into the house. The dog suffices to explain the chaos, without positing another entity such as a burglar.

Ockham justified his move toward nominalism by appeal to the razor. If I can see and talk about individual objects like three clouds, there is no need to posit the existence of something else called the "form of cloud." The relation of such ideas to scientific method is complicated—Ockham's contemporary Roger Bacon, the clearest precursor of modern scientific method at the time, was an extreme realist—but this emphasis on not going beyond one's data is at least an attitude with which modern scientists would sympathize.

Just as Scotus' emphasis on God's will had affinities with the decreasing importance he gave to universals, so his belief in God's absolute power connects with Ockham's move toward nominalism. If God is full of surprises and need not follow any rules, then a philosopher had better look at each particular object and not make grand assumptions or universal conclusions. Someone who believes that God can be arbitrary has to look at each individual to see what God has done this time. Thus, against Aquinas' belief that we can know only universals, Ockham thought we can know individual objects more certainly than anything else.

None of this implied the denial of any traditional doctrines, and Ockham did not question them, but he did bring a new theological attitude. Reason had a smaller role in theology. We must simply take God's revelation on faith more often. Moreover, nominalism raised questions about the social order. Realists who believed that the way we order the universe corresponds to an eternal and true order tended to think of institutions and hierarchies as eternal and good as well. But if those three things in the sky are all "clouds" simply because we have decided to give them the same name, then maybe the pope is the pope simply because we have decided to give *that* name to *him.* "It is up to men," Ockham declared, "to designate a particular person as Pope and to decide who will elect him and who will correct him if he needs correction."[5] (He was not, incidentally, using "men" in a limited sense, for he thought women should be represented in a general council too.[6]) More traditional theologians argued that ordinary folk should not presume to correct the pope, for the pope and the church hierarchy generally would never diverge from the spirit of Christ. Had not Christ promised his apostles he would be "with you always"? But Christ did not, Ockham replied, promise always to be with the pope. Christ's promise would be fulfilled even if only one believer held to the truth, or even if true faith existed only potentially in baptized infants.[7] Just as God has not given us an eternally ordered world but left us to order it for ourselves, so God has not given us a perfect church to be obeyed, but left the task of shaping the church to us. In the Middle Ages, the idea that social structures rest on our choices, not an external order, contained the seeds of revolution, and one of Ockham's fellow exiles at the emperor's court, Marsilius of Padua, wrote one of the most radical political treatises of the time. All authority derives from the people, Marsilius said, and the people or their leaders ought to correct the church whenever they see it in need of correction. Thus in different ways principles of both modern science (stick close to observed data) and modern democracy (the people decide how things should be ordered) began with nominalism and the belief in the absolute power of God.

PATHS TO SALVATION

Nominalism had a more immediate impact on theological theories of salvation. In the past, most theologians had taught that Christ saves humanity by uniting it with divinity or changing humanity's relationship with God. Now nominalism implied that there is no such thing as "humanity," merely a great many particular individuals. Ockham still believed that Christ saves us, but he rejected theories like Anselm's which tried to show how it was appropriate or reasonable that God should save us by acting in this particular way. God simply chooses to save us in this way, Ockham said. If he had wanted to, he could have saved us by becoming an ass instead of becoming a human being—a melodramatic phrase from a book that reflects Ockham's ideas, though he may not have written it himself.[8] It follows that God need not follow any rules in salvation. Judas, one of the twelve apostles, can betray Christ, while Paul becomes a saint. Yet having made that point in principle, Ockham and his followers retreated. "God *can* do many things that he *will not* do," Ockham explained.[9] God *can* do *anything,* but normally he follows rules, and one rule is that people who have tried to lead good lives are more likely to be saved. "If he should choose to," wrote the English theologian Robert Holcot, "God could deviate from his law," but ordinarily, "according to God's established law the pilgrim who does whatever he can to dispose himself for grace always receives grace."[10] That meant that our efforts contribute to our salvation. As Ockham's admirer Gabriel Biel put it late in the fifteenth century, "Though the passion of Christ is the *principal* merit on account of which grace is infused, the kingdom opened, and glory granted, yet it is never the *sole and complete* meritorious cause. If we do not add our merits to those of Christ, the merits of Christ will not only be insufficient, but nonexistent."[11]

A contemporary of Ockham's, the English writer Thomas Bradwardine, published a book denouncing this emphasis on our contribution to our salvation as Pelagianism, the heresy of believing that we can win salvation through our efforts, which Augustine had fought centuries before. "I am not unaware," he noted grimly, "how the pestilential Pelagians . . . will strive to tear this small treatise with their savage teeth."[12] Bradwardine argued that Augustine had shown how Pelagius would replace our gratitude for God's grace with human pride, and how the only way to avoid that error is to insist that we cannot earn God's grace in any sense. It goes to those to whom God chooses to give it, without regard for merit. Now theologians associated with nominalism like Ockham, Halcot, and Biel were rejecting Augustine and going back to Pelagius.

This debate may point to an underlying psychological tension. Augustinians like Bradwardine thought that the world has an eternal order, established in the mind of God. Even if God chooses the saved arbitrarily, therefore, their world did not fall into complete anarchy. The nominalists, on the other hand, believed that the order we make of things rests on our choices, a much less secure position, and therefore they needed to think that there are rules and patterns in the process of salvation. If one tried to be a nominalist and an Augustinian at the same time, the world seemed so chaotic that it could drive one to the edge of madness—as it did to an Augustinian monk trained in nominalism named Martin Luther.

When theology grew more confused and questions arose about the saving of "humanity," mystical experience could offer an immediate confidence at least in one's own salvation. Not surprisingly, many, from sophisticated intellectuals to the common folk, turned to mysticism in the fourteenth century. Around 1300 the German Dominican Meister Eckhart urged his readers to turn away from the world and look to the spark of their soul deep within them, for there God will be found. "In that core is the central silence, the pure peace, an abode of heavenly birth. . . . God enters the soul with all that he has."[13]

> The seed of God is in us. Given an intelligent farmer and a diligent fieldhand, it will thrive and grow up to God whose seed it is, and, accordingly, its fruit will be God-nature. Pear seeds grow into pear trees; nut seeds into nut trees, and God-seed into God.[14]

Such language, especially when preached in German to a popular audience, made some church leaders nervous. God is God, they insisted, and we are God's creatures, separate from God. In saying that a spark within our souls can become God, Eckhart risked losing that distinction between God and creatures. Mysticism may be, in fact, the only field in which metaphysics is more controversial than sex. No one challenged those, like Bernard of Clairvaux, who used the language of physical love and sexual *union* to describe the relationship between God and a human being, but references like Eckhart's to metaphysical *unity* raised suspicions of heresy. In union the two partners remain distinct; in unity they merge, and the idea of humans merging into God, common in the early and Eastern churches, now seemed too daring.

Although charged with heresy, Eckhart remained loyal to the church. He recognized that mystical experience is not the most important part of Christian life. "If a person were in such a rapturous state as St. Paul once entered, and he knew of a sick man who wanted a cup of soup, it would be far better to withdraw from the rapture for love's sake, and serve him who is in need."[15] If the church hierarchy remained chronically nervous about mysticism, it was partly because the claim to direct encounter with God always risked rendering the hierarchy irrelevant. Even in its completely orthodox form, respectful of the hierarchy, mysticism had a democratic flavor; one did not need education or influence to seek God within. Jean Gerson, chancellor of the University of Paris at the very end of the fourteenth century, argued for the superiority of mystical theology over the "scholastic theology" of theologians like Scotus and Ockham precisely because, in addition to being more conducive to real piety, it was open to more Christians. He tried to reorganize the university's curriculum to increase its practical emphasis on the development of the religious life. Women, denied access to the kind of education that made participation in many theological debates possible, could report with authority on their own experience. Julian of Norwich, for instance, an English-woman born about 1340, had lived a simple pious life until the age of thirty, when she had a series of visions of the dying Christ in which God revealed some of the mysteries of the faith to her. "I am a woman, trusting, feeble and frail," she acknowledged. "But I know well this that I say; I have it on the revelation of him that is the sovereign teacher."[16] Julian (like Anselm) often used feminine language of God; she regularly talked of Jesus as our mother.

> The mother's service is nearest, readiest and surest; nearest: for it is most kind; readiest: for it is most of love; surest: for it is most of truth. . . . The mother can give her child to suck of her milk. But our precious Mother Jesus, he can feed us with himself; and doth, full courteously and tenderly, with the Blessed Sacrament.[17]

Such language aroused no protests. As already noted, the worry about mysticism was that it operated outside the usual structures of the church. But those structures were undergoing a major crisis.

COUNCILS AND REBELS

In 1309 a French pope moved the papal court from Rome to Avignon in southern France. The political situation in Rome had reached such a point that the pope could no longer feel safe in the city, but the move away from Rome with all its traditions somehow lowered papal prestige, and other countries suspected that popes living in Avignon would fall too far under French influence. In 1378 Pope Gregory XI died while on a visit back to Rome. When the cardinals met to elect a successor, a angry mob surrounded the building, demanding the election of an Italian pope who would return the papal court, together with all the business it generated, to Rome. The cardinals complied, electing the archbishop of Bari, who became Pope Urban VI. Afterwards, however, many claimed that they had acted in fear of their lives, and a majority of the cardinals slipped out of town, declared the original election invalid, chose a French pope, and returned to Avignon.

Each pope soon excommunicated his opponent's supporters, and Europe divided, with some countries generally supporting one candidate, some the other. Both sides had their share of reasonable arguments, and popes had traditionally claimed that no one but God could judge the pope, so who could adjudicate between them? Some scholars, particularly at the University of Paris under its chancellor Jean Gerson, suggested that a general council might settle the matter. Only the pope could call a general council, however. As one writer, Conrad of Gelnhausen, explained, "It is impossible for the general Council to be held . . . without the authority of the Pope. But to convene such a council in the present case the authority of the Pope cannot step in, because no single person is generally recognized as Pope."[18] Gradually some "conciliarists" (those who supported the idea of a council) began to ask whether only the pope could call a council. After all, the Emperor Constantine had convened the Council of Nicaea. Besides, suppose the pope were captured by the Muslims, and no one knew if he remained alive, or suppose he went mad or became a heretic. In such an emergency, someone else would have to call a council. Did not the split of the church represent as great a crisis?

The conciliarists, however, could not agree on just how far to carry such ideas. Some thought the pope remained in all ordinary circumstances head of the church, and only the odd case of having two popes at once justified appealing to a council. A cardinal named Uguccione, for instance, explained that people other than the pope were usually forbidden to call a council because it would divide the church if all sorts of people claimed this right. But "that justification fails in the present case, for the cardinals do not choose a council to disturb the unity of the church, but to restore it. . . . The case of the present schism has no parallel in the law nor in the chronicles. . . . Therefore human ingenuity must find a way out of the said schism by any reasonable means."[19] Other conciliarists, however, went beyond the particular emergency to argue that no one individual should rule the church without checks and balances even in normal circumstances. In the blunt words of Dietrich of Niem, "the Pope . . . is a man of the earth, clay from clay, a sinner liable to sin, but two days ago the son of a poor peasant. . . . The Pope cannot become an angel. A Pope as Pope is a man and as Pope can sin even as a man can err."[20] Therefore a council ought to meet regularly to supervise the pope.

Behind all these disputes lay a deeper problem of church corruption. Earlier in the Middle Ages increasing papal power had seemed the best way to correct abuses, for only a strong pope could achieve effective reforms. To some extent that program had succeeded, but a stronger centralized administration had required a steadily larger bureaucracy, and popes had to devise more and more ways of obtaining money to support that bureaucracy. It seemed, one contemporary observer noted, "as though the Lord, instead of driving the buyers and sellers from the Temple, had rather shut them up inside it."[21] Perhaps the greatest tragedy of the schism was that disputes between rival popes and conciliarists diverted attention from such more basic difficulties.

In 1410 a council meeting at Pisa deposed both popes and elected another. Unfortunately, both of the previous incumbents rejected the council's legitimacy, so it succeeded only in increasing the problem by fifty percent. In 1415, however, a council at Constance managed to unify the whole church behind its choice for pope, Martin V. The council further declared that it, not the pope, headed the church:

> This holy synod, constituting the general council of Constance
> ... declares that ... it holds power directly from Christ; and that
> everyone of whatever estate or dignity he be, even papal, is
> obliged to obey it in those things which belong to the faith, and
> to the eradication of the ... schism, and to the general reform of
> the ... church of God in head and members.[22]

The council required the pope to call a council at regular intervals in the future, the next in five years. Constance claimed authority as an assembly representing the church—authority even over the pope. That gave official sanction to the radical idea, proposed earlier by Marsilius of Padua, that authority might flow upward rather than down from above. On the other hand, it would be wrong to call the council "democratic," for it included only high officials in the church and it asserted the authority of the hierarchy over popular protest in the most dramatic way possible by burning the popular leader John Hus at the stake.

The story of Hus and his condemnation can be understood only against the background of earlier protest movements. The plagues and food shortages of the fourteenth century had produced a long series of passionate religious outbursts. Troupes of flagellants traveled from city to city, decrying the sins of the time and beating themselves until the blood flowed. Secret societies awaited the coming or the return of some great leader who would put things right. Many expected the second coming of Christ in the near future. Some groups attacked the clergy; they denounced sinful priests and denied the efficacy of the sacraments they performed. Others even raised questions about the whole existing order of society. A later chronicler reported the speech of John Ball, the leader of the English peasants' revolt of 1381:

My friends, the state of England cannot be right until everything is held communally, and until there is no distinction between nobleman and serf, and we are all as one. Why are those whom we call lords masters over us? ... We are all descended from our first parents, Adam and Eve; how then can they say that they are better lords than us, except in making us toil and earn for them to spend?[23]

Such popular uprisings had little lasting success, however, and they often seemed intellectually confused. They mixed democratic ideals with hopes for a great emperor and combined dreams of equality with nightmares of vicious anti-Semitism. Indeed the church hierarchy often had to try to protect Jews from the assaults of such groups.

In England John Wyclif, who died in 1384, developed more of an intellectual foundation for protest against the church hierarchy. Wyclif joined many others in denouncing the wealth and corruption of the church. "If Christ would have not so much as a little house in which to rest his head," he asked, ". . . how should Christ's vicar be so great a lord in this world?"[24] "The wicked Pope is the anti-Christ and the devil, for he is both lying itself and the father of lies."[25] Wyclif based his attacks on Augustine's doctrine of predestination. Those predestined to salvation, and no others, will be saved—and therefore all the efforts of the institutional church cannot really help or hinder our salvation. Rather than turning to the church as our authority in matters of faith, Wyclif urged turning to the Bible. "Every Christian ought to study this book because it is the whole truth."[26] For everyone in England to study the Bible, of course, it would have to be translated into English—and why not? "Christ and his apostles taught the people in the tongue that was best known to them. Why should men not do so now?"[27] It is not clear just how much translating Wyclif himself did, but he inspired the work which others completed.

Wyclif hoped that the state might force the church to reform. He supported John of Gaunt, the leader of a party that opposed papal power and sought to confiscate church property. People with motives less honorable than his own may have taken advantage of Wyclif, but he himself, while demanding greater democracy in the church, took care not to apply his democratic principles to the kingdom. In any event, the political winds soon shifted, and Wyclif, finding himself without powerful friends, retired to a country church. He had followed Augustine in believing that the bread and wine of the Eucharist became Christ's body and blood only in a spiritual sense, and by this time the church had adopted transubstantiation as doctrine, so shortly after Wyclif's death he was declared a heretic and the teaching of his works was forbidden at Oxford. His movement lost its intellectual side, and it survived only among popular preachers, the Lollards, who traveled in poverty around England, carrying the English translation of the Bible to the ordinary people.

John Hus, who was born in Bohemia about 1372, roughly twelve years before Wyclif died, and who greatly admired the Englishman, found much wider support for a similar program of reform. The Czechs of Bohemia had for some time struggled to assert their own national identity against the Germans, and that effort merged with an attack on church corruption. Hus preached in Czech, denouncing "priests . . . who shamefully squander pay for requiem Masses in fornication, in adorning their concubines, priestesses, or prostitutes . . . from the tithes and offerings of the poor."[28] Hus and his followers formulated a series of demands. No one should interfere with popular preaching. All the people should receive wine as well as bread in the Eucharist. (The custom that only the priest drank the wine had begun in an effort to avoid spilling Christ's blood, but it had for some become a symbol of the gap between priests and ordinary Christians.) The clergy should give up their wealth, and their sins should be properly punished.

The Council of Constance charged Hus with heresy and ordered him to come to face the charges. The emperor guaranteed his safety, but he was betrayed, arrested, and burned at the stake. "They will roast a goose now," he cried ("Hus" means "goose" in Czech), "but after a hundred years they will hear a swan sing,"[29] and Luther wrote his first protests almost exactly a hundred years later. Hus' trial had been a farce. He was convicted of agreeing with Wyclif, but he consistently rejected Wyclif's teaching on the Eucharist, the only point that had ever been declared heretical. It seems as if, perhaps unconsciously, the leaders of the council, having taken a radical stand by opposing papal authority, had to establish their moderation and respectability by finding someone even more radical to condemn.

Hus' movement continued among the Czechs, and, after a long guerrilla war reached a stalemate, the pope granted a number of their demands. Thus they finally had more success than the conciliarists, who had had their greatest victory at Constance. Only the crisis of the schism had drawn moderate support for the power of a council, and now the schism had ended. When the Council of Basel a few years later tried to reassert the rights claimed by Constance, Pope Eugenius IV easily defeated it. As mentioned above in Chapter 7, he entered into negotiations with the Eastern church and invited the council down to Florence to ratify the union of East and West. Half of the council went, but the other half distrusted the pope and stayed up in Switzerland. A council had triumphed over a divided papacy, but now a pope could easily triumph over a divided council, and Eugenius proclaimed that the pope holds "the primacy of the whole world, and that the Roman pontiff is the successor of blessed Peter, prince of the apostles, and the true vicar of Christ, the head of the whole Church."[30]

The German philosopher and mystic Nicholas of Cusa defended the pope's triumph. Like many mystics, Cusa believed that God lies beyond the capacities of our understanding. We speak of God best from a "learned ignorance" that acknowledges how little we can know of him. We usually apply our intellects to finite things, which are one thing and not another—large and not small, straight and not curved. But God is infinite, and in him all opposites come together and achieve reconciliation. Cusa applied that idea of the reconciliation of opposing forces to church politics. The best governance, he said, is not one of absolute papal power, or of absolute democracy, or of domination by any one group, but the cooperation of all parties in the church. He began as a conciliarist, for he thought a general council best represented such a concord. By the time of Eugenius, however, he said that the pope and the part of the council which had come to Italy represented the concord of the whole church better than the rump council still in Basel.

In defeating the conciliar movement, however, the popes won a hollow victory. For most Christians, the central problem was the corruption of the church, which often took too much of their money and in return provided ignorant or corrupt priests who scarcely inspired confidence as the guardians of the means of salvation. Popes and councils had spent so much time fighting each other that they had little left over for the task of reform, and now popes feared to call a council to organize a major reform lest they begin conciliarism all over again.

TOWARD HUMANISM AND SIMPLE PIETY

While philosophers and theologians debated increasingly technical issues, and popes and councils feuded, many Christians turned away from all the technicalities and all the politics. Surely, they thought, Christ cared more about how we live our lives and how we try to love each other. A group of related movements centered in the Netherlands, loosely called the "Modern Devotion," gathered lay men and women together, often to live communally and to devote themselves to prayer and charity. Unlike nuns or monks or friars, most of them did not take permanent vows. They kept their jobs, and sometimes their families, while trying to live in obedience to Christ. "We are not Religious," one wrote (meaning monks or nuns), "but we wish and strive to live in the world religiously."[31] That mattered more than details of doctrine. In the words of the most famous book of this movement, *The Imitation of Christ,*

> If thou knewest the whole Bible by heart and the sayings of all the philosophers, what would it profit thee without the love of God and without grace? . . . Indeed a humble husbandman that serveth God is better than a proud philosopher who, though occupied in studying the course of the stars, neglecteth himself.[32]

That practical emphasis, together with their refusal to withdraw from the world of jobs and families, indicated the beginnings of a new kind of Christian ideal.

A similar new spirit dominated much of the religious thought of the Renaissance. In any history of art, the Renaissance would fill one of the longest chapters. A history of theology can touch on it rather briefly. That in itself says something: Theology did not lie at the center of this period's creative energies. Still, the Renaissance did not represent a return to paganism or a move to heresy. Given the view of "humanism" as an enemy of Christianity often heard these days, it is important to emphasize that most of the great Renaissance humanists shared a deep piety and an orthodox theology. They did not represent a new philosophical point of view so much as a new set of interests, above all a commitment to study the classical texts with an interest in their literary value. The typical humanist was the secretary of some nobleman or city-state, interested in developing eloquence and literary style on classical models. He might hold any sort of philosophy, or none at all, but he was almost certainly a Christian.

Like the Modern Devotion, however, the Renaissance humanists often paid more attention to the practical affairs of this world than, say, the ideal medieval monk. One Italian humanist, Benedetto Morandi, conveyed the new spirit in his interpretation of the passage in Genesis where God puts Adam and Eve to work cultivating the earth. The traditional reading made the need to work part of the punishment for their sin, but Morandi thought it a good thing that we should lead our lives

> not in enfeebling leisure but always in doing something. . . . What therefore does it profit a man to know, to feel, to believe if there

was nothing to be done by man? . . . And since man is a social animal it befits him to build palaces, homes and cities, to cultivate fields . . . , to cross rivers with bridges, to purge cities with sewers.[33]

One would not describe Bernard of Clairvaux or Francis of Assisi as living in "enfeebling leisure," but they did not devote their lives to building bridges or sewers either. This life had been mostly a preparation for the next, this world an evil place to test our patience. Now fifteenth-century writers were suggesting that we ought to get to work on improving this world. "The world and all its beauties seem to have been first invented and established by Almighty God for the use of man," wrote Giannozzo Manetti, "and afterwards gratefully received by man and rendered more beautiful and much more ornate and far more refined."[34] Any orthodox theologian would have praised the world God created, but it was something new to suggest that we might improve on God's efforts. That way of looking at the world as raw material to be remade rather than a glory to be contemplated would have profound effects.

Perhaps people turned to such new hopes in part because the old hopes seemed so shaky. Nominalism had raised basic questions about the nature of the order we see around us. Do we see an eternal order there, or merely invent one for our own purposes? Theologians continued to debate the role of human efforts in salvation, and their very inability to agree undermined confidence that anyone knew the answers. Division and corruption in the church further decreased confidence that a church full of rich bishops and illegally married priests could really bear God's salvation to God's people. If people had lost interest in religion, none of this would have mattered much. It was precisely because people in the fifteenth century cared so much about their salvation that they found themselves so often frustrated with their church and its theology.

FOR FURTHER READING

INTRODUCTIONS. For two excellent surveys of the period, Francis Oakley, *The Western Church in the Later Middle Ages* (Cornell University Press, 1979), and Steven E. Ozment, *The Age of Reform* (Yale University Press, 1980), which, in defiance of the usual periodization, covers the period from about 1250 through the Reformation. Norman

Cohn, *The Pursuit of the Millennium* (Essential Books, 1957), describes the wilder apocalypticists with real verve.

COLLECTIONS OF ORIGINAL SOURCES. C. M. D. Crowder, *Unity, Heresy and Reform, 1378–1460* (London: Edward Arnold, 1977); Ray C. Petry (ed.), *Late Medieval Mysticism* (Westminster Press, 1957); Heiko Oberman, *Forerunners of the Reformation* (Holt, Rinehart & Winston, 1966); and Matthew Spinka (ed.), *Advocates of Reform* (Westminster Press, 1953).

IMPORTANT BUT MORE DIFFICULT. E. F. Jacob, *Essays in the Conciliar Epoch,* 2d ed. (Manchester: Manchester University Press, 1953), goes far beyond conciliarism. The many works of Gordon Leff are central to the scholarship of this period. The two-volume *Heresy in the Later Middle Ages* (Manchester: Manchester University Press, 1967), is probably his masterpiece. Heiko Oberman, *The Harvest of Medieval Theology* (Harvard University Press, 1963), is a study of the nominalist theologian Gabriel Biel but really ranges far more widely. Charles Trinkaus, *In Our Image and Likeness,* 2 vols. (London: Constable & Co., 1970), is the best work on religion in the Italian Renaissance.

NOTES

1. Quoted in Johan Huizinga, *The Waning of the Middle Ages* (London: Edward Arnold, 1924), p. 24. My translation.
2. Thomas Aquinas, *Truth* q.3, a.8, tr. by Robert W. Mulligan, Vol. 1 (Henry Regnery Co., 1952), p. 166.
3. John Duns Scotus, *Ordinatio* 1, dist. 8, part 2, q.1.24, in *Opera Omnia,* Vol. 4 (Vatican City: Typis Polyglottis Vaticanus, 1956), p. 325.
4. William of Ockham, *Reportatio* 3.51 (this is the later part of Ockham's commentary on the Sentences of Peter Lombard); quoted in Gordon Leff, *William of Ockham* (Manchester: Manchester University Press, 1975), p. 476.
5. William of Ockham, *A Dialogue Between Master and Disciple on the Power of the Emperors and Popes* 3.1.2.20; quoted in Paul E. Sigmund, *Nicholas of Cusa and Medieval Political Thought* (Harvard University Press, 1963), p. 95.
6. Ibid., 1.6.85; quoted in Alan Gewirth, *Marsilius of Padua,* Vol. 1 (Columbia University Press, 1951), p. 177.
7. Ibid., 3.1.3.11 and 1.5.35; quoted in Gewirth, op. cit., p. 289.
8. William of Ockham (?), *Hundred Theological Sayings,* conclusion 7A; quoted in Heiko Oberman, *The Harvest of Medieval Theology* (Harvard University Press, 1963), p. 250.
9. William of Ockham, Quodlibet 6.1; quoted in Gordon Leff, *The Dissolution of the Medieval Outlook* (New York University Press, 1976), p. 63; emphasis added.
10. Quoted in Francis Oakley, *The Western Church in the Later Middle Ages* (Cornell University Press, 1979), p. 131.

11.   Gabriel Biel, *Prepared Epitome and Collection on the Four Books of Sentences* 3.19.1.2.5, and *Sermons on the Festivals of Christ* 2G; quoted in Oberman, *The Harvest of Medieval Theology*, p. 268; emphasis added.

12.   Thomas Bradwardine, *On the Cause of God Against Pelagius*, preface 1; quoted in Gordon Leff, *Bradwardine and the Pelagians* (Cambridge: Cambridge University Press, 1957), p. 14.

13.   Meister Eckhart, Sermon, *This Is Meister Eckhart from Whom God Hid Nothing*, in *Meister Eckhart*, tr. by Raymond B. Blakney, (Harper & Brothers, 1941), p. 97.

14.   Meister Eckhart, *The Aristocrat*, ibid., p. 75.

15.   Meister Eckhart, *The Talks of Instruction* 10, ibid., p. 14.

16.   Julian of Norwich, *Revelations of Divine Love, The Shorter Version* 6 (Heidelberg: Carl Winter Universitätsverlag, 1978), p. 48; I have modernized the language.

17.   Julian of Norwich, *The Revelations of Divine Love*, ch. 60, tr. by James Walsh (London: Burns & Oates, 1961), pp. 163–164.

18.   Conrad of Gelnhausen, *Letter of Concord* 2; quoted in E. F. Jacob, *Essays in the Conciliar Epoch*, 2d ed. (Manchester: Manchester University Press, 1953), p. 9.

19.   Cardinal Uguccione, *Address to the Three Estates of England*, as recounted in *St. Albans Chronicle*; quoted in C. M. D. Crowder, *Unity, Heresy and Reform, 1378–1460* (London: Edward Arnold, 1977), p. 49.

20.   Dietrich of Niem, *Ways of Uniting and Reforming the Church*, tr. by James Kerr Cameron, in Matthew Spinka (ed.), *Advocates of Reform* (Westminster Press, 1953), p. 155.

21.   Henry of Herford, *Book of Memorable Things or Chronicle*; quoted in Norman Cohn, *The Pursuit of the Millennium* (Essential Books, 1957), p. 133.

22.   Council of Constance, *Haec sancta*, in Crowder, *Unity, Heresy and Reform*, p. 83.

23.   Jean Froissart, *Froissart's Chronicles* 73, tr. by John Jolliffe (Modern Library, 1968), p. 237.

24.   John Wyclif, *Of Ministries in the Church*, in *Select English Works*, Vol. 2 (Oxford: Clarendon Press, 1871), p. 395; I have modernized the language.

25.   John Wyclif, *On Speech and the Purging of the Church* 4, in *John Wyclif's Polemical Works in Latin*, Vol. 1 (London: Trübner & Co., 1833), p. 349.

26.   John Wyclif, *On the Truth of Sacred Scripture* 1.109; quoted in John Stacey, *John Wyclif and Reform* (Westminster Press, 1964), p. 74.

27.   John Wyclif, *The Pastoral Office* 2a, tr. by Ford Lewis Battles, in Spinka, *Advocates of Reform*, p. 50.

28.   John Hus, *On Simony*, ibid., p. 251.

29.   Quoted in Martin Luther, *Commentary on the Alleged Imperial Edict*, tr. by Robert R. Heitner, in *Luther's Works*, Vol. 34, ed. by Lewis W. Spitz (Muhlenberg Press, 1960), p. 104.

30.   Eugenius IV, *Laetentur coeli*, in Crowder, *Unity, Heresy and Reform*, p. 171.

31.   *De coercendis inconstancie filii*; quoted in Oakley, *The Western Church in the Later Middle Ages*, p. 112.

32. *The Imitation of Christ* 1.3 and 2.1, tr. by Brother Leo (Macmillan Co., 1937), pp. 2–3.

33. Quoted in Charles Trinkaus, *In Our Image and Likeness,* Vol. 1 (London: Constable & Co., 1970), pp. 281–282.

34. Ibid., p. 247.

12

FAITH ALONE,
SCRIPTURE ALONE

Even if the whole world goes to smash, God can make
another world.

—Martin Luther[1]

Luther & Zwingli
Should be treated singly:
L hated the Peasants,
Z the Real Presence.

—W. H. Auden[2]

On April 18, 1521, a monk named Martin Luther, a university lecturer
in New Testament, stood before Emperor Charles V, ruler of half the
world, and the nobles of Germany, assembled in the city of Worms.
Emperor and nobles had joined the pope in demanding that Luther
retract some of his theological views; refusal could mean death. Luther refused:

Unless I am convinced by the testimony of Scripture or by clear
reason, for I do not trust either in the pope or in councils alone,
since it is well known that they have often erred and contradicted themselves, my conscience is captive to the Word of
God. I cannot and will not retract anything. . . . I cannot do
otherwise, here I stand, may God help me. Amen.[3]

By refusing to back down, Luther changed the history of Christian
theology, but his stand at Worms was only one episode in a life full
of dramatic conflicts—just as Luther himself was but one figure in an
era full of passionate controversialists.

Luther's theology, indeed, developed in a series of controversies,
from his own early struggles over the meaning of justification to his
debate with humanists like Erasmus about free will to quarrels with

more radical reformers like Andreas Carlstadt and Thomas Müntzer over questions of authority to his dispute with the Swiss reformer Huldreich Zwingli about the Lord's Supper. Through all those controversies Luther pursued a program of reform, but some of his contemporaries did not think he went far enough and proposed more radical changes in Christianity. His own followers, on the other hand, sometimes found that any effort to produce a systematic "Lutheran" theology had to trim back some of Luther's passionate and occasionally inconsistent declarations. This chapter will trace the controversies, introduce the radical opposition, and conclude with a look at Lutheranism after Luther.

LUTHER AGAINST THE WORLD

Like his near contemporary Columbus, who found a new world by accident, Luther began without any intention of making a religious revolution. In 1505 he had entered a monastery, fulfilling a vow made in a moment of terror in the midst of a thunderstorm. He had tried to be a good monk, fulfilling every discipline, but it hadn't seemed to work. He could always think of one sin left unconfessed, doubt the sincerity of his contrition, imagine one more demand God might make. "Love God? I hated him."[4]

The largely nominalist theology Luther had studied taught that, with the help of grace, we earn our own salvation through our works. Luther found he couldn't do it. In the presence of God, none of his works seemed worthy. Then, studying Paul's letter to the Romans, he realized he didn't need to earn salvation.

> Night and day I pondered until I saw the connection between the justice of God and the statement that "the just shall live by his faith." Then I grasped that the justice of God is that righteousness by which through sheer grace and sheer mercy God justifies us through faith. Thereupon I felt myself to be reborn and to have gone through open doors into paradise.[5]

To claim to earn one's own salvation is "to please and enjoy oneself in one's own works and to adore oneself as an idol."[6] We are not righteous, we are sinners. We can be counted righteous only because God in his grace declares us righteous, like a judge freeing a guilty defendant. Our justification thus comes as a gift, not an accomplishment. "Therefore we must be taught a righteousness that comes completely from the outside and is foreign. And therefore our own righteousness that is born in us must first be plucked out."[7] The law condemns us; the gospel of grace sets us free.

Luther's reflections on these themes led him, in 1517, into a conflict over indulgences. In the medieval system of penance, a sinner felt ashamed, confessed to a priest, and then received forgiveness and the assignment of some penance to do. If the church or some worthy charity needed money or other help, however, the sinner could be let off all or part of the penance in return for a contribution to a good cause. That release from a penance was the "indulgence." In 1095, for instance, the Council of Clermont offered an indulgence to all those who went on a crusade to Jerusalem. Gradually a theory emerged to explain this practice. The church came to teach that Christ, Mary, and the saints had done more than they needed to do to achieve salvation and had thus accumulated a "treasury of merits" that the church could distribute in indulgences for the sake of worthy purposes— though the treasury of merit became part of official doctrine only in 1343.

Purgatory had become an important doctrinal interest in the same period. Saints go straight to heaven when they die, and unredeemed sinners straight to hell, but the church now taught that others, who were on their way to salvation at death, go to an intermediate place, purgatory, to work off their remaining demerits before entering heaven. After 1476 one could also buy indulgences for souls in purgatory, and this provided the church with an obvious source of additional revenue. In 1517 the pope and a German bishop named Albert of Brandenburg both needed money, so they hired a Dominican named John Tetzel to sell indulgences around Germany. Tetzel could have taught Madison Avenue a thing or two about the hard sell:

Listen to the voices of your dear dead relatives and friends, beseeching you and saying, "Pity us, pity us. We are in dire torment from which you can redeem us for a pittance." . . . Remember that you are able to release them for

As soon as the coin in the coffer rings,
The soul from Purgatory springs.[8]

Luther wrote a series of ninety-five theses criticizing the selling of indulgences. It was not just the corruption and abuse of the indulgence system; the very idea of indulgences seemed to imply that we can earn our salvation and thus, to Luther's mind, denied the grace of God. Movable-type printing had appeared in Europe a few years before, and German presses quickly reproduced his attacks. As he said later, "They went through the whole of Germany in a fortnight, for the whole world complained about indulgences. . . . This is the first, real, fundamental beginning of the Lutheran rumpus."[9]

At first, Luther did not recognize the radical implications of his conclusions. He hoped that the church would acknowledge that he was right. Then in 1519 the great scholar John Eck came to Leipzig to debate him, and Eck persuaded even Luther that his views were contrary to the official teachings of the church. By this time, however, Luther had such confidence in his conclusions that, if they contradicted popes and councils, so much the worse for the popes and councils. And so, in the scene in 1521 described at the beginning of this chapter, he refused to recant. He soon drew widespread support from many directions. Corruption had filled the church, and many people eagerly sought some kind of fundamental change in such a contaminated system. In Germany in particular, the absence of a strong central government left people at the mercy of church taxation, which they deeply resented.

Luther also won initial support from many of the German humanists, the heirs of the Renaissance tradition. As good humanists, they valued the authority of ancient texts. Now Luther wanted to question the authority of the pope and base theology on the text of the Bible. Further, the humanists disliked "superstitions," and they felt uncomfortable with selling indulgences or kissing the relics of saints, practices that Luther too opposed. In the end, however, many of the humanists did not follow Luther. Erasmus, the famous Dutch biblical scholar and the best known humanist in northern Europe, provides the most famous example. It was partly a matter of personal style. Erasmus had carefully edited the Greek New Testament, collected classical proverbs, and written witty dialogues ridiculing the abuses in the church. He wanted peace and tolerance; he admitted that he lacked the courage to be a martyr. Luther had little patience with this. If you are defending the truth, he said, it doesn't matter "if you tread on Peter's foot or even slug an angel in the mouth."[10]

But their differences ran deeper. Erasmus sought to clear away corruption and superstition in order to restore a simple, ethical Christianity in which people would try to follow Christ and be decent to each other. Luther had just survived a cataclysmic psychological crisis in which he had discovered that he could not lead a decent life, but had to throw himself on God's grace. He did not hold a complete determinism; he admitted that we can decide what to wear or whom to marry. But when Erasmus urged people to turn away from sin, Luther insisted that no one can do it. At this point, "It is a profound and blind error to teach that the will is by nature free and can, without grace, turn to the spirit, seek grace, and desire it."[11] Augustine had been right; God helps those who cannot help themselves.

Erasmus disagreed. "Although free will has been wounded through sin," he wrote, "it is not extinct; though it has contracted a paralysis, making us before the reception of grace more readily inclined towards evil than good, free will has not been destroyed."[12] Luther and Erasmus shared an interest in biblical scholarship and opposition to corruption, but Erasmus wanted to persuade people they could be better if they only tried, while Luther had found all such human efforts to be futile. As Luther came into ever deeper conflict with Rome, everyone wanted Erasmus to choose a side. He could only protest, "I have sought to be a spectator of this tragedy,"[13] and, like many other humanists, he remained cautiously loyal to Rome.

Luther faced even more bitter disputes about questions of authority, both political and religious. In its early days, his movement depended on the support of the German princes for its survival. Only the protection of the Elector of Saxony kept Luther alive. Luther argued for the right of princes to interfere in religious affairs to make necessary church reforms. Further, he urged Christians to be obedient subjects of their princes in nearly any circumstances. To be sure, if the state orders you to act contrary to Scripture, you should refuse. If called upon to fight in an unjust war, for instance, "You shouldn't fight or serve. 'Nay,' you say, 'my lord compels me, takes my fief, does not give me any money, pay, or wages, and besides I am despised, put to shame as a coward. . . .' I answer, 'You must take that risk.' "[14] Unless you are ordered to act contrary to the Bible, however, you should accept any injustice to which you are subjected: "For no matter how right you are, it is not for a Christian to appeal to law or to fight, but rather to suffer injury and endure evil."[15] Christ, who endured suffering and death, should serve as a model. Thus Luther would always support the status quo against a political rebellion. "For insurrection lacks discernment; it generally harms the innocent more than the guilty. Hence no insurrection is ever right no matter how right the cause it seeks to promote. It always results in more damage than improvement, and verifies the saying, 'Things go from bad to worse.' "[16] In other words, I must not do wrong myself, but, if the government does wrong, I must put up with it, rather than participate in a rebellion in which I would end up causing my neighbors suffering. A critic might ask if I do not in a way cause them suffering by letting injustice continue, but Luther would leave such questions to God. A Christian, Luther insisted, lives in "two kingdoms," and they should not be confused. The church, as the representative of the kingdom of God, should exercise no temporal rule and employ no coercion. The state, the human kingdom, necessarily employs coercion but should not interfere in questions of faith.

Luther's essential conservatism on social issues early became apparent in his conflicts with Andreas Bodenstein von Carlstadt. Carlstadt was Luther's senior colleague at the University of Wittenberg, but he had had a checkered career. One year he had even managed to draw his full salary while spending the whole time in Italy. When Luther, having refused to recant, went into hiding, Carlstadt briefly took charge of the reformation party in Luther's city of Wittenberg. He felt that Luther's reformation implied an end not only to the authority of the pope but to all institutional authority whatever. He wore a worker's clothing and urged his students to call him "Andreas." More important, he said that each individual congregation should determine the course of its own reformation. "We here were not obliged to refrain either in teaching or activity from carrying out God's commands until our neighbors and the guzzlers at Wittenberg followed. [By this time Carlstadt had moved to a neighboring town.] Each congregation, however little or great it may be, should see for itself that it acts properly and well and waits for no one."[17] Such decisions need not even appeal to the authority of the Bible, for Carlstadt thought that the voice of the Holy Spirit could speak directly to any Christian. "This is the way it was with the apostles." Christians did not need to consult bishops or councils or educated biblical scholars; the Spirit might speak through any peasant or shopkeeper. Luther thought this a recipe for chaos, with each local congregation going off its own way, at the mercy of any claim to have heard the voice of the Spirit, and hurried back to Wittenberg to put Carlstadt under control.

Luther always retained a kind of affection for his old colleague Carlstadt, but he had no such fondness for Thomas Müntzer. Like many a young humanist, Müntzer had been caught up in the excitement of Luther's ideas, but, like Carlstadt, he soon began to place a greater weight on the inner voice of the Spirit than on the Scriptures. "If a man in his whole life had neither heard nor seen the Bible," he wrote, "he could nevertheless have an undeceivable Christian Faith through the teaching of the Spirit—like those who wrote the Scripture without any books."[18] Luther lacked the Spirit, and therefore could not understand the Bible even if he swallowed a hundred thousand copies. (Müntzer, Luther replied, seemed to have "swallowed the Holy Ghost, feathers and all."[19])

Like Carlstadt, Müntzer valued the authority of the Holy Spirit in part because the Spirit could speak even to those who lacked the education needed for biblical scholarship. Increasingly, he thought that the poor, those who had suffered, would understand Christ best, for Christ spoke not of comfort, but of bitterness and suffering. Luther seemed to him the symbol of comfortable Christianity.

> Doesn't he realize that men whose every moment is consumed in the making of a living have no time to learn to read the Word of God? The princes bleed the people with usury and count as their own the fish in the stream, the birds of the air, and the grass of the field, and Dr. Liar says, "Amen!" What courage has he, Dr. Pussyfoot, the new pope of Wittenberg, Dr. Easychair, the basking sycophant.[20]

In a way it was a classic case of generation gap; Müntzer could no longer imagine the young Luther, that daring, tortured rebel.

Like many Christians who have identified with the oppressed and suffering and put their faith in the voice of the Spirit, Müntzer came to think the end of the present age and the second coming of Christ near at hand. The church, he said, had been corrupt since the generation after the first apostles and would soon be destroyed. When peasants throughout Germany revolted in 1525, he became a sort of chaplain to the peasant army, proclaiming the revolt a holy crusade. The peasants lacked trained leaders and armed themselves only with clubs and sticks; not surprisingly, they were quickly defeated. Müntzer tried to escape, but was captured and killed.

At the beginning of their rebellion, many of the peasants appealed to Luther for support, and he acknowledged the justice of many of their complaints, telling the German princes, "You do nothing but flay and rob your subjects in order that you may lead a life of splendor and pride, until the poor common folk can bear it no longer."[21] Nevertheless, he could not support a rebellion against political authority, and, in a burst of anger, urged the princes,

> Let everyone who can smite, slay and stab, secretly and openly, remembering that nothing can be more poisonous, hurtful or devilish than a rebel. It is just as when one must kill a mad dog; if you do not strike him, he will strike you, and a whole land with you.[22]

Luther had set the limits of his reformation. He would appeal from popes and councils to Scripture, but not from Scripture to the inner voice of the Spirit. He would attack the church hierarchy, but rebellion against political authorities struck him as wrong and dangerous.

ZURICH AND ZWINGLI

Along with Luther, other reformers had also set to work. In Switzerland the city of Zurich called a young humanist and Swiss patriot named Huldreich Zwingli to be their preacher in 1518. Zwingli set to work to end practices like the cults of the saints and the emphasis on elaborate rituals and to make the Bible the sole authority for Christian faith. Zurich delayed his appointment as preacher, incidentally, when a young woman from his previous hometown accused him of robbing her of her virginity. Zwingli had supposedly been a priest vowed to celibacy at the time, but a letter from a number of young men swearing they had reason to know that the lady had not been a virgin satisfied the Zurichers, and he got the job.

Zwingli shared much of Luther's program of reform, but with different emphases. Luther had begun with justification by faith and turned to the authority of Scripture because he found that principle clearly enunciated there. Zwingli began with the absolute authority of Scripture. He lacked Luther's sense of the desperation of sin; indeed, he even denied that original sin is really sin, since we are not ourselves responsible for it. He thought of it rather as a disease. In some ways Zwingli stood more in the tradition of Erasmus, more concerned with cleansing the church of "superstitious" or "corrupt" practices. Zwingli believed in God's sovereign control of all human activity if anything even more absolutely than Luther did, but his conviction had a different origin. Luther's religious experience taught him the powerlessness of human efforts and the power of divine grace. Zwingli started rather from a philosophical conviction that God is omnipotent, which implies that God determines the course of all events.

More immediate differences between the two arose from their different political situations. Luther lived as the subject of a prince. Zwingli's Zurich had a considerable degree of democracy. Thus Luther thought about politics primarily in terms of when one should obey authority, while Zwingli had to ask how the government should move in religious matters. He himself favored reforming the city gradually—ending private confessions, taking down statues of the Virgin and the saints, and so on, slowly enough so that the more conservative citizens would not become alienated and split off and divide the city religiously. He acknowledged that this involved compromises: "The contemporary state does not, of course, correspond to the ideal of Christianity, but we are living in a world in which, for the time being, there can be nothing but half-measures."[23] One young citizen of Zurich, Conrad Grebel, found this disgusting. Zwingli, he said, appealed to the Bible, but then he allowed the continuation of parts of the old Catholic Mass, the collection of forced tithes instead of voluntary offerings to support the church, and much else he acknowledged to be unscriptural. Above all, Grebel insisted that the Bible mentions only the baptism of adults who have confessed their faith, not the baptism of infants. Grebel and some of his friends therefore denied the validity of infant baptism and began to rebaptize each other.

Grebel and his friends sought purity; they wanted to follow the Bible as they understood it without compromise and create a community of the committed who had made a personal decision to join and submitted to rebaptism. Zwingli cared more about unity among Christians. He feared the results "if it should come to pass that every hot-headed crank should form a new group as soon as any new or strange idea came into his head."[24] He was willing to delay reforms to hold the city together, and he sought the baptism of all the children of the Christian community of Zurich. In Zurich Zwingli won. Some of Grebel's followers were killed—some were drowned with mordant jokes about their views on baptism—and Grebel fled only to die shortly afterward. In general in the sixteenth century, victory lay with those, like Luther, Zwingli, and later Calvin, and Cranmer in England, who sought to reform a whole territory with the help of its rulers, rather than with the radicals like Grebel who sought to separate out the pure.

On that issue Luther and Zwingli agreed, but they utterly disagreed about the Lord's Supper. Zwingli taught that the bread and wine represent or symbolize Christ's presence. Christ is present spiritually, he said, but not physically, for Christ is physically in heaven at the right hand of God. "Christ announced where he would be until the last judgment," Zwingli insisted. "Never did he give us to understand that he would be anywhere else but at the right hand of God. We are hardly being pious if we look for Christ elsewhere than in the place where he said he could be found."[25] Luther had rejected the Catholic theory of transubstantiation, which used the categories of Aristotle's philosophy: normally, as when ice melts to water, a substance remains the same but its accidents change. In the Mass, however, the accidents remain the same—the elements still look and taste like bread and wine—but the substance changes, and it is now the body and blood of Christ. Luther rejected transubstantiation because he distrusted the introduction of philosophical theories into theology. We should simply accept what the Bible says. "How he is in the bread, we do not know, and are not to know. We should believe the word of God, and not dictate ways and means to him."[26] At the same time, Luther insisted that Christ had declared, "This is my body," and meant what he said. Zwingli claimed that "is" really meant "symbolizes," but with that kind of interpretation, Luther observed, "God" could mean "cuckoo," "created" could mean "ate," and "heavens and earth" could mean "hedgehog," so that the opening verse of the book of Genesis could be interpreted to mean, "The cuckoo ate the hedgehog."[27] Luther would have none of it, and when political leaders anxious to form an alliance among all Protestants brought him together with Zwingli to seek a compromise, he wrote, "This is my body," on the table and pointed to it whenever called upon to speak. Christ, he said, does not exist only in heaven "like a stork in a treetop."[28] Rather Christ, as divine, is present everywhere. Most of the time Christ's presence remains hidden from us; the power of the Eucharist is that in the words of institution Christ's presence in the elements is revealed to us—a real presence, not just a symbolic one. Neither Luther nor Zwingli would budge, and the efforts of the Protestant princes and cities to form an alliance collapsed.

THE RADICAL REFORMATION

In 1531 Zwingli met his death in a battle against the Catholic forces in Switzerland, but his work survived in Zurich. By the end of the 1530s, indeed, "Reformed" Christianity more or less on Zwingli's pattern was spreading through Switzerland and into Germany, while "Lutherans" dominated several parts of Germany and had spread into Scandinavia. During the same period, other reformers sought different kinds of changes in Christianity, but they rarely became the dominant force in any territory. Historians classify together as the "radical reformers" an odd collection of pacifists and violent revolutionaries, eccentric individualists and tightly knit communities, biblical literalists and those who followed the inner voice of the Spirit. It is tempting to consider the "Radical Reformation" simply a grab bag filled with everyone who lost, that is, everyone who failed to establish a territorial church. But most of the radicals did not want to win on those terms anyway. Luther and Zwingli may have divided the church universal, but they wanted to hold the local Christian community together. Almost everyone in Saxony became a Lutheran; nearly all the people of Zurich automatically became part of Zwingli's reform. In the religious wars of the following generation, in fact, this principle generally provided the basis for the peace settlement—the ruler's faith became the faith of a whole territory.

Many of the radical reformers, in a way already described in connection with Conrad Grebel in Zurich, wanted to establish a church made up only of the truly committed, even if that left out most of their neighbors. They often argued that the whole church had been corrupt at least since the conversion of Constantine and perhaps since just after the first generation of apostles. Merely clearing away some medieval practices as Luther and Zwingli had done didn't go nearly far enough in purifying the church. For some of the radicals, adult baptism provided a particularly vivid symbol of limiting the church to committed believers.

George H. Williams, the greatest modern historian of the Radical Reformation, has divided the radicals into Anabaptists, Spiritualists, and anti-Trinitarians or rationalists. The Anabaptists ("re-baptizers") were those, like Conrad Grebel and his friends in Zurich, who believed in rebaptizing adults who had already been baptized in infancy, on the grounds that infant baptism could not either involve a real commitment of faith or be justified by Scripture. In the 1530s, for instance, a wandering preacher named Melchior Hoffmann traveled around northern Germany proclaiming that the Bible did not recognize the validity of infant baptism and rebaptizing adults who confessed their faith. Others compromised on the issue. Thomas Müntzer, for instance, urged postponing baptism until adulthood but did not rebaptize those who had already been baptized as infants. Anabaptists in the strict sense spread their ideas through Switzerland and Germany in the 1520s, often suffering persecution, and then in the early 1530s in the German city of Münster had a temporary success that later proved a disaster. Northern German Anabaptists had always been wilder than the Swiss variety. Melchior Hoffmann, for instance, had had a strong apocalyptic streak and proclaimed himself the prophet Elijah returned. In 1534 a group of Anabaptists took over the city of Münster and declared the beginning of the kingdom of God on earth. They adopted the Old Testament as their law code, even to permitting polygamy. They drove out the upper classes and punished by death everything from blasphemy to scolding one's parents or complaining, yet some of their leaders apparently participated in wild sexual activities. Reading eyewitness accounts, it is difficult not to think that they all went crazy. Soon the alarmed neighboring states surrounded the city, starved them into submission, and massacred a good part of the population, but the example of Münster left many people convinced that Anabaptists were dangerous lunatics.

South German and Swiss Anabaptists, however, had always been quite different. A visitor named John Kessler recorded a description of the Anabaptists of St. Gall in the late 1570s:

> They avoid ostentatious clothes, despise delicate food and drink, clothe themselves with coarse cloth, decking their heads with broad felt hats, their way and conversation quite humble. They carried no weapon. . . . They swore not, not even to the authorities, the civic oath. And if anyone transgressed among them, he was banned; for there was the practice of daily excommunication among them. In their talk and disputation they were grim and hard bitten and so unyielding that they would rather have died than have yielded a point.[29]

Kessler may not have liked these people, but he showed a grudging respect for them, and he mentioned most of their characteristic practices. They tended to withdraw from ordinary society, dressing in a way that set them apart, and refusing to fight in the army or take part in any governmental affairs. When one of them broke the rules of their community, the others subjected the offender to the "ban"—they refused to speak until the person in question had properly repented. (Kessler's phrase "daily excommunication" means that they excluded people from daily conversation, not just the Lord's Supper.) In the 1540s, after the debacle at Münster, a former priest named Menno Simons traveled around the Netherlands and northern Germany establishing Anabaptist communities on this Swiss model, and the whole movement gradually took on his name, so that they survive today as the Mennonites.

Like the Anabaptists, those who can be grouped together as "Spiritualists" did not try to impose their sort of reformation on a whole territory in the way that Luther or Zwingli did. The Anabaptists, however, usually withdrew into closed communities and emphasized the literal authority of the Bible, while the Spiritualists stood for the freedom of the individual and followed the guidance of the inner voice of the Holy Spirit. Carlstadt and Thomas Müntzer had explored some such themes in the earliest days of the Reformation, but later Spiritualists rejected the revolutionary politics prominent at least in Müntzer and concentrated on the life of the individual. A Silesian nobleman named Caspar Schwenckfeld, for instance, followed Luther in the 1520s but soon came to feel that all the parties of the Reformation had bogged down in disputes over outward ceremonies and institutions. "To my mind," Schwenckfeld wrote, "I am one with all churches in that I pray for them, in that I despise none, because I know that Christ the Lord has his own everywhere, be they ever so few."[30] The Holy Spirit will never reach more than a minority, but members of that minority can be found in every church group. So why should all the churches keep fighting? Schwenckfeld so regretted disputes over the Lord's Supper that he stopped celebrating it altogether as a symbolic protest, a suspension his followers in the Schwenckfelder church continued until 1877. He did not really mind suspending the ceremony, since he cared about inner spiritual realities, not outward forms. He would have sympathized with another Spiritualist, a gardener from the city of Strassburg named Clement Ziegler, who wrote that wherever there is faith in Christ, "in the heart of anybody, regardless of where that person is—hewing timber or cleaning a stall, washing dishes or sweeping the house . . . that person with certainty tastes the body and the blood of Christ, and he does so although there be no priest, no altar, and no outward sign."[31]

A small community of Schwenckfelders survives today in Germany and Pennsylvania, but the Spiritualists did not in general spread their influence widely or even found organized communities. Their impact came, when it did, through the introduction of new ideas of tolerance. The same might be said of a third general type of radical reformers, those who rejected the Trinity. Starting in the 1550s some among Anabaptist groups in Poland and Hungary began to question the traditional doctrine of the Trinity. Some of them held views like those of Arius in the fourth century: while they considered Christ divine, they denied his full equality with the Father. Others went further and supposed that Jesus had been no more than a very good man dedicated to the doing of God's will. In their early stages, these groups retained many of the social characteristics of other Anabaptists. They founded isolated communities and refused to have anything to do with ordinary forms of government.

In the 1570s, however, an Italian named Faustus Socinus (Fausto Sozzini) began to exert a deep influence on Eastern European anti-Trinitarianism. Theologically, he taught that Christ did not have a "divine nature" but simply did God's work. He also denied that God demanded Christ's suffering and death as a price for the forgiveness of humanity, as Anselm and so many others had taught. According to Socinus, the human soul is by nature mortal and would ordinarily cease to exist at death. The work of Christ does not have to do primarily with sin but consists in giving the soul immortality. Socinus modified the earlier Anabaptist pattern of withdrawal from society. He permitted people to hold government office as long as they did not sentence anyone to death and even permitted some military service.

He ended all special styles of dress, asking only that people avoid extravagance. Anti-Trinitarianism even became the official religion of Transylvania in the 1570s, and its "Socinian" form remained influential for some time in Poland.

This tradition distinguished itself by its tolerance. "Dogmas do not constitute the essence of Christianity, but devout living," wrote its most eloquent exponent of religious toleration, the Pole Samuel Przypkowski. "No man is in measure to fathom the nature of God, thus . . . we must not impose 'spiritual censure' on anybody, for each of us has a right to his own individual evolution."[32] Such attitudes, as well as the Socinian position on the Trinity, became influential in the seventeenth century, especially in England, but the immediate impact of anti-Trinitarianism was limited. Indeed, the same could be said for all the radical reformers. Some raised intellectual questions that would become important in subsequent centuries; others founded small communities that still survive, but none gained support equal to that of the Lutherans or the Reformed tradition begun by Zwingli. In large part, this derived from a general inability in the sixteenth century to think that there might be religious diversity within the same political territory. Christendom was split, but religious and political loyalties remained tightly bound together. Most people just couldn't believe in the political loyalty of those who didn't share their ruler's religion, and thus the withdrawal of the Anabaptists and the individual tolerance of the Spiritualists or the anti-Trinitarians led to suspicions of political disloyalty and thus to persecution.

LUTHERAN DEVELOPMENTS

The greatest influence of ideas from the Radical Reformation, therefore, lay in the future. Chapter 14 will have more to say about the Reformed tradition Zwingli began. Here we need to conclude by tracing some subsequent developments in Lutheran theology. In the years after his initial break with the Roman Catholic Church, Luther's most influential acts were probably translating the Bible and getting married. His translation not only made the Scriptures accessible to ordinary Germans, it helped shape the German language for centuries. Clerical celibacy had seemed to separate the clergy from the laypeople and in practice had occasioned endless corruption. Luther's marriage provided the most vivid possible symbol of the equality implied in the Lutheran doctrine of the "priesthood of all believers," and its great happiness set a pattern of ideal family life that has served civilization—and imposed burdens on the wives and children of ministers—ever since.

Increasingly, the leadership of Luther's movement fell to his young friend Philip Melanchthon, who had come to Wittenberg in 1518 at a precocious twenty-one to teach Greek. Their relationship had its tensions. Impatient with Melanchthon's caution and moderation, Luther once exclaimed, "Be a sinner and sin boldly, but believe and rejoice in Christ even more boldly."[33] For his part, Melanchthon once wrote to a friend, "Oh that Luther would keep silent! I did hope that with age, experience, and so many troubles, he would grow more moderate; but I see he becomes the more violent."[34] Still, Melanchthon always loved and admired Luther, and Luther said that Melanchthon was by far a better theologian than he was and that the *Loci communes,* Melanchthon's summary of Lutheran theology, deserved a place second only to the Bible.

After Luther's death, Melanchthon's willingness to compromise got him into a series of troubles. In 1547 Catholic forces took control of the area around Wittenberg and permitted the university to stay open only if certain Catholic practices like not eating meat on Fridays and Saturdays during Lent were restored. Melanchthon argued that, as long as the basic theology of justification by faith remained, one could compromise on such nonessentials *(adiaphora).* Others thought that he had betrayed the basic principles of Lutheranism.

Then in the 1550s even the principle of justification by faith came under examination, initially because of Andreas Osiander, who had led the early reformation in Nuremberg but whose abrasive personality had won him enemies wherever he had gone, raised another question about justification. Like Luther himself, Melanchthon believed that we are justified though we remain sinners because God *imputes* Christ's righteousness to us. To be sure, in our lives as Christians we may turn gradually away from sin (this involves "sanctification" and "regeneration"), but that comes later and does not contribute to our justification, which derives not at all from our efforts. Osiander argued that justification is itself an inward process in which our hearts are changed and God *infuses* love within us. He defended "infused righteousness" over "imputed righteousness." That captured something important in Luther's experience of a justification so overpowering that it changed his innermost being, but it also made it sound as if we are justified because we become better people, not because God justifies us even in our sins. At any rate, neither Melanchthon nor anyone else much agreed with Osiander.

Around 1560 a Lutheran pastor named Victorinus Strigel set off a more widespread debate about justification. Luther had taught that we are utterly powerless apart from God's grace. Melanchthon had agreed, but he added that when we receive God's grace, we then cooperate with it and thus contribute to our salvation. In salvation, he said, "Three causes are conjoined: The Word, the Holy Spirit, and the will, not wholly inactive, but resisting in its own weakness. ... God draws but draws him who is willing ... , and the will is not a statue, and that spiritual emotion is not imposed upon it as though it were a statue."[35] Another Lutheran theologian, Matthias Flacius Illyricus, argued that this compromised Luther's unqualified emphasis on grace. The sinner, he said, can do nothing to contribute to salvation, for the sinner has no capacity for free choice. Indeed, sinners have in essence ceased to be human beings—sin has become their very substance.

Luther himself had died in 1546, and Melanchthon died in 1560. Strigel claimed to be following in Melanchthon's footsteps when he insisted that even a sinful human being remains a human being, a creature of God and therefore retaining some capacity for doing good. Some of Luther's followers charged that any idea that our wills participate in salvation returns to a concept of justification by works, and thus Strigel (and perhaps Melanchthon as well) was betraying Luther.

By 1580 Lutherans reached a general consensus which they expressed in the Formula of Concord. It condemned Melanchthon's compromise on nonessentials, condemned Osiander, and, while admitting that people are not statues and that grace does not act on them as if they were, opposed Melanchthon and Strigel by denying that a sinner's will can cooperate with grace.

None of this contradicted Luther's views, yet somehow, perhaps inevitably, something of his spirit had been lost. He had always spoken with the passion of the moment. Any effort to make his ideas systematic, to explain them through philosophical terminology, inevitably changed them. He had championed faith alone and Scripture alone, and so did later Lutherans. But for Luther faith meant a personal relationship with God. Increasingly it came to mean assent to a set of propositions. We "have faith" if we believe x and y and z. Similarly, Luther had proclaimed the authority of Scripture, but he often interpreted it very freely. He dismissed the letter of James as an "epistle of straw" because it talked about the importance of works as well as faith, and he admitted that the book of Revelation had never seemed particularly revealing to him. To many later Lutherans, the authority of Scripture came to mean the truth of everything the

Bible said. "They are trying to make me into a fixed star," Luther once complained. "I am an irregular planet."[36]

FOR FURTHER READING

INTRODUCTIONS. Steven Ozment's *The Age of Reform*, mentioned at the end of the last chapter, continues through this period. Roland H. Bainton, *The Reformation of the Sixteenth Century* (Beacon Press, 1952), is a popular account. G. R. Elton, *Reformation Europe* (Harper & Row, Harper Torchbooks, 1963), sets the political and historical context. Bernard M. G. Reardon's *Religious Thought in the Reformation* (Harlow, Essex: Longman Group, 1981), concentrates on the theological issues. On Luther, Roland H. Bainton, *Here I Stand* (Abingdon-Cokesbury Press, 1950), remains a superb popular biography. John M. Todd, *Luther* (Crossroad Publishing Co., 1982), is the most up-to-date account.

COLLECTIONS OF ORIGINAL SOURCES. Two works collect a wide variety of texts from the Reformation period with helpful editorial comments: Hans J. Hillerbrand, *The Reformation in Its Own Words* (London: SCM Press, 1964), and Lewis W. Spitz, *The Protestant Reformation* (Prentice-Hall, 1966). Martin Luther, *Three Treatises*, tr. by C. M. Jacobs, A. T. W. Steinhaeuser, and W. A. Lambert (Fortress Press, 1947, 1960), gathers three crucial texts. *Erasmus-Luther, Discourse on Free Will*, tr. by Ernst F. Winter (Frederick Ungar, 1961), presents both sides of a famous debate. For works from other reformers, see the following volumes from The Library of Christian Classics: Wilhelm Pauck (ed.), *Melanchthon and Bucer* (Westminster Press, 1969); G. W. Bromiley (ed.), *Zwingli and Bullinger* (Westminster Press, 1953); and George Huntston Williams (ed.), *Spiritual and Anabaptist Writers* (Westminster Press, 1957).

IMPORTANT BUT MORE DIFFICULT. Of the making of books on Luther, there seems to be no end. Two that deal with his theology at a fairly easy level in a biographical framework are James Atkinson, *Martin Luther and the Birth of Protestantism* (Harmondsworth, Middlesex: Penguin Books, 1968); Heinrich Boehmer, *Martin Luther*, tr. by John W. Doberstein and Theodore G. Tappert (Meridian Books, 1957). Roland H. Bainton, *Erasmus of Christendom* (Charles Scribner's Sons, 1969), like all Bainton's works, combines careful scholarship and a readable style. G. R. Potter, *Zwingli* (Cambridge: Cambridge University Press, 1976), is the most recent and careful account. George Huntston Williams, *The Radical Reformation* (Westminster

Press, 1962), has the virtues and faults that result from a determination to include nearly everything. It can seem ponderous, but it is the standard work. Franklin H. Littell, *The Origins of Sectarian Protestantism* (Macmillan Co., 1964), focuses on the Anabaptists. Gordon Rupp, *Patterns of Reformation* (Fortress Press, 1969), is an entertaining study of two wayward radicals, Müntzer and Carlstadt.

NOTES

1. Quoted in Roland Bainton, *Erasmus of Christendom* (Charles Scribner's Sons, 1969), p. 192.

2. From W. H. Auden, "Academic Graffiti," *W. H. Auden: Collected Poems,* ed. by Edward Mendelson (Random House, 1976), p. 514. Copyright © 1976 by Edward Mendelson, William Meredith and Monroe K. Spears. Used by permission of Random House, Inc.

3. Martin Luther, *Luther at the Diet of Worms,* tr. by Roger Hornsby, in *Luther's Works,* Vol. 32 (Muhlenberg Press, 1958), pp. 112–113. Scholars debate the authenticity of these remarks.

4. Quoted in Roland H. Bainton, *Here I Stand* (Abingdon-Cokesbury Press, 1950), p. 59.

5. Ibid., p. 65.

6. Quoted in Philip S. Watson, *Let God Be God!* (Fortress Press, 1947), p. 90.

7. Martin Luther, *Lectures on Romans,* tr. by Jacob A. O. Preus, in *Luther's Works,* Vol. 25 (Concordia Publishing House, 1972), p. 136.

8. Quoted in Bainton, *Here I Stand,* p. 78.

9. Martin Luther, *Against Hanswurst,* tr. by Eric W. Gritsch, in *Luther's Works,* Vol. 41 (Fortress Press, 1966), p. 234.

10. Martin Luther, Sermon 17 (for June 5, 1535), in *D. Martin Luthers Werke,* Vol. 41 (Weimar: Hermann Bohlaus Nachfolger, 1964), p. 192; quoted in Mark U. Edwards, Jr., *Luther and the False Brethren* (Stanford University Press, 1975), p. 122.

11. Martin Luther, *Defense and Explanation of All the Articles,* tr. by Charles M. Jacobs, in *Luther's Works,* Vol. 32, p. 93.

12. Erasmus, *A Diatribe or Sermon Concerning Free Will,* in Ernst F. Winter (ed.), *Erasmus-Luther, Discourse on Free Will* (Frederick Ungar Publishing Co., 1961), p. 26.

13. Quoted in Bainton, *Here I Stand,* p. 255.

14. Martin Luther, *Whether Soldiers, Too, Can Be Saved,* tr. by C. M. Jacobs, in *Works of Martin Luther,* Vol. 5 (A. J. Holman Co., 1931), p. 68.

15. Martin Luther, *An Admonition to Peace,* tr. by C. M. Jacobs, ibid., p. 233.

16. Martin Luther, *A Sincere Admonition by Martin Luther to All Christians to Guard Against Insurrection and Rebellion,* tr. by W. A. Lambert, in *Luther's Works,* Vol. 45 (Muhlenberg Press, 1962), pp. 62–63.

17. Andreas Carlstadt, *Whether One Should Proceed Slowly and Avoid Offending the Weak on Matters That Concern God's Will,* in Ronald J. Sider

(ed.), *Karlstadt's Battle with Luther* (Fortress Press, 1978), p. 56.

18. Thomas Müntzer, *Expressed Exposure of False Faith in an Untrue World;* quoted in Gordon Rupp, *Patterns of Reformation* (Fortress Press, 1969), p. 216.

19. Quoted in Bainton, *Here I Stand*, pp. 264, 261.

20. Ibid., p. 277.

21. Luther, *An Admonition to Peace*, in *Works of Martin Luther*, Vol. 5, p. 220.

22. Martin Luther, *Against the Robbing and Murdering Hordes of Peasants*, tr. by C. M. Jacobs, in *Works of Martin Luther*, Vol. 4 (A. J. Holman Co., 1931), p. 248.

23. Quoted in Oskar Farner, *Zwingli the Reformer* (Philosophical Library, 1952), p. 60.

24. Ibid., p. 59.

25. Huldreich Zwingli, *Amica exegesis, id est: expositio eucharistiae negocii ad Martinum Lutherum*, in *Corpus Reformatorum*, Vol. 92 (Leipzig: M. Heinsius Nachfolger, 1934), p. 695; quoted in Jaques Courvoisier, *Zwingli* (John Knox Press, 1963), p. 70.

26. Quoted in Reinhold Seeberg, *The History of Doctrines*, tr. by Charles E. Hay (Baker Book House, 1977), Vol. 2, p. 322.

27. Quoted in Farner, *Zwingli the Reformer*, p. 114.

28. Quoted in Rupp, *Patterns of Reformation*, p. 26.

29. John Kessler, *Sabbata;* quoted in George Huntston Williams, *The Radical Reformation* (Westminster Press, 1962), p. 323.

30. Caspar Schwenckfeld, Third Letter to Leo Judd (Sept. 10, 1533), in *Corpus Schwenckfeldianorum*, ed. by Chester David Hartranft et al., Vol. 4 (Leipzig: Breitkopf & Härtel, 1914), pp. 830f.; quoted in Williams, *The Radical Reformation*, p. 257.

31. Quoted in Williams, *The Radical Reformation*, pp. 337–338.

32. Samuel Przypkowski, *De pace et concordia ecclesiae;* quoted in Stanislas Kot, *Socinianism in Poland*, tr. by Earl Morse Wilbur (Starr King Press, 1957), p. xxv.

33. Martin Luther, Letter to Philip Melanchthon, Aug. 1, 1521, tr. by Gottfried G. Krodel, in *Luther's Works*, Vol. 48 (Fortress Press, 1963), p. 282.

34. Philip Melanchthon, Letter to Camerarius, April 11, 1526, in *Corpus Reformatorum*, Vol. 1 (Halle: C. A. Schwetschke & Sohn, 1834), col. 793; quoted in Clyde Leonard Manschreck, *Melanchthon* (Abingdon Press, 1958), p. 120.

35. Quoted in Manschreck, *Melanchthon*, p. 296. I am unable to verify Manschreck's reference.

36. Quoted in Bainton, *Here I Stand*, p. 296.

13

THE CATHOLIC REFORMATION

Strive always to choose, not that which is easiest, but that which is most difficult;
Not that which is most delectable, but that which is most unpleasing . . .
Not that which is a desire for anything, but that which is a desire for nothing.

—John of the Cross[1]

Histories of Christianity often contrast the "Protestant Reformation" with the "Catholic Counter-Reformation," as if the Catholic Church of the sixteenth century opposed and defeated reform. But one need not have been a Protestant to find the corruption of the church around 1500 a scandal. Luther offered one sort of cure for the church's problems: Give up the authority of popes and councils for that of Scripture and turn to a theology of justification by faith alone. Many Christians, however, wanted to purify the papacy rather than abandon it and thought that the need for reform called for the hard work of human efforts that would be stifled by a theology that said you have to leave everything to the grace of God. Even before Luther, Catholic humanists had begun efforts at reform, from the simple piety of the Modern Devotion to Erasmus' work on the Greek New Testament. But that kind of moderate humanism did not in the end dominate Catholic reform. The Protestant challenge called for a tough response, and the spirit of Erasmus yielded to that of Loyola. Part of Luther's success had come from the fact that he presented a clear and coherent theological point of view. His Catholic opponents needed to shape an equally clear alternative, and that process produced a more militant, less tolerant church.

THE COUNCIL OF TRENT

From 1512 to 1517, just before Luther began his rebellion, the Fifth Lateran Council had met and set forth some admirable goals: Only worthy people should become bishops; cardinals and papal officials should adopt a stricter mode of life; and church officials should stop giving (or selling) so many exceptions to church rules. Still, merely setting such goals did not provide the energy to accomplish them. In the 1530s Pope Paul III appointed a flock of cardinals concerned about reform. One of them, Gaspero Contarini, had undergone a psychological crisis and discovery of the central importance of faith rather like Luther's. Like Luther, he had concluded that "no one can at any time justify himself through his works. . . . We must justify ourselves through the righteousness of another, that is, of Christ."[2] At the same time, Contarini thought we must strive for justification with "such little love as we are capable of," not just depend on faith alone, and he emphasized the importance of union with the church in the process of justification. He was searching for a way to respond to Luther's concerns in a more traditional Catholic context.

In 1537 Contarini and some other cardinals wrote the pope a memorandum (the *Consilium de emendanda ecclesia*) in which they laid out the need for reform with startling bluntness:

> Flatterers have led some Popes to imagine that their will is law; that they are the owners of all the benefices so that they are free to dispose of them as they please without taint of simony. This conception is the Trojan horse by means of which numerous abuses have penetrated into the Church.[3]

Therefore in the future the pope must ordain only the qualified, choose bishops to provide souls with shepherds and not to provide papal income, require bishops to live in their dioceses, grant indulgences only in special circumstances, improve education, control literature through censorship, and reform the monks, nuns, and friars. It is far more important, they said, to get on with the business of reform than to try to defend every previous papal action.

> Rest assured that nothing will disarm the calumnies of the Lutherans and intimidate the King of England more effectively than a reform of the Curia [the papal bureaucracy] and the clergy. The attempt to justify all the actions of all the Popes would be an arduous and in fact an endless undertaking. We cast no stones

at your predecessors, but from you the world expects better things![4]

Four years later the pope sent Contarini to Regensburg to negotiate with the Lutherans, and Contarini and Melanchthon arrived at a compromise on justification. Most medieval theologians had thought of righteousness as a property people either have or don't have and which Christians ought to try to develop. Luther had said we *cannot* develop a righteousness of our own; we can be saved only through *Christ's* righteousness. Implicitly, the Regensburg compromise acknowledged two righteousnesses: an inherent righteousness, which grows within us, and Christ's righteousness, which is imputed to us. We are justified by faith, but not by faith alone; rather, by "faith rendering itself efficacious in love." Our good works do not win justification, but God will reward the good works we do.[5]

No pope or council had ever made an official statement on justification, so there Contarini had room to maneuver and produced this cautious collection of carefully balanced phrases. When discussion turned to the Eucharist, however, the Lutheran rejection of transubstantiation ran squarely into the fact that the Fourth Lateran Council had declared it doctrine in 1215, and the negotiations collapsed. Catholic theology would be formulated at Trent, not at Regensburg, and in opposition to the Lutherans, not in compromise with them.

The Council of Trent stands forever as a refutation of all those nasty jokes about the incompetence of committees. Popes delayed calling the council for decades, and then it took months for even a modest number of bishops to show up. The deliberations began in 1545 but had to adjourn at various times because of wars, plagues, and all sorts of political squabbles, dragging on until 1563. The assembly included no really first-rate theologians, and debates could become chaotic—at one point one bishop even yanked out part of a colleague's beard. Nevertheless, Trent managed to set forth doctrinal statements on Scripture and tradition, original sin, justification, and the sacraments that have provided the basis of Catholic theology ever since, and it laid the foundation for practical reform of the church.

Scripture and Tradition. Nothing so symbolized Luther's revolt as his refusal to accept the authority of popes and councils, yet some of those who gathered at Trent agreed that nothing else could match the Bible's authority for Christians. "To put Scripture and Tradition on the same level," cried Bishop Noichianti of Chioggia, "is ungodly."[6] Most of the bishops, however, insisted on the independent authority of the church's traditions. After all, they said, the earliest Christians had known what to believe before the New Testament had even been written, having learned the traditions passed down by word of mouth from the apostles. Particularly in regard to liturgical practices, the church still had all sorts of customs it assumed went back to New Testament times but which were not mentioned in the Bible. The council therefore declared that Christian faith rests on "truths and rules . . . contained in the written books *and in the unwritten traditions.*"[7] To Luther's cry of "Scripture alone!" Trent replied, "Scripture and tradition!"

Original Sin. Protestants sometimes claimed that the Catholic emphasis on working toward salvation risked denying the doctrine of original sin. If we can do good works, have we really been hopelessly corrupted? Trent affirmed that Adam had been corrupted in body and soul by his first sin, and that "men would not be born unjust, if they were not born through propagation of the seed of Adam, since by that propagation they contract through him, when they are conceived, injustice as their own."[8] Even infants can be cleansed of original sin only by baptism. However, while Luther taught that original sin had destroyed free will, so that we are now incapable of doing good, Trent said that free will, "weakened as it was in its powers and downward bent, was by no means extinguished."[9] Further, Luther said that even after justification we still remain sinners, for we still have a desire to sin. Trent responded that the mere desire to sin is not in the regenerate truly and really sin.[10] "For in those who are born again God hates nothing."[11] Thus, while acknowledging the doctrines of grace and original sin, the council preserved a place for moral striving and thereby for the whole system of penance in the process of achieving salvation.

Justification. "The significance of this Council in the theological sphere," its chairmen wrote to the pope in June of 1546, "lies chiefly in the article on justification, in fact this is the most important item the council has to deal with."[12] History has agreed with that judgment. The bishops believed that salvation cannot be achieved without grace, but they rejected Luther's claim that justification comes from grace alone. Human efforts matter too.

> For God does not command impossibilities, but by commanding thee to do what thou canst and to pray for what thou canst not . . . aids thee that thou mayest be able. . . . Wherefore, no one ought to flatter himself with faith alone, thinking that by faith alone he is made an heir.[13]

Grace comes first, an awakening and assisting grace that begins the process of justification, but people must consent to and cooperate with that grace. Justification, in turn, "is not only a remission of sins but also the sanctification and renewal of the inward man through the voluntary reception of the grace and gifts whereby an unjust man becomes just and from being an enemy becomes a friend."[14] Luther had focused on an instant of justification, in which God saved sinners by pure grace but left them sinners—they were justified only because Christ's righteousness was imputed to them. Trent pictured justification as a process in which divine grace and human efforts cooperate at every step and not only lead God to count us as justified but also begin to transform us so that we more nearly deserve that status.

Sacraments and Reform. Most of the council's decrees concerned the sacraments, but here Trent only made systematic and official what the church had already come to teach. There are seven sacraments: baptism, confirmation, the Eucharist, penance, marriage, ordination, and extreme unction (the sacrament of the dying). The council affirmed transubstantiation and declared that Christ's sacrifice is repeated on the altar every time the Eucharist is celebrated. (Protestants said that the sacrifice had happened only once, on the cross.) Some of the dead go to purgatory, and prayer and indulgences can help them get out sooner, though the council warned against abuses in such matters. Having said that we can cooperate in our salvation, the bishops clarified the system of sacraments which helps us to do so.

The council also demanded a whole series of reforms. Bishops must live in their dioceses and preach regularly, in a simple style and in the language of their people. Priests must not keep mistresses, education must be improved, and everyone must attend Communion more often. If the church and sacraments were to help the people toward salvation, they would have to be put in order. Oddly enough, the issue most dreaded ahead of time, the relation between popes and councils, never aroused much fuss. Some of the bishops recognized the pope as the vicar of Christ, and said that bishops received their authority from him. Others said that the pope is only the chief among the vicars of Christ, and that, just as the apostles received authority from Christ, not Peter, so all the bishops have their authority directly from God. While the church had desperately needed reform, this question had seemed of central importance, but now, with the reform underway and a theological program set forth, Trent felt it possible to leave the relation between popes and bishops unresolved.

JESUITS AND MYSTICS

Trent provided the platform for a Catholic reformation; the Jesuits provided the shock troops. Their founder, Ignatius Loyola, was born sometime in the early 1490s, a Spanish aristocrat who dedicated himself in medieval fashion to the ideals of knighthood. Reading about Loyola's life brings to mind that another Spaniard wrote *Don Quixote* only a generation later. As Loyola later wrote of himself, "Up to twenty-six years of age he was a man given to the vanities of the world and his chief delight was in martial exercises with a great and vain desire to gain honor."[15] Then he received a painful leg wound in battle and spent the months of recuperation wondering about the purpose of his life and reading lives of saints and *The Imitation of Christ*. He decided to become a different kind of knight, dedicated himself to Christ, practiced extreme asceticism, and planned to walk barefoot to Jerusalem.

First, though, he went to Paris to get himself a better education. His classmates first found this ragged, middle-aged soldier just starting school a source of amusement, but gradually some turned to him for advice in their spiritual development. He began to assemble his *Spiritual Exercises* for their guidance. It is a remarkable book. Much of it has all the literary eloquence of a cookbook, and a similarly practical intent, designed as it is for spiritual directors to use in guiding people through a religious retreat. The *Exercises* prescribe a series of daily reflections and prayers, moving from contemplation of one's sins to meditation on the life of Christ. At every stage, they urge the exercise of the imagination. Do not think of the birth of Christ merely in the abstract; "form a mental image of the scene and see in . . . imagination the road from Nazareth to Bethlehem. . . . consider its length and breadth, and whether it is level or winding through valleys and over hills."[16] In a more famous passage, Loyola urged one to imagine hell:

> To see in imagination the great fires. . . . To hear the wailing, screaming, cries, and blasphemies. . . . To smell the smoke, the brimstone, the corruption and rottenness. . . . With the sense of touch to feel how the flames surround and burn souls.[17]

Ignatius organized his followers into the Society of Jesus, the Jesuits, and they resolved to go on pilgrimage to Jerusalem or, if that proved impossible, to offer themselves to the pope, to be used as he might see fit. He demanded incredible endurance through hardship on occasion, but he insisted that his companions get plenty of sleep and food when they could, and he had no patience with medieval self-tortures. "Until a man has once given himself over completely to God," he wrote, "he loves to suffer and to endure physical pain and hardship. But when he has finally given himself over to God he treats his body better, but now no longer as a thing of his own, but as God's property."[18] Unlike earlier religious orders, the Jesuits did not spend a good part of each day saying the office of daily prayers. One Dominican of the period, indeed, denounced them as "an order of loungers, whose members go to and fro about the streets like other people."[19] But Loyola refused to separate prayer from practical activity—in preaching or teaching the Jesuits were living a life of prayer, and he had little patience with anything that distracted them from the task at hand.

To that end, he might compromise on many points, but on obedience he was uncompromising. The Jesuit "ought to allow himself to be carried and directed by Divine Providence through the agency of the superior as if he were a lifeless body which allows itself to be carried to any place and to be treated in any manner desired."[20] He must never criticize his superiors, for, even if they deserve such criticism, it will "give rise to murmuring and scandal rather than to edification."[21] In short, "If we wish to be sure that we are right in all things, we should always be ready to accept this principle: I will believe that the white that I see is black, if the hierarchical Church so defines it."[22]

At the same time, few organizations have ever given subordinates so much flexibility. As he sent out missionaries, Loyola repeatedly insisted that they must adapt their instructions to the circumstances they encountered. He sought an obedience so deep in spirit that it could feel free to break any rule for a good reason. As a result, wherever they went, Jesuit missionaries adapted themselves to the customs of the people they met. Francis Xavier, one of Loyola's first followers, traveled to India and Japan. Matteo Ricci, one of the Jesuit missionaries to China, adopted the dress of a Confucian scholar, taught Western astronomy as an aid to Chinese astrology, showed a deep respect for Chinese culture, and wrote a "Treatise on the True Idea of God" which deliberately did not discuss "all the mysteries of our holy faith" but only "such as can be proved and understood by the light of natural reason."[23] Other religious orders attacked the Jesuit missionaries, partly out of jealousy (for the Jesuits tended to gain influence at the top of a society), but partly because this willingness to tailor preaching to the attitudes of different societies seemed to them to compromise the faith. For a long period, however, Catholic missionaries generally remained remarkably adaptable. In 1659 the *Congregatio de Propaganda Fide,* the papal office in charge of missionary work, wrote from Rome to missionaries all over the world,

> Do not regard it as your task, and do not bring any pressures to bear on the peoples, to change their manners, customs and uses, unless they are evidently contrary to religion and sound morals. What could be more absurd than to transport France, Spain, Italy, or some other European country to China? Do not introduce all that to them, but only the faith.[24]

That proved a high-water mark. Not again until the twentieth century would Christian missionaries so clearly distinguish between Christian faith and European culture.

The Jesuits sought practical accomplishments—influence, conversions—but their practical successes grew out of the spiritual discipline Loyola had established. Other Catholics in the sixteenth century also vividly manifested such a combination of spirituality and practical drive, and none more so than the Spanish nun Teresa of Avila, born in 1515. She was a mystic, but it is hard to imagine anyone less like the popular stereotype of a contemplative withdrawn from the world. She spent her life traveling around Spain founding new convents and shaping up old ones, walking or riding in all weather and writing her books at high speed and with a total and irresistible lack of self-consciousness. If obedience "sends you to the kitchen," she wrote her nuns, "remember that the Lord walks among the pots and pans."[25] That image of kitchen work should not imply that Teresa encouraged only a modest domesticity. "My daughters," she declared, "I want you to be strong men. If you do all that is in you, the Lord will make you so manly that men themselves will be amazed at you."[26] When a male friend ignored her advice, she wrote him impatiently, "Although we women are not of much use as counselors, we are occasionally right."[27]

Teresa regularly saw visions but did not consider them of much importance. Images, she found, played a role only in the lower stages of contemplation and could prove a distraction. At higher levels, not only the imagination but all our faculties fail us. Yet we do not experience that "failure" as a loss.

> When the Lord suspends the understanding and makes it cease from its activity, he gives it something which . . . keeps it busy,

so that, without reasoning in any way, it can understand more in a short time than we with all our human efforts in many years.[28]

A young monk of Teresa's order (the Carmelites) named John of the Cross further developed her account of mystical experience. He stood only five feet, two inches, and when he and another monk arrived to help her, Teresa exclaimed that now she had the assistance of a monk and a half. But his theological education encouraged him to develop a more theoretical analysis of mysticism, and his feel for language made him one of the greatest of Spanish poets. Opponents of Teresa's reforms threw him into prison and subjected him to regular beatings, but precisely in the solitude and pain of his imprisonment John found the best opportunity for mystic exploration. "In order to preserve our spirituality," he wrote, ". . . there is no better remedy than to suffer and work and be silent, and to close the senses by the practice of solitude."[29]

That practice, as John came to understand it, often proves difficult. There comes a point where any imagery distracts the soul from the contemplation of God, but we derive great pleasure from religious images, so advancing to higher levels of contemplation often involves periods of great frustration. The subjects on which one used to meditate now seem worthless and empty, though for a time nothing may take their place. But such "dark nights of the soul," however agonizing, show that the soul is focusing more on God, just as "the more directly we look at the sun, the greater is the darkness which it causes in our visual faculty."[30] Without any familiar landmarks, then, the mystic must travel alone toward God, and that can be terrifying. Nevertheless, John could write of his soul's agonizing journey in the language of a lover's ecstasy:

> O night that was my guide!
> O night more friendly than the dawn!
> O tender night that tied
> the lover and the loved one,
> loved one in the lover fused as one!
>
> On my flowering breasts
> which I have saved for him alone,
> he slept and I caressed
> and fondled him with love,
> and cedars fanned the air above. . . .
>
> I lay, forgot my being,
> and on my love I leaned my face.

All ceased. I left my being,
leaving my cares to fade
among the lilies far away.[31]

CONTINUING DEBATES

Teresa of Avila and John of the Cross shaped the theory of mysticism, and of course other Catholic writers made other contributions, but the Jesuits remained at the center of formulating the Catholic response to Protestantism. Aquinas had delineated a system of cooperation between faith and reason, church and state, and grace and free will. Luther denied that reason had much of a role in the religious life. He insisted that Christians must obey their rulers unless ordered to disobey Scripture. And he taught that sin destroys free will, and that we are saved by grace alone. Catholic theologians debated all of these issues.

The effort to defend the role of human reason in theology proved difficult, for philosophical criticisms raised in the later Middle Ages and thereafter made it hard to explain even how we can talk about God. Aquinas had taught that we talk about God "analogically." When we say God is "wise," for instance, we aren't using the word "wise" in exactly the same sense that we would if we applied it to a human being, but our meaning is not completely different either—it is analogous. Later Catholic theologians divided analogies into analogies of proportionality and analogies of attribution. To stick with the example of divine wisdom, in an analogy of proportionality, I admit that I do not know just *how* God is wise, but I do know that God's wisdom is related to God's being as human wisdom is related to human being, and this gives me a rough framework for thinking about God's wisdom. Analogy of attribution is easiest to explain with a nontheological example: We talk about "healthy people," but we also talk about "healthy food." Now food isn't healthy in the same sense in which people are, but we call food "healthy" (by analogy) when it *causes* health in people who eat it. Similarly, God isn't wise in the same sense in which people are, but we can call God wise because he causes (creates) human wisdom.

In the early 1500s the Dominican Cardinal Cajetan argued that analogy of attribution doesn't really work. We cannot infer much about a cause from the properties of its effects. True, God created people who are wise, but after all God created ice too—it doesn't follow that we should talk about God as cold and easily melted.

Around 1600 the great Spanish Jesuit Francisco Suárez defended the analogy of attribution but attacked the analogy of proportionality. The analogy of proportionality, he said, looks like a neat mathematical equation until you realize that we don't know what God's being is, any more than we know what God's wisdom is. With two elements in the equation unknown, those ratios cease to provide much help.[32] Cajetan, moreover, denied the possibility of a philosophical proof of the immortality of the soul, and Suárez thought that Aquinas' argument for the existence of God as the first mover (everything that moves is moved by something else . . . and therefore there must be a first mover, itself unmoved, which we call God) didn't hold up, since some things in the world at least appear to move themselves.[33] Both Cajetan and Suárez produced theological systems of great sophistication, but anyone who accepted the criticisms raised by both would be left with a very limited role for reason in theology.

For Aquinas, just as reason and revelation supplemented each other, so church and state cooperated in achieving human goods. Suárez and other Jesuits faced the new situation of Catholics living under the authority of Protestant rulers and raised some tough questions about the religious justification of many of the governments of their time. Suárez denied that kings rule by divine right. The power to make laws, he said, "resides, not in any individual man, but rather in the whole body of mankind."[34] Therefore, for a king or anyone else to have the right to rule, "it must necessarily be bestowed upon him by the consent of the community."[35] If a ruler had usurped power and was harming the whole community and there was no other way of getting rid of him, one could justly kill him.[36] Suárez discussed this only on a highly abstract level, but another Spanish Jesuit, Juan Mariana, praised the assassination of King Henry III of France, declaring, "It is a salutary reflection that the princes have been persuaded that if they oppress the state . . . they can be killed not only justly but with praise and glory."[37] Such talk might proclaim the people's liberty against tyrants, but it also embarrassed Catholicism by seeming to justify Protestant charges that Catholic subjects could not be trusted, since the "evil Jesuits" urged them to murder Protestant rulers.

Whatever fears such charges aroused, in France a debate about works and grace seems to have produced even greater passions. Luther had taught that in such matters sinners have no free will, and apart from grace we can do nothing but sin. The Council of Trent, on the other hand, had declared that human beings must freely cooper-

ate with grace in order to achieve justification. Loyola had urged his
Jesuits:

> We ought not to emphasize the doctrine that would destroy free
> will. We may therefore speak of faith and grace to the extent that
> God enables us to do so, for the greater praise of His Divine
> Majesty. But, in these dangerous times of ours, it must not be
> done in such a way that good works or free will suffer any
> detriment.[38]

The Jesuit theologian Luis Molina eagerly followed Loyola's advice
to protect belief in good works and free will. He insisted that even
in a state of nature humans could seek and in some measure achieve
morality and happiness, though only grace could lead us on to the
further goals of salvation and the vision of God. Human efforts can
therefore accomplish something worthwhile even without grace.
Molina further argued that, when God gives us grace, that doesn't
automatically assure our salvation. Only if we cooperate with it does
grace become efficacious.

A Belgian bishop named Cornelius Jansen considered Molina and
his followers Pelagians who were betraying the great Augustine.
Jansen's book *Augustinus,* published in 1640 shortly after his death,
proclaimed that free will apart from grace could lead only to sin and
that God's grace did not require active human cooperation to succeed. Though a long book that might have gone unnoticed and virtually unread, it drew the interest of a circle centered on the French
convent of Port Royal, just outside Paris. Antoine Arnauld, the
brother of the young abbess of Port Royal, wrote: "The Catholic
interpretation is that grace cooperates with the will by causing it to
determine to do good. . . . The Pelagian interpretation is that grace
cooperates with the will by helping it after the will has determined
on its own to do good."[39] He left little doubt that he considered Jansen
"Catholic" and Molina and the Jesuits "Pelagian."

Arnauld's criticism of the Jesuits went beyond their theology of
grace. Port Royal dedicated itself to a rigorous piety, with fasting and
long prayers, and Arnauld and his friends thought the Jesuits partly
to blame for the appallingly lax morality of the French society around
them. The Jesuits sought influence with those in power, and they tried
not to discourage people's religious efforts by making excessive demands. Theories of repentance had distinguished between *contrition*
(repenting of a sin because you genuinely regretted doing it) and
attrition (repenting of a sin only because you were afraid of the

punishment). It had sometimes been uncertain whether mere attrition sufficed for genuine repentance, but the Jesuits now assured people that it did. They also said that one could not commit a sin without the intention to do so. They then developed the theory of "probabilism." Aquinas had taught that one who had any suspicion that an act might be a sin and then went ahead and did it was guilty of sin. Many confessors found that some overscrupulous people could think of a way in which *anything* might be a sin. They started to teach that, as long as one thought an act *probably* not sinful, one did not intend to sin. In the sixteenth century a Spanish Jesuit named Medina went a step further in saying that one did not intentionally commit a sin if there were any plausible interpretation according to which the act was not sinful.

This seemed to mean that a sufficiently imaginative confessor could get one off nearly anything. At any rate, Arnauld thought so. "The Jesuits," he wrote, ". . . make a game of penitential discipline. People do not fear God's punishment, because they are persuaded on the faith of these fathers that it is easy to receive absolution."[40] Under assault, the Jesuits counterattacked. They charged that the Jansenist doctrine of grace was really Protestantism in disguise and secured a papal condemnation of the Jansenists.

About this time, the Jansenists won the support of one of the geniuses of the age, Blaise Pascal. Pascal was one of the greatest mathematicians in history; his experiments on vacuums and atmospheric pressure made important contributions to the science of his day, and he did everything from inventing a calculating machine to establishing the first public trolley service in Paris. As a young man, he had had little interest in religion, but when his sister joined the convent at Port Royal, he came to respect the Jansenists there. One night in 1654 something happened to him. Since he never discussed it, all we can know we learn from a scrap of paper found sewn into the lining of his coat when he died:

Year of Grace 1654.
    Monday, 23rd of November, Feast of St. Clement . . .
    From about half past ten in the evening until about half past twelve.

FIRE

    God of Abraham, God of Isaac, God of Jacob, not of the philosophers and scholars.
    Certitude. Certitude. Feeling. Joy. Peace . . .[41]

The experience changed his life, and he committed his energies to defending Christianity and the Jansenists. In his *Provincial Letters* he satirized the Jesuit confessors who sought to free people from "the 'painful' obligation to love God."[42] The proper approach to a Christian life, he said, is "neither so cruel as that of Calvin, nor so soft as that of Molina."[43] Christ does not, after all, call us to an easy path. Pascal recalled the agony in the garden of Gethsemane: "Jesus seeks companionship and comfort from men. This is the sole occasion in all His life, as it seems to me. But He receives it not, for his disciples are asleep. Jesus will be in agony until the end of the world. We must not sleep during that time."[44]

Pascal devoted the last years of his life to writing an unfinished defense of Christianity. He began with a bleak picture of the human state:

> Let us imagine a number of men in chains, and all condemned to death, where some are killed each day in the sight of others, and those who remain see their own fate in that of their fellows, and wait their turn, looking at each other sorrowfully and without hope. It is an image of the condition of men.[45]

Life may bring fame or accomplishment, but "the last act is tragic, however happy the rest of the play is; at the last a little earth is thrown upon our head, and that is the end for ever."[46] Pascal the scientist even rejected the idea of a hierarchically ordered universe with the earth at its center. We live on a tiny planet somewhere in the midst of a void, and "the eternal silence of these infinite spaces frightens me."[47]

Yet there is another side to the human condition. "Man is but a reed, the most feeble thing in nature; but he is a thinking reed."[48] The universe may dwarf me, but I can imagine the totality of that universe. I may be doomed, but I am conscious of my fate, and that makes me special. Even "if the universe were to crush him, man would still be more noble than that which killed him, because he knows that he dies. . . . The universe knows nothing of this."[49] In sum:

> What a chimera then is man! What a novelty! What a monster, what a chaos, what a contradiction, what a prodigy! Judge of all things, imbecile worm of the earth, depository of truth, a sink of uncertainty and error; the pride and refuse of the universe.[50]

Reason cannot make sense out of these contradictions, Pascal said; the only explanation comes from Christian faith. Only the idea that a creature made in God's own image has fallen into a state of sin can explain the paradoxical mixture of features that makes up human beings.

Pascal thought that faith often leads to more profound insights than reason. Philosophers, he said, want to prove what is true or else remain skeptics, but neither of these alternatives turns out to be possible. Every argument begins with assumptions, which could be proven only by another argument that would involve additional assumptions. We cannot achieve a definitive proof. But neither can we live as skeptics. The pretended skeptic proves himself a fraud as soon as he reaches for a cup of coffee or dodges a falling rock. We all believe some things to be true. How can this be justified if we can't prove anything? Pascal appealed to intuition. "The heart has its reasons, which reason does not know."[51] In mathematics or science—or religion—we start with what we sense or feel to be true. But in religion, someone might protest, surely it is best to remain a skeptic and admit that one cannot be sure. Pascal replied that it is much like a wager. Either God exists or he doesn't. If God exists, belief will win us eternal joy, while disbelief will bring eternal punishment. If God does not exist, the believer will still lead a good life, and the unbeliever will gain nothing. Belief has everything to win and nothing to lose.[52] Pascal's "wager" has often been taken out of context and ridiculed, but he knew well enough that no one comes to faith by a careful calculation of the odds. The point he wanted to make is that skepticism too represents a decision, with consequences should it prove mistaken. If someone has the intuition of faith, the resulting position cannot be condemned as less rational than any other.

However powerful Pascal's defense of Christianity, in the short run his arguments for Jansenism failed. The Jansenists sounded too much like the hated Calvinists, and in 1653 Pope Innocent X issued a bull, *Cum occasione,* which denied that people cannot do good works apart from grace, that grace is irresistible, and that the Jesuits are Pelagians. That did not, however, end the theological disputes within French Catholicism. A very different problem soon emerged around the person of Jeanne Marie Bouvier de la Motte, born in 1648. A few years after she married a man named Guyon, he died, leaving her with three small children. Feeling a call to a special life of piety, she left the children behind and set off on a life of mystic contemplation. She soon attracted admirers of every sort, from poor peasants to Fénelon, one of the greatest writers of France, and her views, known as "Quietism," became the subject of great debate.

Mme. Guyon dismissed the importance of every aspect of the Christian life except the highest form of contemplation. Mystics like

Teresa of Avila and John of the Cross had taught that in the highest kind of contemplation the soul transcends any images. Now Mme. Guyon taught that the "prayer of simple regard," free of any will or image, was the only really good kind of prayer, and that even meditating on the life of Christ is only a distraction and should be avoided. In true prayer, she said, we should surrender ourselves to God so completely that we cease to care whether we will be saved or damned. Increasingly, she even denied the importance of acts of charity. Visiting the sick, she felt, only distracted her from seeking pure submission to God. Once she even blurted out, "Let no one speak to me of humility; the virtues are not for me." At the highest level of mystical contemplation, the soul "has no desire to procure the glory of God, leaving it to God to procure his own glory."[53] The soul must become completely passive, "must simply suffer itself to be possessed, acted upon, and moved without resistance . . . letting itself be led at all times and to any place."[54]

At some level this may all be true. A few mystics may reach a kind of self-surrender in which they feel that God does everything and lose themselves in adoration. But the French bishops, led by the great Bossuet, judged that Quietism should not be proposed as a general model for the Christian life. In 1695 they issued a condemnation, declaring that Christians should not be indifferent to their own salvation. They should have beliefs and hopes and not lose themselves in an all-encompassing love. Extraordinary states of prayer do not represent the only road to salvation; contemplation of the life of Christ can be helpful to Christians. Rules for beginners may not apply to the most advanced mystics, but neither can the special experiences of a few be made the general rule.[55]

Mme. Guyon represents a tendency which regularly reappears in Christianity—a tendency to claim a special relationship with God to which the usual rules do not apply. In rejecting her appeal to the authority of her own experience and her argument for utter passivity in contemplation, the church reaffirmed some of the basic principles of the Catholic Reformation. Luther had appealed to Scripture alone as the basis for a theology of salvation by faith alone. In response Catholics appealed to both Scripture and the traditions of the church as the basis for a theology of salvation through the cooperation of grace and human efforts. Jansenist insistence on pure grace or Quietist appeals to individual experience and passivity had to be rejected. Such defenses of church tradition and the importance of human efforts preserved the significance of the church and sacraments as means to salvation. In that sense, Catholics defended the past. But in the new energy they brought to that defense and the reforms they achieved in the church, they too had undergone a significant reformation.

FOR FURTHER READING

INTRODUCTIONS. A. G. Dickens, *The Counter Reformation* (Harcourt, Brace & World, 1969), provides a basic survey. Michael Foss, *The Founding of the Jesuits* (Weybright & Talley, 1969), is a popular account of Ignatius and his first followers.

COLLECTIONS OF ORIGINAL SOURCES. John C. Olin, *The Catholic Reformation: Savonarola to Ignatius Loyola* (Harper & Row, 1969), brings together a selection of primary texts. Other works by authors mentioned in this chapter: Ignatius Loyola, *Spiritual Exercises*, tr. by Anthony Mottola (Doubleday & Co., Image Books, 1964); Teresa of Avila, *Interior Castle*, tr. by E. Allison Peers (Doubleday & Co., Image Books, 1972); John of the Cross, *Dark Night of the Soul*, tr. by E. Allison Peers (Doubleday & Co., Image Books, 1959); Blaise Pascal, *Pensées*, tr. by A. J. Krailsheimer (Harmondsworth, Middlesex: Penguin Books, 1966).

IMPORTANT BUT MORE DIFFICULT. Pierre Janelle, *The Catholic Reformation* (Bruce Publishing Co., 1963), surveys the field at a level a bit more advanced than Dickens' book. Frederick Copleston, *A History of Philosophy*, Vol. 3, Part 2 (Doubleday & Co., Image Books, 1963), provides a clear account of Suárez. Hubert Jedin, *A History of the Council of Trent*, tr. by Ernest Graf, 2 vols. (B. Herder Book Co., 1957, 1961), is a massive piece of scholarship. Ronald A. Knox, *Enthusiasm* (Oxford: Clarendon Press, 1950), ranges from the Marcionites to the present but provides a wonderfully entertaining account of Jansenism and Quietism.

NOTES

1. John of the Cross, *The Ascent of Mount Carmel* 1.13.6, in *The Complete Works of Saint John of the Cross*, tr. by E. Allison Peers (Newman Press, 1946), Vol. 1, p. 61.
2. Contarini to Giustiniani, Sept. 22, 1511; in Hubert Jedin, "Contarini und Camaldoli," in *Archivio italiano per la storia della pieta*, Vol. 2 (Rome: Edizioni di Storia e Letteratura, 1959), p. 117.
3. Quoted in Hubert Jedin, *A History of the Council of Trent*, tr. by Ernest

Graf, Vol. 1 (B. Herder Book Co., 1957), pp. 424–425.

4. Ibid., p. 431.

5. Dermot Fenlon, *Heresy and Obedience in Tridentine Italy* (Cambridge: Cambridge University Press, 1972), pp. 54–55.

6. Quoted in Hubert Jedin, *A History of the Council of Trent,* tr. by Ernest Graf, Vol. 2 (B. Herder Book Co., 1961), p. 86.

7. *Decree Concerning the Canonical Scriptures,* in H. J. Schroeder (ed.), *Canons and Decrees of the Council of Trent* (B. Herder Book Co., 1941), p. 17.

8. *Decree Concerning Justification,* ch. 3, ibid., p. 31.

9. Ibid., ch. 1, p. 30.

10. *Decree Concerning Original Sin,* sec. 5, ibid., p. 23.

11. Ibid.

12. Quoted in Jedin, *A History of the Council of Trent,* Vol. 2, p. 171.

13. *Decree Concerning Justification,* ch. 11, in Schroeder, *Canons and Decrees of the Council of Trent,* pp. 36–37.

14. Ibid., ch. 7, p. 33.

15. Quoted in Michael Foss, *The Founding of the Jesuits* (Weybright & Talley, 1969), p. 64.

16. Ignatius Loyola, *The Spiritual Exercises of St. Ignatius,* tr. by Anthony Mottola (Doubleday & Co., Image Books, 1964), pp. 70–71.

17. Ibid., p. 59.

18. Quoted in Hugo Rahner, *Ignatius the Theologian,* tr. by Michael Barry (Herder & Herder, 1968), p. 22.

19. Quoted in Foss, *The Founding of the Jesuits,* p. 134.

20. Ignatius Loyola, *The Constitutions of the Society of Jesus,* tr. by George E. Ganss (St. Louis: The Institute of Jesuit Sources, 1970), pp. 248–249.

21. Ignatius Loyola, *Rules for Thinking with the Church,* in *The Spiritual Exercises of St. Ignatius,* p. 140.

22. Ibid., p. 141.

23. Quoted in Foss, *The Founding of the Jesuits,* p. 214.

24. Ibid., pp. 216–217.

25. Teresa of Jesus, *Book of the Foundations,* ch. 5, in *The Complete Works,* tr. by E. Allison Peers (London: Sheed & Ward, 1946), Vol. 3, p. 22.

26. Teresa of Jesus, *Book Called Way of Perfection,* ch. 7, ibid., Vol. 2, p. 35.

27. Teresa of Jesus, *The Letters of Saint Teresa of Jesus,* tr. by E. Allison Peers (London: Burns & Oates, 1951), p. 223.

28. *The Life of the Holy Mother Teresa of Jesus,* ch. 12, in *The Complete Works,* Vol. 1, p. 72.

29. John of the Cross, Letter 6, in *The Complete Works,* Vol. 3, p. 272.

30. John of the Cross, *The Dark Night of the Soul* 2.5.3, ibid., Vol. 1, p. 406.

31. John of the Cross, "Black Night," in *The Poems of St. John of the Cross,* tr. by Willis Barnstone (Indiana University Press, 1968), pp. 39–41. Used by permission of Willis Barnstone. The first line, "O night, my guide!" has been emended here at the translator's request.

32. See Frederick Copleston, *A History of Philosophy,* Vol. 3, Part 2 (Doubleday & Co., Image Books, 1963), p. 182.

33. Ibid., p. 183.

34. Francisco Suárez, *A Treatise on Laws and God the Lawgiver* 3.2.3, in

Selections from Three Works, tr. by Gwladys L. Williams, Ammi Brown, and John Waldron, Vol. 2 (Oxford: Clarendon Press, 1944), p. 373.

35. Ibid., 3.4.2, p. 384.

36. Francisco Suárez, *A Defence of the Catholic and Apostolic Faith,* 6.4.7, ibid., p. 711.

37. Juan de Mariana, *The King and the Education of the King,* tr. by George Albert Moore (Country Dollar Press, 1948), p. 149.

38. Ignatius Loyola, *Rules for Thinking with the Church,* in *The Spiritual Exercises of St. Ignatius,* p. 141.

39. Quoted in Alexander Sedgwick, *Jansenism in Seventeenth-Century France* (University Press of Virginia, 1977), p. 69.

40. Ibid., p. 149.

41. Blaise Pascal, *Mémorial,* in *Oeuvres complètes* (Paris: Librairie Gallimard, 1954), pp. 553–554.

42. Blaise Pascal, *The Provincial Letters,* tr. by Thomas M'Crie (Modern Library, 1941), p. 464.

43. Blaise Pascal, *Ecrits sur la grâce,* in *Oeuvres complètes,* p. 956.

44. Blaise Pascal, *Pensées* 552, tr. by W. F. Trotter (E. P. Dutton & Co., 1958), p. 148.

45. Ibid., 199, p. 60.

46. Ibid., 210, p. 61.

47. Ibid., 206, p. 61.

48. Ibid., 347, p. 97.

49. Ibid.

50. Ibid., 434, p. 121.

51. Ibid., 277, p. 78.

52. Ibid., 233, pp. 66–68.

53. All these passages are quoted in Ronald A. Knox, *Enthusiasm* (Oxford: Clarendon Press, 1950), p. 279.

54. Ibid., p. 263.

55. Ibid., pp. 341–342.

14

GOD'S GOVERNANCE

[Geneva,] I neither fear nor am ashamed to say, is the most perfect school of Christ that ever was in the earth since the days of the Apostles. In other places, I confess Christ to be truly preached; but manners and religion to be so sincerely reformed I have not yet seen in any other place.

—John Knox[1]

By the end of the sixteenth century Scandinavia and parts of Germany followed Luther's church. Much of Eastern Europe kept to its own ancient traditions. Italy, Spain, and most of France retained their allegiance to the papacy. The radical Reformation survived only in isolated pockets. Much of Switzerland and the Netherlands, parts of Germany along the Rhine, Scotland, and—with all sorts of qualifications—England shared what is usually called the Reformed tradition, which later shaped much of the early religious heritage of the United States. Zwingli began it, but John Calvin at Geneva became its greatest theologian.

CALVIN

Calvin grew up in a moderately wealthy French family, studied in Paris, at the same school as Loyola, and joined a circle of French humanists. At some point he became a Protestant. It is characteristic that Luther provided a vivid account of his religious development while Calvin mentioned this conversion, which changed his life and put him at some risk of death, only once or twice in passing. He was always eager to talk about God but often reluctant to talk about himself.

Protestants were not altogether safe in France, and Calvin left in pursuit—so he always said—of the quiet life of a scholar. He passed

219

through the Swiss city of Geneva, intending only to spend the night. Geneva had just gone Protestant but lacked any clear theology or religious leadership. The leaders of the city asked Calvin to stay and take charge. He refused, pleading his "natural shyness and timidity,"[2] until someone said that God needed Calvin in Geneva and would curse him if he fled his duty. The Genevans soon realized they had gotten more than they bargained for. Calvin set out to reorganize worship and education, improve morals, and persuade all to accept a common statement of faith. When one prominent citizen raised doubts that God had really called this imperious Frenchman, Calvin replied, "If you entertain some doubts . . . it is enough for me that it is quite clear to my own satisfaction."[3] The Genevans grew restive. "If I simply said it was daytime at high noon," Calvin wrote later, "they would begin to doubt it."[4] They drove Calvin out but three years later, in 1541, pleaded for his return. They were an isolated, vulnerable, and tiny Protestant enclave surrounded by Catholic France. They needed leadership and confidence, and Calvin was the man to provide it.

Reading Calvin seldom evokes the emotive response so often roused by reading Luther or Augustine. There is, rather, the cumulative effect of a clear and systematic mind at work, fitting together all the pieces into a way of looking at the world. That picture begins with an overpowering sense of God's glory. "Nearly all the wisdom we possess"—Calvin's masterpiece, the *Institutes of the Christian Religion,* begins—"that is to say, true and sound wisdom, consists of two parts: the knowledge of God and of ourselves."[5] We cannot understand ourselves if we ignore God, and we cannot understand God without facing up to the truth about ourselves. The sad truth is that "the whole man is overwhelmed—as by a deluge—from head to foot, so that no part is immune from sin."[6] The order of the universe proclaims the glory of God, but we fail to see it. We deny God, and then, finding our lives falling apart, we invent something to put in God's place. The mind of man is a factory of idols; people "worship and adore their own ravings."[7] Plato had taught that we sin out of ignorance; Calvin said that we are ignorant because we have sinned. Our sin prevents us from seeing the world aright. Therefore the Scriptures provide the only guide to understanding God or ourselves—like glasses that correct our vision. Calvin acknowledged that the Bible might be wrong about matters of detail that did not affect doctrine, but he insisted on its authority concerning what to believe. Yet faith cannot be merely "belief in the existence of God and in the truth of the narratives concerning the

Christ";[8] we must also sense that God can change our lives.

Christ stood at the center of Calvin's faith, but in contrast to Luther's sharp distinction between law and gospel, he emphasized that we still stand within the same covenant God first made with Abraham. For Luther, the Law served only negative functions: it convicts us of our sins, and it helps keep order among sinful people who without some law would just murder each other. Calvin insisted on a third use of the law. For the Christian, "the law remains a constant sting that will not let him stand still."[9] It guides and shapes a morally better life. Christians should not, of course, follow the Law out of fear or in hopes of earning salvation.

> Those bound by the yoke of the law are like servants assigned certain tasks for each day by their masters . . . [who] dare not appear before their masters unless they have fulfilled the exact measure of their tasks. But sons, who are more generously and candidly treated by their fathers, do not hesitate to offer them incomplete and half-done and even defective works, trusting that their obedience and readiness of mind will be accepted by their fathers. . . . Such children ought we to be.[10]

God's grace alone saves us, but in gratitude we then try to do God's will. That grateful effort, indeed, was so important to Calvin that he even reversed Luther's usual order and discussed sanctification (the change in our lives) before justification (the initial bestowal of God's grace)—without for a moment implying that we are justified *because* we have reformed our lives.

Reflections on how we come to be saved led to the doctrine of predestination. Most people think of this doctrine as occupying a far more important place in Calvin's thought than it actually did. He dealt with predestination late in the *Institutes* and not at all in one of the catechisms he wrote, and this certainly was not the starting point of his theology. Still, when it followed, or seemed to, as a logical consequence of other conclusions, he did not hesitate. Why are some people saved? Surely not because of their own works.

> The saints, when it is a question of the founding and establishing of their own salvation, without regard for works turn their eyes solely to God's goodness. . . . For if they begin to judge it by good works, nothing will be more uncertain or more feeble.[11]

And yet, as Calvin bluntly said, "in actual fact, the covenant of life is not preached equally among all men, and among those to whom it is preached, it does not gain the same acceptance either constantly or in equal degree."[12] Scripture talks about goats as well as sheep, and our experience suggests that God's grace does not transform everyone. But if some are saved and others damned, and salvation has nothing to do with merit, it can only be because God has predestined some to salvation and others to damnation. "If we ask why God has pity on some, and why he lets go and leaves others, there is no answer except that it pleases him to do so."[13] No one gets less than they deserve, for we are all sinners and deserve damnation. Some get more than they deserve, because God chooses to act mercifully—in some cases.

Why only some? Why this particular number? Calvin refused to speculate. "To seek any other knowledge of predestination than what the Word of God discloses is not less insane than if one should purpose to walk in a pathless waste, or to see in darkness."[14] Only God knows who stands among the elect. We cannot look around in the world and identify them. Sometimes Calvin thought that Christians could at least be confident of their own salvation. "When it pleases God to imprint the certitude of his promises on our hearts . . . he declares to us that we are of that little number whom he has reserved for himself."[15] At other times, he entertained a terrifying possibility: "Experience shows that the reprobate are sometimes affected by almost the same feeling as the elect, so that even in their own judgment they do not in any way differ from the elect . . . because the Lord, to render them more convicted and inexcusable, steals into their minds to the extent that his goodness may be tasted without the Spirit of adoption."[16] It is a thought to make the blood run cold, but Calvin had an important point to make. There are enough cult messiahs convinced that God has spoken to them to show that inner certainty does not suffice to prove a divine calling. So how can one be certain of salvation? It is a question Calvin never really answered. For many of his followers the search for a way to identify the elect, or at least to be certain for oneself, became crucial. It is remarkable that Calvin himself so focused on the glory of God that he could leave even his own salvation a matter of secondary importance.

Thus the fact that our moral efforts cannot have any effect on whether or not we will be saved does not make them unimportant, for they can contribute in a small way to God's glory. Christ is the head of the church, and therefore any corruption within the church brings a kind of dishonor on him. Therefore the church, and the Christian state, ought to work to improve the morals of those within them, and in particular the church should examine the morals of those admitted to Communion, for nothing would more dishonor Christ than that the unrepentant should take part in any way in the sacrament of his body and blood.

Calvin's theology of the sacraments and his theories of church organization generally followed those of his friend Martin Bucer, the leader of the reformation at Strassburg, with whom Calvin, in the time when the Genevans had thrown him out, spent the happiest years of his life. One could make a case for Bucer as the central figure of the Reformation: he had a deep influence on Calvin, he worked hard to reconcile the Lutherans and Zwinglians, and he ended his life in England as an elder statesman advising the course of the reformation there. In Strassburg he organized elders to cooperate with the ministers in running the church and to take a lead in the moral improvement of the city. In trying to reconcile Lutherans and Zwinglians, he sought to avoid any specific account of what happened to the bread and wine, insisting only on Christ's presence. Whenever our bodies eat the bread and wine, he said, our spirits receive the body and blood of Christ—let us speculate no further. In an age of violent religious dispute, Bucer stood out for his tolerance. "Flee formulas," he proclaimed, "bear with the weak. While all faith is placed in Christ the thing is safe. It is not given for all to see the same thing at the same time."[17] Many who had been persecuted elsewhere found a haven in Strassburg, and one cannot help admiring this side of Bucer. Yet one can also see why Luther and others came to distrust him. As a negotiator he had a fatal flaw. Not content with hoping for unity, he would pretend he had achieved it, writing slightly different letters to each side and trying to slip through an ambiguous formula.

Concerning what happens at the Lord's Supper, Calvin also sought a position between Luther and Zwingli. He could not agree with Zwingli that the bread and wine simply symbolize Christ's body and blood, but he also could not accept Luther's ideas that, since Christ is divine, Christ's body is present everywhere, and therefore bodily present in the bread and wine. "The Holy Spirit," Calvin insisted, "teaches that the body of Christ from the time of his resurrection was finite, and is contained in heaven even to the last Day."[18] A body that is everywhere at once, Calvin suspected, is not really a human body, and thus Luther's theory of the sacrament endangered Christ's full humanity. "And why (they say) cannot God make the same flesh occupy many and divers places, be contained in no place, so as to lack measure and form? Madmen, why do you demand that God's power make flesh to be and not to be flesh at the same time!"[19] Like Bucer, therefore, Calvin said that we should not ask *how* Christ is present but simply accept that whenever we eat and drink the bread and wine he is.

The church maintained its discipline by regulating whom it admitted to the Eucharist. The Genevan church had four kinds of officials: ministers, teachers, elders, and deacons. Within each congregation deacons concerned themselves with charity and elders with church government and morals. The ministers met regularly for Bible study and theological discussion, but the real power lay in a regular gathering of ministers and representative elders (in Geneva called the "consistory" but among later English and Scottish Calvinists called the "presbytery"). The consistory and the elders of each congregation could punish members, but only by exclusion from Communion, and Calvin urged that even in this, "there should be no strictness that may in any way burden anyone, and even none but medicinal corrections, in order to recall sinners to our Lord."[20]

The city government would punish more serious moral lapses through the criminal law. The state, after all, Calvin observed, does not exist merely so that "men may breathe, eat, drink, and be warmed. . . . But it also exists so that idolatry, sacrilege of the name of God, blasphemies against his truth and other public offences against religion may not emerge and may not be disseminated."[21] In the sixteenth century everyone took it for granted that the state would legislate morality; what was unusual about Geneva was that the rules were enforced, even against the rich and powerful.

TWO CALVINISTS: KNOX AND ARMINIUS

In Geneva, church and state could cooperate, but French Calvinists found themselves ruled by a Catholic king. Even in such circumstances, Calvin generally urged obedience to constituted authority. Rulers "have a mandate from God, have been invested with divine authority, and are wholly God's representatives."[22] Besides, "We know that there is such perversity in human nature, that everyone would scratch out his neighbor's eyes if there were no bridle to hold him."[23] On occasion, however, Calvin took a different attitude, and those passages became crucial for many later Calvinists. Like Luther and many others, he taught that Christians should disobey a government which ordered them to betray their faith. Ordinarily, however, a citizen faced with injustice should simply put up with it. As a good humanist, though, Calvin recalled that in ancient Rome the tribunes had been charged with defending the rights of the common people.

If there are officials charged with such a responsibility in a government, Calvin said,

> I am so far from forbidding them to withstand, in accordance with their duty, the fierce licentiousness of kings, that, if they wink at kings who violently fall upon and assault the lowly common folk, I declare that their dissimulation involves nefarious perfidy, because they dishonestly betray the freedom of the people, of which they know that they have been appointed protectors by God's ordinance.[24]

French nobles or English members of Parliament, reading that, could become convinced they had a religious duty to fight their kings. Calvin even allowed that on rare occasions God directly commissions prophets to denounce injustice and call for action. If revolution comes, the results may, as Luther had feared, be dreadful. Nevertheless, "however these deeds of men are judged in themselves, still the Lord accomplished his work through them alike when he broke the bloody scepters of arrogant kings and when he overturned intolerable governments. Let the princes hear and be afraid."[25] Some later Calvinists seized upon such principles with an enthusiasm which would probably have horrified Calvin himself.

None more so than John Knox in Scotland. Scotland had a notoriously corrupt church, a weak government, and a tradition of some social democracy. Knox was one of the country's first Protestants; he first appears in history as a bodyguard of the early Protestant martyr George Wishart, carrying a two-headed ax. Captured by Catholic forces, he spent two years as a galley slave. He had no patience with those who urged patience and obedience in the face of a ruler's acts contrary to God's will.

> Now the common song of all men is, "We must obey our kings, be they good or be they bad; for God hath so commanded." But horrible shall the vengeance be that shall be poured forth upon such blasphemies of God's holy name and ordinance. For it is no less blasphemy to say that God hath commanded kings to be obeyed when they command impiety, than to say that God by his precept is author and maintainer of all iniquity.[26]

It is not even enough to avoid impiety oneself, for the Old Testament makes clear that God punishes even individually righteous people if they live in corrupt nations. "The whole tribe of Benjamin perished with the adulterers. . . . Whole Amalek was commanded to be destroyed."[27] Christians have a duty to oppose bad government. Knox reminded the nobles of Scotland of their duty "to vindicate and deliver your subjects and brethren from all violence and oppression."[28] Little wonder that Mary Queen of Scots protested to Knox, "Then I perceive that my subjects shall obey you, and not me; and shall do what they list and not what I command: and so must I be subject to them, and not they to me."[29]

In Scotland and France, and later in England, political conditions drove Calvin's followers to think about their relations to an unfriendly government. In Holland, Calvinism became the official religion, and attention turned to the doctrine of predestination. The debate came to center on an Amsterdam minister named Jacob Arminius. Some of his parishioners would tell him that, while they wanted to stop sinning, they guessed they were not predestined to do so! The doctrine, he concluded, "restrains . . . all zeal and studious regard for good works . . . , extinguishes the zeal for prayer . . . , [and] takes away all that most salutary fear and trembling with which we are commanded to work out our own salvation."[30]

Arminius conceded that in a state of sin, "the free will . . . is not only wounded, maimed, infirm, bent, and weakened; but it is also imprisoned, destroyed, and lost."[31] Therefore we can accomplish nothing without grace. When God offers us grace, however, "It always remains within the power of the free will to reject the grace bestowed."[32] Since God knows everything, God knows who will accept grace and who will turn it down. In that sense salvation and damnation are predestined. But Arminius denied what Calvin had affirmed: that God determines who will accept grace and who will refuse it.

In 1610, a year after Arminius' death, his followers wrote up a "Remonstrance" which set forth the principles of Arminian theology. Christ died for all, they said, and grace is offered to all, but grace is not irresistible, and some people reject it. The Synod of Dort in 1619, composed mostly of Dutch Calvinists but with delegates from Germany, Switzerland, and England, condemned Arminius and the "Remonstrants" and laid out the five basic principles of Calvinist orthodoxy:

    1.   Unconditional election: Salvation and damnation rest only on God's free decision "before the foundation of the world."
    2.   Limited atonement: The efficacy of Christ's atonement extends only to the elect.

3. Total depravity: The Fall has left human beings in corruption and helplessness.

4. Irresistible grace: Regeneration is wholly the work of God; we cannot reject it when it is offered.

5. The perseverance of the saints: God so preserves the elect that they do not fall away from grace.[33]

It was an uncompromising faith, making brutally explicit some things even Calvin would have left as mysteries, but full of awe at the power and grace of God, determined to be logical, and willing to live with the consequences.

REFORMATION IN ENGLAND

Many believe that England became Protestant because Henry VIII wanted a divorce which the pope would not grant. Like much of what everyone knows about history, this is not particularly true. The tradition of reform begun by Wyclif in the fourteenth century had never died out entirely, and Protestant ideas imported from the continent had reinforced it from the earliest days of the Reformation. If the divorce question had never arisen, Henry VIII might well have had to lead the Catholic opposition to a strong Protestant party. But, needing a divorce, Henry broke from the pope's authority in the early 1530s and declared himself supreme head of the church in England. As a result the theology of the monarch came to have a dramatic effect on the theology of the Church of England. To oversimplify an exceedingly complex story: Henry at one point had some Lutheran sympathies but grew steadily more Catholic as he grew older. Under his young son Edward VI English theology moved closer to Calvin. When Edward died, his sister Mary returned England to Roman Catholicism. On Mary's death in 1558 her sister Elizabeth secured a Protestant compromise. Thus, to take some examples, the "Bishops' Book" of 1543 (under Henry) affirmed transubstantiation, denied salvation by faith alone, and asserted freedom of the will—all Catholic positions. Henry later even sought to require that all priests be celibate. The Forty-two Articles of 1553 (under Edward), on the other hand, presented a rather Calvinist view of the Lord's Supper, defended salvation by grace alone, and argued for predestination, though with an Arminian interpretation—Christ died for all, not just the elect.[34]

Most of this movement took place while Thomas Cranmer was

Archbishop of Canterbury. One contemporary remarked of Cranmer
that it was "difficult to determine with precision, at any given time,
the exact phase of a mind so shifting."[35] Cranmer had far more Protestant sympathies than Henry, and he also had a wife—whom, legend
had it, he kept hidden in a trunk during the time when Henry insisted
on clerical celibacy—but his loyalty held his king's affection. His
interests lay less in systematic theology than in church history, especially the history of liturgy, and in writing the Book of Common
Prayer he produced the foundation of much English religion and one
of the glories of English prose. When Edward died and his Catholic
sister Mary came to the throne, however, England seemed lost to
Protestantism. Cranmer recanted his Protestant faith but then recanted his recantation and went to the stake, thrusting into the fire
the hand with which he had signed his first recantation. Mary's persecution of many Protestants and her marriage to the king of Spain
identified Catholicism, however unfairly, with persecution and the
hated Spanish in the minds of many English people. Under Elizabeth,
an independent church and some sort of Protestantism became part
of the English tradition, but its theological details remained somewhat vague.

The Thirty-nine Articles, adopted in 1571 and the basic doctrinal
document of the Church of England, compromised on some issues and
admitted of several interpretations on others. Article 17, for instance,
declared that some are predestined to salvation but did not say if the
rest are damned by God's decision or their own wills. It neither
affirmed nor denied Calvin's doctrine of *double* predestination. Article 28 rejected transubstantiation while affirming the real presence of
Christ's body and blood in the sacrament—though in a "heavenly and
spiritual manner." Anglicans could hold any theology from near
Catholic to Calvinist; most were probably moderate Arminians. In
the late 1500s Richard Hooker's *Laws of Eccesiastical Polity* set out
a "middle way" between the extremes of Catholicism and Calvinism,
a thoughtful and moderate theology that rejected the authority of
popes for that of Scripture alone but drew heavily on Christian writers of the first several centuries in interpreting the faith. Such scholarly attention to the early church has been characteristic of English
theology ever since, and the theological compromises developed by
Hooker and others produced a degree of peace. Some questions of
liturgy and church organization, however, could not be compromised
—one either had bishops or did not, knelt to pray or remained standing, and so on—and these issues therefore became the center of
English theological debate.

FROM PURITANS TO QUAKERS

In such controversies the Puritan party desired to purify the church —purify it of theological vagueness, moral laxity, elaborate liturgy, and bishops. The English Puritans often claimed to follow Calvin, but Calvin had acknowledged the legitimacy of a number of different forms of church organization and liturgical style. Increasingly, the Puritans insisted that worship should not include anything not explicitly mentioned in the Bible and therefore opposed kneeling or special vestments or stained glass windows. They also argued that in the New Testament no minister stood superior to any other, and therefore that independent congregations or "presbyteries" (regional conferences of ministers and elders as in Scotland or Geneva) were allowable, but not bishops. Further, they put more emphasis on personal religious experience, especially for ministers. As one early Puritan, William Perkins, put it, "Wood that is capable of fire does not burn unless fire be put to it: and he must first be godly affected himself who would stir up godly affections in other men."[36]

"Puritan" has come to denote a character type as much as a theological position. The Puritan character in one play of the period, "Sir Thomas Bitefig," advises

> First then,
> I charge thee, lend no money; next, serve God;
> If ever thou hast children, teach them thrift:
> They'll learn religion fast enough themselves.[37]

Puritans, in other words, worked hard and saved their money. The great sociologist Max Weber argued for a connection between Protestantism, especially Calvinism, and the beginnings of capitalism, claiming that people who believed in hard work and in frugal living inevitably built up supplies of surplus money to invest. Historians continue to debate Weber's thesis, and it is at least a problem that Catholics in Florence took to capitalism with as much enthusiasm as Calvinists in Amsterdam, but there can be no doubt that Puritans thought of their jobs as divine callings. To quote Perkins again: "As in a camp, the general appoints to every man his place and standing . . . , even so it is in human societies: God is the general appointing to every man his particular calling . . . though it be but to sweep the house or keep sheep."[38] From thinking of one's job as a divinely appointed vocation, it could be but a step to thinking of success in that job as a sign of divine grace. Calvin's reading of history had taught him that the saints had most often been among the poor and oppressed, and that therefore, "it is (spiritually) much more dangerous to be rich than to be poor,"[39] but *some* Puritans risked identifying material success with a sign of grace.

Of course Puritanism produced a reaction against itself. In the early 1600s Archbishop William Laud tried to tighten up church order and force the Puritans into line. Great preachers like John Donne and Lancelot Andrewes perfected an elegant, metaphysical style of Anglican preaching very different from the deliberately plain Puritan sermons. Anglicans appealed to Hooker's *Laws of Ecclesiastical Polity* for the historical and theological underpinnings for the Church of England's "middle way" between Rome and Geneva. In attacking bishops or elaborate ceremony, the Puritans appealed to the model of the earliest church. Hooker had argued that we cannot know for sure the form of the New Testament church. The evidence is too vague. What we can know is that for over a thousand years the church had many of the customs the Puritans now opposed. "A very strange thing sure it were," he pointed out to his Puritan opponents, "that such a discipline as you speak of should be taught by Christ and his apostles in the word of God, and no church ever found it out ... till this present time."[40] Hooker did not accept the Roman Catholic position that tradition has an authority independent of Scripture, but he did use it as a reliable guide to the interpretation of Scripture, while the Puritans wanted to read their Bibles unencumbered by traditional assumptions.

Like many people anxious for reform, the Puritans knew what they were against more clearly than they could define what they were for. Some wanted to work for reform within the Church of England; others separated their congregations from a church they considered hopelessly corrupt. Some would tolerate properly reformed bishops; others insisted on presbyterian organization like that of Scotland or Geneva; still others favored independence for each local congregation. Some, like John Rogers, admitted to communion only those who had had a clearly definable religious experience: "Every one to be *admitted* gives out some *experimental* Evidences of the work of *grace* upon his *soul* (for the *Church* to judge of) whereby he (or she) is *convinced* that he is *regenerate* and *received* of God."[41] Others, like Richard Baxter, were convinced that this amounted to "taking a very few that can talk more than the rest, and making them the church."[42] Baxter favored admitting anyone who would affirm the church's teaching and lead a reasonably good life. Some accepted infant baptism; others baptized only adults who had made a declaration of faith, and the origins of today's Baptists lie principally among these radical English Puritans.

Inevitably, theology came to be mixed up with politics. In the 1640s Parliament defeated King Charles and called together the Westminster Assembly to define a faith for England. The resulting document, the Westminster Confession, has become a key statement of faith for Scottish and American Presbyterians, but it never really took hold in England. It tried to impose a moderate Presbyterianism, but Parliament owed its victory primarily to the army of Oliver Cromwell, which included many Separatists, who insisted that each congregation should be independent, and Baptists, who could not accept Westminster's defense of infant baptism. Cromwell introduced a general religious toleration of all Protestant groups. (He also distinguished himself by his tolerance of Jews, though he continued to mistrust and persecute Catholics.)

Cromwell soon began to have regrets about his principle of tolerance. Just as in the early days of Luther's reformation, some people began to apply the principles of religious reform to social issues. For those called "Levellers," distrust of aristocratic bishops turned into an attack on economic inequality. "The rich lock up the treasures of the earth," wrote the popular preacher Gerrard Winstanley, and tell the poor to wait for a reward in heaven. "Why may not we have our heaven here (that is, a comfortable livelihood in the earth) and heaven hereafter too?"[43] Winstanley led one group of Levellers, the "Diggers," to seize some land and set up an agricultural commune with all property in common. His theology was as radical as his economics. He considered much of Scripture—the story of Adam and Eve, for instance, or the virgin birth, or Christ's physical resurrection —as allegory. "Whether there were such outward things or no, it matters not much."[44] What really matters is not events that might have happened long ago, but the spirit of Christ within each person today:

> The whole creation . . . is the clothing of God. . . . The Father is the universal power that hath spread himself on the whole globe; the Son is the same power drawn into and appearing in one single person. . . . This is the excellency of the work, when a man shall be made to see Christ in other creatures as well as himself.[45]

Religious authority became a crucial issue dividing moderate and radical Puritans. The moderates emphasized the authority of Scripture. The radicals, often pointing out that the poor lacked the time or education to study Scripture, appealed to the individual's experience.

"To a poor soul," John Rogers wrote, "all such things as are in the soul are made known by experience."[46] As another radical Puritan put it, "It was the same Spirit I now felt . . . that did write the Scriptures."[47] More moderate Englishmen had their doubts. In a surviving account of a debate in an English parish during this period, one speaker, challenged to prove his point, said he "found it by experience," but his opponents firmly declared, "We desired him to prove it by the scriptures, for we would not be ruled by his fancy."[48] Such debates no doubt occurred repeatedly.

The longest-lasting group of those appealing to inner experience is the Society of Friends, the Quakers. Their origins lie among the Ranters, wild wandering preachers in rebellion against moderate Puritan repression, who exploded in loud opposition to established preachers. George Fox, the greatest early Quaker leader, tells how he would stand up in a "steeple house" (since the *people* really make up the church, he refused to call any *building* a church) after the minister "had donn his stuffe" and speak out as the spirit called him.[49] Another early Quaker leader, James Naylor, described his call:

> I was at the Plow, meditating on the things of God, and suddenly I heard a voice saying unto me, "Get thee out from thy kindred and from thy Father's House." . . . Without any money, having neither taken Leave of Wife or Children . . . , I was commanded to go into the West, not knowing . . . what I was to do there . . . , and ever since, I have remained, not knowing today what I was to do tomorrow.[50]

The early Quakers heard voices, experienced the dramatic tremblings that gave them their name, and on occasion walked naked through cities "for a sign" to urge repentance. They were mystics rather than primarily social reformers in any usual sense. Yet they made extreme commitments to the principle of social equality. They refused to remove their hats in the presence of social superiors. According to the customs of the time, a poor man would address a rich one as "you," while the rich man would say "thou" in reply. The Quakers would " 'thee' and 'thou' all men and women, without any respect to rich or poor, great or small."[51]

Early Quakers minimized the importance of the Bible and denied bodily resurrection after death, saying that everyone has the spirit of Christ within and that in good people the resurrection has already taken place in this life. They believed that real conversion left one certain of salvation and free from moral faults. Not surprisingly, they concluded that many ministers had not really been converted. They appealed to the Inner Light within each person, insisting that that Light gave women as much right to preach as men. Many of their great missionaries, indeed, were women, and Margaret Fell, who eventually married George Fox, expressed their central principle as eloquently as anyone: "Now friends, deal plainly with yourselves, and let the Eternal Light search you . . . , for this will deal plainly with you; it will rip you up and lay you open . . . naked and bare before the Lord God."[52] Such sentiments had come a long way from the beginnings of Puritanism.

None of the Puritans got what they wanted. The moderate Presbyterians did not impose the Westminster Confession and Presbyterian governance on England, and none of the radical groups succeeded in transforming their society. Cromwell, who hoped for tolerance, ended by persecuting Winstanley and James Naylor, and shortly after Cromwell's death in 1658 the Puritan Commonwealth collapsed and Charles II came back to be king. Most moderate Puritans decided they could live with bishops and vestments more easily than with social and religious chaos, and something like the Elizabethan compromise returned. Yet ideas about individualism and religious diversity had been released into the air and would not be fully shut away again.

FOR FURTHER READING

INTRODUCTIONS. On Calvin, see T. H. L. Parker, *John Calvin, A Biography* (Westminster Press, 1975). A broader survey is given in John T. McNeill, *The History and Character of Calvinism* (Oxford University Press, 1967). A standard introduction is A. G. Dickens, *The English Reformation* (Schocken Books, 1964).

COLLECTIONS OF ORIGINAL SOURCES. John Dillenberger (ed.), *John Calvin, Selections from His Writings* (Doubleday & Co., Anchor Books, 1971); T. H. L. Parker (ed.), *English Reformers* (Westminster Press, 1966); Leonard J. Trinterud (ed.), *Elizabethan Puritanism* (Oxford University Press, 1971).

IMPORTANT BUT MORE DIFFICULT. François Wendel, *Calvin*, tr. by Philip Mairet (Harper & Row, 1963), is the best introduction to Calvin's theology. Two intellectual biographies are Carl Bangs, *Arminius* (Abingdon Press, 1971); Jasper Ridley, *John Knox* (Oxford University Press, 1968). Two books on the political side of this theology: Christopher Hill, *The World Turned Upside Down* (London: Maurice Temple Smith, 1972); Michael Walzer, *The Revolution of the Saints* (Atheneum Publishers, 1972). Owen Watkins, *The Puritan Experience* (Schocken Books, 1972), approaches the Puritans through their autobiographies. Hugh Barbour, *The Quakers in Puritan England* (Yale University Press, 1964), introduces the early Quakers.

NOTES

1. John Knox, Letter to Mrs. Anna Locke, Dec. 9, 1556, in *The Works of John Knox,* ed. by David Laing, Vol. 4 (Edinburgh: Bannatyne Club, 1855), p. 240.

2. Quoted in T. H. L. Parker, *John Calvin* (Westminster Press, 1975), p. 53.

3. Quoted in Michael Walzer, *The Revolution of the Saints* (Atheneum Publishers, 1972), p. 64.

4. Calvin to Bullinger, Sept. 1553 (Letter 1790), in *Corpus Reformatorum,* Vol. 41 (Brunswick: C. A. Schwetschke & Sohn, 1875), col. 611.

5. John Calvin, *Institutes of the Christian Religion* 1.1.1. Unless otherwise indicated, this and subsequent quotations from Calvin's *Institutes* are taken from *Calvin: Institutes of the Christian Religion,* ed. by John T. McNeill and tr. by Ford Lewis Battles, Vols. XX and XXI of The Library of Christian Classics (Westminster Press, 1960). Copyright © MCMLX W. L. Jenkins. Used by permission of The Westminster Press.

6. Ibid., 2.1.9.

7. Ibid., 1.4.3.

8. John Calvin, *Christianae Religionis Institutio* (1536 ed.), in *Corpus Reformatorum,* Vol. 29 (Brunswick: C. A. Schwetschke & Sohn, 1863), col. 56.

9. Calvin, *Institutes* 2.7.12.

10. Ibid., 3.19.5.

11. Ibid., 3.14.18 and 19.

12. Ibid., 3.21.1.

13. John Calvin, *Sermons on the Letter to the Ephesians,* Second Sermon, in *Corpus Reformatorum,* Vol. 79 (Brunswick: C. A. Schwetschke & Sohn, 1895), col. 259.

14. Calvin, *Institutes* 3.21.2.

15. John Calvin, *Sermons on Deuteronomy,* Sermon 53, in *Corpus Reformatorum,* Vol. 54 (Brunswick: C. A. Schwetschke & Sohn, 1883), col. 524.

16. Calvin, *Institutes* 3.2.11.

17. Quoted in Hastings Eels, *Martin Bucer* (Yale University Press, 1931), p. 340.

18. Calvin, *Institutes* 4.17.26.

19. Ibid., 4.17.24.

20. Quoted in François Wendel, *Calvin,* tr. by Philip Mairet (Harper & Row, 1963), p. 78.

21. John Calvin, *Christianae Religionis Institutio* (1536 ed.), in *Opera Selecta,* ed. by Peter Barth (Munich: Chr. Kaiser Verlag, 1926), p. 260.

22. Calvin, *Institutes* 4.20.4.

23. Calvin, *Sermons on Deuteronomy,* Sermon 142, in *Corpus Reformatorum,* Vol. 56 (Brunswick: C. A. Schwetschke & Sohn, 1885), col. 211.

24. Calvin, *Institutes* 4.20.31.

25. Ibid.

26. John Knox, *The Appellation from the Sentence Pronounced by the Bishops and Clergy,* in *The Works of John Knox,* Vol. 4, p. 496.

27. John Knox, *A Godly Letter of Warning or Admonition to the Faithful in London, Newcastle, and Berwick,* in *The Works of John Knox,* ed. by David Laing, Vol. 3 (Edinburgh: Bannatyne Club, 1854), pp. 189–190.

28. John Knox, *Letter to Glencairn, Lorne, Erskine of Dun, and Lord James,* Oct. 27, 1557, in *John Knox's History of the Reformation in Scotland,* ed. by William Croft Dickinson (Philosophical Library, 1950), Vol. 1, p. 135.

29. *John Knox's History of the Reformation in Scotland,* Vol. 2, p. 17.

30. James Arminius, *Declaration of Sentiments,* in *The Works of James Arminius,* tr. by James Nichols and W. R. Bagnall, Vol. 1 (Baker Book House, 1977), p. 231.

31. James Arminius, Disputation 11, ibid., p. 526.

32. Quoted in Carl Bangs, *Arminius* (Abingdon Press, 1971), p. 216.

33. See John T. McNeill, *The History and Character of Calvinism* (Oxford University Press, 1967), p. 265.

34. A. G. Dickens, *The English Reformation* (Schocken Books, 1964), pp. 184–185, 251–252.

35. Cardinal Gasquet, quoted in Dickens, op. cit., p. 187.

36. Quoted in William Haller, *The Rise of Puritanism* (Columbia University Press, 1938), p. 116.

37. William Cartwright, *The Ordinary,* act 5, scene 1, in *The Plays and Poems of William Cartwright,* ed. by G. Blakemore Evans (University of Wisconsin Press, 1951), p. 338.

38. Quoted in Walzer, *The Revolution of the Saints,* pp. 166, 214.

39. Quoted in McNeill, *The History and Character of Calvinism,* p. 222.

40. Richard Hooker, *Of the Laws of Ecclesiastical Polity,* preface 4.1, in *The Works of Richard Hooker,* Vol. 1 (Oxford: Oxford University Press, 1845), pp. 155–156.

41. Quoted in Owen C. Watkins, *The Puritan Experience* (Schocken Books, 1972), p. 29.

42. Ibid., p. 30.

43. Gerrard Winstanley, *The New Law of Righteousness,* in *The Works of Gerrard Winstanley* (Cornell University Press, 1941), p. 181.

44. Quoted in Christopher Hill, *The World Turned Upside Down* (London: Maurice Temple Smith, 1972), p. 115.

45. Ibid., p. 112.

46. Quoted in Hugh Barbour, *The Quakers in Puritan England* (Yale University Press, 1964), p. 3.

47. Quoted in Geoffrey F. Nuttall, *The Holy Spirit in Puritan Thought and Experience* (Oxford: Basil Blackwell, 1947), p. 29.

48. Ibid., p. 35.

49. George Fox, *The Journal of George Fox,* ed. by Norman Penney, Vol. 2 (Octagon Books, 1973), p. 32.

50. Quoted in Barbour, *The Quakers in Puritan England,* p. 115.
51. George Fox, *The Journal of George Fox,* ed. by John L. Nickalls (Cambridge: Cambridge University Press, 1952), p. 36.
52. Quoted in Barbour, *The Quakers in Puritan England,* p. 98.

15

REASON AND ENTHUSIASM

The universal disposition of this age is bent upon a rational
religion.

> —Thomas Sprat, *History of the Royal Society*[1]

Sir, the pretending to extraordinary revelations and gifts of
the Holy Ghost is a horrid thing, a very horrid thing.

> —Supposed remark of Bishop Butler to John Wesley[2]

One morning in 1774 the French writer Voltaire persuaded a friend
to join him in climbing a nearby hill to see the sunrise. As glorious
colors spread across the horizon, Voltaire took off his hat, knelt, and
cried, "I believe! I believe in you! Powerful God I believe! As for
monsieur the Son and madame His Mother, that's a different story."[3]
The incident exemplifies a number of the characteristics of much
Christian theology in the late seventeenth century and during the
eighteenth century. Voltaire believed in God, he found the evidence
for his belief in nature rather than in the Bible, he doubted a good bit
of traditional doctrine—and he didn't treat religion all that seriously.
Even for many who were theologically far more conservative than
Voltaire, religion no longer stood at the center of their lives or the
way they understood the world.

It is that shift in the *place* of religion rather than changes in any
particular doctrine that makes this period, often called "the Enlightenment," one of the watersheds in the history of Christian theology.
To be sure, it was also a time of great religious revivals—Pietism in
Germany, Methodism in England, the Great Awakening in the United
States. But even those caught up in revivals understood the world in
a way different than earlier Christians had done. In the Middle Ages
and the Reformation, believers thought that their own lives mattered
only because they fit into the story of God's activity in history. Now

they tended to think that God mattered because he could be fit into the story of *their* lives—whether as a rational guide to a moral life or as the cause of a conversion experience. Many of the details might remain the same, but the center of the story moved from God to human beings.

At least five factors contributed to this change. First, what historians call the "wars of religion" tore Europe apart in the early 1600s. A third of the population of Germany died. Then in the mid-1600s a civil war brought England near to chaos. It is not clear that religion really "caused" all this warfare. After all, Protestants and Catholics often fought on both sides, and the king of France even made an alliance with the Turks. Still, religion got much of the blame, and many thoughtful people doubted that doctrinal disputes could be worth all that bloodletting. Second, the wars of religion left Europe religiously divided. People off in the neighboring kingdom, people passing through as traders, now might belong to a different church. Once you knew such folk, it grew harder to believe they were consigned eternally to hell. That could make faith in the doctrines of your own church seem less crucial.

Third, new philosophical attitudes encouraged people to question inherited beliefs. In the mid-1600s the French philosopher René Descartes argued that we can achieve certain knowledge only if we begin by doubting everything. Only if we examine all our beliefs skeptically can we be sure that we do not take for granted some unexamined belief that turns out to be false. In the end, belief in God played a central role in Descartes' philosophy, and his conclusions posed little threat to traditional theology, but his skeptical method challenged religious appeals to authority, whether of the Bible or the church. Fourth, a century of scientific geniuses produced accomplishment after accomplishment, and people couldn't help comparing the progress of science with theology, where the same old debates seemed to continue interminably. Fifth, the nations of Europe were trying to centralize their power. That involved dismantling all sorts of special privileges and exemptions held by nobles and guilds and other individuals and institutions. States sought to bring the church under government control as well, and that tended to make religion seem secondary in importance to the affairs of state.

THE RELIGION OF REASON

In the middle of the 1600s, during the civil war between Puritans in Parliament and an Anglican king, England suffered particularly from religious conflict. A group of English philosopher-theologians called the "Cambridge Platonists" (Benjamin Whichcote, Henry More, John Smith, Ralph Cudworth, and others) questioned the importance of the doctrinal details that had apparently occasioned so much bloodshed. "Vitals in religion are few," Whichcote wrote.[4] And except for those few "vitals" nothing mattered ultimately. As Cudworth put it, "No man shall ever be kept out of Heaven . . . if he had but an honest and good heart, that was ready to comply with Christ's commandments."[5] The Cambridge Platonists took religion seriously. Their study of Plato and their own mystical experience left them with a strong sense of the divine. "God is more inward to us than our very souls," Whichcote insisted.[6] But they based their religion on reason and confined themselves to a simple, ethically centered faith. In particular, they had no place for the doctrine of predestination, which seemed to make God arbitrary and unfair and to deny the value of human moral efforts. Predestination pictured an "unreasonable" God and human beings who were not basically good, and that challenged increasingly common assumptions of the age.

The Cambridge Platonists influenced Isaac Newton, the greatest scientist of the age. Their concept of God's "immensity" stretching infinitely in all directions and unchanged for all eternity seems to lie behind Newton's idea of absolute space and time, important for his own physics and one of the points where Einstein would attack it centuries later. Indeed, religion played an important role in many aspects of Newton's life. He wrote far more about theology than about science and spent much of his life trying to work out a chronology of the world based on the prophecies in Daniel and Revelation. Only the existence of a God "very well skilled in mechanics and geometry," he thought, could explain the continuing order of the solar system.[7] When he wrote his physics, he explained to a friend, "I had an eye upon such principles as might work with considering men for the belief of a Deity, and nothing can rejoice me more than to find it useful for that purpose."[8]

On the other hand, Newton found the Nicene Creed unintelligible and denied the full divinity of Christ. He believed in a God of nature, a God of the whole universe, and he could not believe that the truth about God had been revealed only through Christ. "There is but one law for all nations," he once wrote, "the law of righteousness and charity, dictated to the Christians by Christ, to the Jews by Moses, and to all mankind by the light of reason, and by this law all men are to be judged at the last day."[9]

Newton was not a great theologian, but he exemplified his age both in what he affirmed and in what he denied. Nearly everyone thought that the new scientific discoveries provided ever more evidence of the existence and greatness of God. If telescopes revealed the universe to be far larger than we had imagined, if microscopes disclosed the complex structures of creatures too small for the naked eye to see, it all showed just how amazing God's power and wisdom are. As Newton's friend Samuel Clarke put it, science could only "confirm, establish, vindicate against all objections, those great and fundamental truths of natural religion."[10] Yet the term "natural religion" is important. Increasingly, scientists and theologians alike distinguished between "natural religion," the basic truths about the existence of God and human morality known to good people in all societies, and "revealed religion," the particular historical claims and doctrines of Christianity and other religions—to the disadvantage of revealed religion. Reason, they thought, could establish the truth of natural religion, while revealed religion rested on the authority of Scripture or the church—and scientific method taught them to question authority. Thus they tended to emphasize morality more than doctrine, and that emphasis combined with an optimistic view of human nature to make them reject original sin and predestination and feel no need for a Christ who was more than a great teacher.

Politics as well as science affected theology during this period. In nearly every country the ruler sought to centralize political power, and that usually involved efforts to bring the church under governmental control. In Germany the peace treaty of 1648 ended religious warfare by declaring that each territory should adopt the religion of its ruler. In France, Louis XIV in 1682 proclaimed the "Gallican articles," which considerably limited the power of the pope in France, and then began persecution of French Protestants three years later. Both Protestants (who rejected the king's religion) and popes (who claimed authority over it) posed threats to the king's absolute power. Even in Russia, Peter the Great brought the Russian Orthodox Church under state control at about the same time.

The English situation had become more complicated. In the 1640s the Puritans in Parliament had started a civil war and executed King Charles I. When Charles II returned to rule in 1660, the radical Puritan sects and even the orthodox Calvinists had acquired a bad reputation among many as the principal cause of the turmoil the country had suffered. Many would have agreed with the preacher who had warned Charles I's archbishop, "Predestination is the root of Puritanism, and Puritanism is the root of all rebellion and disobedient intractableness and all schism and sauciness in the country."[11] On the other hand, most English people regarded Catholicism with even greater suspicion, for they still associated it with foreigners and potential traitors. When Charles II's brother and successor James II, himself a Catholic, tried to introduce official toleration of Catholicism, the people drove him from his throne. After that revolution of 1688 the Toleration Act of 1689 set the limits of English toleration. The Church of England would keep its theology vague enough to include as many groups as possible and tolerate the presence of some dissenting groups like Anabaptists and Quakers, though not Catholics. Allowing theological diversity within fairly broad limits seemed to the "Latitudinarians"—those who favored allowing plenty of latitude in theology—the best way to keep the peace. The preacher at the funeral of the great Latitudinarian Archbishop Tillotson could think of no higher compliment to pay him than to say that Tillotson "thought the less men's consciences were entangled and the less the communion of the church was clogged with disputable opinions or practices, the world would be the happier, consciences the freer, and the church the quieter."[12] Inevitably it seemed that religion functioned principally to maintain decency and moral order. In the early 1700s the essayist Joseph Addison explained the value of the Sabbath in such terms:

> It is certain the country people would soon degenerate into a kind of savages and barbarians, were there not such frequent returns of a stated time, in which the whole village meet together with their best faces, and in their cleanliest habits, to converse with one another upon indifferent subjects, have their duties explained to them, and join together in adoration of the supreme Being.[13]

Religion was socially useful, even—the half-conscious qualification that never became explicit—if it wasn't true.

Nearly all the attitudes of the time came together in John Locke, the most influential English philosopher of his day, who worked out the philosophical underpinnings of Newtonian science, wrote political essays justifying in advance the moderate revolution of 1688, and defended Latitudinarianism in religion, always arguing that "reason must be our best judge and guide in every thing."[14] Locke distinguished that which we can prove by reason, that which we can prove to be contrary to reason, and mysteries "above reason" which our rational powers cannot determine one way or the other.[15] Reason, he thought, establishes the existence of God with a force "equal to mathematical certainty."[16] If anything is contrary to reason, we must reject it no matter what religious authority it claims. God can, however, reveal to us truths above reason, though even here reason must be our guide. We believe such truths because the people who proclaimed them performed miracles, and our reason tells us that anyone who can perform miracles must have divine authorization, and therefore what they tell us must be true.[17]

In *The Reasonableness of Christianity* Locke turned to the Bible and found a simple faith and the call to a moral life, with nothing contrary to reason. Jesus exposed the errors of polytheism and idolatry, established a clear and rational morality, and reformed the worship of his time, ridding it of superstitious elements. He brought encouragement to those who try to lead a virtuous and pious life: "If we do what we can, he will give us his Spirit to help us to do what, and how we should."[18] But Jesus was not just a moral teacher. No one can perfectly fulfill the moral law, and therefore we would all be subject to condemnation. The good news of the gospel is that, if we believe Jesus to be the Messiah and try to lead better lives, "by the law of faith, faith is allowed to supply the defect of full obedience; and so the believers are admitted to life and immortality as if they were righteous."[19] According to Locke, morality and the promise of forgiveness if we have faith in Jesus as Messiah and try our best were the essence of biblical religion. He could find, he said, no mention of the Trinity or any number of other doctrines in the Bible.

Like many moderate reformers, Locke soon found that the enthusiasm of his own supporters was passing him by. Locke had allowed that God might reveal truths above reason and that faith in Jesus as Messiah might save us in spite of our inability to obey the moral law. The Deists, many of whom cited Locke as their hero, saw no need to go beyond natural religion to any revelation or any distinctively Christian faith. A generation or so before Locke, Lord Herbert of Cherbury had set forth the principles of natural religion, which he thought were shared by good people everywhere in the world:

There is a Supreme God.
This Sovereign Deity ought to be worshipped.
The connection of virtue and piety . . . is and always has been held to be, the most important part of religious practice.
The minds of men have always been filled with horror for their wickedness. Their vices and sins have always been obvious to them. They must be expiated by repentance.
There is reward or punishment after this life.[20]

Why go beyond that? Some, like Matthew Tindal in *Christianity as Old as Creation,* insisted that natural religion is in fact identical with Christianity properly understood, and "that the Excellency of the Latter, did consist in being a Republication of the Former."[21]

Others attacked Christianity as inferior to natural religion. Locke and other rational theologians had argued that the biblical reports of miracles and the fulfillment of prophecies count as good evidence for the truth of biblical teaching, for only God could perform miracles or enable people to foretell the future. The radical Deist Anthony Collins replied by analyzing biblical prophecies in detail and arguing that the "fulfillment" often bore so little relationship to the natural meaning of the original prophecy that nearly anything, apparently, would have counted as a "fulfillment." Many Deists brought to bear on the biblical miracle stories all the prestige of the scientific discovery of laws of nature and all of the skepticism historians were increasingly applying to their work. Few were as blunt as Thomas Woolston, who dismissed the raising of Lazarus as "a fraud" and Jesus' resurrection as "the most barefaced imposture ever put upon the world,"[22] but many grew dubious about arguments for miracles that claimed to establish violations of natural laws on the basis of limited historical evidence. Was not the order of nature as Newton had discovered it miracle enough?

The Deists distrusted appeals to authority and the miraculous, but they also turned away from anything beyond natural religion in part for moral reasons. If Christian faith, as opposed to the universal principles of natural religion, is necessary to salvation, then God has abandoned most of humanity, which has never even heard about Christianity, to damnation, and that's just "inconsistent with the universal and unlimited goodness of the common parent of mankind."[23] Further, they could never forget all the persecution and warfare for which they judged Christianity responsible. French Deists, with Louis XIV's persecutions in the near past, tended to be more violent on this subject. "Every sensible man, every decent man," Voltaire wrote, "must hold the Christian sect in horror."[24]

The Deists' attacks on Christianity went much farther than most of their contemporaries were prepared to go. But even many of their opponents shared some of their assumptions and their style of argument—an emphasis on reason and ethics. Joseph Butler, for instance, perhaps the greatest English theologian of the eighteenth century, showed by the use of reason that all the arguments the Deists brought against revealed religion applied just as much to natural religion. If argument from Scripture involved some questionable assumptions, well, after all, the move from a world full of plagues and earthquakes and wars to the existence of a beneficent creator was not all that obvious either. We cannot prove anything, Butler concluded, in either natural or revealed religion. We have to be satisfied with probabilities. But there lies no fatal flaw in that, for in all sorts of contexts we live our lives on the basis of probable judgments. Butler then constructed a good lawyer's brief for Christianity, careful and impressive, but hardly full of visible passion.

ENTHUSIASM: PIETISTS AND METHODISTS

Butler would not have apologized for that lack of passion. "Enthusiasm" was a dirty word in the eighteenth century. The philosopher David Hartley defined it as "a mistaken persuasion in any person that he is a peculiar favorite with God; and that he receives supernatural marks thereof."[25] Some identified enthusiasm with seeing visions or hearing voices or crying out in the midst of a revival service, but others regarded even going to church too often or reading the Bible too much as suspicious signs. Reasonable, moderate people agreed that enthusiasm was a bad thing. Newton's friend Samuel Clarke assured his readers that anyone who carefully studies the life of Jesus "cannot without the extremest malice and obstinacy in the world charge him with enthusiasm."[26] Nevertheless, enthusiasm changed the face of eighteenth-century religion.

The story begins in Germany, where Lutheran orthodoxy had increasingly defined faith as assent to a set of doctrines. In addition, Luther's emphasis on justification by faith made many Lutherans suspect any call to moral improvement as a move toward works-righteousness. When rationalism appeared in Germany, it grew out of the complex metaphysics of philosophers like Leibniz and Christian Wolff and produced complex, abstract theology and preaching.

German Pietism reacted against all these developments. In 1600, Johann Arndt's *True Christianity* called his readers to faith as an act of personal trust. Of course our justification depends on God's grace, but Arndt urged people to work at being better Christians. Of course, as the doctrine of "baptismal regeneration" teaches, baptism begins our life in faith and transforms us, but the true Christian life might also involve a moment of conversion, of being "born again," just as important in its way as baptism. Arndt advised all people to set aside some time each day for meditation and to reform their lives, but he organized no movement to put his ideas into effect. That task fell to Philipp Jakob Spener, whose *Pia desideria* (1675) established the

Pietist movement. Spener attacked excessive intellectualism in preaching and an emphasis on the objective validity of the sacraments—the fact that the sacraments "work" regardless of how much thought or emotion we bring to them—which led to indifference about making the sacraments meaningful experiences in people's lives. He organized groups of laypeople within congregations devoted to studying the Bible and helping each other in spiritual growth. His supporters saw a spiritual revival; his opponents accused him of splitting congregations apart.

Pietism spread all over Germany, and soon the educational reformer and theologian August Hermann Francke made the schools and university of the little city of Halle a great center of Pietism. In 1710 a young boy named Nicholas Zinzendorf, the son of a nobleman, arrived at school in Halle. Little Nicholas claimed to have had a deep sense of faith in Jesus from earliest childhood, and his teachers, convinced that everyone had to go through a period of sin in order then to experience conversion, accused him of spiritual pride. Their conflicts continued, but Zinzendorf remained at the school and learned much from the Pietists. When he inherited the family estates and some religious refugees from Bohemia and Moravia came to live on his lands, he encouraged them to preserve and develop their religious traditions, which went indirectly back to John Hus. Soon he opened his lands to all sorts of religious refugees and set up a community dedicated to piety. He could not quite decide his attitude to other church bodies. He encouraged the Moravians to keep up their own customs, but he got himself ordained a Lutheran minister and welcomed Lutherans, Schwenckfelders, and others into the fold. He apparently sought not so much to found a church as to create a fellowship of pious folk who would spread through all denominations.

Zinzendorf emphasized a personal relation with Jesus, the Lamb of God, and being saved by his blood. Indeed, to the unsympathetic reader Moravian hymns often seem awash in the blood of the Lamb. For a time in the 1740s the community sought to recover a childlike Christianity, calling Zinzendorf "Papa" and talking again and again about the "Lambkin" Jesus. They soon shook off the excesses of this "Sifting Time," however, and began a remarkable burst of missionary activity throughout the world, devoting particular attention to black slaves and others ignored by other Christians.

One group of Moravian missionaries traveling to the American colony of Georgia in 1735 met a young English priest named John Wesley, also setting off for missionary work. At Oxford, Wesley had founded the "Holy Club," a group of young men dedicated to prayer, fasting, Bible-reading, and visiting prisoners, whose "enthusiasm" and methodical approach to religious observance led people to dub them the "Methodists." In spite of his work with the Holy Club, religious doubts still tormented Wesley. Confronted by the confident faith of the Moravians during a storm at sea, he admitted that he was afraid to die.

> I have a fair summer religion. I can talk well; nay, and believe myself while no danger is near. But let death look me in the face, and my spirit is troubled. . . . What if the Gospel is not true? A dream, a cunningly-devised fable . . .[27]

His experiences in Georgia did not increase his self-confidence. While he tried to decide whether to marry one of the young women in his congregation, she married someone else. Wesley accused her of dishonesty and refused to admit her to Communion. Her father took him to court, and Wesley left the colony under indictment.

Wesley's relations with women remained unhappy. His wife left him and tried to humiliate him. But his religious life took a dramatically more positive turn. One evening in 1738, he was listening to a reading from Luther's preface to Romans at a meeting in London.

> About a quarter before nine, while he was describing the change which God works in the heart through faith in Christ, I felt my heart strangely warmed. I felt I did trust in Christ, Christ alone for my salvation; and an assurance was given me that He had taken away my sins, even mine, and saved me from the law of sin and death.[28]

Wesley denied baptismal regeneration. Baptism, he said, provides only an outward sign, not the actual beginning of new life in Christ. The real change comes when we experience "not . . . a cold, lifeless assent, a train of ideas in the head; but also a disposition of the heart. . . . So that he who is thus justified, or saved by faith, is indeed *born again.*"[29] Luther had taught that those who are justified through faith in Christ will remain nevertheless sinners, whose lives may improve but will never be completely purified. But Wesley insisted that those who experience such a transformation can go on to experience "Christian perfection" or "full sanctification" in which "they feel all faith and love; no pride, no self-will, or anger; and . . . have continual fellowship with God"[30] and "cannot voluntarily transgress any command of God."[31] If anyone doubted, Wesley had his evidence marshaled: "The habitual drunkard, that was, is now temperate in all things. The whoremonger now flees fornication. He that stole, steals no more. . . . These are demonstrable facts. I can name the men, and their several places of abode."[32]

As that appeal to "facts" suggests, the eighteenth century's emphasis on reason influenced Wesley too. His emotional preaching appealed to people's hearts, but like the Latitudinarians he shifted emphasis from doctrine to the moral quality of Christians' lives. He believed in the Trinity but would not require others to do so, and he rejected "the blasphemy clearly contained in the *horrible decree* of predestination. . . . I would sooner be a Turk, a Deist, yea an atheist, than I could believe this."[33] Predestination turned God into a tyrant and preaching into hypocrisy, for the preacher called all his people to be saved when some of them could not be. Wesley accepted the Arminian view that grace is not irresistible: "Every child of God has had at some time, 'life and death set before him,' eternal life and eternal death; and has in himself the casting voice."[34]

That brought Wesley into conflict with his friend George Whitefield. The son of a poor innkeeper, Whitefield had joined Wesley's Holy Club at Oxford. His powerful voice and emotional style made him one of the great preachers of history, converting thousands in England and America. He admired Wesley and tried to defer to him, but they found themselves increasingly at odds. Whitefield could not accept Wesley's doctrine of "Christian perfection," for he continued to feel the struggle with sin within himself. Whitefield wanted to improve the lot of slaves but defended slavery; Wesley strongly opposed it. They feuded most bitterly over predestination, for Whitefield agreed with Calvin's doctrine and could not accept Wesley's Arminianism.

Whitefield was the more successful preacher, but no one could match Wesley as an organizer. Wherever he went—and by one estimate he traveled 225,000 miles and preached over 40,000 sermons— he established a Methodist society of the converted to pray together and help each other in moral improvement. Wesley remained a member of the Church of England, though he ordained Methodist missionaries to go to America despite the fact that in the Church of England only a bishop could properly perform ordinations. But he seems to have recognized that the Methodists would inevitably become a separate church eventually, as they did shortly after his death. Whitefield, on the other hand, principally shaped the piety of the "Evangelical" wing of the Church of England.

THE END OF THE AGE OF REASON

Wesley and Whitefield changed the shape of popular religion in England and North America, but they made little impact on the attitudes among most intellectuals. In the late eighteenth century, however, four philosophers—Hume, Rousseau, Lessing, and Kant—in very different ways began to challenge some of the assumptions of the age of reason.

The Scotsman David Hume asked some embarrassing questions about scientific method. The great edifice of modern science rested on the inductive method. If I repeat an experiment several times and it always yields the same result, I can assume that it will continue to do so. If my pen always falls when I let go of it, I am confident that it will not rise the every next time I release it. But how do I know? Hume did not doubt it, but he insisted that such predictions rest on inclinations and assumptions. We cannot *prove* them, but there may be nothing wrong in that. In life we can manage quite well without proofs, guided by our instincts and intuitions, but we should learn to be a bit less dogmatic and certain about what we believe.

Such skepticism applied to any beliefs, but Hume singled out some traditional religious arguments for particular attack. One of the basic arguments of natural religion was that the order of the universe proves the existence of an infinite, perfect God. Hume pointed out that the universe contained a good bit of tragedy and disorder. Even if it implies the existence of a creator, it hardly shows that creator to be perfect. He also attacked arguments that miracles have occurred. Historical arguments, he said, always appeal to probabilities. We conclude that a particular event must have happened when this is the most probable explanation of our data. But a miracle is by definition an utterly improbable event. Therefore, those who want to prove that a miracle took place are caught in a dilemma: to argue that it happened, they must show its probability, but to argue that it was a miracle, they must show its complete improbability. Their two sets of arguments will inevitably cancel each other out.

Hume did not deny the possibility of miracles, or even the truth of Christianity. He might be a skeptic himself, but he would admit that science and his own philosophy rested on unprovable assumptions too. But philosophy is at least safer than the superstitions of religion.

> For as superstition arises naturally and easily from the popular opinions of mankind, it seizes more strongly on the mind, and is

often able to disturb us in the conduct of our lives and actions. Philosophy, on the contrary, if just, can present us only with mild and moderate sentiments. . . . Generally speaking, the errors in religion are dangerous; those in philosophy only ridiculous.[35]

Philosophers at least don't murder each other over their views.

The thought of the eighteenth century had held that science would inevitably advance civilization. Hume questioned some of the assumptions of science; his French contemporary Jean-Jacques Rousseau became famous with an essay that doubted the value of civilization. Civilization, he proclaimed, has only corrupted and enslaved human beings. We were happier and more virtuous in a state of nature. In one of his most popular books, *Emile,* Rousseau described the ideal education. The boy Emile grows up freely in nature, growing self-reliant out of doors and learning through his natural curiosity, not books or lectures. Toward the end of the book he meets an old Catholic priest who sets forth a religion of God and the soul based on intuitive feelings. Indeed, a turn from reason to intuition dominated much of Rousseau's philosophy and makes him one of the precursors of the later Romantic movement. For all his love of nature, however, Rousseau did not defend the usual eighteenth-century "natural religion," which he regarded as an artificial creation of philosophers. The old priest will continue to be a Catholic, and he urges Emile to join in Protestant worship, though each should be tolerant of all other religions. Accepting the religious traditions of your own community really represents the most "natural" path. Rousseau thus did not present himself as an enemy of religion, but his conviction that people are naturally good was irreconcilable with any belief in original sin and left little sense of a need for a redeemer.

Rousseau was not alone in believing that people ought to follow their own religious traditions while respecting the truth of others. A few years later the German playwright and philosopher Gotthold Lessing, in his play *Nathan the Wise,* had the Moslem emperor Saladin ask the Jew Nathan which religion is best. In reply, Nathan told the story of a father who had a magic ring that made its wearer beloved by God and man. The father loved all three of his sons, and on his death they found he had given each an apparently identical ring. Which had the magic ring? The wise judge to whom they posed the problem replied that each should live as if he had the magic ring himself. Perhaps someday, in a thousand thousand years, a better judge would determine the truth. In the meantime, each might, by his own actions, earn the favor of God and man. In other words, Christians, Jews, and Moslems should all serve God and humanity in their own ways. Perhaps none of their faiths contains the ultimate truth. Human beings may not be destined for possession of the truth. Lessing suspected that an eternal search for truth suits us better, anyway.

> The worth of a man does not consist in the truth he possesses, or thinks he possesses, but in the pains he has taken to attain that truth. . . .
>   If God held all truth in his right hand and in his left the everlasting striving after truth . . . and said to me, "Choose," with humility I would pick on the left hand and say, "Father grant me that. Absolute truth is for thee alone."[36]

Lessing did not identify any religion with "absolute truth," but he did not on that account retreat to natural religion. He thought that each religious tradition contributes something to the "education of the human race." All authentic religious insights reveal something of the truth, but none tells the whole story.

For Lessing, Christianity too had great insights to contribute—regardless of the historical accuracy of the Gospel accounts. He published posthumously a manuscript by a scholar named Hermann Samuel Reimarus, which claimed that Jesus had expected God's intervention to end the world as he went to the cross. He had been wrong, but the disciples had discovered that preaching yielded a better life than fishing and so invented the story of the resurrection to keep themselves in business. Lessing did not agree with Reimarus, but he wanted to shock people into realizing the fragility, and also the irrelevance, of basing hopes for eternal truth on the inevitably shaky ground of historical arguments, which can be probable at best.

Another German writing at the end of the eighteenth century, the philosopher Immanuel Kant, also sought a religion independent of the historical facts about Jesus. Kant had been raised and educated by Pietists, and he always retained a deep admiration for their moral seriousness, but he came to think many of their beliefs superstitious and thought their emphasis on conversions led to hypocrisy, for people pretended to have experiences they did not really have. For Kant religion really began with ethics. He rejected the traditional arguments for the existence of God but developed his own "moral argument." We ought to act virtuously, he said, and virtue means doing our duty, fulfilling the moral law, regardless of the consequences. If we act to bring pleasure to ourselves, or even to someone else, we are not acting according to pure ethical duty. At the same time, we should never treat human beings simply as means to an end. We should never just "use" people. But this can create a moral dilemma: If the virtuous action leads to human unhappiness, should we abandon virtue for happiness? (No!) or sacrifice human beings to the principle of virtue? (Not that either!) The only way to preserve moral integrity, Kant concluded, is to assume that somehow, if we act virtuously, that will ultimately serve the human good. But nothing in nature guarantees that acting morally increases happiness. Only the direction of the world by an all-powerful and good being could assure that. Without such an assumption, one could have to choose between abandoning virtue and sacrificing human beings to moral principles —both immoral courses of action. "Therefore, it is morally necessary to assume the existence of God."[37]

Kant further believed that morality really demands perfection from us. The moral law does not just say that we ought to be fairly good; its account of what we *ought* to do implies that we ought to be perfect. Yet none of us ever manages to be perfect. Does that mean that morality demands the impossible? That would seem to render it absurd.

> The injunction that we *ought* to become better men resounds unabatedly in our souls; hence this must be within our power, even though what *we* are able to do is in itself inadequate and though we thereby only render ourselves susceptible of higher, and for us inscrutable, assistance.[38]

Higher and inscrutable assistance—in other words, grace. We are called to perfection, but we can never achieve it. Only grace can save the moral demand from absurdity.

Kant believed in God and grace, but not in most of Christian theology. His ethical arguments, he said, held regardless of the historical facts about Jesus, and therefore concern about those facts is irrelevant. Moreover, while Christianity teaches people their moral duty, it tells them to act this way because God commands it (and perhaps in hope of a reward) and not simply because it is right—and this cheapens morality. Religion also tends to introduce cults and rituals, which distract people from their moral duty. Kant admitted that,

> by reason of a peculiar weakness of human nature, pure faith can never be relied on as much as it deserves, that is, a church cannot be established on it alone. . . . Because of the natural need and desire of all men for something *sensibly tenable* . . . some historical ecclesiastical faith or other, usually to be found at hand, must be utilized.[39]

In other words, we probably have to have institutional religion, but Kant regretted this consequence of human weakness.

Such ambivalence characterized all these thinkers of the end of the eighteenth century. Hume rejected superstition but admitted that science and philosophy could prove their basic assumptions no better. Rousseau argued optimistically for the essential goodness of human nature but saw civilization as a corrupting force. Lessing doubted that we could ever determine the truth of any religion but saw revelation in history as a valuable part of the education of the human race. Kant rejected much of institutional religion but saw the need for God and grace as foundations of morality. Obviously, many of the assumptions of the age of reason were coming into question.

FOR FURTHER READING

INTRODUCTIONS. Gerald Cragg has written a number of fine books on this period; perhaps the most useful as an introduction is *From Puritanism to the Age of Reason* (Cambridge: Cambridge University Press, 1966). The first volume of Peter Gay's *The Enlightenment: An Interpretation* (W. W. Norton & Co., Norton Library, 1977), focuses on religion; Gay writes intellectual history full of verve and excitement.

COLLECTIONS OF ORIGINAL SOURCES. Gerald R. Cragg (ed.), *The Cambridge Platonists* (Oxford University Press, 1968); Peter Gay (ed.), *Deism* (D. Van Nostrand Co., 1968); Albert C. Outler (ed.), *John Wesley* (Oxford University Press, 1964).

IMPORTANT BUT MORE DIFFICULT. Two books by F. Ernest Stoeffler, *The Rise of Evangelical Pietism* (Leiden: E. J. Brill, 1965), and *German Pietism During the Eighteenth Century* (Leiden: E. J. Brill, 1973), provide the best account of "enthusiasm" in Germany. There are a great many books on Wesley. William R. Cannon, *The Theology of John Wesley* (Abingdon-Cokesbury Press, 1946), centers on Wesley's views on justification. Two particularly fine studies of thinkers mentioned in the last section of this chapter are Henry E. Allison, *Lessing and the Enlightenment* (University of Michigan Press, 1966), and Allan W. Wood, *Kant's Moral Religion* (Cornell University Press, 1970). Hans W. Frei, *The Eclipse of Biblical Narrative* (Yale University Press, 1974), discusses, with unusual sensitivity, changes in the way people read the Bible.

NOTES

1. Quoted in Ernest Campbell Mossner, *Bishop Butler and the Age of Reason* (Macmillan Co., 1936), p. xii.

2. Quoted in William Ragsdale Cannon, *The Theology of John Wesley* (Abingdon-Cokesbury Press, 1946), p. 216.

3. Quoted in Peter Gay, *The Enlightenment: An Interpretation,* Vol. 1 (W. W. Norton & Co., Norton Library, 1977), p. 122.

4. Benjamin Whichcote, *Moral and Religious Aphorisms,* No. 1008 (London: Elkin Mathews & Marriot, 1930), p. 113.

5. Ralph Cudworth, *Sermon Preached Before the Honorable House of Commons at Westminster,* Mar. 31, 1647, in *The Cambridge Platonists,* ed. by Gerald R. Cragg (Oxford University Press, 1968), p. 379.

6. Benjamin Whichcote, *Works,* Vol. 3 (Aberdeen: Thomson, 1751), p. 178; quoted in W. C. de Pauley, *The Candle of the Lord* (London: S.P.C.K., 1937), p. 9.

7. Newton to Bentley, Dec. 10, 1692, in *The Correspondence of Isaac Newton,* Vol. 2 (Cambridge: Cambridge University Press, 1961), p. 235.

8. Ibid., p. 233.

9. Isaac Newton, *A Short Scheme of the True Religion,* in *Theological Manuscripts* (Liverpool: Liverpool University Press, 1950), p. 52.

10. Samuel Clarke, *Dedication,* in *The Leibniz-Clarke Correspondence,* ed. by H. G. Alexander (Manchester: Manchester University Press, 1956), p. 6.

11. Quoted in Gerald R. Cragg, *From Puritanism to the Age of Reason* (Cambridge: Cambridge University Press, 1966), p. 16.

12. Ibid., p. 83.

13. Joseph Addison, *The Spectator,* No. 112 (July 9, 1711), ed. by Donald F. Bond (Oxford: Clarendon Press, 1965), p. 460.

14. John Locke, *An Essay Concerning Human Understanding* 4.19.14 (London: George Routledge & Sons, 1909), p. 595.

15. Ibid., 4.17.23, p. 582.

16. Ibid., 4.10.1, p. 528.

17. Ibid., 4.16.13, p. 566.

18. John Locke, *The Reasonableness of Christianity* (Stanford University Press, 1958), p. 70.

19. Ibid., p. 30.

20. Edward, Lord Herbert of Cherbury, *De veritate,* in *Deism,* ed. by Peter Gay (D. Van Nostrand Co., 1968), pp. 32–38.

21. Quoted in Gay, *The Enlightenment,* Vol. 1, p. 380.

22. Quoted in Gerald R. Cragg, *Reason and Authority in the Eighteenth Century* (Cambridge: Cambridge University Press, 1964), p. 86.

23. Matthew Tindal, *Christianity as Old as Creation;* quoted in Henry E. Allison, *Lessing and the Enlightenment* (University of Michigan Press, 1966), p. 14.

24. Voltaire, "Examen Important de Milord Bolingbroke," in *Oeuvres complètes,* Vol. 26 (Paris: Garnier Frères, 1879), p. 298.

25. David Hartley, *Observations on Man* (Scholars' Facsimiles & Reprints, 1966), Vol. 1, p. 490.

26. Ibid.

27. Quoted in V. H. H. Green, *John Wesley* (London: Thomas Nelson & Sons, 1964), p. 51.

28. John Wesley, *The Journal of John Wesley*, May 24, 1738 (Moody Press, 1974), p. 64.

29. John Wesley, Sermon 1, June 18, 1738, in *The Works of John Wesley*, Vol. 5 (Zondervan Publishing House, 1958), pp. 9, 12.

30. John Wesley, *The Journal of John Wesley*, Nov. 29, 1761, in *The Works of John Wesley*, Vol. 3 (Zondervan Publishing House, 1958), p. 75.

31. John Wesley, Sermon 19, in *Sermons on Several Occasions* (London: Henry G. Bohn, 1845), p. 95.

32. John Wesley, *An Answer to the Rev. Mr. Church's Remarks*, in *The Works of John Wesley*, Vol. 8 (Zondervan Publishing House, 1958), p. 402.

33. Quoted in Green, *John Wesley*, pp. 114, 116.

34. Quoted in Cannon, *The Theology of John Wesley*, p. 107.

35. David Hume, *A Treatise of Human Nature* (Oxford: Clarendon Press, 1978), pp. 271–272.

36. Gotthold Lessing, *Lessing's Theological Writings*, tr. by Henry Chadwick (Stanford University Press, 1957), pp. 42–43.

37. Immanuel Kant, *Critique of Practical Reason*, tr. by Lewis White Beck (Bobbs-Merrill Co., 1956), p. 130.

38. Immanuel Kant, *Religion Within the Limits of Reason Alone*, tr. by Theodore M. Greene and Hoyt H. Hudson (Harper & Row, Harper Torchbooks, 1960), pp. 40–41.

39. Ibid., pp. 94, 100.

16

THE CITY ON A HILL

Indeed I tremble for my country when I reflect that God is just.

—Thomas Jefferson[1]

An eighteenth-century Italian visitor named Francesco Caraccioli once remarked that England had sixty different religions, and only one sauce. The mind boggles at what he might have said about the United States, which has supported nearly every religion of the Old World and many more besides. One could write a history of Christianity in the United States by tracing the rise and development of all its denominations. But that would be a very long book rather than just a chapter. It would also study church politics and organization more than theology. The idea of "denomination" itself, incidentally, really developed in the United States. In Europe after the Reformation each country tended to have an established "church" and various minority "sects." The United States evolved a more or less equal competition among various "denominations": Catholics, Quakers, Congregationalists, Methodists, and so on. Long lists of such names do not make for interesting history. This look at theology in the United States will try to focus on intellectual issues that have transcended any particular denomination, and on a few denominations that introduced radically new theological ideas.

NEW ENGLAND'S COVENANT WITH GOD

That means beginning with New England Puritans. While Anglicans and Methodists in the South and Quakers, Presbyterians, or Lutherans in the Middle Colonies may have been as numerous and socially important, they generally sought to preserve the religious traditions of the "old country." The Puritans of New England consciously sought to make something new.

Puritanism itself, of course, did not begin in New England. Many in England had opposed ceremonialism, episcopacy, and moral decay in the Church of England. Some "Puritans" (in a narrow sense of the word) wanted to purify the church from within. Others—the Separatists—broke off to form independent congregations. Both groups came to New England—Separatists to Plymouth in 1620 and Puritans to Boston in 1630, for instance—but with an ocean separating all of them from the English hierarchy, the distinction between them tended not to matter very much. Similarly, conflicts between Presbyterians, with their regional assemblies, and Congregationalists, who insisted on the independence of each local congregation, mattered less on the western side of the Atlantic. "Puritan" can serve as a general term for all these groups, for they shared a common dream. During the voyage of the first Boston settlers in 1630, their governor, John Winthrop, wrote:

> Thus stands the case between God and us: we are entered into covenant with Him for this work; we have taken out a commission. . . . We shall find that the God of Israel is among us. . . . For we must consider that we shall be as a city upon a hill, the eyes of all people are upon us.[2]

They had not come for the sake of religious liberty, but for religious purity—to set up an ideal commonwealth according to God's laws, an example to inspire the whole world.

The idea of "covenant," an agreement freely entered by both parties (we would probably say "contract" today), played a crucial role in their thought, shaping their thinking in two different areas. First, they rejected the idea that a person belonged to a church simply by being born into its territory. A church consisted only of those who had made a commitment—entered into a covenant—to join it. Second, they defined a person's relations with God in terms of covenant. Calvin's view was that God saves whomever he chooses without regard for merit. That implied the terrifying thought that nothing one could do has any effect on salvation. Some English and Dutch Calvinists had looked for some modification of this doctrine that would still preserve God's freedom, and they hit upon covenants. In a contract, after all, the parties freely choose to sign, but once they sign, the contract binds them. So it is with God, according to these "federal theologians" (from *foedus*, the Latin word for "contract"). God is indeed absolutely free, but "it has pleased the great God to enter into a treaty and covenant of agreement with us his poor creatures,"[3] and if we fulfill our part of the agreement by believing in him, he will reward us with salvation. As Thomas Hooker, the first minister at Cambridge, Massachusetts, declared, "We have the Lord in bonds, for the fulfilling of his part of the covenant: He has taken a corporal oath of it, that He will do it."[4]

Both these uses of the idea of covenant soon generated controversy in New England. The idea of our covenant with God produced conflict first. John Cotton, the first minister at Boston, rejected federal theology in favor of pure Calvinism. No human efforts, he said, can prepare one for grace, and nothing about the moral quality of one's life indicates whether or not one stands among the saved. The other ministers, led by Thomas Hooker, favored federal theology. They believed that God follows rules in the process of salvation. First, we must recognize our sin and repent before God will send grace. Second, once we receive grace, it will make a recognizable difference in our lives. We will be morally better. As Hooker said, "Wherever fire is, it will burn, and wherever faith is, it cannot be kept secret. . . . There will be a change in the whole life."[5]

A woman named Anne Hutchinson came to Boston from England with her husband and twelve children to hear Cotton preach pure grace. She was horrified at the views of the other ministers. Grace follows no rules, she said. It may come to the town drunk or a prostitute as likely as to the most respectable citizen. Attacked by her opponents, she began to report prophecies and visions confirming her views. In 1637 a synod of the colony's ministers exiled her to Rhode Island, where she died in an Indian massacre six years later. John Cotton compromised with federal theology, and pure Calvinism had lost the day. The New England dream was to produce that city on a hill as an inspiring example of a proper Christian community. That required a discipline that the preaching of unpredictable grace seemed to threaten. "I know there is wild love and joy enough in the world," Hooker wrote, "as there is wild thyme and other herbs, but we would have garden love and garden joy, of God's own planting."[6]

Soon the other sense of covenant, the covenant of church membership, produced another crisis. To preserve the ideals of this religiously based community, only those who could testify to a conversion experience were counted as full church members, with the right to vote, take Communion, and have their children baptized. The rigors of the ocean crossing ensured that the first generation would consist mostly of the truly committed, but the next generation included many who were New Englanders only by accident of birth. The percentage of members kept dropping, and the children of nonmembers could not even be baptized. The dream of New England as God's special commonwealth seemed about to collapse.

New Englanders sought a variety of solutions. In 1662 a synod of the churches of eastern Massachusetts approved what came to be called the "Half-way Covenant." If you affirmed the church's doctrines and tried to lead a good life, you could come halfway into the church even if you had never had a conversion experience. You could not take Communion or vote, but your children could be baptized. At about the same time, at Northampton in western Massachusetts, Solomon Stoddard abandoned federal theology for a purer Calvinism and decided that, if "the mere pleasure of God" decides who will be predestined to salvation, this "cannot be made evident by experience to the world."[7] We cannot identify the elect, and Stoddard therefore let everyone into Communion. Let God sort out the saved.

Both approaches began to compromise the earlier rigor, and by around 1700 the whole issue seemed to be fading away. Standards of church membership grew more lax, and some New Englanders began admiring the greater sophistication of England, which their forebears had fled as a place of corruption. Puritanism seemed to be slowly yielding to rationalism. Then in the 1740s the Great Awakening changed the shape of American religion. Its story is intertwined with that of America's greatest theological genius, Jonathan Edwards.

Born in Connecticut in 1703, Edwards proved precocious, writing a scientific study of spiders as a schoolboy and studying Locke and Newton as a teenage student at Yale. His faith grew out of both his father's Puritan sermons and his own meditations on nature. One day, after talking with his father, he tells us,

> I walked alone, in a solitary place in my father's pasture, for contemplation. And as I was walking there, and looking up on the sky and clouds, there came into my mind so sweet a sense of the glorious majesty and grace of God, that I know not how to express.... There seemed to me ... [the] appearance of divine glory in ... all nature. ... I often used to sit and view the moon for continuance; and in the day, spent much time in viewing the clouds and sky, to behold the sweet glory of God in these things; in the meantime, singing forth, with a low voice my contemplation of the Creator and Redeemer.[8]

In 1729 his grandfather Solomon Stoddard died, and young Edwards took over the most famous church in western Massachusetts.

As the last chapter explained, many of his contemporaries thought that the new scientific discoveries called for the modification of a good bit of traditional theology. Edwards argued that in fact the most orthodox Calvinism fit best with modern science. For example, to many science implied materialism. The scientist talks about the world we can see and touch, and that is the most clearly real world. Spirits and souls and God came under suspicion as perhaps only imaginary. Edwards, however, insisted that science, as represented by John Locke's philosophy, taught that all our knowledge begins with experience. It is experience—ideas and the minds that have ideas—of whose existence we are most sure. A *really* consistent empiricist will rather have doubts about the existence of matter. (The philosopher Bishop George Berkeley was developing a similar view in Britain at about the same time. His influence on Edwards remains unclear pending the clear dating of Edwards' early works.)

Similarly, many of Edwards' contemporaries concluded that a reasonable God just would not predestine some to hell, and therefore modern theology must give up predestination. On the contrary, Edwards maintained, Newton's philosophy implies that the universe is a system in which everything follows necessarily from prior causes. Therefore, the choices of people who live in the universe as described by Newton must be predetermined from the beginning of time. This does not imply that humans lack freedom, for freedom means doing what you want, and if what we want is determined (Edwards believed this to follow from both Calvinism and Newtonianism), we nevertheless remain free.

His opponents protested that it would be unfair for God to send some to hell. Edwards replied that we all *deserve* hell, for we all inherit the consequences of Adam's original sin. God simply gives some better than they deserve. But is it fair that we should suffer the consequences of something Adam did? Edwards replied that for modern empirical philosophy the way one thinks about something defines the identity of an individual. Sometimes I think of my arm as one "thing," my leg as another; other times, I treat them both as "parts" of my body. One of the implications of the empiricist rebellion against earlier metaphysics is that neither is wrong; both define the individual for a particular purpose. Now, "God in each step of his proceeding with Adam, in relation to the covenant or constitution established with him, looked on his posterity as being *one with him*."[9] God thinks of humanity as one individual in this context, and individual identity is something that can be defined in any consistent way. Therefore it makes no sense to protest that we get punished for the deed of someone else.

These ideas suggest how radical Edwards could be in "defense" of

Calvinism, setting traditional doctrines in a new metaphysical context. He believed in a God so powerful he left no room for anything else. God was not, he kept saying, one agent, one entity among others. A stone or a horse or a human being is "nothing but the Deity, acting in that particular manner, in those parts of space where he thinks fit."[10] "But I had as good speak plain: I have already said as much as that space is God."[11]

Edwards was usually an intellectual and unemotional preacher, but in 1734 his people in Northampton experienced a great revival, a burst of conversion experiences. That proved only a prelude. In 1740 George Whitefield traveled the length of the colonies, inspiring a "Great Awakening" marked by conversions from Massachusetts to Georgia—perhaps the first "national" experience shared by all the colonies. It soon generated opposition from those who found the shouting and weeping undignified and the attacks on "unconverted" ministers disruptive. Edwards rose to the revival's defense with a detailed empirical report. He described the experiences of conversion and the changes in people's lives and concluded, "We must throw by our Bibles, and give up revealed religion; if this be not in general the work of God."[12] The Great Awakening, he proclaimed, led people from theories about religion to the experience of it.

The story ended in tragedy. Excesses of emotionalism gave the Awakening a bad name. A young minister named James Davenport traveled about screaming, moaning, and stripping himself half naked as he preached, ending up judged insane by a Boston court. Even in Northampton, long-simmering frustration boiled over when Edwards reversed the practice of his grandfather Stoddard and admitted to Communion only those who could establish a conversion experience. The causes of tension between Edwards and his congregation ran deeper. Practical people out to cut down the forests in the name of progress could not understand his wonder at the divinity of nature. Practical people who wanted results could hardly understand a theology that left everything to unmerited grace. In 1750 they fired him, and he went into a kind of exile at Stockbridge on the edge of the wilderness. In 1758 the trustees of a new college in New Jersey—later to become Princeton—called Edwards to be their president, but he caught smallpox and died about a month after taking office. His followers tried to defend predestination and revivalism, but they ignored most of the philosophical underpinnings Edwards had developed. Edwards combined a defense of religious revivals with appeals to the most advanced philosophy. In subsequent generations in the

United States, intellectual sophistication and revivalistic passion tended to go their separate ways.

RATIONAL RELIGION IN THE UNITED STATES

In intellectual circles on the East Coast, the Great Awakening proved only a temporary delay in the advancing march of rational religion. By the time of the struggles for independence, many American leaders were more or less Deists. Asked about the divinity of Christ, Benjamin Franklin admitted, "It is a question I do not dogmatize upon, having never studied it, and think it needless to busy myself with it now, when I expect so soon [he wrote this as a very old man] an opportunity of knowing the truth with less trouble."[13] He would have agreed with Thomas Jefferson that "he who steadily observes those moral precepts in which all religions concur, will never be questioned at the gates of heaven, as to the dogmas in which they all differ."[14] Jefferson even produced a special edition of the New Testament, which included Jesus' teachings but left out all the miracles.

In spite of such attitudes, in 1776 every state except Rhode Island still required some sort of religious affirmation from anyone seeking public office, and Connecticut (until 1818), New Hampshire (until 1819) and Massachusetts (until 1833) still recognized an established church with special privileges and tax support. People like Jefferson and Franklin naturally sought to limit the churches' influence on the state, but it was principally the sheer fact of religious diversity which ruled out an established church on the national level. Congregationalists dominated Massachusetts, Anglicans Virginia, and so on, but no denomination had a dominant position in the whole country. As a result, while few Americans moved as far in the direction of Deism as Jefferson or Franklin, a least-common-denominator Christianity rather like Deism came to characterize public occasions in the United States.

To that extent, rationalism in religion made its mark on the whole country, but in the early 1800s it took an institutional form in Unitarianism. Unitarians have remained few in number and have not spread far—giving rise to the gibe that they believe in the Fatherhood of God, the brotherhood of man, and the neighborhood of Boston—but their influence on American intellectual life has been out of all proportion to their numbers. They began with an emphasis on reason and divine benevolence. They rejected the Trinity as irrational. They insisted that a good God would not let everyone fall into sin because of

Adam's fault or predestine anyone to damnation. In the words of William Ellery Channing, minister of the Federal Street Church in Boston for forty years and the most distinguished spokesman of Unitarianism, "A natural constitution of the mind unfailingly disposing it to evil . . . would absolve it from guilt . . . and argue unspeakable cruelty [on God's part]; and . . . to punish the sin of this unhappily constituted child with endless ruin would be a wrong unparalleled by the most merciless despotism."[15] Unitarians read their Bibles and believed in miracles, but they approached these matters rationally too. Good evidence proved that miracles had occurred, and the miracles in turn established the authority of whoever performed them. "Christianity," Channing wrote, ". . . is not a deduction of philosophy . . . intelligible but to a few. It is . . . sealed by miracles . . . which are equally intelligible, striking, and appealing to all."[16]

REVIVALS ON THE FRONTIER

Many Americans on the frontier would have found Channing's rational religion neither intelligible nor striking nor appealing. Both Puritans and Unitarians preached to the same congregation week after week and could gradually educate their audience, but sermons on the frontier came only with the occasional visit of a traveling preacher. These itinerants had little chance to give much theological instruction; they focused on immediate conversions. Beginning in the 1820s two Yale theologians, Nathaniel W. Taylor and Lyman Beecher, organized revival campaigns throughout Connecticut and beyond. Jonathan Edwards had believed that a revival would come in God's predestined time; Beecher and Taylor thought that effective preaching and good organization could create a revival. Beecher urged the clergy "no longer to trust Providence, and expect God will vindicate his cause while we neglect the use of appropriate means."[17] Effective preaching involved telling people they had the freedom to choose between salvation and damnation. "The people did not need high-toned Calvinism on the point of dependence; they . . . needed a long and vigorous prescription of free-agency."[18] Revivalists, like Unitarians, moved away from predestination.

At about the same time in upstate New York, Charles Grandison Finney carried the new style of revivalism several steps further. Finney prided himself on his lack of theological education. He thought that intellectual subtlety just gets in the way of good preaching. "We must have exciting, powerful preaching, or the devil will have the people, except what the Methodists can save."[19] Finney pioneered new techniques, like the "anxious bench" where those deemed near conversion came forward to sit and receive the focused attention of the whole congregation, and praying for recalcitrant relatives and friends by name. "Revival," he insisted, "is not a miracle, or dependent on a miracle in any sense. It is a purely philosophical [we would say "scientific"] result of the right use of the constituted means."[20]

Under the influence of Finney and others, the "burned-over" district of upstate New York ("burned over" by the fires of successive revivals) came to have the reputation southern California has today as the natural home of all sorts of religious cults. Already in 1774 Mother Ann Lee had established a community of Shakers at New Lebanon. Back in England, Ann Lee Stanley had converted to Quakerism and then had a series of visions which persuaded her that she, like Jesus, was God incarnate, this time in a woman to capture the female aspect of divinity. Her followers, the Shakers, granted women full equality, shared all their goods, opposed war, corporal punishment, and the use of tobacco and alcohol, and lived celibate lives. In the 1840s John Humphrey Noyes founded at Oneida another community in which all goods were shared. Defending "the right of a woman to dispose of her sexual nature by attraction instead of by law and routine and to bear children only when she chooses,"[21] Noyes made every adult at Oneida the spouse of every adult of the opposite sex. This "complex marriage" was supposed to overcome possessive love and lay the basis for scientific procreation. The new movements of the burned-over district combined abolitionism, revivalism, communism, attacks on the use of alcohol, and concern for women's rights in ways that seem surprising today.

All these new movements sought the creation of a perfect community, inspired by a sense that dramatic events lay near at hand. Soon a Baptist named William Miller began to preach that the present age of the world would come to an end in 1843. When his calculations, mostly based on the book of Daniel, proved apparently in error, his followers explained that he had been wrong only concerning the nature of the event. At the appointed time Christ had in fact brought one age to an end by entering the Holy of Holies in the heavenly sanctuary. The Millerites joined the followers of a visionary from Portland, Maine, named Ellen White to establish the Seventh Day Adventists, with a number of distinctive beliefs, many of them reminiscent of early Jewish Christianity. The Adventists celebrate the

Sabbath on Saturday, follow a good bit of Jewish dietary law, and emphasize Jesus' role as high priest.

Joseph Smith founded the largest group to come out of that upstate New York milieu. His family had migrated to New York in 1816, when Joseph was eleven. To his neighbors the boy seemed a wild dreamer, always looking for buried Indian gold or claiming to have a magic stone that enabled him to predict the future. Smith announced that the angel Moroni had appeared to him and disclosed the existence of hidden golden tablets, which a magic stone allowed him to translate from the "reformed Egyptian." Smith's "translation," the Book of Mormon, tells how the descendants of the ancient Israelites had come to America, and how Christ had appeared in America after his crucifixion.

Smith's followers, the Church of Jesus Christ of Latter-day Saints, or Mormons, moved first to Ohio, then to Missouri, then to Nauvoo, Illinois. They opposed slavery in slave-owning Missouri, tried to exercise influence in Illinois politics, and roused all sorts of suspicions. Following Old Testament precedent, Smith and a few others took more than one wife. A bitter story of persecution culminated in the lynching of Smith and his brother in Carthage, Illinois, in 1844.

Mormonism has produced a new sacred book, nearly as complex as the Bible, and so much new theology that some argue it is not a new Christian group but a different religion altogether. After learning that the usual Hebrew word for God is "Elohim," grammatically a plural form, Smith argued that the Old Testament clearly teaches that there are many Gods, some male and others female. His inquiries into Hebrew also convinced him that the word in Genesis usually translated "create" really means "organize," and he concluded that the "creator" did not make a world out of nothing but organized eternally existing matter. Many worlds have come and gone, and many Gods developed on them. "God himself," Smith preached, "was once as we are now. . . . If you were to see him today, you would see him like a man in form. . . . God himself, the Father of us all, dwelt on an earth, the same as Jesus Christ himself did."[22] Indeed, we all have the capacity to become Gods ourselves someday.

All this may seem a long way from John Locke or Thomas Jefferson, but Smith's optimism about human nature and his rejection of predestination and original sin agreed with the rationalism of moderate Deists. In Europe or Boston "reason" might mean Newton's physics, but out on the frontier "science" meant amateur archaeology, pamphlets on Indian history, and popular lectures on the Hebrew language—just the context in which Smith developed his ideas.

ROMANTICISM IN AMERICA

As the next chapter will indicate, rationalism came under challenge in Europe in the nineteenth century, in large part from a complex of new attitudes historians lump together under the term "romanticism." That romantic challenge made its impact in America too. The romantic spirit turned from reasoned analysis to appeals to immediate intuition and from individualism to a new emphasis on the unity of communities, of humanity, and indeed of the whole universe.

Rationalist Unitarians like William Ellery Channing had argued from the Bible and the evidence of its miracles. In the 1830s Transcendentalists like Ralph Waldo Emerson appealed instead to immediate intuition, which told Emerson that "the world is ... the product of one mind ... everywhere active, in each ray of the star, in each wavelet of the pool."[23] I don't need to turn to the Bible to find revelation, Emerson said; I can look within myself. "Men have come to speak of revelation as somewhat long ago given and done, as if God were dead. . . . In how many churches . . . is man made sensible that he is an infinite soul; that the earth and the heavens are passing into his mind; that he is drinking forever the soul of God."[24] Why single out a few events long ago as miracles when Jesus "felt that man's life was a miracle"? The rationalist idea of a miracle as a violation of some law of nature is a "monster. It is not one with the blowing clover and the falling rain."[25] Religion does not provide some external standard by which I judge myself, for "no law can be sacred to me but that of my own nature."[26] Indeed, "I become a transparent eye-ball. I am nothing. I see all. The currents of the Universal Being circulate through me; I am part or particle of God."[27]

Transcendentalism inspired many young Bostonians impatient with Unitarian rationalism, but it led them in many different directions. Theodore Parker became a popular lecturer who praised Jesus as a teacher of love but insisted that Christianity really concerns what we make of our lives now. "If it could be proved ... that Jesus of Nazareth had never lived, still Christianity would stand firm."[28] Orestes Brownson pursued interests in sacred mystery and tradition to one logical conclusion and became a Roman Catholic. But the romantic turn from reason to intuition and from individualism to community ran through the whole movement.

In the little town of Mercersburg, Pennsylvania, two college teachers from the German Reformed Church, John Williamson Nevin and Philip Schaff, developed romantic themes in a different way. They argued that American Protestantism had strayed far from the principles of the Reformation. American ministers generally followed no set order of service and rarely celebrated Communion. Worship focused on the sermon, and the point of the sermon was to produce conversions. In Nevin's words, "Religion is not regarded as the life of God in the soul, that must be cultivated in order that it may grow, but rather as a transient excitement to be renewed from time to time by suitable stimulants presented to the imagination."[29] But sin, Nevin insisted, is not a matter of individual people doing evils acts; it is a state into which all humanity has fallen. Therefore its cure must lie in Christ's power to transform all of humanity. The search for that cure led Nevin back to the study of the theology of the atonement and a new emphasis on the sacraments. All this utterly bewildered most of his contemporaries, who were suspicious of metaphysics and even more suspicious of anything that suggested Roman Catholicism. By the middle of the nineteenth century, revivalism, with its emphasis on individual conversions and its suspicion of complicated theology, had become so traditional to most American Protestants that Nevin's appeal back to the Reformation struck them as an eccentric innovation.

In those decades just before the Civil War a Hartford minister named Horace Bushnell was also attacking individualism and the emphasis on revivals and raising questions about rationalism in religion. Bushnell rejected both traditional Calvinism and Unitarianism. Both, he said, take much of the Bible and creeds as statements of literal facts. The Calvinists then affirm them, and the Unitarians deny them. But in religion, according to Bushnell, language can offer "only hints, or images" of truth.[30] Therefore we should treat the books of the Bible, not as "magazines of propositions," but as "poetic forms of life."[31]

He argued that the emphasis on conversions treated people as isolated individuals who could be changed in an instant. In fact, we grow up in families and communities which shape who we are. Therefore, religion ought to be a corporate experience, not a purely individual one, and it ought to grow gradually in us from earliest childhood. Bushnell's *Christian Nurture* became an important text for the emerging Sunday school movement, which at first rebelled against the exclusive emphasis on revivals.

Bushnell also presented the doctrine of the atonement in more corporate terms. The fact that Christ's suffering paid the debt of our sin had come to seem utterly arbitrary to many. Particularly in the aftermath of the Civil War, Bushnell set the atonement in a more general context of human experience. For over two hundred years the United States had permitted slavery; now thousands had died in this terrible war. Somehow, people can and do die for the sins of others, and sometimes reconciliation and redemption can emerge out of such tragedy. The atonement will not have a living meaning for us, Bushnell suggested, unless we can relate it to such general patterns of human experience. In seeking to bring doctrine alive by tying it to human experience, and in moving from individualism to a renewed sense of humanity's corporate character, Bushnell too was reflecting the new romantic attitudes.

SLAVERY AND BLACK RELIGION

Bushnell's concern about the moral implications of slavery serves as a reminder that, in the words of the greatest contemporary historian of American religion, "Any history of America that ignores the full consequences of slavery and non-emancipation is a fairy tale."[32] Christian theology too played its part in the history of slavery. The authors of the Bible had lived in an age that took slavery for granted. The laws of Israel demanded that Jewish slaves be freed every seven years, and Paul urged Philemon to forgive his newly baptized slave Onesimus for running away and treat him as a brother in Christ, but no biblical text explicitly opposed slavery, and Paul did send Onesimus back to his master.

Ancient slavery, however, existed within an economic and social system so different from the modern world that one should make comparisons with the greatest caution. And ancient slavery had nothing to do with race. A slave in Rome was as likely to be a Briton as a Nubian. Indeed, until the sixteenth century no Christian text suggested that any race was better suited to slavery than any other. By then slavery had virtually disappeared in Europe, when a variety of factors suddenly encouraged the use of African slaves in the American colonies, and Europeans searched around for justifications of an institution that had seemed about to disappear. Philosophers cited Aristotle's references to those who are slaves by nature. Scientists claimed to prove the natural inferiority of blacks. Theologians discovered in an obscure passage in Genesis (Gen. 9:25), in which Noah cursed either his son Ham or Ham's son Canaan, a justification for enslaving black people—a way of reading this passage that had never occurred to Christians before.

In England the evangelical party led the attack on the slave trade, and John Wesley's strong views against slavery encouraged a continuing opposition among Methodists. In America, however, only the Quakers (starting in the 1750s) really demanded that people either free their slaves or get out of the church. In 1818 the Presbyterian General Assembly unanimously declared slavery "utterly inconsistent with the law of God" but also warned against "hasty emancipation" and approved of the deposition of one Southern minister for his too-outspoken attacks on slavery.[33] One could cite similar episodes from most denominations.

It therefore seems remarkable that blacks who encountered Christianity first in the persons of whip-bearing traders and slave owners —and most slaves later said that Christian owners were generally more brutal—so often accepted Christian faith. Yet why would they not have understood the story of the Israelites fleeing from bondage and the agony of Christ crucified? Slave owners often hoped that preaching would make their slaves more obedient, but another message kept breaking through. As one slave preacher recalled years later:

> When I starts preachin' I . . . had to preach what massa told me and he say tell them niggers iffen they obeys the massa they goes to Heaven but I knowed there's something better for them, but daren't tell them 'cept on the sly. That I done lots. I tell 'em iffen they keeps prayin' the Lord will set 'em free.[34]

The best-documented slave revolts were led by black preachers, and black churches provided the one institution the slaves could call their own. The Baptists, whose lack of educational requirements or complicated procedures for ordination made it especially easy for blacks to become ministers, won a loyalty from black Americans that continues to this day.

Nothing symbolizes the unfulfilled character of the Puritan dream of America as the city on a hill, inspiring all the earth, so well as slavery. Yet in spite of slavery and much else, Americans have continued to think of themselves as a chosen people, set apart by God. Jonathan Edwards and other early Puritans, however, understood that God chooses without regard to merit, and the chosen should feel gratitude rather than pride. But that is a theological lesson Americans have found it hard to remember. Some prophetic voices have tried to remind them. Near the end of the Civil War, Abraham Lincoln, looking back on America's dreams and failures, declared:

> Fondly do we hope—fervently do we pray—that this mighty scourge of war may speedily pass away. Yet, if God wills that it continue, until all the wealth piled up by the bond-man's two

hundred and fifty years of unrequited toil shall be sunk, and until every drop of blood drawn by the lash, shall be paid by another drawn with the sword, as was said three thousand years ago, so still it must be said "the judgments of the Lord, are true and righteous altogether."[35]

For nations as for individuals, the awareness that we deserve the worst we get, and all else is grace, remains one of the hardest lessons of Christian theology.

FOR FURTHER READING

INTRODUCTIONS. The definitive work on American religion for a long time to come is Sydney E. Ahlstrom, *A Religious History of the American People* (Yale University Press, 1972). Shorter introductions are Jerald C. Brauer, *Protestantism in America* (Westminster Press, 1953), and Robert T. Handy, *A Christian America* (Oxford University Press, 1971).

COLLECTIONS OF ORIGINAL SOURCES. Two general collections are: Sydney E. Ahlstrom, *Theology in America* (Bobbs-Merrill Co., 1967); H. Shelton Smith, Robert T. Handy, and Lefferts A. Loetscher, *American Christianity*, 2 vols. (Charles Scribner's Sons, 1960, 1963). On particular periods, see the following collections of texts: Perry Miller and Thomas H. Johnson, *The Puritans* (American Book Co., 1938), and Perry Miller, *The Transcendentalists* (Harvard University Press, 1950). Some collections from important individual writers are: *Jonathan Edwards*, ed. by Clarence H. Faust and Thomas H. Johnson (American Book Co., 1935); John Williamson Nevin, *Catholic and Reformed* (Pickwick Press, 1978); *Horace Bushnell*, ed. by H. Shelton Smith (Oxford University Press, 1965). Emerson's essays are available in a host of editions.

IMPORTANT BUT MORE DIFFICULT. The works of Perry Miller remain the greatest studies of Puritan New England. See especially his *The New England Mind: The Seventeenth Century* (Beacon Press, 1961), *The New England Mind: From Colony to Province* (Beacon Press, 1961), and *Jonathan Edwards* (William Sloane Associates, 1949). Henry F. May, *The Enlightenment in America* (Oxford University Press, 1976), provides a superb survey of that period. Whitney R. Cross, *The Burned-Over District* (Harper & Row, Harper Torchbooks, 1965), studies that crucible of American revivalism. Fawn M. Brodie, *No Man Knows My History* (Alfred A. Knopf, 1945), still provides the fairest account of Joseph Smith. On slave religion, see Albert J. Raboteau, *Slave Religion* (Oxford: Oxford University Press, 1980).

NOTES

1. Thomas Jefferson, *Notes on the State of Virginia;* quoted in Henry F. May, *The Enlightenment in America* (Oxford University Press, 1976), p. 300.
2. John Winthrop, *A Modell of Christian Charity,* in Perry Miller and Thomas H. Johnson (eds.), *The Puritans* (American Book Co., 1938), pp. 198–199.
3. Quoted in Perry Miller, *The New England Mind: The Seventeenth Century,* (Beacon Press, 1961), p. 377.
4. Ibid., p. 380.
5. Thomas Hooker, *The Activity of Faith,* in Sydney E. Ahlstrom (ed.), *Theology in America* (Bobbs-Merrill Co., 1967), p. 126.
6. Quoted in Miller, *The New England Mind: The Seventeenth Century,* p. 48.
7. Quoted in Perry Miller, *The New England Mind: From Colony to Province* (Beacon Press, 1961), p. 234.
8. Jonathan Edwards, *Personal Narrative,* in *Jonathan Edwards,* ed. by Clarence H. Faust and Thomas H. Johnson (American Book Co., 1935), pp. 60–61.
9. Jonathan Edwards, *Original Sin* (Yale University Press, 1970), p. 389.
10. Quoted in Perry Miller, *Jonathan Edwards* (William Sloane Associates, 1949), p. 91.
11. Jonathan Edwards, *Of Being,* in *Scientific and Philosophical Writings* (Yale University Press, 1980), p. 203.
12. Jonathan Edwards, *The Distinguishing Marks of a Work of the Spirit of God,* in *The Great Awakening* (Yale University Press, 1972), p. 268. Edwards later grew more cautious in drawing such conclusions.
13. Benjamin Franklin, Letter to Ezra Stiles, March 9, 1790, in *Autobiography, Poor Richard, Letters* (D. Appleton, 1900), pp. 394–395.
14. Thomas Jefferson, Letter to Mr. William Canby, Sept. 18, 1813, in *The Writings of Thomas Jefferson,* Vol. 6 (Taylor & Maury, 1854), p. 210.
15. William Ellery Channing, *Unitarian Christianity,* in *The Works of William E. Channing,* Vol. 3 (James Munroe, 1846), p. 86.
16. William Ellery Channing, *The Essence of the Christian Religion,* in Ahlstrom, *Theology in America,* pp. 199–200.
17. Quoted in Sidney Earl Mead, *Nathaniel William Taylor* (Archon Books, 1967), p. 76.
18. Lyman Beecher, *Autobiography,* Vol. 2 (Harper & Brothers, 1874), p. 187.
19. Quoted in Whitney R. Cross, *The Burned-Over District* (Harper & Row, Harper Torchbooks, 1965), p. 174.
20. Charles Grandison Finney, *Lectures on Revivals of Religion* (Belknap Press, 1960), p. 13.
21. Quoted in Cross, *The Burned-Over District,* p. 335.

22. Joseph Smith, *King Follett Discourse*, in *Discourses of the Prophet Joseph Smith* (Deseret Book Co., 1965), p. 263.

23. Ralph Waldo Emerson, *Divinity School Address*, in Ahlstrom, *Theology in America*, p. 299.

24. Ibid., pp. 305, 307.

25. Ibid., pp. 302–303.

26. Ralph Waldo Emerson, *Self-Reliance*, in *The Collected Works of Ralph Waldo Emerson*, Vol. 2 (Belknap Press, 1979), p. 30.

27. Ralph Waldo Emerson, *Nature*, in *The Collected Works of Ralph Waldo Emerson*, Vol. 1 (Belknap Press, 1971), p. 10.

28. Quoted in William R. Hutchison, *The Transcendentalist Ministers* (Beacon Press, 1965), p. 109.

29. John Williamson Nevin, *The Anxious Bench*, in *Catholic and Reformed: Selected Theological Writings of John Williamson Nevin* (Pickwick Press, 1978), p. 57.

30. Horace Bushnell, *God in Christ* (Scribner, Armstrong & Co., 1877), pp. 46, 74.

31. Quoted in William A. Johnson, "Nature and the Supernatural in the Theology of Horace Bushnell," *Encounter* 26 (Winter 1965), p. 67.

32. Sydney E. Ahlstrom, *A Religious History of the American People* (Yale University Press, 1972), p. 13.

33. Ibid., p. 648.

34. Anderson Edwards, quoted in Albert J. Raboteau, *Slave Religion* (Oxford: Oxford University Press, 1980), p. 232.

35. Abraham Lincoln, Second Inaugural Address, in *Abraham Lincoln: His Speeches and Writings* (World Publishing Co., 1946), p. 793.

17

THE CLAIMS OF HISTORY

> Why should I become a mind of pure reason when my sole
> wish is to be human, and when in knowledge and belief I
> am just what I am in my being, drifting like a wave in the
> sea of history?
>
> —Johann Gottfried Herder, writing in 1780[1]

Historians often classify the eighteenth century as the age of reason,
a time when many people contrasted the rationality of their own age
with the superstition of earlier times. As already noted, much eighteenth-century theology fit the style of its time—a reasonable belief
in the existence of God, often supported by arguments from the order
of the universe and the evidence of miracles. Earlier chapters have
indicated how some of those rationalistic assumptions came under
question at the end of the century and how romanticism changed
American theology in the nineteenth century. This chapter will trace
nineteenth-century developments in Europe. It was a time of new
awareness of history and new appreciation for emotion and intuition.
Revolutions in America and France made people vividly aware of
historical change, and the terror that followed the French revolution
suggested that change is not always for the best. A new spirit of
nationalism created new interest in various national traditions—the
brothers Grimm scoured the countryside for old folktales, composers
incorporated folk tunes in their symphonies. Romantic poets attacked
scientific analysis in the name of feeling.

Inevitably, all this affected theology. At the beginning of the nineteenth century Friedrich Schleiermacher in Germany and Samuel
Taylor Coleridge in England appealed to romanticism to defend
Christianity against the claims of natural religion. Just as poets and
artists were rediscovering the emotional power of their national traditions, so theologians could find the Christian tradition newly attrac-

tive. But if one presented Christianity as the religious tradition of a particular culture, what claim could it make to absolute, universal truth? A series of philosophers beginning with Hegel were worrying about the general question of how, given the fact that each society sees the world differently, one could make any claim to absolute truth, and religion often provided the test case for their theories. The question of Christianity's relation to its culture arose on a more practical level too. The Roman Catholic Church made strong claims to a truth that transcended any particular historical period, but critics then accused it of ignoring the realities of the modern world. The Church of England, on the other hand, adapted in many ways to its society, and critics claimed it was betraying the Christian faith. In the second half of the nineteenth century the moderately liberal theology of Albrecht Ritschl and his students dominated the German scene and was attacked from both sides—for distorting Christianity and for failing to face the full implications of modernity. The new awareness of history, which had offered such promise at the beginning of the century, now seemed a threat to even the possibility of Christian theology.

TWO ROMANTICS: SCHLEIERMACHER AND COLERIDGE

Friedrich Schleiermacher grew up in a deeply pious Moravian community, studied theology, and in the 1790s fell in with the poets and literary critics of Berlin, the writers at the forefront of German Romanticism. He wanted to be up-to-date, but he also wanted to be a Christian; he did not desire that "the tangle of history so unravel that Christianity becomes identified with barbarism and science with unbelief."[2] In his *Speeches on Religion,* published in 1799, he sought to persuade his sophisticated friends that they should not reject religion. They criticized its doctrines and institutions, but these do not lie at the heart of religion. "You must transport yourself into the interior of a pious soul and seek to understand its inspiration. . . . Otherwise you learn nothing of religion."[3] Anyone who does so will find that scientific theories and historical facts matter little to religion, which is a matter of feeling, a "sense and taste for the infinite," a "life in the infinite nature of the Whole, in the One and in the All, in God."[4] Simple pious folk had long known what Romantic poets were just discovering, that facts and logic are less important than intuitively sensing one's unity with the Universe. To the truly religious, every event is a miracle, and "every intuition and every original feeling" is a revelation.[5] But this does not mean we should turn to some universal "natural religion." Every culture, every individual, needs to express its own particular genius. We do not try to water down art or literature to some lowest common denominator; likewise, we should treasure the particular traditions and insights of our own religious traditions.

In the 1820s an older and somewhat more conservative Schleiermacher published *The Christian Faith,* presenting most traditional Christian doctrines, but often interpreted in a new way. Of his theology Schleiermacher said: "[It] is based entirely on the inner experience of the believer; its only purpose is to describe and elucidate that experience."[6] The Bible and the church are important, but only because they play a role in the Christian's experience. At the basis of all my experience, Schleiermacher said, lies a "feeling of absolute dependence." I sense that I did not create myself or shape myself, and, beyond all my relations with particular objects in the world, I have a relation with the ground or source of them all, God. Thus the feeling of absolute dependence is God-consciousness. That feeling lies within each of us, but we often lose sight of it. We get caught up in daily affairs and lose sight of that which underlies all our experience. Theologians, Schleiermacher explained, call this "sin." We fall into this sin in large part because we live in a corrupt and distracting society, and according to Schleiermacher that social corruption is the real meaning of original sin: "What appears as the congenital sinfulness of one generation is conditioned by the sinfulness of the previous one."[7]

Jesus, however, had an absolutely pure God-consciousness or feeling of absolute dependence. That's what it means to say that he was divine. Only by a miraculous divine intervention could such a pure God-consciousness come into existence in the midst of sinful humanity. By founding the community that became the church, Jesus then communicated that pure God-consciousness to others. Schleiermacher offered an analogy: The existence of a nation implies that some genius at some point grasped a new sense of national identity (thought of himself or herself, for instance, as "an American" rather than "a Massachusetts colonist") and communicated that feeling to others so that "there arises among them a new corporate life, but also . . . each of them becomes in himself a new person—that is to say, a citizen."[8] Similarly, Jesus' communication of pure God-consciousness to everyone in the community he founded makes each of them a new person—a Christian. All this put traditional theology into a new shape, but it tried to *reinterpret* traditional doctrines like original sin and salvation through the church, rather than rejecting them as natural religion had often done.

At about the same time as Schleiermacher, the English poet Samuel Taylor Coleridge was also reinterpreting Christianity in terms of the romantic spirit. Coleridge attributed his sympathy for traditional doctrines not to conservatism but "to my having gone much further than the Unitarians, and so having come round to the other side."[9] He made a distinction between understanding and reason and used it to reject the tendency of eighteenth-century theology to base Christianity on argument and the evidence of miracles. Understanding gathers individual facts and connects them with careful logic. Reason intuitively inspires our moral life and enables us to see the value and ultimate meaning of things. Religion lies within the realm of reason, and therefore is not a matter of scientific or historical detail. The factual accuracy of the Bible does not much matter, for it can give us Truth in the way a great poem can. "Whatever *finds* me, bears witness for itself that it has proceeded from a Holy Spirit . . . [and] in the Bible there is more that *finds* me than I have experienced in all other books put together."[10]

Some of Coleridge's contemporaries had begun to ask why the British government should use tax money to support the Church of England. Coleridge replied that government does not exist just to provide armies and a postal service. It should also aim "to secure and improve that civilization, without which the nation could be neither permanent nor progressive."[11] What Coleridge called "the clerisy"— the church, the universities, and other cultural institutions—develop the national ideals and values. The church provides, after all, a preacher in every community, relatively independent of economic pressures since he has a guaranteed salary, who addresses the public regularly on moral issues and the values of their traditions. That is "an aid and instrument, which no State or Realm could have produced out of its own elements . . . a *God-send.*"[12] Like Schleiermacher, Coleridge was defending Christianity, over against natural religion, in terms of its place in its culture. It was a defense that risked implying—though both Schleiermacher and Coleridge would have rejected the implication—that Christianity was simply the religion of one culture, with no absolute or universal claim to truth.

HEGELIANS AND ANTI-HEGELIANS

Nineteenth-century philosophers worried about the relation of history to claims of absolute truth in a more general way. It seems that each society, each era, sees the world differently, and those who compare these world views inevitably see them from the perspective of their own society. Is there any way to judge among them? Georg Wilhelm Friedrich Hegel, perhaps the century's greatest philosopher, thought that one could make claims to absolute truth only if one could find a perspective that disclosed all of history as a rational system. If you can see how all history fits together in a pattern, then you can judge the significance of the pieces of that pattern. But that is not easy, Hegel admitted, for history "forms a picture of most fearful aspect, and excites emotions of the profoundest and most hopeless sadness."[13] How can this bloody succession of wars and disasters be a rational process? Because, Hegel answered, all that tragedy contributes to our understanding of ourselves. History is the process by which we come to self-understanding.

A generation earlier Kant had already acknowledged that the philosopher cannot describe the eternal structure of reality. He instead defined the philosopher's task as laying out the characteristics of the world of our experience. Beyond that world of experience, he said, lies a world of things-in-themselves, which we can never know or talk about but which somehow generate our experience. Kant limited philosophy to the world of experience, but he though that the basic structures of the experienced world remain the same in all times and places.

Hegel wanted to take history more seriously, to allow for more basic change in the way we experience things, and he also argued that, if we cannot know or talk about things-in-themselves, Kant really could not know they exist or talk about them. No, Hegel argued, all there is is a world of experience and subjects having that experience. That is all the reality we know. Therefore all reality has a three-stage form: (1) There is a thinking subject; but (2) in order to think, that subject has to have an object to think about; but (3) that object is part of the experience of the subject and therefore not really separate from it. Reality is therefore not static but intrinsically a process of change and conflict. That is the shape of my own experience. I exist as a thinking subject only as I think about the world, but my mind shapes the world I think about. God's activity has the same form. In order to be God, God has to create a world, but that world is God's creation and therefore not ultimately separate from God. "We define God when we say, that He distinguishes Himself from Himself, and is an object for Himself, but that in this distinction He is purely identical with Himself, is in fact Spirit."[14] The dialectic of these three stages—Hegel himself rarely used the now traditional terms thesis, antithesis, and synthesis—provided the basic pattern of all reality.

Christianity, Hegel explained, had already grasped this in the doctrine of the Trinity: the Father; the Son, who becomes a particular object; and the Holy Spirit, who unites them both in love—three persons yet one God. Hegel believed that his philosophy revealed the basic truth of Christianity, but, whereas Christian theology expressed that truth in images and metaphors, he presented it in clear concepts. Religion had given birth to philosophy, but later on philosophy turned temporarily against religion. "When the wings of thought have become strengthened, the young eaglet flies away for himself to the sun of Truth; but like a bird of prey he turns upon Religion and combats it." But then, in Hegel's philosophy, "latest of all Philosophy permits full justice to be done to the content of Religion."[15] That justice, to be sure, involved turning Christianity into a sort of illustrated children's version of Hegelian philosophy, without full conceptual clarity.

In 1835 a young Hegelian named David Friedrich Strauss published a *Life of Jesus*. Until Strauss, people trying to explain the miracles in the New Testament had said either that they happened just as described, that they happened but had some "rational" explanation— the power of Jesus' personality cured psychosomatic illness, etc.—or, as Reimarus had proposed, that these stories resulted from deliberate fraud. Given those options, it was not hard to defend the truth of the narratives. Strauss offered another alternative. Much of the Gospels consisted of myths—not deliberate lies but the sort of legends that naturally grew up around a charismatic figure in earlier societies. They are not historically true, Strauss said, but Hegel has taught us that that doesn't matter. What matters is the idea they express, the idea of God coming into the world and making it one with himself. "The supernatural birth of Christ, his miracles, his resurrection and ascension, remain eternal truths, whatever doubts may be cast on their reality as historical facts."[16] "This is the key to the whole of Christology, that, as subject of the predicate which the Church assigns to Christ, we place, instead of an individual, an idea."[17] As Strauss interpreted him, Hegel implied that to treat the Gospels as historically accurate would be to take metaphors and images as literal truth. Thus Hegel permitted Strauss to hold on to the "real" truth of Christianity while reaching skeptical conclusions about the historical accuracy of the Gospels.

Then in 1841 another German philosopher applied an even more radical analysis. Ludwig Feuerbach said that Hegel had everything exactly backward. Hegel said that God posited human beings, indeed everything in the world, as objects. According to Feuerbach, human beings invent the idea of God. *"Theology is anthropology.* . . . Man's God is nothing other than the deified essence of man."[18] Our idea of God really consists just of all our highest ideals put together and personified. When we say, "God loves human beings," or, "God is wise," we are really saying that we think the love of human beings and wisdom are good things. Feuerbach reversed the dialectic: now humans created God but then realized that it was humanity that is really divine. Therefore, we ought to cast aside the superstitious attitudes toward God that interfere with the full development of humanity.

Feuerbach can seem trivial today. After all, many college sophomores come up with the same idea—that God is just a projection of the human imagination. But that may indicate not Feuerbach's triviality but the pervasiveness of his influence. One may not agree with Feuerbach's answer, but his question is hard to ignore. He did not raise questions just about religion, either, but about the ways we understand any assertion. When religious people talk about God, Feuerbach does not say that their statements are false—he explains what those statements "really mean" as claims about human ideals. Such analysis, which says that we do not really mean what we think we mean, but that someone else has uncovered the "real" meaning of what we say, can be applied to anything from politics to literature to science to dreams. It has influenced all kinds of intellectual movements, from Marxist analysis to Freudian psychology to several schools of literary criticism; it has certainly proven immensely fertile intellectually. Yet it invariably risks poisoning a discussion, for the temptation is always to ignore your opponents' arguments as you explain their hidden motivations. What is interesting is that in the nineteenth century Feuerbach's arguments, which really apply to any truth claims, were rarely applied to anything but religion. No one sought the hidden meanings of science, but pervailing cultural attitudes left religion open to Feuerbach's attack.

Strauss and Feuerbach both lost their jobs in the ensuing uproar. In England, H. L. Mansel wrote satirically of all this new theology in Germany,

> Where Strauss shall teach you how martyrs died
> For a moral ideal personified,
> A myth and a symbol, which vulgar sense
> Received for historical evidence . . .

> Where Feuerbach shows how religion began,
> From the deified feelings and wants of man,
> And the Deity owned by the mind reflective
> Is Human Consciousness made objective.
>   Presbyters, bend,
>   Bishops, attend;
> The Bible's a myth from beginning to end.[19]

But for some, even Strauss and Feuerbach did not go far enough. The young Karl Marx, deeply influenced by radical Hegelian thought, insisted that, while Feuerbach replaced God with that deified essence of humanity, that still remained too abstract, too removed from the concrete realities of how people clothe and feed themselves. Feuerbach remained a philosopher; he still wanted to find the answer to the world's problems through thought. But for Marx, "the philosophers have only *interpreted* the world, in various ways; the point, however, is to *change* it."[20] Marx wanted to interpret history as a process of economic conflict in which religion figured only as an illusion which those in power offered to the oppressed to keep them in line.

Marx's contemporary, the Danish writer Søren Kierkegaard, made equally radical criticisms of Hegel, but his led him back to Christianity. Young Kierkegaard was haunted by his father's confession that once, in a moment of despair, he had cursed God. Søren studied for the ministry but never sought ordination; he got engaged but then broke off the engagement. "The thing is to understand myself," he wrote; "to see what God really wishes *me* to do; the thing is to find a truth which is true *for me,* to find *the idea for which I can live and die.*"[21] In that Hegel did not offer much help. His system could explain everything—after it happened—but it could not tell anyone what to do next. Hegel could interpret life; the point, however, is to live it.

When Kierkegaard asked his fellow Danes about how to live, they all said they had the answer—they were Christians. "People who perhaps never once enter a church, never think about God, never mention His name except in oaths . . . are all of them Christians, call themselves Christians."[22] Kierkegaard thought all these comfortable, middle-class people bore little resemblance to the apostles and martyrs. So he undertook the difficult task of trying to teach Christianity to people convinced they were already Christians. Obviously, he could not go about that task directly. No one would listen. So he wrote a series of books under different pseudonyms, showing from within the lives of different sorts of people who weren't really Christians, showing how their lives remained incomplete, empty. He started with the "aesthetic stage," describing young poets and lovers who live for the pleasures of the moment, a seducer always searching for one more conquest, yet always dissatisfied, unfulfilled. Then he portrayed the "ethical stage," describing an elderly judge, happily married, who had devoted his life to universal moral principles. Yet in following those principles, the judge has always done what duty demanded, what "the good person" would do in any situation, and he has somehow lost his individuality.

In trying to describe a "religious stage," Kierkegaard recalled from Genesis the story of how Abraham set off to sacrifice his son Isaac. Now from the ethical point of view, Abraham was a father about to murder his son. Only faith can offer a different interpretation—that this individual had a special command from God. Faith goes beyond the universal categories of ethics to make the individual matter again. But it is the odd character of Abraham's faith that he went off to kill his only son, the basis of all his hopes, and that nevertheless he did not despair, he remained confident that somehow all would finally be well. That this is absurd, Kierkegaard agreed. But the highest form of religion is absurd, for it involves believing in a paradox with all one's passion. "The absurd is . . . that God has come into being, has been born . . . and this absurdity, held fast in the passion of inwardness, is faith."[23] A faith that could be shown reasonable or probable would be trivialized; people would avoid the need to make a real decision for or against it and thus it would not be faith at all. Christians cannot prove their faith, and certainly they cannot show that it is probable. They cannot follow Hegel in turning their faith into a system. They can only grasp a paradox with passion. That is a hard message, and Kierkegaard had little influence on his contemporaries, but in the twentieth century, when Hegel's account of history as rational came to seem increasingly absurd, many turned to Kierkegaard's paradoxes with new interest.

ROMAN CATHOLIC AND ENGLISH THEOLOGY

Nineteenth-century romanticism produced new interest in tradition and new respect for the Middle Ages, and that offered the potential of new sympathy for Catholic thought. The relations between church and state, however, provided one serious problem for Catholic theology and pointed to a larger set of problems about the relation between Christianity and culture. To the popes it seemed that their political independence as rulers of a good part of central Italy gave them freedom and authority no other religious leader could match. But it also risked compromising their spiritual authority by forcing them into political or military alliances to protect their interests. The rise of a strong sense of national loyalty in many countries posed particular problems for Catholics, who owed some sort of allegiance to this "foreign" ruler.

The debates emerged most clearly in France. Back in 1682 the Gallican articles had limited papal control within the French church in return for government support of the Catholic Church. During the French Revolution, the state cut off church funds, closed Catholic schools, and curtailed the religious freedom of Catholics. Then in 1801 Napoleon signed an agreement with the pope that essentially restored the Gallican articles. But many French Catholics had come to mistrust the idea of resting their security on an alliance with the state. An "Ultramontane" party (their loyalties lay "across the mountains"—in Italy) argued that only full papal power could protect the church. Most Ultramontanes were political conservatives who looked to the papacy as a bastion of traditional order against the tendencies of liberal French governments. Around 1830, however, a passionate priest named Félicité de Lamennais began arguing that church independence could be a liberal cause. He proposed cutting all ties between church and state. "Religion administered like tariffs and taxes, the priesthood degraded . . ., the church, in a word, deprived of its necessary independence. . . . What is this, if not death?"[24] Let the church renounce all benefits and privileges from the state, secure its own freedom, and identify the church with the needs of the poor against their oppressors in society. "People tremble before liberalism; well, Catholicize it and society will be reborn."[25]

Lamennais eventually left the church, which refused to consider accepting independence if that meant sacrificing privilege. Pope Gregory XVI declared that Catholic rulers should not give equal rights to all religions. Error simply does not have equal rights with truth. When Pius IX was elected pope in 1846, however, liberals initially expected great things. As a bishop, he had fought for reform and helped the poor. Unfortunately, he had to flee Rome in a brief revolution in 1848, and Italian nationalists increasingly demanded that he give up the Papal States so that Italy could be united. He felt that many of the forces of the modern world were conspiring against him. In 1864 he issued a "Syllabus of Errors," a list of eighty propositions Catholics ought to reject. The Syllabus condemned rationalism, indifference to religious doctrine, compromises of traditional Christian ethics, and attacks on papal power, and ended by denouncing the idea that "the Roman Pontiff can and should reconcile and harmonize himself with progress, with liberalism, and with recent civilization."[26]

Pius IX created the modern papacy in spite of himself. He increased the pope's theological authority as he lost political power. In 1854, when he proclaimed the immaculate conception of the Virgin Mary (the belief that at the moment of her conception a miracle had freed Mary from the taint of original sin), he affirmed something that the vast majority of Catholics had long believed anyway. But he declared this dogma on his own authority. Thus he anticipated the proclamation by the First Vatican Council in 1870 that the pope is infallible "when he defines a doctrine regarding faith and morals to be held by the universal church."[27] Also in 1870, however, Italian armies conquered the last of his territory and occupied Rome, and Pius retreated, an angry recluse, into the Vatican. He could not believe that the loss of territorial independence, and with it the need to participate in political and military alliances, might make the pope's voice more influential.

Yet problems concerning Catholic attitudes to modern society continued. Near the end of the century Pope Leo XIII denounced a society in which "working men have been surrendered, isolated and helpless, to the hard-heartedness of employers and the greed of unchecked competition."[28] Writing to American Catholics, however, he urged them to seek special legal privileges for Catholicism over against other groups and advised that, "unless forced by necessity to do otherwise, Catholics ought to prefer to associate with Catholics."[29] Leo XIII also condemned the "Modernists," a group of Catholic writers who had sought to bring Catholic theology more in line with recent developments in philosophy and historical scholarship. The modern age brought good and bad, things worth adopting and things deserving criticism. It was hard to sort them out, and Leo XIII sometimes, like Pius IX, imposed blanket condemnations.

In many ways the Church of England in the nineteenth century had a set of virtues and faults opposite to those of Rome. It could adapt to its society, but found it hard to criticize. In the 1830s a group of scholars called the Oxford movement began to ask if English Christianity had not compromised too much with its society. In a rhetorical flourish, one of them, John Henry Newman, even declared that England would improve "were it vastly more superstitious, more bigoted, more gloomy, more fierce in its religion, than at present it shows itself to be."[30]

Issues of church and state again focused the problem. Parliament essentially had final authority over the Church of England. In 1833

Parliament reorganized the Irish churches, eliminating a few bishops and reassigning some revenues. On a practical level, the reforms probably made sense, but Newman's friend John Keble pointed out that they showed how completely the state could control the church, a situation made worse as liberal reforms increasingly gave equal political rights to people who were not members of the Church of England, so that that control might not even be administered by church members. Let them "take every pound, shilling and penny and the curse of sacrilege along with it," Keble wrote to Newman, "only let us make our own bishops and be governed by our own laws."[31] Newman agreed that the church is "not an institution of man . . . not a creature of the state . . . but . . . a great work of God, a true relic of Christ and His Apostles."[32] He mistrusted state control of the church and also the general "liberal" sense that one could be indifferent to doctrine, that you could believe what you chose as long as you led a decent life.

Newman saw many faults in the Church of England, but at first he retained many traditional suspicions of Roman Catholicism as corrupt and superstitious. He thought that the Church of England preserved the beliefs of the earliest church in purer form, without medieval and later accretions. But then his study of early theology began to persuade him that doctrine had developed even in the earliest church. New questions had always forced the church to provide new answers. Heresy, Newman concluded, had arisen not from "new doctrine" but from splitting off from the universal church to form a group represented in only part of the Christian world. In his own time, the Church of England might claim the authority of antiquity for its beliefs, but Rome had universality. Newman therefore decided to become a Roman Catholic. He tore the Oxford movement apart, and indeed all England shook as its most famous preacher joined a church many still associated with treason and the Spanish Armada. Newman retreated into seclusion and devoted himself to developing the philosophical foundations of his faith.

We cannot prove the truth of religion, he admitted, but we cannot prove the truth of many of our most fundamental beliefs. How do I *know* that England is an island? How do I *know* I can trust my closest friend? I may have forgotten the evidence that persuaded me, and many factors, including emotional ones, may have played a part. None of this implies that I ought to abandon these beliefs. In life we can rarely run one definitive experiment. We start with unexamined assumptions, make use of a variety of arguments, each leading to only a probable conclusion, and commit ourselves to accepting that conclusion in part because of the example of a trusted friend or because it just feels right.

> Life is for action. If we insist on proofs for everything, we shall never come to action; to act you must assume and that assumption is faith. . . . Why we are so constituted that faith, not knowledge or argument, is our principle of action, is a question with which I have nothing to do; but I think it is a fact.[33]

Critics of religion may attack theologians for making such unproven assumptions, but such assumptions are in fact a necessary part of the structure of the beliefs that guide *anyone's* life.

Though Newman's conversion shook it badly, the Oxford movement remained influential in the Church of England as the basis for the "high church" party, with emphasis on doctrine and liturgy. The "evangelical" party continued the spirit Wesley and Whitefield had introduced in the previous century, with an emphasis on evangelism and conversions. One English theologian of the middle nineteenth century, Frederick Denison Maurice, rejected both parties. The Evangelical wing, he said, talked only of sin and the need for conversion. The Oxford movement called for asceticism and moral self-discipline. That might be fine for Oxford professors, Maurice observed sarcastically, but should the priest of a working class parish

> tell wretched creatures, who spend eighteen hours out of the twenty-four in close factories and bitter toil . . . that if they spent the remaining six in prayer—he need not add fasting—they may possibly be saved. How can we insult God and torment men with such mockery?[34]

Maurice insisted that instead we must find a way to proclaim the good news that Christ has died to save us all. "The truth is that every man is in Christ; the condemnation of every man is, that he will not own the truth; he will not *act* as if this were *true*."[35] Maurice proclaimed a powerful message, but he did not really come to terms with many of the new developments of his time. He made little use of contemporary biblical scholarship, and he had little to say about the work of Charles Darwin, which was shaking the intellectual world of England.

The publication of Darwin's *The Origin of Species* in 1859 raised awkward questions not only about how to interpret Genesis but also about how to understand God's action in history generally in the light of modern science. In a famous debate at Oxford in 1860, Darwin's champion T. H. Huxley listened while Bishop Samuel Wilberforce sarcastically asked if he were descended from an ape on his father's side or his mother's. Huxley jumped up and replied:

> A man has no reason to be ashamed of having an ape for his grandfather. If there were an ancestor whom I should feel shame in recalling, it would rather be a man . . . who . . . plunges into scientific questions with which he has no real acquaintance, only to . . . distract the attention of his hearers from the real point at issue by . . . skilled appeals to religious prejudice.[36]

Wilberforce was demolished, and Huxley sat down to cheers. Yet his triumph was in part only a rhetorical one. On scientific issues, Darwin and Huxley carried the day, but neither they nor anyone else very clearly explained the philosophical and theological implications of these new scientific conclusions. They simply set one more item on the agenda of how to fit Christianity to culture.

LIBERAL THEOLOGY AND ITS CRITICS

In Germany the theologian Albrecht Ritschl and his students dominated much of the religious thought of the second half of the century, and Ritschl tied Christianity closely to the culture of his time. He sought to move theology away from metaphysical theories to contact with people's lives, but he would have agreed with Maurice in attacking an exclusive emphasis on justification and conversion experiences. Christianity, he said, is more like an ellipse with two foci: God's action in redeeming us, *and* our response in working to create the kingdom of God. Theology which seeks only conversions and ignores social change is incomplete. Ritschl's student Adolf von Harnack wrote a monumental history of Christian doctrine guided by the view that the ethical teachings of Jesus had been distorted and corrupted by the admixture of Greek speculation. For Harnack, "that Jesus' message is so great and so powerful lies in the fact that it is so simple and on the other hand so rich." Basically, it consists of three points:

> Firstly, the kingdom of God and its coming.
> Secondly, God the Father and the infinite value of the human soul.
> Thirdly, the higher righteousness and the commandment of love.[37]

That pictured a simple and attractive version of Christianity, but a number of problems concerning it were emerging. For one thing, German scholars of the "history of religions school" were discovering the complexity of the history of Christianity. Harnack claimed he could discover a single "essence of Christianity." "History of religions" theologians like Ernst Troeltsch concluded that Christianity had emerged gradually out of a context of Jewish and other eastern Mediterranean religions. And, once formed, it continued to develop and has taken many different forms at different times. Earlier theologians, Troeltsch wrote, had failed to acknowledge "how thoroughly individual is historical Christianity after all, and how invariably its various phases and denominations have been due to varying circumstances and conditions of life. . . . It is a purely historical, individual, relative phenomenon."[38] Christianity cannot claim any eternal essence or absolute truth; it is simply the religious manifestation of our culture. "Christianity . . . stands or falls with European civilization. . . . We cannot live without a religion, but the only religion that we can endure is Christianity, for Christianity has grown up with us and has become a part of our very being."[39] That hardly made an enthusiastic case.

Some developments in New Testament scholarship were also raising questions. Ritschl had assumed that by "the kingdom of God" Jesus meant a better world that would emerge gradually, with God's help, out of our efforts at moral reform. Biblical scholars like Johannes Weiss and Albert Schweitzer now argued that Jesus had thought in the context of apocalypticism—the expectation that the world will get steadily worse until God brings a cataclysm down from heaven to inaugurate the new age. Schweitzer concluded that Jesus had simply been wrong: he expected that the world was about to end dramatically, and here we all are, two thousand years later. At any rate, it seemed that Jesus could not be simply identified as a teacher of nineteenth-century liberal ethics.

Most of Christianity's critics, however, at least acknowledged that Christian ethics had improved humanity. But the philosopher Friedrich Nietzsche denounced the Christian praise of meekness, lowliness, and pity. "Christianity," he declared, "has sided with all that is weak and base, with all failures; it has made an ideal of whatever *contradicts* the interest of the strong life to preserve itself."[40] Everything that Christians had considered moral progress Nietzsche dismissed as decadence, leading ever downward to the nadir of "God as god of the sick, God as a spider, God as spirit."[41] Nietzsche offered instead the ideal of the "healthy" overman, strong and faithful to the things of the earth.

Most philosophers of the nineteenth century had, like Hegel, assumed that history was progressing. If we do not have the truth, at least we are closer to it than previous generations. Nietzsche said only that truth varies from one place to another, and there can be no standard for judging one version to be superior to another. Indeed, "truth" is simply whatever a society agrees to call "true"—the socially accepted lie.

> In some remote corner of the universe, poured out and glittering in innumerable solar systems, there once was a star on which clever animals invented knowledge. That was the haughtiest and most mendacious minute of "world history"—yet only a minute. After nature had drawn a few breaths, the star grew cold, and the clever animals had to die.[42]

The fascination with history that had seemed to hold such promise at the beginning of the nineteenth century thus seemed to end in despair. Schleiermacher had appealed to new sympathy for tradition to defend the claims of Christianity against natural religion, and Hegel had traced a pattern of rational development through history that culminated in Christianity. Now historical research into the New Testament led to skepticism or the conclusion that Jesus had been wrong, and the very method of history seemed to lead to a relativism that made claims to absolute truth or even to progress impossible. This disquiet among scholars might not have been taken very seriously, but in the trenches of World War I all of Europe learned to be suspicious of claims about progress and optimism about history.

FOR FURTHER READING

INTRODUCTIONS. Most good books on nineteenth-century theology are difficult. Paul Tillich, *Perspectives on Nineteenth and Twentieth Century Theology* (Harper & Row, 1967), presents a reasonably simple account from Tillich's perspective. On the Protestant side the most current work is Claude Welch, *Protestant Thought in the Nineteenth Century*, Vol. 1 (Yale University Press, 1972). Bernard M. G. Reardon, *From Coleridge to Gore* (London: Longman Group, 1971), is the best survey of British developments. E. E. Y. Hales, *The Catholic Church in the Modern World* (Doubleday & Co., Image Books, 1960), is a good introduction, especially helpful on church-state relations.

COLLECTIONS OF ORIGINAL SOURCES. Bernard M. G. Reardon, *Religious Thought in the Nineteenth Century* (Cambridge: Cambridge University Press, 1966), is an excellent collection of brief passages from primary sources. Some starting points for reading other authors discussed in this chapter are: Friedrich Schleiermacher, *On Religion,* tr. by John Oman (Harper & Row, Harper Torchbooks, 1958); G. W. F. Hegel, *Reason in History,* tr. by Robert S. Hartman (Liberal Arts Press, Library of Liberal Arts, 1953); Søren Kierkegaard, *A Kierkegaard Anthology,* ed. by Robert Bretall (Modern Library, 1959); John Henry Newman, *Apologia pro vita sua* (Doubleday & Co., Image Books, 1956); Adolf Harnack, *What Is Christianity?* tr. by Thomas Bailey Saunders (Harper & Row, Harper Torchbooks, 1957); Friedrich Nietzsche, *The Portable Nietzsche,* tr. by Walter Kaufmann (Viking Press, 1968).

IMPORTANT BUT MORE DIFFICULT. Karl Barth, *Protestant Theology in the Nineteenth Century,* tr. by Brian Cozens and John Bowden (London: SCM Press, 1972), is sometimes eccentric but often brilliant. It deals almost entirely with Germany. John Martin Creed, *The Divinity of Jesus Christ* (Cambridge: Cambridge University Press, 1938), is a remarkable definition of the central issues. Many fine scholars have done work on individual authors mentioned in this chapter. For Protestants, the bibliographical footnotes in Claude Welch's book provide a thorough introduction to the available works. On Catholic thought generally, see Gerald A. McCool, *Catholic Thought in the Nineteenth Century* (Seabury Press, 1977). Some important studies of Catholic figures are: Christopher Hollis, *Newman and the Modern World* (Doubleday & Co., 1968); Bernard M. G. Reardon, *Roman Catholic Modernism* (London: Adam & Charles Black, 1970); Peter N. Stearns, *Priest and Revolutionary* (Harper & Row, 1967), on Lamennais; Alec R. Vidler, *A Variety of Catholic Modernists* (Cambridge: Cambridge University Press, 1970).

NOTES

1. Johann Gottfried Herder, *Briefe über das Studium der Theologie,* in *Sämmtliche Werke,* Vol. 10 (Berlin: Weidmannsche Buchhandlung, 1879), p. 290; quoted in Karl Barth, *Protestant Theology in the Nineteenth Century,* tr. by Brian Cozens and John Bowden (London: SCM Press, 1972), p. 326.

2. Friedrich D. E. Schleiermacher, *On the Glaubenslehre: Two Letters to Dr. Lücke,* tr. by James Duke and Francis Fiorenza (Scholars Press, 1981), p. 61.

3. Friedrich Schleiermacher, *On Religion,* tr. by John Oman (Harper & Row, Harper Torchbooks, 1958), p. 18.

4. Ibid., pp. 39, 36.

5. Ibid., p. 89.

6. Friedrich Schleiermacher, *The Christian Faith,* various translators (Edinburgh: T. & T. Clark, 1928), p. 428.

7. Ibid., p. 288.

8. Ibid., p. 429.

9. Samuel Taylor Coleridge, *Specimens of the Table Talk,* June 23, 1834, Vol. 1 (Harper & Brothers, 1835), p. 166.

10. Quoted in Basil Willey, *Samuel Taylor Coleridge* (W. W. Norton & Co., 1972), p. 244.

11. Samuel Taylor Coleridge, *On the Constitution of the Church and State,* in *Collected Works,* Vol. 10 (Princeton University Press, 1976), p. 44.

12. Ibid., p. 55.

13. Georg Wilhelm Friedrich Hegel, *Lectures on the Philosophy of History,* tr. by J. Sibree (London: George Bell & Sons, 1890), p. 22.

14. Georg Wilhelm Friedrich Hegel, *Lectures on the Philosophy of Religion,* tr. by E. B. Speirs and J. Burdon Sanderson, Vol. 2 (Humanities Press, 1962), p. 327.

15. Georg Wilhelm Friedrich Hegel, *Hegel's Lectures on the History of Philosophy,* tr. by E. S. Haldane, Vol. 1 (Humanities Press, 1955), p. 78.

16. David Friedrich Strauss, *The Life of Jesus Critically Examined,* tr. by George Eliot (Fortress Press, 1972), p. lii.

17. Ibid., p. 780.

18. Ludwig Feuerbach, *Lectures on the Essence of Religion,* tr. by Ralph Manheim (Harper & Row, 1967), p. 17.

19. H. L. Mansel, "Phrontisterion"; quoted in Bernard M. G. Reardon, *From Coleridge to Gore* (London: Longman Group, 1971), p. 225.

20. Karl Marx, *Theses on Feuerbach,* in *Marx and Engels on Religion* (no translator given) (Schocken Books, 1964), p. 72.

21. Søren Kierkegaard, *The Journals of Søren Kierkegaard,* Aug. 1, 1835, tr. by Alexander Dru (London: Oxford University Press, 1938), p. 14.

22. Søren Kierkegaard, *The Point of View for My Work as an Author,* tr. by Walter Lowrie (Harper & Brothers, Harper Torchbooks, 1962), p. 22.

23. Søren Kierkegaard, *Concluding Unscientific Postscript,* tr. by David F. Swenson and Walter Lowrie (Princeton University Press, 1941), p. 188.

24. Félicité de Lamennais, *On the Separation of Church and State,* Oct. 18, 1830, *L'Avenir* (Rome: Edizioni di Storia e Letteratura, 1967), pp. 27–28.

25. Quoted in Peter N. Stearns, *Priest and Revolutionary* (Harper & Row, 1967), p. 63.

26. Pius IX, *Syllabus of Errors,* in *Dogmatic Canons and Decrees* (Tan Books & Publications, 1977), p. 209.

27. First Vatican Council, First Dogmatic Constitution on the Church of Christ, ibid., p. 256.

28. Leo XIII, *Rerum novarum* (May 15, 1891), in *The Papal Encyclicals 1878–1903,* ed. by Claudia Carlen Ihm (McGrath Publishing Co., 1981), p. 242.

29. Leo XIII, *Longinqua* (Jan. 6, 1895), ibid., p. 368.

30. John Henry Newman, Sermon 24, in *Parochial and Plain Sermons,* Vol. 1 (London: Longmans, Green & Co., 1891), p. 230.

31. Quoted in Christopher Dawson, *The Spirit of the Oxford Movement* (London: Sheed & Ward, 1945), p. 73.

32. John Henry Newman, Sermon 17, in *Parochial and Plain Sermons,* Vol. 7 (London: Rivingtons, 1868), p. 242.

33. John Henry Newman, *An Essay in Aid of a Grammar of Assent* (Doubleday & Co., Image Books, 1955), p. 91.

34.   Quoted in Alec R. Vidler, *F. D. Maurice and Company* (London: SCM Press, 1966), p. 97.

35.   Frederick Denison Maurice, Letter to his mother, Dec. 9, 1833, in *The Life and Letters of Frederick Denison Maurice*, Vol. 1 (Charles Scribner's Sons, 1884), p. 155.

36.   Leonard Huxley, *Life and Letters of Thomas Henry Huxley*, Vol. 1 (D. Appleton Co., 1901), p. 199.

37.   Adolf Harnack, *What Is Christianity?* tr. by Thomas B. Saunders (Harper & Row, Harper Torchbooks, 1957), p. 51.

38.   Ernst Troeltsch, *Christian Thought: Its History and Application* (Meridian Books, Living Age Books, 1957), pp. 51–52.

39.   Ibid., pp. 54–55.

40.   Friedrich Nietzsche, *The Antichrist,* tr. by Walter Kaufmann, in *The Portable Nietzsche* (Viking Press, 1968), p. 571.

41.   Ibid., p. 585.

42.   Friedrich Nietzsche, *On Truth and Lie in an Extra-Moral Sense,* ibid., p. 42.

18

THE END
OF WESTERN CHRISTENDOM

In a world full of Nazis one can be forgiven for being a
Barthian.

—Peter Berger[1]

In September of 1914 a young Swiss pastor named Karl Barth first
learned of a manifesto signed by ninety-three prominent German
intellectuals proclaiming their enthusiastic support of the Kaiser's
war policy. He discovered with horror that the signers included many
of the leading German theologians, including most of his own teachers. Barth dashed off a note to his friend Eduard Thurneysen: "The
unconditional truths of the gospel are simply suspended for the time
being and in the meantime a German war-theology is put to work."[2]
Something, Barth concluded, had to be wrong with a theological
tradition that led to this. Most twentieth-century theologians have
come to share that conclusion.

Nineteenth-century theology had often tried to identify Christianity
with the forces of progress and the best in Western civilization. The
twentieth century has become considerably more skeptical about
both progress and Western civilization, and theologians have often
sought to keep their distance. Barth himself sought to distinguish the
grace of God in Christ as radically as possible from any claims about
the superiority of Christians or their societies. Theologians in the
United States have sought to criticize American culture from stand-
points as varied as fundamentalism and the social gospel. Other
theologians in Germany, such as Rudolf Bultmann, borrowed their
categories from existentialist philosophy. To be sure, that meant
adopting ideas from the surrounding milieu, but they were ideas
which turned from optimism to talk of boundary situations and crises
and our responsibility as we face death alone. Catholic theology grew

291

less confident that its doctrine embodied the final truth or that salvation could come only within the church. Theologians in Africa, Latin America, and Asia, and women and blacks in the United States as well, moved theology away from the assumptions of traditional European culture. At the beginning of the century, Ernst Troeltsch had argued that Christianity would endure as long as Western culture. That no longer seemed so encouraging a thought, and Christian theology looked for new ways to define its own identity.

BARTH AND BONHOEFFER

The story has to begin with Karl Barth. Even before 1914, Barth had already had his doubts about the liberal theology of the nineteenth century. He had become active in the local labor movement and sympathetic with the socialists, and liberal theology seemed too inclined to accept the established values of contemporary society. At the same time, the more he studied the Bible the more he found a "strange new world" there, "something very ancient, early oriental, indefinably sunny, wild, original."[3] In comparison, most modern theology seemed tame stuff. Liberal commentators tried to sort out the parts of the Bible that reflected the author's own biases or the assumptions of his culture, with the hope of eliminating the residue of that earlier culture and restating Christianity in terms appropriate to our modern society. In a radical commentary on Romans, Barth argued that *everything* reflects Paul's biases and cultural assumptions. Nevertheless, Paul knew something about God and managed to communicate it through biased, inadequate human words.

Every preacher, Barth said, does the same thing. "As ministers we ought to speak of God. We are human beings, however, and so cannot speak of God."[4] The search for adequate theological categories is doomed to failure. Yet God has called Christians to preach the gospel, and they must try to obey. Barth preserved both sides of that dialectic in a style full of paradoxes and passion. "Faith," he wrote, "is . . . beyond all human ideas and affirmations . . . , beyond every positive religious achievement. . . . It is always a leap into the darkness of the unknown, a flight into empty air."[5] We cannot prove that Christ, as a human being, was more remarkable than Mohammed or the Buddha or St. Francis. His resurrection remains utterly incomprehensible. Every effort to show the ethical superiority of Christianity to other religions or ideologies collapses in failure. Barth rejected all the nineteenth century's efforts to show the cultural superiority of Christianity and honed theology down to the claim that through this very ambiguous, imperfect Christian faith God chooses to be revealed.

Barth's commentary on Romans, first published in 1918 and completely revised in 1921, had an explosive impact on theology. Young theologians like Emil Brunner and Friedrich Gogarten and the New Testament scholar Rudolf Bultmann offered their support to the cause of "dialectical theology," and Barth accepted a professorship in theology in Germany, though he feared that among all those great scholars he would seem like a "wandering gypsy . . . with only a couple of leaky kettles to call his own who to compensate occasionally burns a house down."[6] Increasingly he distrusted his allies as people who wanted only to replace one philosophy, one kind of cultural Christianity, with another. To his mind, replacing nineteenth-century liberalism with existentialism did not deal with the real problem—it continued to look for human words adequate to God's Word, and there are none. In his *Church Dogmatics,* still unfinished at his death, thirteen volumes and forty years later, Barth attacked all "natural theology," all human efforts to understand God. Religion, he said, represents the ultimate sin, the effort to reach up to God like the tower of Babel. We must accept the fact that we can know of God only what God reveals.

In the 1930s this theological protest could, in Barth's words, "no longer have the slightest vestige of an academic theory. . . . This had of necessity to take on the character of a summons, a challenge, a battle-cry, a confession."[7] The Nazis sought to organize the German churches as part of their propaganda machine, to forbid anyone of Jewish ancestry from serving as a Christian minister, and to make a place for homage to Hitler in Christian liturgy. Nazi ideology owed more to neo-paganism than to Christianity, and the most committed Nazis always intended to follow the murder of the Jews with the destruction of Christianity. Nevertheless, centuries of Christian toleration of anti-Semitism and sermons denouncing the Jews as "Christ-killers" had largely created the anti-Semitic climate. If Christians in the generation before the 1930s had firmly denounced anti-Semitism, the Holocaust could not have happened. That fact must haunt Christian theology for the rest of history.

In the 1930s some German theologians saw cooperation with the Nazis as just another step in the church's need to adapt itself to contemporary culture. A small group called the Confessing Church disagreed, and Barth drafted their manifesto, the Barmen Declaration of 1934:

> Jesus Christ . . . is the one Word of God. . . . We repudiate the false teaching that the church can and must recognize other happenings and powers, images and truths as divine revelation. . . . We repudiate the false teaching that there are areas of our life in which we belong not to Jesus Christ but to another lord. . . . We repudiate the false teaching that the church can turn over the form of her message and ordinances at will or according to some dominant ideological and political convictions.[8]

His attack on cultural Christianity had become a matter of life and death. Barth later regretted that he had not made an attack on Nazi anti-Semitism more central, but he had said enough to cost him his job and force him to flee to Switzerland.

There he continued to emphasize that our knowledge of God begins, not with "human nature" or "modern civilization" or "German culture," but only with Jesus Christ, but he began to put more emphasis on the positive implications of that conviction. In his early years Barth had concentrated on God's character as "wholly other" than human beings. But Jesus Christ was human; therefore, God has authenticated value in humanity. "Nietzsche's statement that man is something that must be overcome is an impudent lie."[9]

> Man . . . can use his senses and understanding to perceive that two and two makes four, and to write poetry, and to think, and to make music, and to eat and drink . . . not as half a man but as a whole man, with head uplifted, and the heart free and the conscience at rest. . . . It is only the heathen gods who envy man. The true God, who is unconditionally the Lord, allows him to be the thing for which he created him.[10]

Human beings cannot reach God, but God has come to human beings, and Barth increasingly found that that fact led him to say positive things about humanity.

And yet, human beings continue to sin. Barth called this an "impossible possibility." He rejected all efforts to explain it or fit it into a system or show that it has some purpose. All that would trivialize or clean up the horror of evil. All a Christian can say about evil, really, is that Christ has defeated it. Barth compared the situation to a battle in which skirmishes continue between isolated units that have not heard that one side has already won the victory. The Christian refuses to set any limit to that victory. Barth rarely criticized Calvin, but he admitted that he thought Calvin had erred in dwelling on the distinction between the elect and the reprobate; that imposes limits on God's grace. Christ became the reprobate, taking on the sins of all.

"The exchange which took place on Golgotha, when God chose as His throne the malefactor's cross, when the Son of God bore what the son of man ought to have borne, took place once and for all . . . and it can never be reversed."[11] Yet Barth never quite affirmed a doctrine of universal salvation. We can *hope* that all will be saved, and we cannot set limits on God's grace, but evil is real and terrible, and we take it far too lightly if we believe that, of course, God will save everyone.

Barth's determination not to let modern culture shape Christian faith often left liberal readers with the sense that he simply repeated biblical language, but he kept conservatives off guard too with his attacks on "religion" and radical reinterpretations of traditional doctrines. In old age he refused to denounce Communism as he had once denounced the Nazis, insisting that the ideology of "anticommunism" posed far more dangerous temptations to most Christians than Communism did. In the last published section of the *Church Dogmatics* he attacked infant baptism as contrary to Scripture and destructive of the health of the church. Barth never ran out of surprises, and he made following him difficult.

Dietrich Bonhoeffer tried to follow one side of Barth, his separation of Christianity from culture and religion, to its radical conclusion. Bonhoeffer participated in church opposition to Hitler but remained in Germany. The Nazis arrested him for playing a minor part in a plot on Hitler's life, but he continued to write theology in letters from his prison cell. He thought that "religion" has come to mean an individualism that turns away from the world to worry about one's own salvation, a metaphysics that talks about some other realm of reality apart from this world, and a basis for privilege that enables "religious" people to claim that they are better than anyone else. In those senses, he concluded, modern people are not interested in religion anymore—and indeed they should not be. In his letters Bonhoeffer tried to define the possibility of a "religionless Christianity." Too often, he said, theologians have fought rear-guard actions, trying to "demonstrate to secure, contented, happy mankind that it is really unhappy and desperate,"[12] and searching for things that science has (so far) failed to explain as proof that we need God after all. All this struck Bonhoeffer as cheap and undignified, a scramble to preserve a place for God on the edges of our lives. "I should like to speak of God not on the boundaries but at the center."[13] In the cross, "God would have us know that we must live as men who manage our lives without him. . . . God let himself be pushed out of the world on to the cross. He is weak and powerless in the world, and that is precisely the way, the only way, in which he is with us and helps us."[14] "Man is challenged to participate in the sufferings of God at the hands of a godless world."[15] Bonhoeffer was looking for a way to preach Christ in a world where all the old assumptions at the foundation of religion no longer seemed to make sense. No one can know what he might have found, for, a few weeks before the end of the war, his Nazi jailers killed him.

AMERICAN DEVELOPMENTS

World War I, which hit many Europeans as a cataclysm, had little impact in America. Even the depression of the 1930s and World War II inflicted on America little of the trauma the Nazi era brought to Germany. Still, even in the United States the early twentieth century brought new challenges to Christian faith.

In the later nineteenth century a group of theologians at Princeton led by Charles Hodge and Benjamin B. Warfield had defined orthodoxy as based on the infallibility of the Bible. Medieval theologians had explored allegorical interpretation, and Luther had interpreted Scripture freely in terms of the principle of justification by faith. Princeton orthodoxy, however, defined the truth of the Bible in terms of the literal truth of its every statement. As Hodge put it, "Inspiration extends to all the contents. . . . It is not confined to moral and religious truths, but extends to the statement of facts, whether scientific, historical, or geographical."[16] Though Hodge rejected many of the conclusions of modern science, he accepted much of its way of thinking. "Truth" meant a collection of facts, and "the Bible is to the theologian what nature is to the man of science. It is his storehouse of facts."[17]

Hodge sometimes recognized nuances in his theory of inspiration. He rejected the "mechanical theory of inspiration," insisting that biblical writers expressed themselves in the language of their culture, not by taking word-for-word dictation from God.[18] He acknowledged that the inspiration of the biblical writers extended only to teaching what God wanted them to teach us; they might have had various erroneous beliefs about science or history.[19] In the subsequent debate, however, such qualifications often got lost, and the leadership of the defense of biblical infallibility moved from the intellectual sophistication of Hodge and Warfield to popular writers suspicious of intellectual theology. After the appearance of a series of widely circulated pamphlets published from 1910 to 1915 called *The Fundamentals,* Americans came to call such defenders of biblical inerrancy "fundamentalists," and in the 1920s fundamentalists in many denominations tried with varying success to require ministers and seminaries to teach fundamentalist doctrine, often summarized in the five fundamental points of biblical inerrancy, the virgin birth, the satisfaction theory of the atonement, bodily resurrection, and the miracles of Jesus. They also led a crusade against the teaching of evolution.

Their opponents often ridiculed the fundamentalists, but it is important to remember the kind of comfortable liberal Christianity they often attacked, with its easy identification of the beliefs and values of modern America with Christian faith. In that respect fundamentalism was part of the general reaction against nineteenth-century theology's comfortable acceptance of its culture.

A very different sort of attack on such Americanized Christianity came from the social gospel movement, which found its greatest spokesman in Walter Rauschenbusch. Most of the urban poor, many of them immigrants, had little connection with any church in the years before World War I, and Protestant churches—the Catholics did better—made little effort to try to reach these people. Deeply moved by his years as a pastor in the slums of New York's "Hell's Kitchen," Rauschenbusch said that Christians had come to pay too much attention to individual salvation and not enough to the call for social change implied in the symbol of the kingdom of God. "Whoever uncouples the religious and the social life," he wrote, "has not understood Jesus."[20] "The wrongs connected with wealth are the most vulnerable part of our civilization. Unless we can make that crooked place straight, all our charities and religion are involved in hypocrisy."[21] Rauschenbusch's emphasis on the kingdom of God had much in common with Ritschl's theology a bit earlier in Germany, but Rauschenbusch made more fundamental criticisms of his society and even found Karl Marx's analyses of social issues helpful. For him, salvation meant above all changing society. "It is not a matter of saving human atoms, but of saving the social organism. It is not a matter of getting individuals to heaven, but of transforming the life on earth into the harmony of heaven."[22]

In 1915, about a generation after Rauschenbusch had begun his pastorate in Hell's Kitchen, a young pastor of the German Evangelical Church from Missouri named Reinhold Niebuhr took charge of a small working-class church in Detroit. Niebuhr shared Rauschenbusch's concern for social reform and became active in liberal and socialist politics, but, both politically and theologically, the social gospel movement's dream of steadily improving society until we achieve the kingdom of God seemed too simple to him. He noted that movements toward social reform tend to treat "our side" (our union, or our political party, or our nation, or whatever) as unambiguously good, whereas in fact all human groups contain imperfection and the potential for dangerous excess. The title of Niebuhr's most famous book, *Moral Man and Immoral Society,* makes the point: "Individual men . . . are endowed by nature with a measure of sympathy and consideration for their kind. . . . Their rational faculty prompts them to a sense of justice. . . . But all these achievements are more difficult, if not impossible, for human societies and social groups."[23] Institutions lead people to perform horrors for the sake of the cause that they would never do on their own behalf.

Niebuhr once remarked that he should have called his book "Immoral Man and Even More Immoral Society," for thinking about the flaws in the easy optimism of social reformers led him to a new appreciation of the doctrine of original sin. "Secularized and moralistic versions of Christianity," he wrote, ". . . cannot understand the doctrine precisely because they believe there is some fairly simple way out of the sinfulness of human history."[24] Changes in society, he insisted, will not make human beings fundamentally good. Niebuhr's political "realism," his conviction that no party or cause can be unambiguously good, drew him farther and farther away from his Marxist friends. When Stalin signed a nonaggression pact with Hitler in 1939, and many American socialists tried to defend it, Niebuhr wrote:

> What appalls us particularly is the spiritual poverty which forces so many people in our era to talk this nonsense in order to save themselves from despair. One must continue to defend and to extend if possible whatever decency, justice and freedom still exist in this day when the lights are going out one by one. One can do that with clearest vision and courage if one has not placed one's faith in some frail reed of human virtue which does not exist.[25]

Niebuhr never lost his passion for social justice, but he grew unwilling to identify Christianity with any social cause—though Karl Barth felt that Niebuhr's reaction against Marxism sometimes tended to identify the Christian cause with anticommunism. Still, Niebuhr's rediscovery of the power of the Augustinian theology of original sin represented the closest American parallel to what Barth did in Germany.

BULTMANN AND EXISTENTIALISM

After World War II, few in Germany followed Barth, whose deter-mination to go his own way made discipleship difficult. Rudolf Bult-mann and his students increasingly took the leading role in German theology. In the 1920s and 1930s Bultmann first made his reputation as a New Testament scholar, a pioneer in the use of "form criticism." The form critics took each Gospel story and tried to figure out why Christians had told this particular tale and when it would have devel-oped in the early history of the church. Thus they studied the New Testament to learn about the development of ideas in the early church, not to learn about the history of Jesus' life. Bultmann indeed doubted that we can know very much about Jesus' history, but such historical skepticism did not seem to him to threaten the foundations of faith, for faith, properly understood, does not involve "the knowl-edge of some fact within the world or the willingness to hold some remarkable dogma to be true."[26] "The man who wishes to believe in God as his God must realize that he has nothing in his hand on which to base his faith. He is suspended in mid-air and cannot demand a proof of the Word which addresses him."[27] For Bultmann, solid histor-ical evidence of the truth of Christianity—if one can even imagine such a thing—would destroy the true nature of faith as a decision, a risk, a personal commitment.

His understanding of personal commitment owed a great deal to existentialism, particularly the work of the German philosopher Mar-tin Heidegger. Existentialism is a complex movement, embracing Christians, Jews, and atheists and tracing its roots to Kierkegaard, Nietzsche, and elsewhere. It defies quick summary. But existential-ists believe at least that we cannot understand human beings in the way a biologist or a chemist, say, understands the natural world, because human beings do not have a "nature." The wolf is aggressive and carnivorous by nature; the plant naturally reaches toward the sun. We neither praise nor blame them. Human beings, on the other hand, have to *decide* what to make of their lives. To quote the French existentialist Jean-Paul Sartre: "First of all, man exists, turns up, appears on the scene, and, only afterwards, defines himself. . . . Man is nothing else but what he makes of himself."[28] That can be a fright-ening thought. As Heidegger always emphasized, we are all going to die, and that means we have finite time; in choosing to do some things, we pass up the chance to do others—and live with the conse-quences, knowing that we are responsible for them. Most people avoid facing up to this fact. They sink into "everydayness," "average-ness," and "idle chatter," worrying about what to have for dinner, what to do this weekend, and never asking what they want to make of their lives. Heidegger called all this "inauthentic existence."

Heidegger was not a Christian theologian, but Bultmann found in his existentialism a set of categories for expressing Christian faith. Given the terrors involved in accepting full responsibility for our own lives, he argued, none of us would ever manage it alone. We look for escape and excuses, and this is a state of sin. Only because God's grace confronts us in Christian preaching, making us aware that God loves us and accepts us as we are can we risk struggling for "authentic existence." Bultmann thought this expressed in existentialist categories Jesus' message of forgiveness, which freed people from the Pharisees' obsession with obeying every detail of the law, and Luther's discovery that salvation is through faith, not works. The realization that God loves us leaves us free to love. "The event of Jesus Christ . . . makes a man free from himself and free to be himself, free to live a life of self-commitment in faith and love."[29] If God loves us even in our sin, we can risk living authentically.

All this provided the context for "demythologizing," the slogan too often thought to represent the whole of Bultmann's theology. People today, he said, cannot believe in many of the features of the New Testament world view: the three-story universe with heaven "up there" and hell "down there," the demons causing illness, and so on. "It is impossible to use electric light and the radio and to avail ourselves of modern medical and surgical discoveries and at the same time to believe in the New Testament world of spirits and miracles."[30] But that does not mean we cannot accept the New Testament message, for the New Testament only uses this mythological language to express something else. "The real purpose of myth is not to present an objective picture of the world as it is, but to express man's understanding of himself."[31] Christian faith does not inform us of new facts about history or science; it challenges us and enables us to live our lives in a new way. The mythological language, properly understood, conveys a new understanding of human possibilities.

Bultmann believed that "an historical fact which involves a resurrection from the dead is utterly inconceivable."[32] Things like that just don't happen. Besides, the "resuscitation of a corpse" wouldn't matter even if it were true. What matters is that after Jesus' death his disciples found themselves able to preach the good news of God's grace in Christ, and their hearers could live a new life in response to that preaching. Christ rose in the church's preaching. At the same time, Bultmann insisted that, while we can know very little about Jesus' life, he does represent the beginning of the new possibility of existence, and Christian faith cannot be separated from its starting point in Jesus Christ. Some of Bultmann's "left-wing" followers, like the American Schubert Ogden, have concluded that Christianity concerns only the possibility of a new way of existing. Christ may provide a particularly vivid way of thinking about God's love, but to think of God as intervening at a particular moment in history to change the possibilities of human existence is a last vestige of the mythology Bultmann was trying to discard. "Right-wing" Bultmannians like Ernst Käsemann and Günther Bornkamm in Germany, on the other hand, agree with Bultmann that Jesus lies inextricably at the foundation of Christian faith, but they argue that this also means that Christians need to make some affirmations about Jesus' life and teaching to explain why he makes such a difference in their lives. Thus, unlike Bultmann himself, they think a good many claims about the "historical Jesus" are important for Christian faith.

Other theologians have also appropriated insights from existentialism for Christian theology. Paul Tillich, who fled from Hitler to begin a new career in the United States, thought of theology as a dialogue. Philosophy—among other fields, like psychology—poses questions about the meaning of human existence, and theology offers Christian answers. Tillich's own wide interests in the arts, psychology, and intellectual history enabled him to arouse the interest of intellectuals in many fields who ordinarily dismissed Christianity as obsolete or meaningless. He acknowledged that all religious language is symbolic, not literal, but he thought we too often dismiss the "merely" symbolic as untrue, failing to realize what artists and poets could teach us: that sometimes only symbols and myths can convey the deepest truths. Tillich did not owe as much to any one philosopher as Bultmann did to Heidegger, but he worked very much in the context of existentialist thought. Existentialism, indeed, has provided many theologians with a powerful way of talking about Christianity, thoroughly modern but without easy optimism or acceptance of the dominant cultural norms.

ROMAN CATHOLIC THEOLOGY TO VATICAN II

In the last twenty years, Roman Catholic theology has probably made the news more often than Protestant thought. Debates about birth control, priestly celibacy, and changes in the Mass have become the stuff of newspaper headlines. A history of theology can perhaps set some of these issues into a wider context. A good starting point might be two apparently unrelated injunctions that Pope Leo XIII delivered at the end of the last century. Catholics, he said, should devote themselves to a renewed study of Thomas Aquinas and a deeper concern for social reform. Surprisingly, those two initiatives often led in the same directions, for careful study of Aquinas revealed a Thomas far more open and exciting than the "Thomism" taught in most Catholic schools.

The Canadian Bernard Lonergan and the German Karl Rahner stand as probably the two greatest living exponents of such new Catholic theology. Lonergan has an odd relationship to twentieth-century thought. Educated in conservative Canadian Catholic schools, he has written many of his major works in Latin, yet he draws on intimate knowledge of contemporary physics, mathematics, and economics. Earlier theology often defined "the truth" in terms of a set of propositions compiled from popes, councils, and great theologians. Lonergan argues that our modern awareness of history makes us realize that we can never get "the truth" once and for all. He therefore proposes that good theology is not that which gets the "right answers" but that which follows the right *method*. People will never agree on all the right answers, but certain basic questions do universally define the method all human beings use to go about finding answers. "When an animal has nothing to do, it goes to sleep; when a man has nothing to do, he may ask questions."[33] Good thinking, good asking of questions, involves being *attentive* to data, being *intelligent* about forming hypotheses on the basis of that data, being *rational* in testing those hypotheses, and being *responsible* about applying the results of our thought. That may seem obvious to the point of triviality, but Lonergan believes that following out the implications of that process—which he finds laid out in Aquinas—avoids all sorts of intellectual traps. It may be harder to condemn people for heresy these days, because we are not sure we have the final truth, but we can criticize them for going astray—ignoring data, acting irresponsibly, and so on. Thus an understanding of proper method provides a way of evaluating even theological proposals.

Lonergan writes in a style of deceptive simplicity, but no one has ever thought of Karl Rahner's prose as simple even for an instant. Yet he has deeply influenced twentieth-century theology. Rahner may be hard to understand in part because he wants to talk about mystery, and that cannot be easy. Too much of Catholic theology, in Rahner's view, had trivialized mystery. There were lists of how many mysteries there are, set out and carefully defined. Rahner thinks that mystery is, well, more mysterious than that, and also more pervasive. We often assume that many areas of our lives are free from mystery—mystery continues only in some awkward corners. Rahner says there is a fundamental mystery, a matter of religious faith, at the heart of all human understanding. Any time one asks a question one is attempting to understand something about reality, and that presupposes that reality can be understood, that the world has some sort of rational pattern that makes sense. But that is a religious claim. Therefore, "in every philosophy men already engage inevitably and unthematically in theology, since no one has any choice in the matter —even when he does not know it consciously."[34]

Rahner insists therefore that religion is implicitly at work far more widely than we usually suppose. He rejects the idea "that grace would no longer be grace if it were too generously distributed,"[35] and speaks of "anonymous Christians" who receive and manifest God's grace whenever they are "really acquainted with unconditional faithfulness, absolute honesty, selfless surrender for the good of others."[36] "Today . . . , when . . . mankind must learn to love completely anew or go under . . . , the love of neighbor, provided it is genuine and accepts its own proper incomprehensible being to the very limit, already contains the whole of Christian salvation and of Christianity."[37]

By the 1960s, then, Lonergan, Rahner, and others were developing a new style of Catholic theology. They talked less about eternal truths and more about a process of inquiry, a search for truth. Some acknowledged that God's grace could work outside the church. They were moving away from a theology that emphasized contrasting opposites (nature/grace, earth/heaven, the world/the church) to a theology that talked about evolutionary growth—nature moving toward grace, the world moving toward the kingdom of God. Then in 1962 Pope John XXIII summoned the bishops of the church to meet in the Second Vatican Council, and the council noted without criticism that "the human race has passed from a rather static concept of reality to a more dynamic, evolutionary one"[38] and talked in new ways about the church, relations with those outside Roman Catholicism, and the need for social reform.

Vatican II tended to define "the church" not as the hierarchy of pope and bishops but as the whole "pilgrim people of God." It gave the laity an increased role in a variety of ways and initiated liturgical reforms—taking the Mass out of Latin and so on—which made the whole community's participation in worship more active.

The council also acknowledged that "at times, men of both sides were to blame" for splits within Christianity and assured other Christians that "the Catholic Church accepts them with respect and affection as brothers."[39] It condemned anti-Semitism and spoke of non-Christian religions with "sincere respect," declaring that they "often reflect a ray of that Truth which enlightens all men."[40] Even with atheists, "whatever goodness or truth is found among them is looked upon by the Church as a preparation for the gospel,"[41] and, "those also can attain to everlasting salvation who through no fault of their own do not know the gospel . . . yet sincerely seek God and, moved by grace, strive by their deeds to do His will as it is known to them through the dictates of conscience."[42]

Christians do not just hope for God's kingdom after they die. "The expectation of a new earth," the council declared, "must not weaken but rather stimulate our concern for cultivating this one. For here grows the body of a new human family."[43] The bishops therefore condemned every type of discrimination and denounced the arms race as "an utterly treacherous trap for humanity," which spends more and more on weapons while the poor still starve.[44] Too many people today, according to the council, are "hypnotized, as it were, by economics," concerned only with their own wealth and indifferent to the miseries of the poor.[45] All these must be important concerns for Christians: "The joys and the hopes, the griefs and the anxieties of the men of this age, especially those who are poor or in any way afflicted, these two are the joys and hopes, the griefs and anxieties of the followers of Christ."[46]

THE CURRENT SCENE

Writing about very recent history poses special problems, for one lacks sufficient perspective to determine the individuals and trends of lasting importance. There is no doubt that Barth, Bultmann's appropriation of existentialism, and Catholic theology leading up to Vatican II will stand among the major landmarks of twentieth-century theology. In the aftermath of Vatican II, Protestant and Catholic theology have grown much closer together. From the time of the Reformation, it has been necessary to present Protestant and Catholic theology as two separate stories. In the last twenty years or so, these two streams (and Orthodox theology as well) have come dramatically together, and there seems genuinely a single theological community. But identifying the major themes and figures in that community would be difficult in any event, and the theology of the last twenty years has been particularly prone to slogans and fads that come and go very quickly. Still, some things seem likely to endure.

In Germany a number of theologians now in their forties and fifties have rebelled against Bultmann and his followers. They criticize him for virtually eliminating the Old Testament as a resource for Christian theology and argue that an alliance with existentialism tends to put too much emphasis on the individual and not enough on social change. As biblical scholarship has rediscovered the importance of eschatology and the kingdom of God in Jesus' preaching, theologians like the Protestant Jürgen Moltmann and the Catholic Johannes Metz have tried to use eschatology as the basis for a theology that would be more open to the new and the unexpected and also more concerned about changing the world, working for reform in society. Eschatology, after all, has to do with the future, and thinking about the future ought to make Christians more open to change and more concerned about improving their world. Moltmann, Metz, and many others have engaged in active dialogue with Marxists about how to bring those changes into reality.

Another German Protestant, Wolfhart Pannenberg, has also drawn on the renewed interest in eschatology, but Pannenberg has concerned himself more with intellectual clarity than with social change. He has attacked Barth, and many others, for retreating into a theological ghetto in which Christians talked to each other without trying to defend their point of view in the wider intellectual community. Pannenberg thinks that the biblical way of understanding history, seen from the perspective of God's final triumph, provides a world view that can be defended in the context of contemporary philosophy.

In England many theologians have devoted themselves to dialogue with the dominant styles of philosophy in that country, where existentialism never made much impact. In the 1930s and 1940s that meant "logical positivism," which taught that only logic, mathematics, and statements that can be verified empirically are meaningful. Thus when religious people talked about God, the logical positivists demanded, "How can we design a scientific experiment to test whether or not God exists?" If no such experiment is possible, they argued, then talk of God is just meaningless. More recently, most British philosophers have come to think that the logical positivists oversimplified things. Particularly under the influence of the later writings of the philosopher Ludwig Wittgenstein, they have recognized how many different ways language can be used meaningfully. If we want to know what language means, they argue, we ought to look at all the different ways in which people in fact use it, not set up rules in advance for how it can be used. This new openness among philosophers has invited theologians to engage in analysis of the uses of religious language.

All these trends, and others, as well as the continuing influence of Barth and Bultmann, have found their way to the United States. Evangelical theology, with a renewed emphasis on the authority, and often the literal inspiration, of the Bible also continues to be an important force in American theology, but it has generally reaffirmed the views Charles Hodge and Benjamin B. Warfield developed in the last century rather than producing new ideas. One really original theological school, "process theology," has developed here under the influence of Alfred North Whitehead. Out of his study of philosophy and also of contemporary physics, Whitehead developed a complex metaphysics which described the world as made up of interrelated processes, not isolated things. The traditional view that the world is made of discrete chunks of stuff, Whitehead maintained, does not fit our ordinary experience very well and certainly does not fit what Einstein and others tell us about ultimate particles. Whitehead attacked theologians too for picturing God as the ultimate case of an isolated unit of substance, a God who never changed, who was untouched by emotion, unaffected by the world. "The Church gave unto God the attributes which belonged exclusively to Caesar."[47] Process theology describes a God who is perfect in that he is perfectly related to everything, who lures actions by love rather than forcing them by power. "He is the poet of the world, with tender patience leading it by his vision of truth, beauty and goodness."[48]

Given the pattern of the last several centuries, it may have seemed natural to begin a survey of the current theological scene by looking at Germany, Britain, and the United States, but that pattern is breaking down. Since the fifth century, really, Europe, and quite recently North America, has dominated the story of Christian theology. But today most Christians live in the southern hemisphere. Theologians in the third world, especially in Latin America, have developed the "theology of liberation." They seek to do what the best theology, from Paul addressing the church at Corinth to Karl Barth denouncing the Nazis, has always done: make Christianity address the particular problems of their societies. The Peruvian Gustavo Gutiérrez has explained that the theology of liberation is "based on the Gospel and the experience of men and women committed to the process of liberation in the oppressed and exploited land of Latin America; it is a theological reflection born . . . of shared efforts to abolish the current unjust situation and to build a different society, freer and more human."[49] Faced with poverty and injustice, these theologians find that they cannot talk about love or hope without participating in the struggle for social change which offers the only hope for their people, the only way they can really show love for those around them. They often find that Marx's analysis of the economic roots of injustice helps them understand their problems and possible solutions, though they disagree among themselves about how much of Marx's philosophy they should accept. They also debate the justification of violence. All agree that the worst violence comes from governments that oppress and starve their people, but they disagree on whether Christians can condone violence when used to overthrow such governments.

Christian theologians in other parts of the third world often share many of the concerns of Latin-American liberation theologians but also face special problems of their own. The fact of poverty, the struggles for economic and social justice, and the need to come to terms with Marxism, which is so important an ideology in their parts of the world, shape their surroundings and their understanding of what it means to be a Christian too. But Asian Christians, for instance, also face the fact of being a religious minority. The question of how Christianity relates to other great world religions, which theologians in Europe and America can treat as an interesting side issue, takes central importance for Japanese or Indian Christians. To complicate the problem, Shinto or Hinduism or Buddhism or Islam is not "just a religion" (if such a phrase really means anything). It shapes the whole society, from family relationships to rules of etiquette to attitudes to government. That generates a whole set of practical problems that are also theological problems. Is giving up traditional Indian customs part of leaving Hinduism to become a Christian—or is it a bogus effort to try to stop being an Indian and become a European? Where the memory of colonialism remains fresh, that of course becomes a particularly touchy issue.

Such tensions between traditional customs and "European" values associated with Christianity, set against the background of rebellion against colonialism, are even more vivid for African Christians. The customs, rituals, and beliefs of a tribe often largely define a traditional African's identity, so that asking people to give up all those customs asks them, in effect, to stop being Africans. Christianity's association with the bitter history of colonial oppression makes Africans understandably suspicious of the advantages of "European values" under the best of circumstances. Yet one cannot always cast the missionary who questions local values as the villain of the story. More equality for women, more rights for the individual, more freedom to choose one's own job and spouse—Christianity often stands for such goals in Africa and Asia. Are those Christian values? European values? both? neither?

All this presents an intimidating list of theological problems, but that should not imply a dismal future for theology in the third world. Theology, as ought to be clear by now, thrives on problems. As a steadily smaller percentage of Christians live in Europe and North America, theology indifferent to the concerns of Christians elsewhere will not really respond to the needs of the church universal—and such theology will probably seem increasingly isolated. At the same time, liberation theology probably needs to overcome a naively romantic view of Marxism if it is to speak to the whole church. Here the experience of Eastern European Christians can remind third-world theologians that a Marxist government too can be oppressive. Still, even in North America and Europe, many of the ideas of liberation theology have become important.

Indeed, liberation theology first drew wide attention in the United States in connection with "black liberation." As noted in Chapter 16, blacks in the United States had long found parallels between Israel's slavery in Egypt and their own experience and drawn strength from Jesus' message to the poor and oppressed. The black churches provided the principal leadership for the civil rights movement of the 1960s, symbolized above all by Martin Luther King, Jr. Indeed, King's "Letter from Birmingham Jail" stands with Barth's Barmen Declaration as one of the century's great conjunctions of theology and history. A number of white ministers had criticized King's nonviolent protest movement as "unwise and untimely," tending to create divisions and lawbreaking. King's reply drew from many sources—the call for justice in the Old Testament prophets, Aquinas' argument that an unjust law may not be a law at all, Reinhold Niebuhr's analysis of the injustice of institutions, arguments for civil disobedience from Socrates to Thoreau and Gandhi, and his own experience as a black American:

> When you have seen vicious mobs lynch your mothers and fathers at will and drown your sisters and brothers at whim; when you have seen hate-filled policemen curse, kick and even kill your black brothers and sisters with impunity; when you see the vast majority of your 20 million Negro brothers smothering in an air-tight cage of poverty in the midst of an affluent society. ... There comes a time when the cup of endurance runs over and men are no longer willing to be plunged into an abyss of injustice where they experience the bleakness of corroding despair.[50]

In such a context, King concluded,

> if today's church does not recapture the sacrificial spirit of the
> early church, it will lose its authenticity, forfeit the loyalty of
> millions, and be dismissed as an irrelevant social club with no
> meaning for the 20th century.[51]

One cannot mistake the power of that message, but in a sense it
was not "black theology." King called on everyone—black *and* white
—to work together toward the fulfillment of a dream in which racial
prejudice and bitterness would come to an end. In the late 1960s,
however, many black writers turned away from that goal of integration—and sometimes, at least in their rhetoric, from King's emphasis
on nonviolence as well. "Black power" became an important political
slogan, and the Black Muslims were pulling some radical blacks
away from Christianity altogether. To some black theologians, establishing their own pride and sense of identity came to seem far more
important than winning acceptance or support from whites—acceptance and support whose depth and sincerity they might doubt in any
event. James Cone's *Black Theology and Black Power,* published in
1969, made the blacks' liberation from their white oppressors its
central theological theme and addressed whites with warnings rather
than pleas for help.

Theologians moving in this direction faced some tough questions.
Was the turn away from integration a temporary strategy, necessary
for a clearer affirmation of black identity, or was it a permanent
commitment to separation? Cone repeatedly used the rhetoric of
black vs. white, but he sometimes acknowledged that

> being black in America has very little to do with skin color. To
> be black means that your heart, your soul, your mind, and your
> body are where the dispossessed are. . . . [It] does not mean that
> one's skin is physically black.[52]

"Black" then becomes a potentially universal symbol. Similarly, in
regard to Jesus—everyone could agree that he was not the northern
European white often pictured in white churches, and that he might
well have been denied service at a segregated lunch counter, but
some black theologians, like Albert Cleague *(The Black Messiah,*
1968) insisted that Jesus was actually black, while others who talked
of Jesus as black referred only to Jesus' identification with the oppressed. Like liberation theologians in Latin America, black theologians also had to decide how they felt about the use of violence
against oppression. They further debated the appropriate attitude to

the history of black churches—had they served to preserve oppression by urging people to accept their lot, or had they kept dreams of freedom as alive as possible in a difficult time? Such issues suggest the complexity of "black theology," and one cannot even classify these theologians very neatly from "more radical" to "less radical." To take one example, a commitment to Marxism often makes a theologian *more* radical in criticizing American society and even in accepting the necessity of violence but *less* inclined to believe in black separatism, since a Marxist will intepret the issues more in terms of economic classes and seek solidarity with other oppressed groups.

By the 1970s, especially in the United States, the movement for women's rights began to gain the same kind of attention that the black movement had received a decade earlier. Feminist theology faced many of the same problems encountered by black theology. Its first goals paralleled Martin Luther King, Jr.'s dream of integration and equality. Women sought the right to be ordained in denominations that did not already permit this. (Methodists and Presbyterians both gave women full rights to ordination in 1956.) They opposed elements in the Christian tradition that discriminated against women —from interpretations of Genesis 2 that "blamed" Eve for the Fall to approaches to Christian ethics that taught women to be subservient and obedient to men. Questions with wider implications arose concerning the "sexism" of much Christian language, with its habit of referring to both God and the believer as "he." Some feminists wanted to fix such problems in the language of theology and liturgy. Others, more radical, came to feel that the male-dominated language of traditional Christianity really reflected a male bias inherent in the tradition. They abandoned altogether the worship of a masculine God who became incarnate in a male human. As Mary Daly—whose earlier *The Church and the Second Sex,* published in 1968, had set out a moderate Christian feminism—now put it in her more radical new perspective, for a woman to seek equality in the Christian church "would be comparable to a black person's demanding equality in the Ku Klux Klan."[53]

Such issues define positions along a spectrum of feminist theology —from those with a pragmatic program for more power for women within the church, to those who want to ask fundamental questions about the "male bias" of Christian language, to those who want to separate from Christianity altogether, sometimes turning to myths of the mother goddess or the traditions of witchcraft as the starting points for a true feminist, post-Christian theology. The more conservative fear that those to their left hurt the image of the whole movement; the more radical may deny that those to their right are really feminists at all.

This review of various strands of liberation theology has indicated an agenda of problems more than describing solutions or even discussing the most important theologians at length. That seems the best that can be done just at the moment, for these theologies are still emerging, and it is too early to tell what directions they will take or which writers will prove to be of greatest importance. A historian ought to be cautious about predictions, but one guess would be that the future does not lie with those exclusively preoccupied with the problems of their own group. A theology that can speak only to women or only to blacks or only to Latin Americans is as limited as a theology that speaks only to white male Europeans. At a minimum, bridges need to be built between different oppressed groups. Looking beyond that, Rosemary Radford Ruether (a prolific theologian committed both to feminism and to Christianity) has written:

> All theologies of liberation, whether done in a black or a feminist or a Third World perspective, will be abortive of the liberation they seek, unless they finally go beyond the . . . model of the oppressor and the oppressed. The oppressed must rise to a perspective that affirms a universal humanity as the ground of their own self-identity, and also to a power for self-criticism. . . . Quite simply, what this means is that one cannot dehumanize the oppressor without ultimately dehumanizing oneself, and aborting the possibilities of the liberation movement into an exchange of roles of oppressor and oppressed.[54]

It is, to be sure, arguably unfair to ask the oppressed to worry about the problems of their oppressors—yet many of the Gospel parables make just such a demand. Only a vision large enough to realize that oppression does wound the oppressor too, that oppressors also need liberation—and also a vision large enough to acknowledge that left-wing governments can sometimes be as oppressive as those of the right—will enable liberation theology to speak to the whole church.

The future of theology lies in the possibility of such greatness of vision, for it has always been a central part of the Christian hope that a divided world might someday learn that all are one in Christ. Liberation theologies will certainly play an important part in the theology of the coming decades—always assuming that nuclear holocaust does not bring us back to apocalypticism with a vengeance. Blacks in the United States and women and others, after all, share with the liberation theologians of the third world a conviction as old as Luther, or Paul, or Moses' cries to Pharaoh—that theology ought to make a difference in people's lives, helping those suffering and in need. As Gutiérrez sees it, "if theological reflection does not vitalize the action of the Christian community in the world by making its commitment to charity fuller and more radical, if . . . it does not lead the Church to be on the side of the oppressed classes . . . , then this theological reflection will have been of little value."[55] The story of Christian theology will certainly continue, but it may have come to a crucial watershed. White males from Europe and North America represent a small and decreasing portion of the church; they may well not dominate the future of theology. As new groups of people do theology in new social contexts, theological issues and methods and conclusions will inevitably change, and new chapters in the history of Christian theology will have to be written.

FOR FURTHER READING

INTRODUCTIONS. William E. Hordern, *A Layman's Guide to Protestant Theology*, rev. ed. (Macmillan Co., 1968); Mark Schoof, *A Survey of Catholic Theology 1800–1970*, tr. by N. D. Smith (Paulist/Newman Press, 1970); Deane William Ferm, *Contemporary American Theologies* (Seabury Press, 1981). Somewhat more difficult surveys are: John B. Cobb, *Living Options in Protestant Theology* (Westminster Press, 1962); John Macquarrie, *Twentieth Century Religious Thought* (Harper & Row, 1963).

READINGS IN ORIGINAL SOURCES. Some good places to start in reading some of the theologians and surveying theological movements mentioned in this chapter are: Karl Barth, *Evangelical Theology: An Introduction*, tr. by Grover Foley (Holt, Rinehart & Winston, 1963); Dietrich Bonhoeffer, *Letters and Papers from Prison*, tr. by Reginald Fuller et al. (Macmillan Co., 1972); Rudolf Bultmann, "New Testament and Mythology," in Hans W. Bartsch (ed.), *Kerygma and Myth*, tr. by Reginald Fuller (Harper & Row, Harper Torchbooks, 1961), pp. 1–44; Paul Tillich, *The Courage to Be* (Yale University Press, 1952). There are any number of interesting journalistic accounts of Vatican II, but none can replace the official documents of the council, collected in Walter M. Abbott (ed.), *The Documents of Vatican II* (Herder & Herder, 1966). Reinhold Niebuhr, *Moral Man and Immoral Society* (Charles Scribner's Sons, 1932); Jürgen Moltmann, *Theology of Hope*, tr. by James W. Leitch (Harper & Row, 1967); Wolfhart Pannenberg,

Faith and Reality, tr. by John Maxwell (Westminster Press, 1977); Antony Flew and Alasdair MacIntyre (eds.), *New Essays in Philosophical Theology* (Macmillan Co., 1964) (contains some famous British analyses of the meaning of religious language); John B. Cobb, Jr., and David Ray Griffin, *Process Theology* (Westminster Press, 1976); Gustavo Gutiérrez, *A Theology of Liberation,* tr. by Caridad Inda and John Eagleson (Orbis Books, 1973); Gayraud S. Wilmore and James H. Cone, *Black Theology: A Documentary History* (Orbis Books, 1979); Cornel West, *Prophesy Deliverance!* (Westminster Press, 1982); Carol P. Christ and Judith Plaskow, *Womanspirit Rising: A Feminist Reader in Religion* (Harper & Row, 1979). For a survey of current issues and theological thinking, see *Christian Theology,* ed. by Peter C. Hodgson and Robert H. King (Fortress Press, 1982).

NOTES

1. Peter Berger, *A Rumor of Angels* (Doubleday & Co., Anchor Books, 1970), p. 18.
2. Barth to Thurneysen, Sept. 4, 1914; in Karl Barth and Eduard Thurneysen, *Revolutionary Theology in the Making* (Their correspondence, 1914–1925), tr. by James D. Smart (John Knox Press, 1964), p. 26.
3. Barth to Thurneysen, Sept. 27, 1917; ibid., p. 43.
4. Karl Barth, *The Word of God and the Word of Man,* tr. by Douglas Horton (Zondervan Publishing House, 1928), p. 186.
5. Karl Barth, *The Epistle to the Romans,* tr. by Edwyn C. Hoskyns (London: Oxford University Press, 1933), p. 98.
6. Quoted in Eberhard Busch, *Karl Barth,* tr. by John Bowden (Fortress Press, 1976), p. 133.
7. Karl Barth, *How I Changed My Mind* (John Knox Press, 1966), p. 46; originally in *The Christian Century,* Vol. 56 (Sept. 13 and 20, 1939), p. 1133.
8. The Barmen Declaration, in John H. Leith (ed.), *Creeds of the Churches* (Aldine Publishing Co., 1963), pp. 520–521.
9. Karl Barth, *The Humanity of God,* tr. by John Newton Thomas and Thomas Wieser (John Knox Press, 1960), p. 52.
10. Karl Barth, *Church Dogmatics,* Vol. 3, Part 3, tr. by G. W. Bromiley and R. J. Ehrlich (Edinburgh: T. & T. Clark, 1960), p. 87.
11. Karl Barth, *Church Dogmatics,* Vol. 2, Part 2, tr. by G. W. Bromiley et al. (Edinburgh: T. & T. Clark, 1957), p. 167.
12. Dietrich Bonhoeffer, *Letters and Papers from Prison,* tr. by Reginald H. Fuller (Macmillan Co., 1967), p. 169.
13. Ibid., p. 142.
14. Ibid., p. 188.
15. Quoted in William Hamilton, "The Letters Are a Particular Thorn," in *World Come of Age,* ed. by Ronald Gregor Smith (Fortress Press, 1967), p. 132.
16. Charles Hodge, *Systematic Theology,* Vol. 1 (Charles Scribner's Sons,

1872), in Sydney E. Ahlstrom (ed.), *Theology in America* (Bobbs-Merrill Co., 1967), p. 277.

17. Ibid., p. 257.

18. Ibid., p. 280.

19. Ibid., pp. 280, 285.

20. Walter Rauschenbusch, *Christianity and the Social Crisis* (Macmillan Co., 1907); in ibid., p. 542.

21. Quoted in Charles Howard Hopkins, *The Rise of the Social Gospel in American Protestantism* (Yale University Press, 1940), p. 212.

22. Rauschenbusch, *Christianity and the Social Crisis;* in Ahlstrom, *Theology in America*, p. 557.

23. Reinhold Niebuhr, *Moral Man and Immoral Society* (Charles Scribner's Sons, 1932), p. xi.

24. Reinhold Niebuhr, *Christianity and Power Politics* (Charles Scribner's Sons, 1940), p. 3.

25. Quoted in D. R. Davies, *Reinhold Niebuhr* (Macmillan Co., 1948), p. 78.

26. Quoted in James D. Smart, *The Divided Mind of Modern Theology* (Westminster Press, 1967), p. 186.

27. Rudolf Bultmann, "Bultmann Replies to His Critics," in Hans W. Bartsch (ed.), *Kerygma and Myth*, tr. by Reginald H. Fuller (Harper & Row, Harper Torchbooks, 1961), p. 211.

28. Jean-Paul Sartre, "Existentialism," in *Existentialism and Human Emotions*, tr. by Bernard Frechtman (Philosophical Library, 1957), p. 15.

29. Rudolf Bultmann, "New Testament and Mythology," in Bartsch, *Kerygma and Myth*, p. 32.

30. Ibid., p. 5.

31. Ibid., p. 10.

32. Ibid., p. 39.

33. Bernard J. F. Lonergan, *Insight* (Philosophical Library, 1970), p. 10.

34. Karl Rahner, "Philosophy and Theology," in *Theological Investigations*, Vol. 6, tr. by Karl-H. and Boniface Krüger (Helicon Press, 1969), p. 79.

35. Karl Rahner, "Nature and Grace," in *Theological Investigations*, Vol. 4, tr. by Kevin Smyth (Helicon Press, 1966), p. 180.

36. Quoted in Anne Carr, *The Theological Method of Karl Rahner* (Scholars Press, 1977), p. 222.

37. Karl Rahner, "Reflections on the Unity of the Love of Neighbor and the Love of God," in *Theological Investigations*, Vol. 6, p. 249.

38. *Gaudiam et spes*, Pastoral Constitution on the Church in the Modern World, introduction 5; in Walter M. Abbott (ed.), *The Documents of Vatican II* (Herder & Herder, 1966), p. 204.

39. *Unitatis redintegratio*, Decree on Ecumenism, 1.3; ibid., p. 345.

40. *Nostra aetate*, Declaration on the Relationship of the Church to Non-Christian Religions, 2; ibid., p. 662.

41. *Lumen gentium*, Dogmatic Constitution on the Church, 2.16; ibid., p. 35.

42. Ibid.

43. *Gaudiam et spes*, part 1, 3.39; ibid., p. 237.

44. Ibid., part 2, 5.81, p. 295.

45. Ibid., part 2, 3.63, p. 271.

46. Ibid., preface 1, pp. 199–200.

47. Alfred North Whitehead, *Process and Reality* (Macmillan Co., 1929), pp. 519–520.

48. Ibid., p. 526.

49. Gustavo Gutiérrez, *A Theology of Liberation,* tr. by Caridad Inda and John Eagleson (Orbis Books, 1973), p. ix.

50. Martin Luther King, Jr., "Letter from Birmingham Jail," *The Christian Century,* Vol. 80 (June 12, 1963), pp. 768–769.

51. Ibid., p. 772.

52. James Cone, *Black Theology and Black Power* (Seabury Press, 1969), p. 151.

53. Mary Daly, *The Church and the Second Sex,* rev. ed. (Harper & Row, 1975), p. 6; quoted in Deane William Ferm, *Contemporary American Theologies* (Seabury Press, 1981), p. 81.

54. Rosemary Radford Ruether, *Liberation Theology* (Paulist Press, 1972), pp. 16, 13.

55. Gutiérrez, *A Theology of Liberation,* p. 307.

INDEX

Abelard, Peter, 144–148
Addison, Joseph, 241
Adiaphora, 195
Albigensians, 148
Ambrose, 112, 129, 131
Anabaptists, 189, 191–192, 241
Analogy, 155, 209–210
Anastasius, 134
Andrewes, Lancelot, 230
Anselm, 142–144, 145, 154
Antiochus Epiphanes, 27
Anti-Semitism, 13, 36, 173, 231, 293–294, 303
Antony, 123
Apocalyptic, 25–26, 28–29, 33–35, 286, 305
Apollinaris, 80–81, 84
Apologists, 59–60, 89
Apostolic succession, 49
Aquinas, Thomas, 142, 152–156, 158, 163, 165, 166, 212, 302, 308
Arianism, 122, 193
Aristotle, 129, 150, 153, 155, 163
Arius, 73–75, 79, 84
Arminianism, 226–227, 228, 247
Arminius, Jacob, 226–227
Arnauld, Antoine, 211
Arndt, Johann, 244
Athanasius, 73–76, 80, 95, 123
Atonement. *See* Jesus Christ, work of
Attrition, 211

Augustine, 70, 79, 101, 108–120, 126–128, 131, 150, 152, 168, 173
Averroës, 151
Avignon, 170

Bacon, Roger, 166
Ball, John, 172–173
Ban, 192
Baptism, 35, 40, 65, 90, 110, 132, 189, 230–231, 246, 257, 295
Baptismal regeneration, 244, 246
Barlaam, 98–99
Barmen Declaration, 293–294
Barth, Karl, 291–295, 298, 305
Basel, Council of, 174
Basil III, Czar, 103
Basil the Great, 76–78, 90, 97, 125
Baxter, Richard, 230
Beecher, Lyman, 262
Benedict of Nursia, 125
Benedictines, 146
Berengar of Tours, 128, 129
Berkeley, George, 259
Bernard of Clairvaux, 146–148, 169
Bible. *See* Scripture
Biel, Gabriel, 168
Bishop, 48, 49, 229
Bishops' Book, 227
Black theology, 267–268, 308–310
Boethius, 150
Bonaventure, 151–152, 165
Bonhoeffer, Dietrich, 295

317

Boniface (missionary), 132
Boniface VIII, 157
Boris, 104
Bornkamm, Günther, 301
Bossuet, Jacques, 215
Bradwardine, Thomas, 168
Brownson, Orestes, 265
Brunner, Emil, 293
Bucer, Martin, 223
Bultmann, Rudolf, 291, 299–301, 304
Bushnell, Horace, 266
Butler, Joseph, 237, 243–244

Caesarius of Arles, 126, 132
Cajetan, Cardinal, 209–210
Callistus, 65
Calvin, John, 103, 213, 219–225, 229, 294
Cambridge Platonists, 239
Canon, 51–52
Canonization, 130
Cappadocians, 76–79
Caraccioli, Francesco, 255
Carlstadt, Andreas Bodenstein von, 186, 192
Carmelites, 208
Cathari, 148
Celibacy, 124, 155, 194, 227
Chalcedon, Council of, 69, 80, 84, 91, 133
Channing, William Ellery, 262, 265
Charlemagne, 134
Charles I, 231, 240
Charles II, 233, 240
Charles V, 181
Church, 15, 48–50, 114, 167, 184, 191, 201, 204, 206, 224, 229, 232, 251, 257–258, 303
Church and state, 15, 21, 36, 38, 64, 114–115, 118–119, 133–136, 156–158, 185, 187, 210, 224–226, 238, 240, 261, 275, 280–283, 293–294
Cistercians, 146
Clarke, Samuel, 240, 244
Cleague, Albert, 309

Clement of Alexandria, 55, 61
Clermont, Council of, 183
Cluny, 146
Coleridge, Samuel Taylor, 272, 275
Collins, Anthony, 243
Communicatio idiomatum, 83, 84
Communion. See Eucharist
Conciliarism, 171–172, 204
Cone, James, 309
Confessing Church, 293
Consilium de emendanda ecclesia, 201
Constance, Council of, 172, 174
Constantine I, 75, 90, 123
Constantine V, 93
Constantinople, Council of, 81, 102
Constantinople, Second Council of, 91
Constantinople, Third Council of, 92
Constantius, 75, 91
Contarini, Gaspero, 201–202
Contrition, 211
Cosmas, 93
Cotton, John, 257
Covenant, 256–258
Cranmer, Thomas, 227–228
Cromwell, Oliver, 231, 233
Cudworth, Ralph, 239
Cum occasione, 214
Cusa, Nicholas of, 175
Cyprian, 113–114, 116
Cyril (missionary), 103
Cyril Lucaris, 103
Cyril of Alexandria, 82–84

Daly, Mary, 310
Damasus, 133
Daniel, 28
Darwin, Charles, 284
Davenport, James, 260
Deacons, 35
Dead Sea Scrolls, 27
Death, life after, 20–21, 26, 62, 130, 155, 193

Deism, 242–243, 261
Descartes, René, 108, 142, 238
Deschamps, Eustache, 162
Dietrich of Niem, 171
Diggers, 231
Dionysius the Areopagite, 95
Dioscurus, 83
Docetism, 47, 49, 68
Dominic, 148, 149
Dominicans, 148, 152, 165
Donatism, 113–115
Donne, John, 230
Dort, Synod of, 226
Dostoevsky, Fyodor, 104

Eck, John, 184
Eckhart, Meister, 169
Edward VI, 227
Edwards, Jonathan, 258–260, 268
Elizabeth I, 227
Elvira, Council of, 124
Emerson, Ralph Waldo, 265
Energeia, 97–98
Enlightenment, 237
Enthusiasm, 244
Ephesus, Council of, 82
Erasmus, 184, 188, 200
Eucharist, 35, 40, 49, 100, 128–129,
    173, 174, 189–190, 193, 204, 223,
    227, 257, 258, 260, 266, 303
Eugenius IV, 174
Eusebius, 50, 90, 93, 119
Eutyches, 83, 84
Existentialism, 299–300, 301, 304–
    305
Ezra, 25

Faith. See Reason, Grace
Faustus, 111
Federal theology, 256, 258
Fell, Margaret, 233
Fénelon, François, 214
Feuerbach, Ludwig, 277–279
Filioque, 101–102
Finney, Charles Grandison, 262–263

Flacius Illyricus, Matthias, 196
Florence, Council of, 100–103, 128,
    174–175
Forty-two Articles, 227
Fox, George, 232
Francis of Assisi, 149, 150
Franciscans, 149–150, 151, 165
Francke, August Hermann, 245
Franklin, Benjamin, 261
Free will, 184, 196, 203, 210–211, 226,
    227, 262
Freud, Sigmund, 108, 278
Fundamentalism, 296–297

Gallican articles, 240, 281
Gelasius, 134
Gerson, Jean, 169–170, 171
Gleb, 104
Gnosticism, 45–49, 68
God, existence of, 142–143, 154, 214,
    250–251
God, nature of, 20–21, 55–56, 60, 62,
    63, 95–96, 154–155, 164–166, 175,
    260, 264, 276, 278, 306
God, sexual language concerning,
    21, 61, 170, 263, 310
Gogarten, Friedrich, 293
Gottschalk, 126–128
Grace, 15, 37, 51, 96, 115–117, 153–
    154, 167–168, 182–183, 203, 211,
    214, 221–222, 226, 244, 251, 257,
    268–269, 300
Great Awakening, 237, 258, 260
Grebel, Conrad, 189, 191
Gregory I, 130
Gregory VII, 135, 136, 146, 148
Gregory XI, 170
Gregory XVI, 281
Gregory of Nazianzus, 76–77, 81, 92
Gregory of Nyssa, 68, 70, 76–77, 95
Gregory Palamas, 97–99
Guitmond of Aversa, 129
Gutiérrez, Gustavo, 306, 312
Guyon, Mme., 214–215

Half-way Covenant, 258
Harnack, Adolf von, 51, 285–286
Hartley, David, 244
Hegel, G. W. F., 150, 273, 276–278, 279, 280
Heidegger, Martin, 299–300
Heloise, 145–146, 148
Henry III, 135
Henry III, of France, 210
Henry IV, 136
Henry VIII, 227
Herbert of Cherbury, 242
Herder, Johann Gottfried, 272
Hermas, 65
Hesychasm, 98
Hilary of Poitiers, 72
Hincmar of Reims, 127, 128
Hippolytus, 65
Hodge, Charles, 296, 306
Hoffmann, Melchior, 191
Holcot, Robert, 168
Holy Spirit, 37, 49, 51, 76, 186–187, 192
Holy Spirit, procession of, 100–101
Homoiousios, 76
Homoousios, 74, 75–76, 77, 78
Homosexuality, 38
Honorius I, 92
Hooker, Richard, 228, 230
Hooker, Thomas, 257
Hosius, 91
Hugh of St. Victor, 147
Humanism, 176, 184, 200
Humbert, Cardinal, 135–136
Hume, David, 248, 252
Hus, John, 172, 174
Hutchinson, Anne, 257
Huxley, T. H., 284–285
Hymn of the Pearl, 45–46
Hypostasis, 78, 79, 83

Iconoclasm, 92–94
Ignatius of Antioch, 48–49
Imitation of Christ, 176, 205

Immaculate conception, 131, 282
Indulgences, 183, 204
Innocent III, 149, 156
Innocent X, 214
Irenaeus, 49, 70, 82

James II, 241
Jansen, Cornelius, 211
Jansenism, 211–213, 214
Jefferson, Thomas, 255, 261
Jerome, 117, 124
Jesuits, 205–207, 209–211, 212
Jesus, historical, 28–30, 250, 265, 277, 286, 299–301
Jesus Christ, person of, 14, 39–42, 47, 68–69, 72–85, 92–94, 261, 274
Jesus Christ, second coming of, 33–35, 39, 187, 263
Jesus Christ, work of, 70–72, 95–96, 143–145, 167–168, 193, 226, 242, 245, 266, 274, 284, 294–295, 300
Joachim of Fiore, 149–150
John XXII, 165
John XXIII, 303
John Cassian, 126
John of Damascus, 92, 93–94, 96
John of Gaunt, 173
John of Paris, 158
John of Parma, 150
John of the Cross, 200, 208
Jovinian, 124
Julian of Eclanum, 109, 117
Julian of Norwich, 170
Justification, 182–183, 195, 201, 202, 203–204, 221
Justin Martyr, 59–60
Justinian, 91, 126

Kant, Immanuel, 142, 250–252, 276
Käsemann, Ernst, 301
Keble, John, 283
Kessler, John, 192
Kierkegaard, Søren, 279–280, 299

King, Martin Luther, Jr., 308–309, 310

Kingdom of God, 29, 285, 286, 297, 304, 305

Knox, John, 219, 225–226

Lamennais, Félicité de, 281

Lanfranc, 129

Lateran Council, Fourth, 129, 202

Lateran Council, Fifth, 201

Latin Averroists, 151

Latitudinarianism, 241

Latreia, 94

Laud, William, 230

Law, 25, 29, 30, 36–37, 51, 182–183, 221, 300

Lay investiture, 135, 136

Lee, Mother Ann, 263

Leibniz, Gottfried, 142, 244

Leo I, 84, 133

Leo III, 134

Leo XIII, 282, 302

Leo the Isaurian, 93

Lessing, Gotthold, 249–250, 252

Levellers, 231

Liberation theologies, 306–307, 308, 310–312

Lincoln, Abraham, 268–269

Locke, John, 241–242, 259

Logical positivism, 305

Logos, 41–42, 58, 60, 69, 80

Lollards, 174

Lonergan, Bernard, 302

Lord's Supper. *See* Eucharist

Louis of Bavaria, 165

Louis XIV, 240

Loyola, Ignatius, 205–206, 211

Luther, Martin, 168, 181–187, 189–190, 194–197, 296

Macarius of Antioch, 92

Manetti, Giannozzo, 177

Manicheanism, 110–112

Mansel, H. L., 278

Marcion, 51–52

Mariana, Juan, 210

Marriage, 100, 155, 263, 264

Marsilius of Padua, 167, 172

Martin V, 172

Martin of Tours, 130

Marx, Karl, 150, 278, 279, 297, 306–307

Marxism, 298, 308, 310

Mary, 81–82, 84, 93, 130–132, 282

Mary, sister of Pachomius, 125

Mary Queen of Scots, 226

Mary I, 227–228

Mattathias, 27

Maurice, Frederick Denison, 284

Maximus the Confessor, 95, 96, 97

Medina, Bartolomeo, 212

Melanchthon, Philip, 195–196

Mercersburg school, 265–266

Methodius, 103

Metz, Johannes, 305

Miller, William, 263

Miracles, 243, 248, 262, 265, 273, 277, 300

Modern Devotion, 175–176, 200

Modernists, 282

Molina, Luis, 211, 213

Moltmann, Jürgen, 305

Monasticism, 93–94, 112, 123–128, 132–133

Monica, 108

Monophysitism, 80, 83–85, 91–92

Monothelitism, 92

Montanism, 50–51, 65

Morandi, Benedetto, 176

Moravians, 245, 273

More, Henry, 239

Mormons, 264

Mt. Athos, 98

Münster, 191

Müntzer, Thomas, 186–187, 191, 192

Mystery cults, 40, 41

Mysticism, 94–99, 169–170, 175, 207–208, 214–215, 232, 239

Nag Hammadi, 46
Natural law, 256
Natural religion, 240, 243, 250, 274, 293
Naylor, John, 232
Negative theology, 95, 154, 175
Nestorius, 80, 81–83, 84–85, 130
Nevin, John Williamson, 265–266
Newman, John Henry, 282–284
Newton, Isaac, 239–240, 259
Nicaea, Council of, 69, 75, 90, 171, 239
Nicaea, Second Council of, 128
Niebuhr, Reinhold, 297–298, 308
Nietzsche, Friedrich, 286–287, 299
Noetus, 72
Noichianti, bishop of Chioggia, 202
Nominalism, 162–167, 182
Noyes, John Humphrey, 263

Ockham, William of, 165–168
Ogden, Schubert, 301
Oikonomia, 90, 94
Olympios of the Cells, 124
Oneida community, 263
Ontological argument, 142–143
Orange, Synod of, 126
Origen, 61–63, 65, 71, 77, 89, 91
Original sin, 70, 82, 96, 115–117, 131, 203, 259, 262, 274, 298
Osiander, Andreas, 195
Ousia, 77, 78, 79, 97
Oxford movement, 282–284

Pachomius, 125
Pacifism, 89, 185, 192, 304
Pannenberg, Wolfhart, 305
Pantaenus, 61
Papacy, 84, 92, 100, 102–103, 133–136, 156, 158, 167, 170–173, 201, 204, 240, 280–282
Papal infallibility, 92, 171, 201, 282
Parker, Theodore, 265
Pascal, Blaise, 212–214
Paschal II, 136

Patriarchs, 102
Patricius, 108
Paul, 32–33, 34, 36–39, 42, 48, 182, 246, 267, 292
Paul III, 201
Pelagianism, 126–128, 168, 211
Pelagius, 115–117
Penance, 132–133, 144, 183
Perkins, William, 229
Persona, 79
Peter of Alexandria, 133
Peter of Blois, 11
Peter the Great, 240
Pharisees, 27, 28
Philip IV, 157
Philo, 27, 41, 80
Philotheus of Pskov, 103
Photius, 100
Physis, 81, 83
Pietism, 237, 244–245, 250
Pisa, Council of, 172
Pius IX, 281–282
Platonism, 56–58, 62, 71, 96, 110, 112, 152, 155, 163, 239
Plotinus, 57
Poverty. See Wealth
Praxeas, 72
Predestination, 115–117, 126–128, 173, 221–222, 226, 227, 228, 239, 247, 259, 260, 261, 262, 294
Presbyter, 48
Presbytery, 224, 229
Priests, 100, 113–115, 135, 174
Probabilism, 211–212
Process theology, 306
Prophets, 22–25, 49–50, 243
Prosōpon, 81, 83
Przypkowski, Samuel, 194
Purgatory, 100, 183, 204
Puritanism, 229–232, 240, 255–256

Quakers, 232–233, 241, 268
Quiercy, Council of, 127
Quietism, 214–215

Radbertus, Paschasius, 128, 129, 131
Rahner, Karl, 302–303
Ratramnus, 128, 131
Rauschenbusch, Walter, 297
Reason, 14, 55–65, 99, 110, 111, 141, 144, 147, 150–156, 158, 164, 166–167, 206, 210, 213, 238–244, 247–252, 259, 261–262, 264, 275, 277, 283–284, 293, 305
Reimarus, Hermann Samuel, 250
Reincarnation, 46, 57, 62–63
Relics, 129–130, 184
Remonstrants, 226
Renaissance, 176–177
Ricci, Matteo, 206
Richard of St. Victor, 147
Ritschl, Albrecht, 273, 285, 297
Robber Council, 83
Rogers, John, 230–232
Rousseau, Jean-Jacques, 249, 252
Ruether, Rosemary Radford, 311
Rupert of Deutz, 140
Russell, Bertrand, 142
Russia, 103–104

Sabellianism, 76, 79
Sabellius, 72
Sacraments, 114, 128–129, 132–133, 135, 204, 223, 245
Sadducees, 27
Saints, 93, 129–130
Samuel, 21
Sanctification, 195, 204, 221, 246
Sardica, Council of, 133
Sartre, Jean-Paul, 299
Satan, 70, 71
Saul, 21, 22
Schaff, Philip, 265
Schleiermacher, Friedrich, 272, 273–275
Schweitzer, Albert, 286
Schwenckfeld, Caspar, 192
Schwenckfelders, 245
Scotus, John Duns, 164–165

Scotus Eriugena, John, 127–128
Scripture, 32, 51–52, 119, 184, 188
Scripture, interpretation of, 60, 62, 173, 186–187, 192, 194, 196, 202, 220, 229, 230, 231, 242, 265, 277, 292, 296–297, 300
Separatists, 256
Seventh Day Adventists, 263
Shakers, 263
Siger of Brabant, 151
Simon of Cyrene, 47
Simons, Menno, 192
Simony, 135
Sin, 110, 115–117, 211–212, 220, 226, 232, 246, 266, 274, 294, 298
Slavery, 247, 267–268
Smith, John, 239
Smith, Joseph, 264
Social gospel movement, 297
Socinus, Faustus, 193
Socrates, 56, 60, 308
Speaking in tongues, 37, 49–50
Spener, Philipp Jakob, 244–245
Spiritualists, 192–193
Stephen, 35
Stoddard, Solomon, 258
Stoicism, 58
Strauss, David Friedrich, 277, 278
Strigel, Victorinus, 196
Suárez, Francisco, 210
Substantia, 79
Syllabus of Errors, 281
Symeon the New Theologian, 88, 98

Taylor, Nathaniel W., 262
Teaching of the Twelve Apostles, 49
Teresa of Avila, 207–208, 209, 215
Tertullian, 51, 55, 64–65, 73, 76, 79, 89, 110, 114
Tetzel, John, 183
Theodore of Mopsuestia, 81, 91
Theodore of Studios, 93–94, 102
Theodosius, 133

Thirty-nine Articles, 228
Thurneysen, Eduard, 291
Tillich, Paul, 301
Tillotson, John, 241
Timē, 94
Tindal, Matthew, 243
Todi, Jacopone da, 141
Toleration Act, 241
Transcendentalism, 265
Transubstantiation, 129, 173, 189, 202, 227, 228
Treasury of merits, 183
Trent, Council of, 201–204, 210
Trinity, 65, 77–79, 97, 100–101, 149, 193, 194, 247, 261, 277
Troeltsch, Ernst, 286, 292

Uguccione, Cardinal, 171
Ulrich of Augsburg, 130
Ultramontanes, 281
Uncreated Light, 98
Unitarianism, 261–262, 275
Universal salvation, 63, 295
Urban VI, 170

Vatican Council, First, 282
Vatican Council, Second, 303
Vigilantius, 129–130
Virgin birth, 40, 69, 116, 131, 231
Vladimir of Kiev, 103–104
Voltaire, 237, 243

Waldo, Peter, 149
War. *See* Pacifism
Warfield, Benjamin B., 296, 306
Wealth, 61, 125, 149, 150, 165, 173, 229–230, 231
Weber, Max, 229
Weiss, Johannes, 286
Wesley, John, 237, 245–247, 267, 284
Westminster Confession, 231
Whichcote, Benjamin, 239
White, Ellen, 263
Whitefield, George, 247, 260, 284
Whitehead, Alfred North, 306
Wilberforce, Samuel, 284–285
Williams, George H., 191
Winstanley, Gerrard, 231
Winthrop, John, 256
Wishart, George, 225
Wittgenstein, Ludwig, 305
Wolff, Christian, 244
Women, place in church, 38, 167, 207, 263, 310
Woolston, Thomas, 243
Wordsworth, William, 44
Worms, Concordat of, 136, 256
Wyclif, John, 173–174, 227

Xavier, Francis, 206

Ziegler, Clement, 193
Zinzendorf, Nicholas, 245
Zwingli, Huldreich, 188–190, 223

CPSIA information can be obtained at www.ICGtesting.com
Printed in the USA
BVOW04s1503100813

328192BV00003B/55/P

9 780664 244965